Praise for *Early Methodist Spirituality*:

"*Early Methodist Spirituality* opens a window into early Methodism that has too long been closed: the profound leadership women provided to the Wesleyan revival. This book is more than an anthology, it is a theologically astute and historically grounded invitation and guide to holistic spirituality in the Wesleyan tradition."
—Kenneth L. Carder, Duke University Divinity School

"Professor Chilcote's remarkable ability to distill essential components of early Methodist spirituality and their connections to love of God, neighbor, and Christ-centered selves offers edification and inspiration to readers."
—Laceye C. Warner, Duke University Divinity School

"This book is a chest of treasures! The last section, 'The Art of Living and Dying,' is worth the price by itself, especially in our death-denying culture that sees the end of life as a mistake rather than as the last step of a spiritual pilgrimage to be faced with faith, hope, and love."
—Gregory S. Clapper, The University of Indianapolis

KINGSWOOD BOOKS

Randy L. Maddox, Director
The Divinity School, Duke University

EDITORIAL ADVISORY BOARD

Joel Green
Asbury Theological Seminary

Richard P. Heitzenrater
The Divinity School, Duke University

Henry Knight
Saint Paul School of Theology

Robin W. Lovin
Southern Methodist University

Rebekah L. Miles
Perkins School of Theology

Mary Elizabeth Mullino Moore
Candler School of Theology, Emory University

Sam Powell
Point Loma Nazarene University

Karen B. Westerfield Tucker
School of Theology, Boston University

Anne E. Streaty Wimberly
Interdenominational Theological Center

Harriett Jane Olson, ex officio
Abingdon Press

Neil M. Alexander, ex officio
Abingdon Press

EARLY METHODIST SPIRITUALITY

SELECTED WOMEN'S WRITINGS

EDITED BY
PAUL WESLEY CHILCOTE

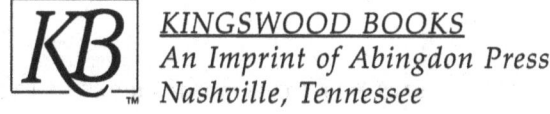

KINGSWOOD BOOKS
An Imprint of Abingdon Press
Nashville, Tennessee

EARLY METHODIST SPIRITUALITY
SELECTED WOMEN'S WRITINGS

Copyright © 2007 by Abingdon Press
All rights reserved.
No part of this work may be reproduced or transmitted in any form or by any means, electronic or mechanical, including photocopying and recording, or by any information storage or retrieval system, except as may be expressly permitted by the 1976 Copyright Act or in writing from the publisher. Requests for permission should be addressed to Abingdon Press, P.O. Box 801, 201 Eighth Avenue South, Nashville, TN 37202-0801, or e-mailed to permissions@abingdonpress.com.

This book is printed on acid-free paper.

Library of Congress Cataloging-in-Publication Data

Early Methodist spirituality : selected women's writings / edited by Paul Wesley Chilcote.
   p. cm.
Includes bibliographical references and index.
ISBN-13: 978-0-687-33416-2 (binding : paperback, adhesive : alk. paper)
   1. Methodist women—History—18th century.   2. Methodist women—History—19th century.
3. Spirituality—Methodist Church—History—18th century.   4. Spirituality—Methodist Church—History—19th century.   I. Chilcote, Paul Wesley, 1954-
   BS8345.7.E27 2006
   248.088'287—dc22

2006026411

All scripture quotations unless noted otherwise are taken from the *New Revised Standard Version of the Bible*, copyright 1989, Division of Christian Education of the National Council of the Churches of Christ in the United States of America. Used by permission. All rights reserved.

07 08 09 10 11 12 13 14 15 16—10 9 8 7 6 5 4 3 2 1

MANUFACTURED IN THE UNITED STATES OF AMERICA

*For the most important women
in my life,
Janet, my wife,
and my five daughters,
Sandy, Rebekah, Anna, Mary, and Ruth.*

Contents

Preface xi
Introduction 1

Part One
Autobiography as Theology

Introduction to Part One 61
A. Agnes Bulmer's Preface to Memoirs of Elizabeth
   Mortimer 65
B. Accounts of Religious Experience
   1. Grace Murray (1718–1803) 71
   2. Sarah Ryan (1724–68) 75
   3. Sarah Crosby (1729–1804) 81
   4. Jane Cooper (1738–62) 87
C. Diaries and Journals
   1. Memoir of Hannah Ball (1733–92) 95
   2. Hester Ann Rogers (1756–94) 104
   3. Mary Entwisle (c. 1770–1804) 123
   4. Isabella Wilson (1765–1807) 131

Part Two
Writings in Practical Divinity

Introduction to Part Two 137

Contents

A. SPIRITUAL INSTRUCTION
1. MEDITATIONS OF MRS. LEFEVRE (1722?–56) .. 143
2. MARY BOSANQUET'S *SPIRITUAL DIRECTION*
   (1739–1815) 148
3. MARTHA HALL'S DISCOURSE ON MEDITATION
   (1706–91) 158
4. MARY TATHAM'S *MEMOIRS* AND BIBLICAL
   COMMENTARY (1764–1837) 161
5. MARY LYTH'S CODE OF LIFE 171
6. MARY HANSON'S MEDITATIONS
   (1786–1812) 173

B. HYMNS AND SACRED POEMS
1. HYMN OF MARY STOKES (1750–1823) 178
2. RELIGIOUS VERSE OF MISS T— 181
3. LAMENT OF PHILLIS WHEATLEY 185
4. LAMENT OF PORTIA YOUNG 186
5. POEMS OF AGNES BULMER (1775–1836) ... 188
6. POEMS OF MARGARET DAVIDSON
   (FL. C. 1760–80) 202
7. POEM BY MARY BARRITT (1772–1851) 207

C. PRAYERS
1. SUSANNAH DESIGN (FL. 1740S) 209
2. MRS. LEFEVRE (1722?–56) 212
3. JOANNA COOK (1732–84) 215
4. MARY GILBERT (1751–68) 218
5. MARGARET DAVIDSON (FL. C. 1760–80) ... 222
6. SARAH CROSBY (1729–1804) 224
7. BATHSHEBA HALL (1745–80) 226
8. HESTER ANN ROE (1756–94) 227
9. ANN CUTLER ("PRAYING NANNY") (1759–94) .. 228

10. ISABELLA WILSON (1765–1807) 231
11. MARY ENTWISLE (C. 1770–1804) 233
12. ELIZABETH EVANS (1776–1849) 234
13. MARY HANSON (1786–1812) 236
D. DREAMS AND VISIONS
   1. THE "ACCOUNT" OF SARAH RYAN (1724–68) . 237
   2. MARY FLETCHER'S JOURNAL (1739–1815) ... 240
   3. THE "ACCOUNT" OF SARAH MALLET (1764–?) 243

PART THREE
THE ART OF LIVING AND DYING

INTRODUCTION TO PART THREE 249
A. ARS VIVENDI: THE SPIRITUAL LIFE IN LETTERS
   1. MRS. LEFEVRE TO MRS. *** [175?] 255
   2. JANE COOPER TO MRS. M. M. (1757) 257
   3. [MARY] B.[OSANQUET] TO A FRIEND (1762) 258
   4. HANNAH BALL TO MISS BEDFORD (1770) .. 260
   5. HANNAH BALL TO ANN BOLTON (1770) ... 262
   6. SARAH CROSBY TO JOHN WESLEY (1773) .. 264
   7. HESTER ANN ROE TO A FAMILY FRIEND
      (1775) 268
   8. HESTER ANN ROE TO [ANN] LOXDALE
      (1779) 273
   9. ELIZABETH RITCHIE TO JOHN WESLEY
      (1782) 277
  10. SARAH CROSBY TO MARY HOLDER (1790) .. 279
  11. MARY FLETCHER TO MRS. DALBY 282
  12. ELIZABETH HURRELL TO FRANCES PAWSON
      (1795) 286
  13. ISABELLA WILSON TO MR. AND MRS. WILSON
      (1800) 289
  14. MARY TAFT TO MARY FLETCHER (1803) ... 291
  15. MARY FLETCHER TO MARY TAFT (1803) ... 293
  16. ANN TRIPP TO FRANCES PAWSON (1806) .. 295

CONTENTS

    17. Mary Fletcher to Elizabeth Collet
        (1807) 298
    18. Mary Hanson to a Friend (1810) 301
    19. Mary Anderson to Mary Taft (1811) ... 305
    20. Elizabeth Mortimer to Mary Holland
        (1817) 306

B. Ars Moriendi: *Accounts of Triumphant Death*
    1. Hester Ann Rogers, "The Dying Bed of a
       Saint and Sinner Contrasted" 309
    2. Sarah Colston, "Some Account of the Death
       of Mary Thomas" (1745) 314
    3. Mary James, "An Account of the Death of
       Mrs. Doyle" (1767) 316
    4. Elizabeth Henson, "Account of the Death
       of Her Mother" (1784) 317
    5. Ann Highfield, "Account of Ann Cutler"
       (1795) 318
    6. Mary Fletcher, *Account of Sarah Lawrence*
       (1800) 323
    7. Ann Tripp, "Account of Sarah Crosby"
       (1804) 331
    8. Mary Tooth, "Account of Mary Fletcher"
       (1815) 335

Abbreviations 341
Notes 345
Selected Bibliography 371
Index 381
Index of Scripture References 391

Preface

The purpose of this collection of women's writings is to provide an introduction for the general reader, as well as for the student of the Wesleyan heritage, to some of the best, but virtually inaccessible, material related to early Methodist spirituality. Although many of the items included in this volume were published in the eighteenth and nineteenth centuries, very few are readily available today. Some manuscript material is presented here for the first time. Most of the women featured in this volume knew one another. They were part of a dynamic network of Methodist Societies committed to the revitalization of the church and could never have conceived themselves apart from these circles of friendship and accountable discipleship. Their spiritual writings reflect a compelling vision of life in Christ—a life of faith working by love leading to holiness of heart and life.

There is no question that women helped make the Wesleyan revival one of the most dynamic Christian movements in the history of modern Protestantism. The vitality and continuing significance of Methodism is due, in large measure, to their presence and influence and to the depth of their spirituality. General ignorance concerning the writings of early Methodist women, however, has left the impression that they have no story to tell. Another purpose of the present volume, therefore, is to dispel this myth and to put the reader in touch with a lost heritage of vital spirituality that can transform lives and the church today. In this sense, this anthology is meant to stand alongside my previous volume, *Her Own Story: Autobiographical Portraits of Early Methodist Women*. While this earlier work touched upon spirituality in a tangential manner, the selections from the writings of early Methodist women that follow here vividly illustrate the richness of their contribution to the life of the church and the legacy of Wesleyan spirituality. The religious accounts, diaries and journals, prayers, hymns and sacred poems, and narrative practical divinity, brought together here for the first time, provide a new vantage point from which to view the exciting spiritual awakening of the Wesleys' day. They reveal a "way of devotion," a way of living out the Christian faith that conjoins personal piety and social action, conversion and growth in grace.

The purpose of part 1 is to introduce the reader to the "early Methodist woman" and to illustrate the centrality of theological biography in the Wesleyan tradition. Four accounts of religious experience and four excerpts from diaries and journals of women demonstrate the importance of the "way of salvation," the holism of the Wesleyan doctrine of salvation, and the importance placed upon the conjunction of faith and works in the tradition. This section also introduces the Wesleyan heritage to the non-Methodist reader. Part 2 gathers together a body of material related to spiritual instruction, hymns and sacred poems, and prayers of early Methodist women. These materials related to Christian instruction and practices reflect concern for meditation, the disciplined regulation of life, and reflection on practical theology lived out in day-to-day relationships. The volume concludes with a section on the art of living and dying. I have divided this material equally into correspondence related to the quest for Christlike living and accounts of triumphant death, written exclusively by women, concerning women.

It is not my intention in this volume to provide an exhaustive introduction to early Methodist spirituality. My primary aim is more descriptive than analytical. But although the volume places these writings more on display for the general reader rather than seeking to interpret them in a systematic fashion, the introduction to the volume as a whole, the three sectional introductions, and the preliminary comments on individual items are meant to set the documents and their authors in context in a way helpful to the reader. The organization of the women's writings into three sections is natural and a reflection of the prominence of these categories within the life of the movement.

Preface

Several principles guided my selection of the documents included here. First, as in *Her Own Story*, I have used the dates of Mary Fletcher (1739–1815) to define the "early Methodist" period. All the women featured here were near contemporaries of this major figure within the movement. Second, all are Wesleyan Methodists or spent significant time in this branch of the evangelical revival—that is, they set themselves under the authority of the Wesley brothers, who exercised spiritual oversight among them. As in the previous volume, I have excluded the works of Selina Hastings, Countess of Huntingdon, and Hannah More. Although their contributions to eighteenth-century evangelical Anglican spirituality were significant, they were only tangentially significant to the Methodism of the Wesleys. Finally, I have done my best to include writings of lesser-known women alongside the better-known works of female icons of early Methodism. It goes without saying that others might have made different choices for inclusion. I have attempted to provide a diversity of voices here with integrity. I have taken a similar approach to that of Susan Hill Lindley in her history of women and religion in America entitled *"You Have Stept Out of Your Place"*; namely, I have assumed that the early Methodist women told the truth about who they were, what they did, and why they did it, unless there is compelling evidence to the contrary. I can only imagine that as this material is discussed in classrooms, reflected upon in small groups, or contemplated in quiet privacy, the spiritual witness of the early Methodist women will elicit a wide range of responses. My hope, however, is that when all is said and done, you will stand in awe of these amazing women as I have come to do.

The editorial principles I have followed in this volume may be summarized as follows. My primary concern throughout has been to honor the distinctive voices of the featured authors in their own contexts. In order to make these writings accessible to the modern reader, however, I have silently modernized the punctuation, capitalization, and spelling in most of the prose selections, and have also, though more rarely, changed awkward syntax. This latter point is particularly true with regard to excessively lengthy sentences that have been broken down into more palatable units. For the same reason I have exchanged archaisms with modern equivalents. All references to "thou" and "thine," for example, have been replaced with "you" and "your." Similarly, for illustration, "dwells" replaces "dwelleth." The only exception to this rule is when the women directly quote texts (most frequently scriptural passages) in which these older forms are present, in which case the original is maintained. I have retained the original texts of all poems and hymns. I have done my best to present these literary works in complete units. In those instances, however, where some attenuation has seemed desirable for economy's sake, elisions are clearly marked. I have retained the original headings as they appeared in editions of material published in the lifetime of the author but have also added some headings to aid the reader in appreciating the content or structure of the particular items. On the basis of these principles, it should be clear that my intent is not to present definitive texts for the scholarly community; rather, my interest lies in a balance of academic and devotional objectives. My hope is that this effort will encourage readers to dive deeply into these readings, to discern connections between the Methodist movement and women's spirituality more generally, and to illumine the larger study of spirituality.

My passion to collect and study these texts quickened during my doctoral studies at Duke University under the direction of Frank Baker, now quite some years ago. The discovery of the women of early Methodism opened the door to a whole new world for me. During a sabbatical, nearly a decade ago, I began the process of collecting writings of these women for the purpose of publication. It quickly became apparent that there was far more material than could be covered in a single volume. This discovery entailed both excitement and frustration. The first fruits of this research was *Her Own Story*, published in 2001. As I prepared that volume, I carefully set aside material with an obvious orientation toward spirituality as I have defined it here, with hopes of publishing it separately. Those materials now fill the pages of this complementary volume.

Several institutions and many individuals have helped me recover the voice of early Methodist women. My first round of thanks goes to the staff of the Methodist Archives and Research Centre, John Rylands University Library of Manchester, particularly Dr. Gareth Lloyd; The Wesley Centre, Westminster Institute of Education, Oxford Brookes University (formerly Westminster

College, Oxford); and Wesley College in Bristol, for their assistance in identifying and providing access to critical collections and documents over the years. In the United States, I am equally grateful to the many who offered their assistance to me at Drew University, Duke University, Garrett-Evangelical Theological Seminary, and Perkins School of Theology. The library staff at Duke Divinity School, particularly Dr. Roger Loyd, have always been so kind to address multiple email requests and sporadic visits on campus. A grant from the General Commission on Archives and History of The United Methodist Church, now seemingly years ago, supported this work in its most nascent stage. I am extremely grateful to Asbury Theological Seminary for a Fall semester sabbatical in 2004 and time set aside from faculty and committee responsibilities that permitted me to bring this project nearly to completion. It has been a great joy to tie up loose ends and complete my work on this volume at Duke Divinity School, where many resources are now right at my fingertips and require only a short walk instead of a long trip.

I developed portions of the introductory material to this book in close conversation with colleagues and dialogue partners across the years. I want to express my appreciation in particular to participants in the Worship and Spirituality working group of the Eleventh Oxford Institute of Methodist Theological Studies, Christ Church, Oxford (August 2002), who graciously accepted a very rough attempt to outline the spirituality of the early Methodist women. Their observations, constructive comments, and suggestions for further study helped refine this material in important ways. Other occasions arose in which I availed myself of the opportunity to share some of these questions and insights, and in which friends led me into new discoveries. Among those that stand out in my memory are several events in the summer of 2003, including the first session of the World Methodist Council/Salvation Army Dialogue, held at Salvation Army International Headquarters, London; the Duke Divinity School Tercentenary Celebration of John Wesley's birth at which I addressed the theme "Women in Early Methodism"; and the Eighth International Conference of Christians for Biblical Equality in Orlando, at which event I was asked to speak on the topic "Winsome Women of the Wesleyan Heritage." My thanks to the many who engaged me in

Preface

conversation about spirituality and the early Methodist women, shared their insights, and stimulated my own thinking, including Tom Albin, Greg Clapper, Karen Greenwaldt, Hal Knight, Margaret Jones, Steve Manskar, Sondra Matthaei, John Newton, Don Saliers, Gordon Wakefield, and Laceye Warner. I am particularly grateful to Steve Harper, Sarah Lancaster, John Lenton, Alison Wilkinson, Kathy Snedeker, David Lowes Watson, and Mary Elizabeth Moore, who graciously read through various redactions of the introductory material and whose insights I have incorporated into the finished manuscript. I completed most of my work on the volume as a charter faculty member of Asbury Theological Seminary in Orlando, Florida. I offer a very special word of thanks to my wonderful colleagues there for their support and encouragement through these past years. I shall never forget you. I have always enjoyed working with the staff of Abingdon Press, and so I offer a special word of appreciation to Kathy Armistead and Suzanne Austin, exceptional editors who have helped me improve the text. My move to Duke Divinity School has enabled me to cultivate new friendships and to celebrate relationships with long-standing friends who are now just down the hall. Of singular importance to me in this regard is my friendship with Randy Maddox, who, in addition to his many other roles, serves as General Editor of Kingswood Books. I have known few people in my life who are as dependable as Randy, and I am deeply grateful for his personal support in this project.

In the final analysis, no women are more important to me than my wife, Janet, and our five girls, Sandy, Rebekah, Anna, Mary, and Ruth. They continue to inspire me and challenge me to consider "the world in which they live" as women and girls. They are all wonderful and winsome Christian disciples. I constantly see reflections of the early Methodist women in the pathos, delight, and love that characterize their lives.

Paul Wesley Chilcote
Birthday of Alice Cambridge,
Irish Methodist Preacher

Introduction

> *O that you would therefore do as Jacob did, be earnest with the Lord, that his love may fill your heart, as the Scripture expresses it, the love of God, shed abroad in your hearts by the Holy Ghost, given unto you. If you get your hearts full of the love of God, you will find that is the oil by which the lamp of faith will be ever kept burning.... Pray, my friends, pray much for this love; and remember that word, "He that dwelleth in love dwelleth in God, and God in him!"*[1]

The story of the early Methodist women must start here, in love. Love is its beginning, and love is its end. The love of God, the love of neighbor, and the love of self-in-Christ are the central elements of their message, and in that order, rediscovered and articulated anew. The words above are those of Mary Fletcher, written in a letter to a Methodist community that needed to be reminded of its source and foundation. What made Mary's words so compelling was the fact that she had experienced the transforming love of God in a deeply personal way in her own life and, like so many of her sisters in the faith, was called to communicate that experience to others. This is a story well worth hearing.

The spirituality of the early Methodist women constitutes the substance of their compelling story. Since "spirituality" is such a problematic and elusive term, it is important for me to be clear about how I am using it. Through the history of Christianity it has been used to cover a breadth of religious experience and a wide range of values, practices, and virtues.[2] According to Gordon Wakefield, on the most basic level "spirituality concerns the way in which prayer influences conduct, our behaviour and manner of life, our attitudes to other people."³ Similarly, Geoffrey Wainwright suggests that spirituality is "the combination of praying and living."⁴ Both definitions emphasize that Christian spirituality reflects a dialectic of movement inward and outward, of personal and social engagement—of an interior life with God manifest necessarily in external relationships of love. The spiritual life is embodied, inclusive, relational, and engaged in the full range of human existence. The texts collected in this volume reflect this conception of Christian spirituality as a dynamic attempt to integrate all aspects of human life and experience.

The very process of collecting material for this volume and making decisions about inclusion and exclusion taught me some interesting lessons about the elusive-yet-distinct nature of spirituality. Taking my clues from the work of Philip Sheldrake, my initial concern was not so much to define spirituality as it was to survey "the complex mystery of human growth in the context of a living relationship with the Absolute" in the lives of the early Methodist women.⁵ I proceeded inductively, laying aside, as best I could, all preconceived notions of what I ought to find. My experience confirmed Sheldrake's conclusions. In practice, all spiritualities are specific and emerge out of the particular attitudes and practices of historic communities of faith. "Spirituality is understood to include," argues Sheldrake, "not merely the techniques of prayer but, more broadly, a conscious relationship with God, in Jesus Christ, through the indwelling of the Spirit and in the context of the community of believers."⁶

I have included in this volume material that points specifically to the intersection of theology, prayer, and practical Christianity. The way in which this conjunction is negotiated is what I am considering the "stuff" of spirituality. To relate these conceptual matters to the specifics of early Methodist spirituality, the simple fact that the Wesleys viewed the evangelical revival as a movement of God's Spirit within the life of the church shaped the way in which the early Methodist women prayed and lived. Their "life of prayer" took on many forms, and the "way they lived" reflected their souls. Their peculiar context—and the value that their leaders placed upon spiritual rediscoveries rooted in the apostolic witness of scripture and the Anglican heritage—defined the Methodists. The spirituality of this movement of renewal may be the most distinctive contribution of the Wesleyan tradition to the life of the church today.

While the spirituality lived and practiced by the early Methodist women reflects all the elements common to the people called Methodists, it also manifests itself in distinctive ways. In order to set the spiritual writings of the women in their proper context, I will explore briefly the social and spiritual context of early Methodism, descriptions of Methodist spirituality, salient themes of the Wesleyan spiritual heritage, and the constellation of women writers gathered in this volume, along with a general description of their writings. I conclude with a discussion of the "voice" of the women and the distinctive tones of their spirituality. The writings of the women are potent expressions of a theology of grace and bear witness to the loving nature of a God who reaches out to us in the person of Jesus Christ and restores our loving nature by means of the indwelling Spirit. The women are amazing mentors with regard to this vision of the Christian life.

EARLY METHODISM IN SOCIAL AND SPIRITUAL CONTEXT

Methodism arose within the Church of England during the eighteenth century as a movement of spiritual renewal.[7] John and Charles Wesley, who gave leadership to the wing of the revival that bore their name, were loyal priests of the church, loved the church with every fiber of their being, and above all else dedicated their lives to the rediscovery of what they called "primitive" or "scriptural Christianity." The movement of renewal they spearheaded within the life of the church paralleled revolutionary developments of the time in the British Isles and beyond.[8] Images of the eighteenth century are often difficult to reconcile, but it is more than safe to say that it was an age of monumental transitions. The renowned British historian Herbert Butterfield used a memorable image to describe this period of English history. The vivid impression is that of broadening sweep and gathering momentum. It is as though a wave, moving only slowly at first—lightly combing the face of the water—collected from the sea increased power and finally arched itself into a thunderous mass. The eighteenth century was an age of tremendous upheaval.

On the political front, concepts of authoritarian rule were giving way to more democratic ideals. Enormous changes in agriculture, industry, and communications reshaped the landscape of the economic world. Tensions created by the wide gulf between the lifestyles of the aristocracy and the common people threatened to shatter the fragile balance of the existing hierarchical society. Whether in the city, town, or village, life was still "nasty, brutish, and short," as the English philosopher Thomas Hobbes purportedly described it in the previous century. Suffering abounded, especially in the hovels that lined filthy and dangerous streets.

Although it is true to say that "folk religion" dominated the spiritual landscape and that the common person found little solace in a church that had become fixated on the maintenance of the status quo, the Established Church of the eighteenth century actually defies easy generalization.[9] Lack of detailed research and the negative portrait painted by later partisan historians of the subsequent century, from opposite wings of the church's life, create as many questions as answers with regard to the state of the church. It can be said rather definitively, however, that complex developments within the life of the church over the course of the two previous centuries had weakened the church's witness and led to a general malaise.[10] Having been established in a more rural and slow-paced world, one of the greatest liabilities of the ecclesiastical system was its visible ineffectiveness in an age of rapid change. Increasingly concerned with institutional preservation, the natural inertia of the church turned away from personal and social transformation and from mission in the world. Monumental demographic shifts were beginning to shake the foundations of the establishment. Rather than finding its vocation in solidarity with the masses of the poor, the church increasingly distanced itself from the least and the lost in society. "The centripetal forces within the church," as Walsh and Taylor claim, "were still vastly more powerful than the centrifugal."[11] Although lacking in a missional culture, however, the Anglican Church was not totally devoid of pastoral zeal. Although many of the clergy and laity practiced a bland form of nominal Christianity, the eighteenth century also witnessed a steady and progressive mobilization of the laity. Overall, there can be no question that religious moderation strengthened the cohesion of the church. But forces that sought to rediscover a more vigorous, robust, and dynamic form of the Christian faith were at work throughout the course of the century.

The "private piety in this period," according to Henry Rack, "remains an unstudied area."[12] What is true of this more discrete area within the study of spirituality can also be said with regard to spirituality as more broadly conceived in this volume. Despite this dearth of research, however, some distinctive characteristics of Anglican spirituality in this period can be affirmed.[13] In exploring the Anglican quest for holiness, several contemporary scholars identify the genius of this tradition with the ability of Anglicans to do their theology "less by the systematic examining of doctrinal structures than by reflecting on the shape of Christian life."[14] After the Bible, no single source exerted more shaping influence on Christian life in the devout English family than *The Book of Common Prayer*. This reservoir of Anglican devotion established the rhythms and gave direction to the essential ethos of the Wesleyan revival as well.[15] Beyond this, two dominant streams of influence within English Christianity continued to shape the spirituality of the Church of England during the eighteenth century: the High Church (or Anglo-Catholic) and the Puritan traditions.[16]

Within the High Church wing of the church, perhaps no group had more continuing influence than the Caroline Divines of the previous century, including renowned devotional writers such as Lancelot Andrews, William Laud, Thomas Ken, George Herbert, and Jeremy Taylor.[17] The contribution of the two latter figures was particularly important to eighteenth-century Anglican spirituality.

George Herbert was born into a noble family, educated in the Cambridge tradition, and destined initially for worldly advancement.[18] He turned his attention instead to serious spiritual concerns in response to the death of King James I in 1625. He is considered to be one of the most authentic representatives of the Anglican *via media* (the middle way) in both its spirit and teaching. *A Priest to the Temple; or the Country Parson*, published posthumously in 1652, is his most famous prose work. It portrays the model priest as sober, learned, temperate, and devout, ideals he sought to emulate in his own brief ministry at Bremerton, near Salisbury. His collection of poems entitled *The Temple* (1633) reveals his own personal struggles of faith, consisting primarily as Richard Baxter once observed of "heart-work and heaven-work."[19] In these devotional writings he consistently emphasized the sense of intimacy with God, the priority of prayer to preaching, the integration of inward grace and outward expression, the exercise of Christian virtue in the supreme act of putting on Christ, and the resolution of life's contradictions in an abiding faith that leads to God.

Jeremy Taylor was best known for his twin works, *The Rule and Exercise of Holy Living* (1650) and *The Rule and Exercise of Holy Dying* (1651).[20] They are characteristic expressions of Anglican spirituality in their balanced sobriety, disciplined piety, and emphasis on moderation in all things. The central theme of the Christian life, in Taylor's view, is God's requirement for believers to live holy lives. Such a life includes temperance and justice as well as godliness. The life of holiness demands a severe regimen and will include the ultimate crucible of suffering and death. His spirituality is oriented around the central Caroline ideal of true piety and sound learning.

The nonjuror, William Law, a contemporary and close friend of the Wesleys, also stood in this High Church tradition.[21] Inspired in part by the teachings of Thomas à Kempis, he published *A Serious Call to a Devout and Holy Life* in 1728, by far his most influential devotional work. In the midst of the Age of Reason, he developed a profound, rational argument for a life of devotion, demanding that serious Christians dedicate the whole and not just a part of their lives to God. He recommends the exercise of the moral virtues, meditation, and ascetical practices. But for him such religious exercises represent only a small part of the spiritual life. He insists on the practice of the virtues in everyday life—particularly temperance, humility, and self-denial; all animated by the intention to glorify God.

The heart of Puritan spirituality was personal religion.[22] Although this label is fraught with difficulties and clouded by later prejudicial images, the central tenets of Puritan devotion can be illustrated by several of its greatest proponents. In his great autobiographical work, *Grace Abounding to the Chief of Sinners*, John Bunyon emphasizes the necessity of conversion—as an experience that is neither achieved nor followed without agony or struggle, but as the fruition of the overwhelming call of God. His more famous classic, *The Pilgrim's Progress*, bears witness to the fact that the Christian life is a journey that requires a covenant community of support and encouragement. Richard Baxter's *The Saints' Everlasting Rest*, composed following an extended illness in 1646, demonstrates the centrality of meditation to Puritan prayer. Likewise, Isaac Watts, one of the greatest Puritans, embodies the introduction of hymnody into English devotional life.[23] The spirituality of Watts's hymns is characterized by a sense of divine transcendence, the glory and majesty of God, and the sweep of God's action in human history with particular focus on the gracious manifestation of God's love through the cross of Christ.

These two great movements within English Christianity set the stage for the eighteenth century. They also shaped the Wesley brothers' theological development and spirituality through several of the prominent representatives. For example, Jeremy Taylor's *Rules and Exercises of Holy Living and Holy Dying* was the initial spark that fired John Wesley's serious religion in 1725 as he stood on the threshold of his ordination. This devotional classic introduced or reacquainted him with the practices of holy living that would be his constant companions through life—namely, the study of the Bible, frequent Communion, disciplined private prayer and public worship, and a general rule of life for the formation of Christian character. Most important, both Wesleys resonated thoroughly with Taylor's identification of the central theme of the Christian life: to live holy lives that are characterized by "purity of intention."

After he became a Fellow of Lincoln College, Oxford, John Wesley immersed himself in the writings of William Law, particularly his *Serious Call*. He was particularly moved by Law's emphasis on self-denial, the imitation of Christ, and the cruciform nature of Christian life. Although the relationship between these two great contemporaries would be strained subsequently, particularly over what Wesley considered to be Law's mystical excesses in later life, Law's formative influence was profound. Law convinced Wesley, as he observed in the *Plain Account of Christian Perfection* (§4), "of the absolute impossibility of being *half a Christian*."

There were other formative influences, of course, that shaped the spiritual terrain of the Wesleys' England, influencing the lives of their followers as well. Two spiritual classics, both of which appear to have been among Susanna Wesley's favorites, were Henry

Scougal's *The Life of God in the Soul of Man*[24] and Lorenzo Scupoli's *The Spiritual Combat*.[25] "True religion," according to Scougal, "is a union of the soul with God, a real participation of the divine nature, the very image of God drawn upon the soul."[26] Scupoli represents a Catholic tradition of "will mysticism," the goal of which is total resignation to God. The primary insight that John Wesley took away from his study of these classical works was the simple fact that the Christian life is a *via devotio* (a way of devotion) that finds its richest and fullest completion in God's love.[27]

Another devotional classic of the Roman Catholic tradition holds a special place in the spiritual development of John Wesley in particular. When he published his *Plain Account of Christian Perfection* in 1766, in the opening paragraphs he identified Thomas à Kempis (in addition to Taylor and Law) as one of the most critical influences of his early life. In conjunction with his ordination in 1725 (despite his mistaken date in the *Plain Account*), Wesley began a close study of à Kempis's *Imitation of Christ*, which initiated him into a form of practical mysticism aimed at perfection in love.[28] He warmed to à Kempis's emphases on humility, the interior life, love, and the Eucharist in the Christian life. Even though the youthful Wesley disagreed with à Kempis's vision of perfection as being too subjective, too self-deprecating, and too individualistic,[29] he remained intrigued with the work, quoted it constantly, and published over twenty editions of his own extracts of it in the course of his life,[30] recommending "that golden treatise" frequently in his letters.[31] Its vision of an inward heart religion that necessitated total dedication to God captured him forever.

Wesley highlights two other critical figures, together with à Kempis, in the opening of his sermon "On the Trinity," in which he describes them as "real, inward Christians."[32] Wesley apparently discovered the first, a Spanish mystic, through the seventeenth-century translation of his biography, *The Holy Life of Gregory Lopez*.[33] The narrative of Lopez's life reflects a number of Wesley's most critical emphases—namely, the concept of holy living as a lifelong quest, a stress on self-denial and contempt for the world, tranquility of soul, identification with the poor, purity of intention in this life, and the equation of holiness and happiness. Gaston de Renty was his other primary exemplar of the "perfect Christian" outside the Methodist movement itself.[34] What was so appealing to

Wesley about de Renty's life was the synthesis of spiritual devotion and practical service.[35] In 1758, he claimed that de Renty's *Life* was his favorite book, and it certainly was one from which he quoted frequently in his later life.[36]

Much farther removed by time, but equally important in the larger context of Anglican spirituality, was the rediscovery of ancient writers and texts. For the Methodists, first and foremost among these sources was Pseudo-Macarius.[37] Wesley knew and loved his *Fifty Spiritual Homilies,* quoting from one of them in his landmark sermon "The Scripture Way of Salvation" (I.7), and publishing twenty-two of them in the first volume of his *Christian Library*.[38] Macarius's spirituality of the heart is concerned primarily with unceasing prayer and the idea of progress toward love in the Christian life. He views the ethical virtues as stages in the soul's development until, through God's transforming grace, the fruit of the Spirit become second nature in the perfect child of God. John Wesley frequently mentions Ephrem Syrus, another early church figure, in conjunction with Macarius.[39] The singular theme of Ephrem's voluminous writings is the full restoration of the lost *imago dei* (image of God) in each human being. Several scholars have begun to explore the resonance of this theme with the spiritual emphases of both John and Charles Wesley.[40] In the fascinating volume *Orthodox and Wesleyan Spirituality,* Kathleen McVey and S T Kimbrough Jr. both explore the spiritual resonance of Charles with Ephrem. But the work has only just begun in this essentially unexplored terrain.

John Wesley not only drank deeply from these various wells of Christian devotion, but also made these works available to the rank and file of the Methodist movement, primarily through his *Christian Library*. From 1749 to 1755, he published this fifty-volume collection, "consisting of extracts from, and abridgements of, the choicest pieces of practical divinity which have been publish'd in the English tongue." The works included in these volumes range from the Apostolic fathers to the English Puritans. They were spiritual classics, as well as more esoteric spiritual writings, and, due to Wesley's use of them, had a wide circulation through the end of the century. From this diverse group came such varying emphases as the importance of spiritual disciplines, the primacy of pure intentions, the role of the affections, and the necessity of participation in God in the quest for holiness of heart and life. The lasting legacy of this spiritual heritage was an emphasis upon the potential triumph of God's grace and the power of a wholehearted love of God and neighbor to displace all lesser loves. Wesley's quest was for Christian wholeness, for holiness of heart and life, for faith working by love. His driving passion was to bring balance and vitality to the Christian life and to restore it to the church he loved. All of these discoveries played a part in the birth of the Wesleyan revival.

Descriptions of Early Methodist Spirituality

The history, theology, and spirituality of early Methodism are so integrally related to one another that it is virtually impossible to separate them without distorting the portrait of the movement. The organizational structure of the Methodist Society—its evolution and function as part of the revival, for example—was a natural extension of Wesleyan theology. Early Methodists learned their theology primarily through the singing of Charles Wesley's hymns; while the unfolding religious experience of the Methodist people shaped the lyrical theology of the movement's cofounder. The Wesleys' concern for a more holistic spirituality stood at the center of their vision and ethos. To examine the history of the movement, therefore, or to explore the evolving theology of the founders, is to study the spirituality of Methodism as the integration of "prayer and life" (one should hear echoes of the Benedictine *ora et labora*).

It is possible to discern a clear set of foundational presuppositions with regard to Christian practice in the writings of the early Methodist people and their leaders. First, early Methodist spirituality is rooted in scripture. Second, the ambiance of their spirituality is derived not from theoretical principles but from their attempt to live out the gospel with integrity in their specific historical and cultural contexts. Third, they locate their personal experiences and spiritual insights within the larger matrix of the Wesleyan heritage and its accents on love, ethical living, service to the poor and oppressed, participation in the sacraments, and community life.

Most interpreters of Methodist spirituality, in one way or another, refer back to these core principles.

At its heart this spirituality has to do with a living, dynamic relationship with God in Jesus Christ, animated by the indwelling Spirit and experienced most fully in community. Having discovered an abundant life of accountable discipleship, the early Methodists reached out in all directions in witness and service as the only possible response to the One whom they believed claimed the whole of their lives—heart, head, and hands. All those who have sought to interpret the Wesleyan heritage affirm this vision of a renewed and holistic way of devotion.

Given the fact that the Wesleys understood the Christian faith to be a *via devotio*,[41] it is actually surprising that so little has been written about Wesleyan spirituality per se. Only a handful of authors' names come immediately to mind. First among them would be the British Methodist Gordon Wakefield. In two classic studies, *Methodist Devotion* and *Fire of Love*, he points to balance and discipline as the keys to understanding this dynamic movement and its founder.[42] According to Wakefield, an emphasis on frequent Communion, study of scripture, mutual encouragement related to ethical conduct, and service to the poor characterize the Wesleys and their followers. In his more recent publication, *Methodist Spirituality*, Wakefield highlights the importance of the means of grace, perfect love, the social gospel, and the rapture and order of the movement reflected in Charles Wesley's hymns and Methodist discipline.

Frank Whaling, in his introduction to the volume *The Classics of Western Spirituality*, devoted to the Wesley brothers, provides one of the most wide-ranging analyses of Wesleyan spirituality. He identifies the "key deposits" that the Wesleys have handed on to their spiritual progeny as:

> Charles Wesley's hymns, the Covenant Service, faith as living reality rather than belief per se, perfect love, mission based on the conviction that "for all, for all, my Savior died," the importance of laymen, fellowship as *koinonia*, the spiritual importance of organization, a creative tolerance based on the notion that true religion is inward and social rather than merely doctrinal, and a pragmatic openness to developing situations.[43]

Introduction

Beyond this detail, Whaling emphasizes that the Wesleys "were unique for the integral nature of their spirituality. They were able to hold together what most Christian groups, even today, tend to keep apart."[44] In similar fashion, in his discussion "The Methodist Synthesis" in *English Spirituality*, David Jeffrey elevates Wesley's ability to hold the "meditative tradition" and the "missionary tradition" of spirituality in dynamic balance.[45]

David Lowes Watson has also made important contributions in this area. In addition to his multiple works on Christian discipleship and the use of small groups in early Methodism, he contributed a lesser-known essay to Frank Senn's *Protestant Spiritual Traditions* in 1986, entitled "Methodist Spirituality."[46] It is a jewel, in my view, one of the most succinct and incisive treatments of this crucial theme. Watson describes Methodist spirituality as a synthesis of an Anglican holiness of intent and a Puritan interior assurance. The spirituality of the early Methodist people, he argues, was shaped by a vital sense of mutual accountability (centered in the Methodist class meeting), the cultivation of a catholicity of grace, the quest for Christian perfection in this life, the constant use of the means of grace, and the celebration of God's pervasive presence through the singing of hymns.

Similar to the work of Watson, Sondra Matthaei's study entitled *Making Disciples* has interfaced Methodist spirituality with formative practices.[47] She argues that the central thrust of the Wesleyan tradition is formation for holiness of heart and life. Three central themes in this "discipleship spirituality" are the search for living faith, the freedom of God's grace in and for all, and the importance of community in the formation of Christian disciples.

The empirical studies of Tom Albin also afford important insights into the spirituality of the Methodist movement. After working through hundreds of accounts of religious experience, he concludes "that the primary force in the Evangelical Revival was laity rather than clergy."[48] The role of the laity in the communication of their spirituality was crucial as well. "The breadth and depth of the revival," Albin observes, "had something to do with the ability of the laity to understand and experience God for themselves and then to enable others to enter into a personal relationship with God as well."[49] It was ordinary people in community, rather than the high-profile leader, who exerted the most influence both inside and outside the movement as they attempted to put their faith into practice in the daily round of life. Albin's ultimate conclusion is "that early Methodist spirituality could be characterized as a positive process in which lay leadership and direction played a key role along with that of the local community rather than sudden experiences related to a fear of death or hell."[50]

It is obvious from these and other interpretations of Methodist spirituality that the vision of the Christian life for the Wesleys and their followers was that of breadth and wholeness.[51] Their principal insight was that no spirituality is complete until God's love—experienced both personally and in the context of community—is carried into the world in concrete acts of compassion and justice.

SALIENT THEMES IN METHODIST SPIRITUALITY

The salient themes in Methodist spirituality include: the foundation of grace, spiritual autobiography and narrative, accountable discipleship and the communal nature of spirituality, works of piety (including prayer and fasting, immersion in scripture, fellowship, and Eucharist), works of mercy, and the gift of song. All of these themes were pervasive in the lives and writings of early Methodist women as a part of their common inheritance in the movement. Before developing a portrait of the authors featured in this volume and examining the distinctive characteristics of their spirituality, it is important to explore these common, salient motifs more thoroughly, especially as they are reflected in the writings of the women themselves.

The Foundation of Grace

Wesleyan spirituality is built upon the foundation of grace.[52] In his sermon "On Working Out Our Own Salvation," Wesley talks about two grand heads of doctrine upon which the Christian life is built.[53] The first is grace as it pertains to the work of God for us in Jesus Christ; the second is grace as it pertains to the work of God in us through the power of the Holy Spirit. Grace is God's unmerited love, restoring our relationship to God and renewing God's own image in our lives. Nothing was more critical to Wesley than this understanding of spiritual restoration founded upon God's unconditional love. When he defined "grace," therefore, in his *Instructions for Children,* he described it simply as "the power of the Holy Spirit, enabling us to believe and love and serve God."[54] Christian discipleship—the arena of God's continuing activity in the life of the believer—is, first and foremost, a grace-filled response to God's all-sufficient grace.

While grace is essentially God's offer of relationship and restoration, in Wesleyan theology grace is understood as prevenient, convincing, justifying, sanctifying, or sacramental, in order to describe the way in which God's extension of love is experienced at various points in the spiritual journey. All of these aspects of grace are reflected in the writings collected in this volume, as we shall see more fully when we examine the narrative of the women's lives. More important than anything else, however, is the understanding that this grace is a free gift.[55] After singing a hymn that celebrates God's infinite, unexhausted love to all, Sarah Crosby confides to her journal: "Since that time I have had no doubt but grace is free for all."[56] Hannah Ball reflects on the foundational nature of God's grace in her life:

> There is no state of life but needs much grace, and no real happiness but what comes from God. A single life is a self-denying life. One day, meditating on what would constitute a person's happiness that had escaped the incidental allurements of youth, it was powerfully applied to my mind, "The grace of God, and nothing else." I have ever found it true. Jesus is all and in all to the believing soul. And where he is, there is no want of comfort to insure which we must always have this conviction, "that it is by grace we stand."

The women frequently refer to their need of "fresh supplies of grace." At a time of deep discouragement in her life, immediately following the difficult delivery of a child, Mary Entwisle confesses to her diary: "I was overcome with fretfulness and discouragements which hurt my soul. How needful it is to be looking for fresh supplies of grace continually." Similarly, Hannah Ball writes to a dear friend:

> I feel I daily stand in need of fresh grace. And I often think the Lord feeds my soul in a spiritual sense, with the manna of his love as he did the children of Israel in the wilderness, day by day. For he gives me my daily bread, and at night I have nothing over. In the morning I am as poor as a beggar. I arise and petition for fresh grace and strength.

The soul is "kept in perfect peace," Hannah reports on another occasion, "by a constant reliance on the Lord for fresh supplies of grace."

Grace elicits the most amazing images and sublime expressions of gratitude. "All glory be to God for grace, free grace," writes Isabella Wilson, "continued to my soul!" The women seek to plumb "the amazing depths of grace." Grace is a light that "shines brighter and brighter to the perfect day." It is a precious gift that the women yearn for in their lives. "Look with compassion on a soul," prays Mrs. Lefevre, "which pants for grace and forgiveness!" Grace can also be fragile, elusive. Mary Hanson reminds her reader that "the grace of God, like a spark in the ocean, can only be kept alive by a miracle." Hetty Roe, reversing this image in a flight of spiritual ecstasy in a letter to her friend, exclaims:

> Great things, indeed, my dear sister, has the Lord done for you, and for your unworthy friend. And yet, O stupendous grace! we have only received a drop from the ocean of his love. An endless prospect, and a maze of bliss, lie yet before us! opening beauties, and such lengths, and breadths, and depths, and heights, as thought cannot reach or mind of man conceive! It is, my friend, the fulness of the triune God, in which we may bathe, and plunge, and sink, till lost and swallowed up in the ever-increasing, overflowing ocean of delights.

Spiritual Narratives

In *Her Own Story*, I discuss women's narratives at length and assert that in the Wesleyan heritage the life of faith is by its very nature autobiographical.[57] Charles Wesley had a particular interest in spiritual narratives. In the early years of the revival, he solicited reflective materials of this nature from the rank and file of the movement on a regular basis. Only recently scholars have begun to bring this corpus together.⁵⁸ These narratives confirm that whenever the Christian faith becomes *my* faith, there lies behind that transformation a story that begs to be told, a narrative to unfold the mystery of life. Methodist spirituality is by definition a narrative spirituality. It is no surprise, therefore, that early Methodist women produced more spiritual autobiography than any other religious community in their time—and perhaps since.⁵⁹ The early Methodists owed much to the English Puritans and the Continental Pietists for the specific form of their narratives. The centrality of testimony concerning one's personal Christian experience in the Puritan heritage had left behind an existing tradition upon which to build. In Pietism, spiritual autobiography served the larger purpose of the movement, which was to rescue a vital faith from an arid orthodoxy. Since the Pietists exerted such a formidable influence upon the Wesleys, it is important to note their most significant contributions to Methodist spirituality.

The Pietist tradition within Lutheranism, manifest among the Methodists primarily through the Moravian communities in London, proclaimed a "religion of the heart." The Pietists maintained that alienation from God is overcome by affective, or "heartfelt," experience. The pivot upon which all else turned in the Christian journey was the experience of conversion, including genuine sorrow over sin (repentance) and personal trust in God through Christ (faith). "The key element in their understanding of religious life, then," claims Ted Campbell, "was their insistence that the 'heart,' denoting the will and affections (or 'dispositions'), is the central point of contact between God and human kind."⁶⁰ Conversion stories in this tradition reflected a specific pattern that generally included deep desire for God, penitential struggle, breakthrough to illumination, and certainty of faith.⁶¹ Pietism provided a language, and Puritanism provided a form for the Methodists to articulate their unique experiences of God in Christ. The Methodists learned about the dynamic nature of Christianity as an "experimental religion." They gained a deeper appreciation for the biological and organic images associated with the Christian life, revolving around terms such as "new birth" or "regeneration" and "growth in grace."

One of the characteristic emphases in the women's writings, therefore, is the experience of conversion—a process involving a call to personal repentance, moral transformation, and concomitant freedom to love. The decisive conclusion to be drawn from these accounts, however, is that the women equated salvation with liberation. This new-found freedom was rooted in the concept of "new creation," developed primarily in the Pauline corpus of the New Testament scriptures. The conversion account of Grace Murray reflects these typical axiological themes:

> One day, however, as I was reading in the fifth chapter of the epistle to the Romans, I was filled with light and love. I saw my lost estate in Adam and my recovery by Christ Jesus. My soul was overpowered and I cried out to those that were with me, "If all the devils in hell were dancing round me, I fear them not." I was as sensible, when the guilt of sin was removed from my conscience, as a man pressed under a load is sensible when it is taken off his shoulders. Now, therefore, God having set my soul at liberty, he opened my lips to praise him. And all that flow of spirits which I had felt in the vanities of the world was directed towards God.

The Wesleyan way of salvation centered on three dynamic movements, summarized by John Wesley in an important piece of correspondence to Thomas Church: "our main doctrines, which include all the rest, are three; that of repentance, of faith, and of holiness. The first of these we account, as it were, the porch of religion; the next, the door; the third is religion itself."[62] Wesley defines repentance as a true self-understanding akin to that experienced by the prodigal son who came to himself in the realization that he was far from his true home. Although it involves remorse and contrition, it carries a strong relational connotation, the initial turning of the heart and life homeward. Faith is the gift of trust in those things we cannot see, especially "Christ's love for me." But the word "faith" often functions as a shorthand symbol among the Wesleyan writers for the more specific concept of justification by grace through faith, which refers to the experience of having been accepted and pardoned by God through faith in Christ alone. Holiness is another shorthand term that refers to the whole process of becoming Christlike in our lives. It includes the idea of sanctification, the process of growing in grace and love, and Christian perfection, perhaps the most important of all Wesleyan concepts, which affirms that the love of God and neighbor can truly fill one's heart and life. The narratives of the women reflect each of these critical movements of God on the soul.

Repentance. The essence of repentance was to place oneself before God, to experience the gaping chasm that separates the sinful creature from the Creator, but to find in God the One who is also close at hand and who truly loves. "Oh crucify in me the whole body of sin!" prays Mrs. Lefeve. "Give me an humble, a mortified, and child-like spirit." In her fascinating apologetic tract, *The Dying Bed of a Saint and Sinner Contrasted*, Hester Rogers paints the lamentable portrait of the unrepentant sinner in hopes of awakening those in spiritual slumber:

> But can I hope to dwell with God? Ah! no, it cannot be. He is holy; I am vile. He is just and will punish the guilty. He called and I refused. He stretched forth his hand and I would not regard.... He often knocked at the door of my heart saying, by an inward whisper, "Thou art wrong; repent, and turn to God. Seek the Lord while he may be found, call upon him while he is near. Turn ye, turn ye, why will ye die?"

In similar fashion, reflecting upon how she had found her true home in a loving God, Hester pleads for the sinner who longs to be free: "It is true that in general the work of repentance is carried on by very slow degrees. Most people are a long time after they are convinced of sin before they are justified. But why is it? Even because of unbelief. The word of faith is nigh you. Fear not, only believe." Because God is a God who seeks to restore all things and is a God of mercy and love, the movement from repentance to faith, the Wesleys believed, is but a step. Contemplation of this merciful God, who responds to the repentant sinner with such grace and mercy, set Mary Stokes's heart in flight with song:

> What wonderous grace! what boundless love!
> What soft compassion this,
> That calls my rebel heart to prove
> A never fading bliss!

> 'Tis mercy bids me seek the Lord;
>   'Tis mercy bids me fly;
> 'Tis mercy speaks the balmy word,
>   "Repent, thy God is nigh."
>
> 'Tis mercy fills my trembling heart,
>   With agonizing pain,
> With keen distress and poignant smart,
>   Nor heave these sighs in vain.
>
> The tears that now in torrents flow,
>   This mercy will repress;
> Remove the load, a pardon show,
>   And speak a healing peace.

Faith. Drawing upon the teachings of his Anglican heritage, John Wesley defined saving faith as a

> true trust and confidence of the mercy of God through our Lord Jesus Christ and a steadfast hope of all good things at God's hand.... This is the true, [living] Christian faith, [which] is not in the mouth and outward profession only, but it liveth and stirreth inwardly in the heart.[63]

The center around which all else revolved for the Methodists was the shared experience of faith-as-trust and salvation by grace. The more that John preached this gospel and Charles wove it into his hymns, the more that people experienced spiritual liberation in their lives. The Spirit of God was alive and at work in the hearts and minds of many people, especially poor people, who had never experienced God as someone real in their lives before.

In the account of her conversion, Hetty Roe asks the existential question:

> But what is faith? O show me how to believe. Show me what is the gospel faith or I am yet undone. I desire not deliverance except in thy own way. I desire no happiness but thy favor. What shall I do? O teach me, O help me, or I am lost!" That word came with divine evidence and sweetness to my heart, "Cast all thy care upon him, for he careth for thee."

Introduction

Mary Tatham sought to answer that question in a meditation on justification and to describe the consequences of God's gift of faith in the believer:

> What is justifying faith? It is a gracious act, whereby a soul under conviction of sin apprehends Christ as his redeemer and lays hold upon him for pardon and reconciliation before God.
> What effect does this justifying faith have upon the heart of every true believer? It fills him with love and with astonishment at the greatness of God's mercy.... Love filling the heart is productive of real holiness, and God being always present with him and his desires going out continually after him, he is kept above the power of temptation and sin. In this state he presses forward to greater degrees of purity and love until the whole soul is changed into the divine image.

"To live by faith," observes Mary Hanson, "is to eye the loving Savior as your wisdom, righteousness, sanctification, and redemption, and to maintain a loving sense of the immediate presence of God, or a walking in a constant remembrance of him who is the fountain of all your mercies." It is to feed every moment on the bread of life. "To live by faith on Jesus," she continues, "[is] to prove all the promises of God, 'Yea and Amen in him.'" Nothing could be more foundational in the life of the Christian than this experience of saving faith. According to Mary Tatham it "purifies the heart, converts the soul, sanctifies the affections, and enlarges the desires towards God and man so that, if it were possible, it would embrace the whole world and bring every soul to taste and enjoy the sweetness of that love of which he so freely partakes."

Having asked what faith was, Hester Roe answered the question herself on the basis of personal experience and bore witness to the liberating nature of life in Christ:

> Then did he appear to my salvation. In that moment my fetters were broken, my bands were loosed, and my soul set at liberty. The love of God was shed abroad in my heart and I rejoiced with joy unspeakable. Now, if I had possessed ten thousand souls I could have ventured them all with Jesus. I would have given them all to him! I felt a thousand promises all my own, more than a thousand scriptures to confirm my evidence.... I could now call Jesus Lord, by the Holy Ghost, and the Father my Father. My sins

were gone, my soul was happy, and I longed to depart and be with Jesus. I was truly a new creature and seemed to be in a new world! I could do nothing but love and praise my God and could not refrain continually repeating, "Thou art my Father. O God, thou art my God!" while tears of joy ran down my cheeks.

Holiness. While justification by grace through faith is the foundation of the Christian life, holiness of heart and life, or sanctification, is the process that leads to the ultimate goal of perfect love in this life. The Wesleyan concept of salvation is that of faith moving toward love. The women's writings are filled with a sense of longing for this ultimate gift of God's grace and with descriptions of such a life. The doctrine of Christian perfection is central to the spirituality of the early Methodist women and can be characterized by the following propositions:[64]

(1) *Love.* Christian perfection is the fullest possible love of God and neighbor—no less, but also no more.

(2) *Purity of Intention.* The essence of Christian perfection is purity of intention; that is, seeking to please God in all thought, word, and action.

(3) *The Definition of Sin.* Christian perfection is freedom from sin "properly-so-called"; that is, "a voluntary transgression of a known law." It is the power not to sin willfully and its concomitant freedom from the tyranny of evil.

(4) *Immediacy.* Despite the fact that Wesley thought the gift of full salvation was normally given in the *articulis mortis* (at the point of death), he was adamant on the point that if perfection is a possibility at all, it must at least be possible in the span of human life.

(5) *Dynamism.* Wesley's basic conception of perfection in the Christian life was dynamic, and not static, in nature. He assumed that growth in holiness would continue within Christian perfection and not just before it.

(6) *Restoration.* Wesley looked to the early church and its understanding of salvation as the restoration of the image of God for his doctrine of Christian perfection. It is essentially conformity to Christ in all things, the believer perennially dependent upon God for whatever level of restoration is made possible through the gracious power of the Holy Spirit.

(7) *Happiness.* Holiness is happiness. The fullest expression of holiness in life was the truest form of happiness. The goal of the

Christian life, therefore, was essentially "a blessed abiding" in God.

The concluding words of John Wesley's first sermon on the subject of Christian perfection epitomize his ultimate vision:

> "Desire not to live but to praise [God's] name; let all your thoughts, words, and works tend to his glory. Set your heart firm on him, and on other things only as they are in and from him." "Let your soul be filled with so entire a love of him that you may love thing but for his sake." "Have a pure intention of heart, a steadfast regard to his glory in all your actions." "Fix your eye upon the blessed hope of your calling, and make all the things of the world minister unto it." For then, and not till then, is that "mind in us which was also in Christ Jesus," when in every motion of our heart, in every word of our tongue, in every work of our hand, we "pursue nothing but in relation to him."[65]

Jane Cooper, featured in this volume, was one of John Wesley's primary exemplars of the Christian perfected in love. Mary Tatham explains Wesley's doctrine and vision of sanctified humanity in a judicious manner. A lengthy quotation from her reflections on the theme is merited:

> If, then, we are justified by faith, by what means are we sanctified? Doubtless, by continuing to believe. If a deliverance from the guilt and dominion of sin, peace with God, and joy in the Holy Ghost follow justification, what is implied in sanctification? Sanctification is a freedom from all sin, love purifying the affections, influencing every action, and filling the heart with a still more abundant measure of peace and joy in the Holy Ghost. How must we continue to believe? By continuing in the love of God. How may we continue in the love of God? By keeping his commandments, and his commandments are not grievous. What are his commandments? "Thou shalt love the Lord thy God with all thy heart, with all thy mind, with all thy soul, and with all thy strength, and thy neighbour as thyself. On these two commandments hang all the law and the prophets." How are we to keep these commandments? By cleaving close to Jesus. By being united to him as the branch is to the living vine, continually receiving life, nourishment, and strength from him, as the branch does from the vine.

Overwhelmed on one occasion by her reflections upon the consolations of the Spirit and the blessed way of holiness, Isabella Wilson expressed the same vision of full restoration, more in the language of Methodist piety:

> This is love unspeakable! His delight is to make us happy. O how does his love exceed all that fancy can form, or imagination paint. The favoured soul is ready to say, I have heard great and glorious things spoken of thee, but, oh, how little was said to what I find! O how unable are the tongues of mortals to set forth the pleasures of those who are united to this Jesus! We joy in his redeeming love. He is most precious, and altogether lovely.[66]

Accountable Discipleship

In defense of his expanding network of Methodist Societies, John Wesley identified small groups as the distinguishing mark of the movement. In addition to organizing a network of itinerant preacher/evangelists, he built up a structure to sustain that ministry, in which his followers were encouraged to "watch over one another in love." The first Societies developed in Bristol initially as small groups that met weekly for worship, fellowship, prayer, and instruction. Originally inspired by the Anglican religious societies made up predominantly of laity, the classes and bands of early Methodism also owed much to their counterparts among the Pietists.[67] Band meetings developed as intimate groups of four to seven members who voluntarily banded together to encourage one another in the quest for holiness of heart and life. Class meetings, typically larger than bands and consisting of approximately twelve members, encompassed the entire membership of the Society and provided a means for the practice and maintenance of disciplinary standards.

The early Methodist hallmarks of mutual encouragement and genuine care are celebrated in the hymn of Charles Wesley:

> Help us to help each other, Lord,
> Each other's cross to bear;
> Let each his friendly aid afford,
> And feel his brother's care.

Introduction

> Help us to build each other up,
> Our little stock improve;
> Increase our faith, confirm our hope,
> And perfect us in love.[68]

Methodist women specialized in this disciple-making enterprise. Grace Murray describes the division of the Methodist Society in Newcastle into these small groups:

> Soon also, the people were again divided into bands, or small select societies; women by themselves, and the men in like manner. I had full a hundred in classes, whom I met in two separate meetings and a band for each day of the week. I likewise visited the sick and backsliders, which was my pleasant meat. The work of God was my delight, and when I was not employed in it I seemed out of my element.

Ann Tripp reports that Sarah Crosby continued to participate in her band meeting into the closing weeks of her life. And when the end was near, "she began praying for her bands, classes, friends, and the church of God, that they might all meet above." Interaction in her classes, however, provided opportunity for her to reveal the most intimate and important concerns of her life:

> Several times in the week she said, "If I die soon, remember such and such things." Thursday and Friday she met both her classes as usual.... In one of the classes she said her time here would not be long, and repeated, "Who first shall be summoned away, my merciful God, is it I?" and said that she found herself more allied to heaven than earth, for though she had many friends here, she had more in glory.

Leaders in these groups had to be persons of spiritual and emotional maturity. When first appointed as a class leader by Wesley himself, Sarah Crosby earnestly sought God's will and prayed for direction in this important responsibility. She assumed that God would "answer me by giving some one a great blessing," and she was not disappointed. "My soul seemed all love," she reminisces, "and I desired nothing so much as to lay down my life for others that they might feel the same." The classes and bands provided an opportunity not only to connect with one another, but also to commune with God through the intimacy of this fellowship. "I have not felt much of the divine presence," confessed Mary Entwisle, "till class time when the Lord was powerfully present with us." Isabella Wilson writes home, "We had blessed times, especially at a class on Friday evening when seven or eight persons obtained purity of heart. Glory be to God, his people here are rising daily!" Accountable discipleship through small groups was a keynote of the Wesleyan revival. The women's accounts of life in these accountability structures reflect salient qualities such as self-denial, transparency, simplicity, sincerity, faithfulness, and immersion in the means of grace. In the intimacy of these small groups women learned what it meant to grow in Christ and, together, plumbed the depths of God's love for them all.

Works of Piety

Fellowship in small groups was just one "means of grace" in a constellation of spiritual practices or disciplines, the purpose of which was richer communion with God through Christ. In addition to Christian fellowship, or conference, John Wesley also included prayer and fasting, Bible study, and participation in the sacrament of Holy Communion among the "instituted means of grace." He also called these "works of piety." These activities nurtured and sustained the women's spiritual growth and also provided the "energy" that fueled the Wesleyan movement as a powerful religious awakening.[69]

Those aspects of Wesleyan spirituality that surface frequently in the pages of the women's writings have to do with the necessity of growth in grace and immersion in the means of grace. In a journal entry of February 18, 1775, Hannah Ball, in characteristic Wesleyan fashion, provides an outline of those means of grace she had found most helpful to her spiritual growth:

> I have received, I trust, an increase of patience. My soul rests in God. To the end that I may improve in the knowledge of him, I read, write, and pray, hear the word preached, converse with the people of God, fast, or use abstinence, together with every prudential help as channels only for receiving the grace of God. But private prayer is in general the most strengthening means of all.

Similarly, Ann Gilbert testifies to the centrality of these works of piety in her life. "Before I conclude," she admonishes her reader, "there is one thing I wish to be particularly remembered; during the course of my pilgrimage, I have always found that the more diligent I was in using the means of Grace, ... the more happiness I have enjoyed in my soul."[70] "I am glad that you give us so particular an account of the means of grace which Raithby affords," writes Elizabeth Mortimer to her newly married daughter. "Use them in faith and you will prosper."

The manuscript journal of Mary Entwisle reflects habituated patterns of piety and remembrance that were typical of the early Methodist women and in this case, are shared with her husband:

> A day to be remembered with gratitude. When I awoke this morning I felt my heart sweetly drawn out after God. I had some very profitable converse with my dear husband. A review of the Lord's gracious dealings with us melted our hearts and we were enabled to praise him. After we arose we spent some time in reading the scriptures and then joined in offering our humble tribute of prayer and praise, in which we were much refreshed. Surely no people in the world have such cause to praise God as we have. Bless the Lord O my soul and forget not all his benefits.

Prayer and Fasting. The prayer of early Methodist women reflects a wide range of styles and forms, and an attempt has been made to retain that breadth in the selections included in this volume. In his journal, John Wesley describes an interesting specimen of a woman at prayer that affected him greatly despite the scene's peculiarity.

> The fire kindled more and more, till Mrs. _____ asked if I would give her "leave to pray". Such a prayer I never heard before; it was perfectly an original: odd and unconnected, made up of disjointed fragments—and yet like a flame of fire. Every sentence went through my heart, and I believe the heart of everyone present. For many months I have found nothing like it. It was good for *me* to be here.[71]

Many of the women were noted for their life of prayer. On the occasion of Sarah Crosby's death, Frances Pawson recalled one of Sarah's unique qualities: "She used to begin prayer with the simplicity of a little child, and then rise to the language of a mother of Israel. Thus she prayed with the Spirit and with the understanding."[72] Elizabeth Mortimer recognized this same gift in Sarah Crosby as well, describing how "she could descend to the capacity of a child, and then rise again to expatiate on the deep things of God, with those that had attained the highest state of grace."[73]

No early Methodist woman, however, was so renowned for prayer as was Ann Cutler, affectionately known by all simply as "Praying Nanny." In the advertisement to William Bramwell's account of her life and work, Zechariah Taft observes that "her peculiar call from Heaven appears to have been chiefly the exercise of importunate believing prayer."[74] Although her public praying tended to be very short, the extent and intensity of her personal devotional life was unparalleled. It was characterized by frequent and often lengthy periods of private prayer, as many as twelve to fourteen such times each day. "For prayer," Bramwell simply concludes, "I never expect to see her equal again."

Hannah Ball describes her own devotional practices that link prayer to ascetic disciplines in her journal:

> Every Friday I set apart as a day of fasting and prayer. This painful task to nature is more than compensated by the divine communications of love to my soul. O transporting thought, to be for ever with the Lord! I long to meditate more on those divine glories which the soul shall be ravished with to all eternity.

Little wonder she confessed on another occasion that "private prayer is in general the most strengthening means of all." "O Lord, keep my soul awake, and athirst for thee!" cries Grace Murray. "It has been my grief to see and feel such deadness and dulness amongst Christians; Jesus Christ was whole nights on the mountain in prayer."[75] Early Methodist women rooted their spirituality in prayer.

Although few of the women actually describe meditative technique or provide direction for contemplative forms of devotion, Martha Hall, sister of the Wesley brothers, did prescribe a particular method of prayer and meditation that may have been adopted by others. As to the benefits of this practice, she maintains that meditation impresses the sense of our duty upon the mind, keeps the conscience tender, and habituates the mind to spiritual objects.

Her own contemplative method takes on a pattern similar to Salesian meditative technique and moves through consideration and affection to resolution. In addition to meditation, recollection is a term related to Anglican spirituality and often used by the women. It denotes the concentration of the soul on the presence of God. In a more restricted sense it applies to a certain stage of prayer in which the memory, understanding, and will are held to be stilled by God's action and the soul is left in a state of peace.

The following excerpt from a meditation in the diary of Hester Ann Rogers powerfully illustrates the spirituality of early Methodist women and demonstrates a wholistic understanding of prayer in the life of the believer:

> O how precious are your ways to my soul, suited to my weakness, worthy of a God! I am nothing! You are all. I live moment by moment upon your smiles and dwell under the shadow of your wings. I desire nothing but to please you, to grow in inward conformity to your will and sink deeper into humble love, to let the light of what your grace has bestowed shine on all around, and to live and die proclaiming God is love.

Immersion in Scripture. "I am determined to be a Bible Christian," John Wesley once claimed, "not almost but altogether."[76] The Wesleyan revival, like other movements of Christian renewal, was at its heart a rediscovery of the Bible. The early Methodist people believed that "their book" was not simply a compilation of letters and histories, of prayers and biographies, of wise sayings and encouraging words. They realized that these ancient words could become the "Living Word" for them as they encountered scripture anew through the inspiration of the Holy Spirit. They understood the Bible to be the supreme authority in matters of faith and practice. In both preaching and personal study, the scriptural text sprang to new life, forming, informing, and transforming their lives with immediate effect and lasting influence.

Scripture was liberating for the early Methodist women. But the freedom they discovered in Christ through the Word often demanded their prophetic witness to the truth in the face of opposition. The defense of their own ministry, for example, ran counter to the accepted social and ecclesiastical norms of their day and required great courage. The Bible was not only the source of their strength, it was a book of promise that held the key to abundant life. The experience of Hester Ann Rogers illustrates this biblical focus:

> Reading the word of God in private this day was an unspeakable blessing. O! how precious are the promises. What a depth in these words: "For all the promises of God in him are yea, and in him, amen, unto the glory of God" [2 Cor. 1:20]. Yes, my soul, they are so to you! The Father delights to fulfil and the Spirit to seal them on my heart. O that dear invaluable truth!
>
> > Ready art thou to receive;
> > Readier is thy God to give.

The Bible figures prominently in the narrative of the women's lives. The scripture index to this volume demonstrates, in part, the diversity of biblical texts upon which the women drew to describe their experience and to understand God's presence in their lives. The words of scripture create, confirm, and communicate God's work of grace. "I went home very serious," Jane Cooper remembers with regard to the inbreaking of faith in her life, "and began to search the scriptures." Similarly, Hannah Ball "applied closer than ever to reading the Bible." While reading the prayer of Moses, she recalls, "divine light was communicated in a greater degree than I had ever known before." In her manuscript journal, Hester Ann Rogers carefully records preaching events, meditates in extended narratives upon important biblical insights, and reflects upon the importance of the Bible in her life. Mary Tatham was noted for her exegetical work and her use of scripture in the class meetings she led. Scripture formed the lives of the women and often provided the necessary stimulus for their transformation as well.

Eucharistic Worship. The Wesleyan revival was both "evangelical" (a rediscovery of God's word of grace) and "eucharistic" (a rediscovery of the sacrament of Holy Communion as a way to experience that grace). The Wesleys believed that sacramental grace and evangelical experience are necessary counterparts in both worship and the Christian life. It is not too much to say that the spirituality of the early Methodist women was eucharistic. The early Methodists sang—and the women bore witness to the testimony of—this Charles Wesley hymn stanza:

> The prayer, the fast, the word conveys,
> When mix'd with faith, Thy life to me;
> In all the channels of Thy grace
> I still have fellowship with Thee:
> But chiefly here my soul is fed
> With fulness of immortal bread.[77]

These "feasts of love," as the women often described them, shaped their understanding of God's love for them and their reciprocal love for God, all powerfully symbolized for them in the sharing of a meal. "I have been much favored this day," recalls Isabella Wilson, "with the means of grace which were feasts of love to my soul. I have fed at the table of the Lord on rich grace with thanksgiving. Oh that I may be more united to Jesus, that I may see him in all things who is altogether lovely." Hannah Harrison explicitly linked her experience of God's sanctifying grace with these instruments of restoration and wholeness of life: "From this time I began to seek for full sanctification; while receiving the Lord's-Supper, I felt the application of those words, 'Thou art sealed unto the day of redemption.'"[78]

Sarah Ryan's spirituality was particularly oriented around the sacrament of the Lord's Supper. She narrates the important encounters with God that she experienced at the sacramental table. Sarah Crosby had invited her to hear John Wesley preach. His sermon touched her heart deeply. What she yearned for more than anything else was a deep assurance of Christ's redeeming love for her. During the sacrament immediately following the service of the word, she availed herself on the altar and encountered God there in a most potent manner:

> And all the way, as I went up with much difficulty to the table, I was still saying, "For *me* Lord; for *me.*" When I came up, my strength being quite gone, I threw my body across the rails, and, being overwhelmed with the power of God, was utterly regardless of outward things. Mr. Wesley offered me the bread, but I was not able to take it. So he passed by me and gave it me when he came back. When he spoke those words, "The blood of the Lord Jesus Christ," they pierced my heart and filled my soul with love to him. Immediately I said, "This is the faith by which the martyrs went to the flames." I felt a change through my whole soul and longed to be alone.

She still struggles, however, to experience the fullest assurance of God's love for which she so desperately seeks. She prays, studies the Word, and seeks Christian counsel from her beloved friends, but remains unsatisfied. For three weeks she immerses herself in all the means of grace. It is not until Easter Eve, however, as she goes forward to receive the sacrament, that God's love overwhelms her with tremendous force. "Immediately I was filled with light and joy and love," she exclaims, "and said with confidence, 'Thou art the resurrection and the life.'" She seeks Sarah Crosby for confirmation, receives it, and concludes her narrative: "I fell back in my seat and was quite overwhelmed with the power and love of God."

The experience of Hester Ann Rogers was remarkably similar, also the consequence of special services of worship during Holy Week. In her case, "As Mr. Simpson was reading that sentence in the communion service, 'If any man sin, we have an advocate with the Father, Jesus Christ the righteous, and he is the propitiation for our sins,'" she recalls that "a ray of divine light and comfort was darted on my soul." She describes how her participation in the sacrament enabled her to believe. "I felt love to God spring up in my heart, and in a measure could rejoice in him," she confesses, "so that I would have given all the world to have died that moment."

Allusions to the Eucharist in the writings of the women reflect the multivalent nature of the sacrament in Wesleyan teaching. Not only does it enable the community to remember the past event of the cross and Christ's redemptive work for all, but also it celebrates the presence of the living Lord in a feast of thanksgiving and orients the community in hope toward the future consummation of all things in the great heavenly banquet to come. These themes of the sacrament as a memorial, a sign and means of grace, and a pledge of heaven are frequently illustrated by reference to Charles Wesley's *Hymns on the Lord's Supper* in the writings of the women.

Works of Mercy

For the women of early Methodism there could be no separation of their personal experience of God and devotion to Christ from their active role as agents of reconciliation and social transformation in the world. Their spirituality was truly incarnational. To the various instituted means of grace, or works of piety, outlined above, John Wesley added "works of mercy," included among his more expansive "prudential means of grace." Authentic Christianity, he believed, consists in a constant inward and outward movement. The primary means by which the Methodists lived out this holistic understanding of the Christian faith was through works of mercy that paralleled the more interior works of piety. In this regard, the women demonstrate a potent balance of vital piety of compassionate ministry. Their lives consisted of active social service, commitment to the poor, and advocacy for the oppressed, as well as attention to the ordinances of God.[79] The women had learned from the Wesleys that authentic Christianity is mission, and sincere engagement in God's mission is true religion. Evangelism was the heart of this missionary vision, fueled by the desire to share the good news they had experienced in Christ with others in both word and deed.

John Wesley mandated that his followers engage in works of mercy, defined in the second of his "General Rules" in the most expansive way possible—"do good." Methodist people were encouraged to do good, "by being in every kind merciful after their power, as they have opportunity doing good of every possible sort and as far as is possible to all men."[80] In their effort to adhere to this spiritual instruction, Methodist women sought out people in need—the poor, the hungry, the destitute, and the neglected. They visited prisons, established orphanages and schools, and practiced their servant-oriented faith in their own particular contexts, thereby extending the ministry of Methodism into the communities they served.

By far the most dramatic manifestation of this missiological spirituality was the establishment of the Leytonstone community of women in London under the direction of Mary Bosanquet. In 1763, when a property near her place of birth became vacant, Mary secured it and moved there with a small circle of women with the intention of establishing an orphanage and school on the basis of Wesley's own prototype at Kingswood. After much careful deliberation the women decided to take in none but the most destitute and hopeless. At first the family consisted of Mary, Sarah Ryan, a maid, and Sally Lawrence. With the addition of five more orphans and confronted with the problem of Sarah's declining health, Ann

Tripp was secured as a governess for the children. They formed themselves into a tightly knit community, adopted a uniform dress of dark purple cotton, and ate together at a table five yards in length. Over the course of five years they sheltered and cared for thirty-five children and thirty-four adults. Their community was a model of vital piety and social service, an important manifestation of the holistic spirituality of the Wesleyan heritage.

Nearly one year into her Sunday school experiment in High Wycombe, Hannah Ball recorded this characteristic resolution in her diary:

> I desire to spend the remaining part of my life in a closer walking with God and in labors of love to my fellow-creatures—feeding the hungry, clothing the naked, instructing a few of the rising generation in the principles of religion, and in every possible way I am capable ministering to them that shall be heirs of salvation.

She also engaged in a prison ministry similar to that of the famous Methodist woman, Sarah Peters, in London.[81] "I this day visited three poor sailors in prison," she writes, "each of them deprived of a limb, apparently ignorant of the scriptures and strangers to the God of their mercies. I pointed them to the Lamb of God which takes away the sins of the world."

The advice of John Wesley to a Methodist woman aspiring to "perfection" is a typical expression of this gospel alongside the poor: "Go and see the poor and sick in their own little hovels. Take up your cross, woman! Remember the faith! Jesus went before you, and will go with you. Put off the gentlewoman: You bear a higher character."[82] It is amazing how many women took this mission in the world with utter seriousness. Charles Wesley memorialized the work of such women in an elegy to Mrs. Mary Naylor, whose representative life so powerfully illustrates the witness of a life committed to the poor:

> Affliction, poverty, disease,
> Drew out her soul in soft distress,
>   The wretched to relieve:
> In all the works of love employed,
> Her sympathizing soul enjoyed
>   The blessedness to give.

> Her Savior in his members seen
> A stranger she received him in,
> An hungry Jesus fed,
> Tended her sick, imprisoned Lord,
> And flew in all his wants to afford
> Her ministerial aid.
>
> A nursing-mother to the poor,
> For them she husbanded her store,
> Her life, her all, bestowed;
> For them she labored day and night,
> In doing good her whole delight,
> In copying after God.[83]

The Gift of Song

"Before we reached the place," writes Grace Murray, "we heard the people singing hymns. The very sound set all my passions afloat, though I did not know one word they uttered, which plainly shows how the affections may be greatly moved while the understanding is quite dark." This reference to the important role that hymns played in the Wesleyan tradition is typical of the women's religious narratives. Methodists sang the keynotes of their heritage in a unique and winsome lyrical spirituality. The Wesleys revolutionized Anglican worship with the rediscovery of congregational singing. "The eighteenth-century revival," Richard Heitzenrater observes, "was to a great extent borne on the wings of Charles' poetry. Charles' hymns not only helped form the texture of the Methodist mind but also, perhaps more importantly, set the temper of the Methodist spirit."[84] The hymns themselves were a powerful tool in the Spirit's work of revival and shaped the spirituality of the Methodist people, perhaps more than any other single force beside the Bible. In a study of a sampling of hymn allusions in the writings of early Methodist women, I identified five primary ways in which the women used the hymns, and these are consistent with the selections presented in this volume.[85] Those motifs most directly related to the spirituality of the women include the hymn as a catalyst for religious awakening, as an act of prayer, and as the language of the heart.

"I still continued to hold the Lord to his promise," confesses Sarah Ryan, "and it was to me according to my faith. Just as I came to the rails, God spoke these words to my soul,

> Lift your eyes of faith, and look
> To the signs he did ordain!
> Thus the bread of Life was broke!
> Thus the Lamb of God was slain!
> Thus was shed on Calvary,
> His last drop of blood for thee!

"Immediately," she continues, "I was filled with light and joy and love, and said with confidence, 'Thou art the resurrection and the life.'"

An excerpt from the account of Sarah Ryan demonstrates the fluid movement from prayer to hymn. "I have been all this day kept in perfect peace," she records in her journal, "and in the evening was much drawn out in prayer for myself and all my dear friends. O my Jesus, you are my all in all!

> Sink me to perfection's height,
> The depth of humble love!"

Hannah Harrison, one of the pioneer Methodist women of York, specifically used a hymn to express the language of her heart. "Thursday morning following, when at private prayer, I was so overwhelmed with the divine presence, that I cried out, 'Lord, can what I feel proceed from any but thee?' and the language of my heart was—

> I yield, I yield,
> I can hold out no more,
> I sink,—by dying love compell'd,
> And own Thee Conqueror."[86]

"Oh! the unbounded love of Jesus to my soul," exclaims Isabella Wilson. "His promises are all precious. My peace flows as a river while he teaches me the lessons of his grace, of faith and holiness. My soul is athirst for all the mind that was in him.

> Lord, take my heart and let it be
> For ever clos'd to all but thee:
> Seal thou my breast, and let me wear
> That pledge of love for ever there."

The hymnody of the movement, and especially the hymns of Charles Wesley, formed the language of their spirituality.

THE WOMEN OF EARLY METHODISM

Painting a portrait of the typical woman of early Methodism is an impossible task.[87] Even the literate women included in this volume represent a wide range of contrasting images, especially in terms of background and status. For several of them, absolutely nothing is known beyond the material presented here.

Gail Malmgreen's study of Cheshire Methodists and their families offers minimal clues to some consistent patterns, although it is a serious question whether they can be generalized.[88] On the basis of her research, the ordinary woman in early Methodism was likely to be unmarried, traveled more widely than would have been expected, and tended to align herself with the Methodists in defiance of her parents' wishes.

Although he does not differentiate with regard to gender, Tom Albin's empirical study of early Methodist people also provides some interesting insights that can be related to the religious experience of early Methodist women.[89] "Typical Methodists" were born to parents who were not disinterested in the Anglican religion they inherited. Providence carried them to an encounter with a Methodist preacher who opened the door to a more serious contemplation of their relationship to God. They joined the Methodist Society as a response to the awakening they experienced. Relationships built in the context of their small groups led them to pray for peace and restoration with God incessantly. They experienced the overwhelming love of God in a conversion to living faith. Feeling as though they have been born again, they sought for God's grace to possess them fully and yearned to love God and neighbor with the fullest possible love. From this general portrait, it is clear that early Methodist women were serious about their spiritual lives, talking about and reflecting upon them constantly.

The writings of three women—Sarah Crosby, Hester Ann Rogers, and Isabella Wilson—appear in all three sections of this volume. The autobiographical vignette of Hester Ann Rogers is strikingly similar to the generic portrait painted above and serves well to provide a concrete illustration of the spirituality of the women. Hetty Roe was born in Macclesfield in Cheshire in 1756. Her father, vicar of the local parish church, was a man of strict morality and high church Anglican piety. Hetty's parents taught her as a child to observe all of the external duties of a devout member of the Church of England, to pray regularly, to read the Bible, and to learn the catechism. But she yearned for an experience of religion that was more direct, more personal, and more uplifting. Her journal chronicles the cataclysmic effect of her father's death when she was nine, the detrimental influence of her "worldly" godmother, and the spiritual turmoil of her quest for peace and assurance. With much of her grief still unresolved, as a young teen she experienced the first of several religious crises.

Returning to her native Macclesfield in the summer of 1773 at seventeen years of age, Hetty discovered that the new curate, the Reverend David Simpson, was reputed to be a Methodist. Having been taught that these "sectarians" were false prophets and enthusiasts, her prejudices welled up against him. Through the winter of 1773–74, however, she sat under his preaching, and her prejudices began to melt away. She began to attend Methodist meetings in secret for fear of her family's retribution. On November 11, 1774, she was struck to the heart by the sermon of Wesley's itinerant preacher, Samuel Bardsley. "I thought every word was for me!" she confesses.

> He spoke to my heart as if he had known all the secret workings there and pointed all such sinners, as I felt myself to be, to Jesus crucified. I was much comforted. My prejudices were now fully removed and I received a full and clear conviction, "These are the people of God, and show, in truth, the way of salvation."

Hester immersed herself thereafter in the activities of the Methodist Society and began to read widely in the literature of the movement, with particular interest in Wesley's doctrine of Christian perfection. Her wholehearted involvement with the Methodists led to harsh persecution and ostracism from family and friends. In the midst of it all, however, her journal reflects a spirit of joy and gratitude. "Last night and this morning I had deep communion with my God," she writes. "I feel I am indeed one with Christ and Christ is one with me. I dwell in Christ and Christ in me. O blessed union with him my soul loves!" It was during this same period that Hester met John Wesley for the first time.[90] Immediately recognizing her spiritual gifts, he employed her as fully as possible, particularly as a class leader. In later years, he identified her primary talent as the ability "to watch over the newborn babes. Although they have much love, they have not yet either much light or much strength."[91] She was also active in the visitation of the sick. In a letter to a friend, Hester describes the benefits related to this ministry in particular.

> In visiting the sick I found a great increase of love to him and the souls for which Jesus died. And at some places, their neighbors coming in, the power of the Lord has been present, and some of them who before were asleep in sin are crying out, What must I do to be saved? And so many fresh ones are sending to beg I will call upon them, that it seems as if my employment would soon be too great for my bodily strength. But if he calls me to the work he will give me strength.[92]

She soon became one of the important pillars of Methodism in Cheshire.

In 1782, John Wesley appointed James Rogers to the Macclesfield circuit. Hester immediately became a close friend of the itinerant and considered his wife, Martha, as a sister. During the ensuing year, Martha's health began to fail, perhaps due to the strain of several births in quick succession. On December 15, 1783, she expressed her strong desire for Hester to marry James if she were to die. In her manuscript journal, Hester confesses that she was astonished, thunderstruck, and speechless. Nine pages of Hester's journal describe the events following her friend's death; James and Hester were married on August 19, 1784, about six months after Martha's death. Nine days after the wedding, Hester began the challenging life of the itinerant preacher's wife in earnest, as the

Rogers family left her beloved Macclesfield for James's new appointment in Dublin. They remained in Ireland, dividing their time between Dublin and Cork in an amazing ministry of tremendous depth and compassion, until 1790, at which time Wesley appointed James to London and Hester to the position of housekeeper at City Road. With the help of Elizabeth Ritchie, Hester attended John Wesley at his death in 1791. In April 1793, she gave birth to a daughter, her fifth child in nine years of marriage, but never fully recovered from complications related to the pregnancy. She died on October 10, 1794. Made famous in Methodist circles through the posthumous publication of her *Experience*, her most fervent prayer was to be filled with all the fullness of God.

I have made a concerted effort to select a representative community of women writers from the extant materials. With regard to those women whose dates are fairly certain, one third were born prior to 1735, another third represent roughly the second generation of the revival (born between 1735 and 1760), and the final third were born after 1760, some of them flourishing more in the early nineteenth rather than in the late eighteenth century.[93] Martha (Patty) Hall, the sister of John and Charles Wesley, was born earliest in 1706 but, like her brothers, lived a long life, dying the same year as John in 1791. Mary Barritt Taft, one of the greatest evangelists of the early nineteenth century, died in 1851, living the furthest into the new century. The vast majority of these women, however, lived the entirety of their lives in the 1700s.

It is not surprising that many of the women were born or spent most of their lives in London, given the critical importance of the city to the movement. But an equal number lived in the north of England, in some of the major centers associated with women such as Leeds, Macclesfield, and throughout Yorkshire. Because of the importance of Bristol in the earliest years of the revival, many of the first generation of Methodist faithful were associated with the Societies in that port city. Hannah Ball lived in High Wycombe, near Oxford; Sarah Mallet came from Norfolk, a historic center of religious fervor; Mary Tooth made Madeley in Shropshire her home with the saintly Fletcher couple. One of the women, Margaret Davidson, was blind and was the first woman preacher in Ireland; and Mary Gilbert came from a family of planters in British Antigua. These women are the daughters of landed gentry and tenant farmers, surgeons and merchants; a substantial number of them are widows. At least one of the women, Phillis Wheatley, was of African descent.

Among the first generation, the most well-known throughout the Methodist connection were certainly Grace Murray, Jane Cooper, and Mrs. Lefevre. A part of their fame was due to their close association with John Wesley. The letters of the latter two were published by their spiritual mentor. Grace was a prototype of female leadership in early Methodism, a spiritual model to whom many women (and men) looked for guidance in the spiritual life. Band and class leader, sick visitor, housekeeper, and itinerant "regulator" of women's groups, she functioned, in effect, as a sub-pastor, providing leadership in acts of worship and service throughout the growing network of Societies. Susannah Designe prepared an account of her religious experience for Charles Wesley in 1742. She was a leader in one of the Bristol bands during the formative decade of the 1740s and was acutely concerned about growth in the spiritual life. Sarah Colston and Mary Stokes were also Bristolians of critical importance to nascent Methodism at the New Room. Joanna Turner was a Calvinist introduced to the Methodist Societies by her cousin, Elizabeth Johnson, the devout class leader in Bristol reckoned one of the most pious women among the Methodists in the west of England.

A fairly large circle of the women were part of the Leytonstone/Cross Hall community, one of the most critical models of vital piety and social service, which included Sarah Ryan, Sarah Crosby, Mary Fletcher, Ann Tripp, Ann Highfield, and Mary Tooth. Sarah Ryan was converted under the preaching of George Whitefield and later became an active member of the Foundery Society in London. In 1762, she joined Mary Bosanquet in her benevolent activities in London and became her close companion in the years that followed. The relocation of the community to Cross Hall in Yorkshire was due in large measure to Sarah's health. Sarah Crosby's associations with this important circle located her in a strategic center of women's activities in the nascent revival and helped catapult her into a preaching ministry of great renown. Ann Tripp was a part of the community nearly from the onset and moved to Yorkshire with the Leytonstone family in 1768. When the group dissolved in 1781, following Mary Bosanquet's marriage to

John Fletcher and her move to Madeley, Ann helped Sarah Crosby transplant the community to Leeds where it continued to flourish. Ann Highfield and Mary Tooth memorialized their two great mentors, Crosby and Fletcher.

At least six of the women, in addition to most in this circle, were preachers. Margaret Davidson of Lisburn was held in high esteem for her ministry of prayer but became instrumental in the great revival that took place in Ballinderry. Reverend and Mrs. Edward Smyth took the blind preacher under their wing and supported her ministry generously over the years. Her keen intellect, retentive memory, and the simplicity of her witness combined to shape a powerful style of preaching. Ann Cutler, affectionately known as "Praying Nanny," was famous among all the Methodists of her day for her ministry among the poor and needy. The account of Elizabeth Evans's spiritual journey reflects personal struggles with a call to preach, but exhortations in prayer meetings held in Derby eventually led to a preaching ministry recounted in the literature of her aunt, Mary Ann Evans (also known as George Eliot). Sarah Mallet was the first woman formally authorized by the Methodist Conference to preach the gospel, while Elizabeth Hurrell traveled extensively throughout Yorkshire, Lancashire, and Derbyshire in a ministry described by one as "irresistibly impressive." Mary Barritt's brand of evangelism combined powerful preaching and meticulous care for her converts. After her marriage to Zechariah Taft in 1802, she became the storm center of controversy over the role of women in the expanding Wesleyan Methodist Church. The story of these women, if not always their writings, was well-known by Methodists into the nineteenth century.

Other well-known women had unique ministries in the life of the movement. Hannah Ball founded a Sunday school movement in her native High Wycombe long before Robert Raikes initiated his experiments in Gloucester. Hester Ann Rogers was famous among the Methodists of her day for her eminent holiness, zeal, and Christian influence. Her fame was due in large measure to the publication of extracts from her journal, first appearing in 1796 as *The Experience of Mrs. Hester Ann Rogers,* one of the most popular devotional publications in early Methodism, on both sides of the Atlantic Ocean.[94] The published life and spiritual letters of Elizabeth Ritchie Mortimer, like those of Hester Ann Rogers, were also well-known in the circles of early Methodism and functioned as important instructional documents. Over the course of more than forty years, Mary Tatham simultaneously led at least three Methodist class meetings. To prepare herself properly for the spiritual direction of those under her care, she provided commentary on the biblical texts under the scrutiny of her groups. John Wesley published seven extracts from the diary of Bathsheba Hall in the *Arminian Magazine* in 1781 after her death. Virtually unknown outside the Bristolian circles of Methodism during her lifetime, her testimony about developments in Methodism during a most critical period, 1765–75, became familiar to most throughout the expanding network of Societies. The writings of these important leaders informed and shaped the lives of many Methodists in the next generations of the movement.

A final cluster of women is noteworthy for the unique nature of their contributions. Both Mary Hanson and Mary Gilbert died much too early in life, but their writings reflect a depth of spirituality beyond their years. Dying shortly after the birth of her first child, at only twenty-five years of age, Mary Hanson's meditations articulate a vision of the Christian life that is transformational to its core. They emphasize the importance of holding heart and mind together in the Christian life and encourage an experiential and contemplative spirituality. Mary Gilbert, "a prodigy of a child" in John Wesley's view, died when she was sixteen, just a month prior to her seventeenth birthday. Wesley published an extract of her journal upon her death, which he described as "a masterpiece in its kind." Agnes Bulmer, one of the greatest Methodist poets of all time, is noteworthy for her massive *Messiah's Kingdom: A Poem in Twelve Books*, published in 1833. This poem, one of the longest poems ever written by a woman, is remarkable for its grandeur and beauty, its rich and harmonious texture. The manuscript journal of Mary Entwisle is an amazing testimony to the trials and tragedies that so many women endured throughout the period of this study. Always pregnant and grieving the loss of children through death, always on the move as the wife of an itinerant preacher and yearning for the security of a stable life, she finds peace and hope in the intimacy of her relationship with God.

THE WRITINGS OF THE WOMEN

I have divided the women's literary works into three basic categories: spiritual autobiography, writings in practical divinity, and letters and accounts related to the spiritual life and death.

All of the materials in part 1 on autobiography as spirituality are extracted from accounts of religious experience, diaries, journals, and published memoirs. Some of these accounts were well-known to the contemporaries of the women, and several of the women featured in this section were something like Methodist icons in their own time. The accounts of Grace Murray and Sarah Ryan come from the early years of the Wesleyan revival. They are narratives of the way of salvation but also reveal some of the dynamic features of the movement of renewal. The selections from Sarah Crosby and Jane Cooper reveal the importance of the Wesleyan doctrine of Christian perfection to these women. Sarah incarnates a vision of the Christian life characterized by a pattern of vital piety and social service. Jane's portrait of the mature Christian helps account for the dynamic nature of Wesley's concept of perfect love of God and neighbor. Four excerpts from the diaries and journals of Hannah Ball, Hester Ann Rogers, Mary Entwisle, and Isabella Wilson follow. Both Hannah's and Hester's lives were well-known to their contemporaries as a consequence of their published *Experiences* and *Memoirs*. Excerpts from Isabella's diary were published in *The Methodist Magazine* following her death. The consistent keynotes of her daily entries are gratitude and thanksgiving in all things; the secret of her life is to be found in her attention to the means of grace. The Entwisle diary manuscript, just thirty-two pages in its entirety, portrays the fragile and tragic nature of life for women of that era. Covering a brief six-year period between 1793 and 1798, it provides a realistic portrait of triumphant discipleship in the midst of tragedy and pervasive uncertainty.

Part 2 focuses on practical divinity, including selections of spiritual direction and instruction, hymns and sacred poems, prayers, and accounts of dreams and visions.[95] Meditations figure prominently in this collection of writings and feature reflections by Mrs. Lefevre from the earliest years of the Methodist revival, as well as Mary Hanson's ruminations about the Christian faith three quarters of a century later. Patty Hall, sister to the Wesleys, devised her own manual of devotion in which a practice of meditation, similar to that of Francis de Sales, is delineated. Mary Bosanquet was one of most widely recognized spiritual counselors in Methodism. A number of items related to spiritual direction are included from her voluminous writings, most particularly excerpts from her devotional tract for single women and her other catechetical writings. Mary Tatham was a noted Methodist apologist and biblical commentator. Selections from her *Memoirs* demonstrate her amazing literary skill and keen spiritual insight. The early Methodists were concerned about the proper regulation of life, certain that a disciplined life would liberate the believer to be able to love more fully. They were known, therefore, for their "rules of life."[96] The Methodists had learned that framing and writing out a set of rules or guidelines helped strengthen Christian praxis. I have selected one such personal, spiritual canon from the writings of Mary Lyth. The rule of life drawn up by Mary Bosanquet for her community in Leytonstone reflects a corporate expression of this ideal.

Seven poets are featured here. They range from those virtually unknown, then and now, to the most famous woman poet within Methodism, Agnes Bulmer. Their hymns, poetry, and religious verse range from a hymn written for the dedication of a Methodist chapel to excerpts from a poem of epic proportions. They celebrate creation, lament the death of the innocent and suffering, rejoice in the grace of God revealed in Jesus Christ, and anticipate the glories of heaven. The prayers of thirteen women reflect the full spectrum of life as well. Some are terse, ejaculatory prayers offered to God in the context of journaling. Others are carefully crafted and designed for repeated use, as is the case with the covenant prayer of Joanna Cook. They mark critical events in the journey of faith, express spiritual desperation in the face of tragedy and grief, call the repentant to faith, encourage the disciple to persevere in growth toward perfect love, acknowledge the presence of God in the minute details of common life, and celebrate the wonder of life's adventure.

This section concludes with three excerpts from the writings of Sarah Ryan, Mary Fletcher, and Sarah Mallet, all of which reflect the important place that dreams, visions, and fits had within their spirituality. In her exhaustive study of the supernatural elements of religious experience, Ann Taves maintains that the Methodists "embraced Wesley's tendency to blur the distinction between the natural and supernatural."[97] The implication is that supernatural elements in early Methodist spirituality were a basic emphasis tied to the "experimental religion" of the movement. Sarah Ryan's journal narrative is filled with visions in which she believes God directs her path, both warning about dangers and encouraging her progress. For Mary Fletcher, dreams generally confirm decisions or courses of action. Such is the case as she contemplates entrepreneurial activities among the poor in London, and a vision of Jesus' majesty, purity, and holiness confirms her revolutionary scheme. Mary also records the dreams and visions of other women, such as an interesting manifestation of God as "the great eye" from the experience of sister Colley. The account of Sarah Mallet's "fits" is one of the most fascinating documents of early Methodism, published by John Wesley in his *Arminian Magazine* in 1788, because it is directly related to her call to the ministry of preaching.

Part 3 of this volume consists of twenty letters related to spiritual direction, illustrating the art of living, and seven published accounts of the deaths of Methodist women, preceded by an evangelistic tract contrasting the deathbeds of a saint and a sinner. All of these demonstrate the art of dying in the Wesleyan heritage. The women of early Methodism excelled as correspondents.[98] Not only was the letter one of the most important literary forms of the age, but also, for the women, it was one of the most important avenues of spiritual reflection and counsel. Letters reveal, therefore, some of the most important aspects of early Methodist spirituality. I selected the pieces of correspondence presented here primarily on the basis of their "spiritual" content. They reflect the Wesleyan way of salvation; discuss the nature of the Christian life and its goal; reveal the ups and downs of the spiritual quest; answer questions posed by their recipients with regard to the spiritual life; provide encouragement for companions in the journey, offer support and guidance to those who are troubled, distracted, or in despair; and bear witness to God's love, peace, and joy.

Ars moriendi (the art of dying) is a unique literary genre.[99] Developed initially in the fifteenth century as a genre of practical, devotional literature to provide guidance and instruction at the approach of death, the early Methodists used accounts of death to confirm the dignity and defend the validity of the Wesleyan vision of life in Christ. The fact that Methodists died well, they all believed, pointed to the ultimate triumph of love and of God's winsome ways. So the *ars moriendi* publications became an important evangelistic tool in the movement as well as in providing a historical record of the ultimate triumph of the Christian disciple in a good death. The accounts presented here provide a balanced portrait of ordinary Methodist women and the most important women leaders of the age. These women speak to us through the ages.

THE VOICES OF THE WOMEN

It is not always easy, however, to hear the voices of women. Complexities surround attentiveness. Any attempt to locate, identify, and amplify the voices of the women will be characterized inevitably by conflicting images and partial truths, as well as breakthroughs. Amazing progress in women's studies in general was made in the last half of the twentieth century,[100] and there is a growing literature on women's spirituality.[101] Very little research has been done, however, on the spirituality of the Methodist women, and any claim to a definitive word concerning this cluster of issues must be suspect. Suffice it to say that some of the lessons learned from women's studies thus far are instructive and help expand our vision of the spirituality that early Methodist women inherited, owned, and challenged. In her seminal and rich account *Women's Faith Development*, Nicola Slee identifies three major generative themes that reveal the core patterns of spiritual development among women: alienation, relationality, and awakening.

The first major theme that emerged from her research was "women's experience of alienation, a profound loss of self, of authentic connection with others, and of faith."[102] While the other themes of faith development that she identifies are more transparent with regard to the early Methodist women, her conclusion concerning this dimension resonates well with many of the writings, and particularly the faith narratives, presented here. "The paradoxical journey imagery used by the women," Slee observes, "not only implicitly rejects the traditional image of the spiritual life as a lonely epic quest, but also holds out hope for a belonging and a homecoming, even if, at present, such a destination remains far off."[103]

Second, the spirituality of women is essentially relational in character.[104] The strong connection that women feel toward others is often manifest in an ethic of nurture and responsibility, frequently rooted in caregiving and the basic human bond it entails. J. L. Surrey, for example, maintains that "self-in-relation" is the core structure of women's identity.[105] A strong sense of connectedness to the other is a dominant theme in the writings of the early Methodist women, and the various aspects of this relational dynamic are manifest throughout this corpus of material. There is a wide range, dynamism, and flexibility of relational conceptualization. Relationality is generative. "Particularly in their understanding of the interdependence of the divine-human relationship and relationships with others," writes Slee, "[women] testify to a conviction of the fecundity of relational energy, which is not depleted as it is expended, but expands to include more and more as it is exercised in the labour of love."[106] Relationship underlies and undergirds the whole of a woman's spiritual journey.

Awakenings—breakthroughs to new consciousness and spiritual vitality—is the third primary theme in Slee's trilogy and is another dominant characteristic in the early Methodist women's accounts of their religious experience.[107] The lives of these women reflect many of the common and defining features of this theme. Ordinary, concrete, and mundane experience is the locus of spiritual awakening. Priority is placed upon intuition and instinct, even upon visions and dreams. Awakenings are experienced in the context of journey, with critical periods of preparation leading to moments of crisis and breakthrough. They are marked by a sense of coherence, wholeness, or integration. These experiences involve taking responsibility for the self and unfold in a way that goes far beyond conscious choice or control. The transformation that awakening entails includes an expansion of consciousness, a liberation of self, and a new definition of reality. Awakening involves a process of being birthed into a whole new world. These are themes of which the reader of this volume needs to be particularly aware.

Serene Jones's observation with regard to mapping feminist theology is instructive at this juncture:

> Listen carefully to the varied experiences of *all* women and avoid too quickly imposing upon them theoretical categories that do not fit. This means attending to women's accounts of their lives *in their own words,* according to their own narratives.... in telling and listening to women's stories, we discover new rules, assumptions, and categories of thought.[108]

In similar fashion, Kathleen Hickok warns against jumping to too many conclusions about the women of the past by virtue of imposing today's values and paradigms of interpretation upon their writings.[109] In her examination of the creation of religious identities among English women poets, Ingrid Hotz-Davies comes to very much the same conclusion. This is particularly true, she maintains, with regard to issues related to women and religion. "Far from reducing women to silence," she writes, "religion can open doors for them not only into speech but also into the assumption of identities freer, larger, and more powerful than otherwise available to them."[110] Despite the fact that difficult interpretive issues such as female subjectivity, authorial repression, and the "gendered self" must be taken with utmost seriousness, it is also important to acknowledge the evidence of profound liberation and empowerment in the women's experience that was directly related to their heritage of Methodist spirituality. They have important lessons to teach us all.

Distinctive Spiritual Tones among Early Methodist Women

What particular contribution do the women of early Methodism make to the spirituality of the movement? What is distinctive about their religious experience and the ways in which they reflect upon life in Christ? While reflecting all the salient themes in Wesleyan spirituality, as we have seen, distinctive tones in their writings bear exploration. As much as is possible, therefore, in this closing section, I am attempting to let the early Methodist women set the agenda for themselves with regard to their spirituality. In her preface to the life of Elizabeth Mortimer, Agnes Bulmer claims that the central thrust of early Methodist women's lives was "a renovated spirit, and a holy life." She provides a simple definition of spirituality that helps frame the distinctive features of the spirituality lived out by women such as the subject of her biography. Spirituality, she maintains, involves every aspect of life that demonstrates "there is a real, a delightful, a transforming intercourse to which the human spirit is admitted with the ever-blessed God." In addition to the various aspects of spirituality held in common with the early Methodist men, the spirituality of early Methodist women is distinctive in the way it revolves around pathos (mystery in life), delight (majesty in life), and love (miracle in life). It is a spirituality that is real, blessed, and loving.

A Spirituality of Pathos—The Mystery in Life

Early Methodist women were masters at practicing the presence of God. Immersed in the "quotidian mysteries" of life[111] and finding God in the common round of daily events, their writings reflect a healthy realism grounded in the ordinary, the ups and downs, the tragedies and triumphs of real life. Their spirituality is preeminently practical and realistic. Margaret Davidson prays: "O compassionate lover of my soul, take the whole matter into your hands—the sole management of my most important and minute concerns! Oh that I could in every condition of life, say, 'Your will be done!'" Such concerns surface repeatedly in their prayers in particular. But the tragic element in life looms large in their writings. The central reality toward which the women's writings point is pathos. It is clear that they approach life as a mystery in which much more is understood than is ever fully comprehended. Nothing brought this closer to home for them than the tragic element that was such a pervasive aspect of their daily experience.

Concerns about health consumed their attention. Smallpox was the great plague of the age, and Hannah Ball suffered the ravages of the disease. "I have been three weeks confined to the house with the small pox," she confides to her journal. "When I first knew it was that disorder, I felt no fear, but rather a joy in hope it was the Master's call to arise and depart for ever to be with the Lord!" Grace Murray reflects upon one of the most common experiences of the women, the death of her child. She describes the way in which she was sustained in the face of this overwhelming grief, but also confesses the debilitating emptiness she felt in the aftermath of such a tragic loss in her life:

> My child sickened, and God was pleased to take her unto himself. When the child was dying I was constrained to kneel down, and having a book with a prayer in it for a departing soul, I read this, and gave up my child into the hands of God. This amazed my sister who had never seen it thus with me before. After the child was interred I was brought into such lowness of spirits that I could rest in no place. I lost my relish for all worldly pleasures, and, though I was taken from place to place to divert me, it was to no purpose. I wanted—but I knew not what.

No selection in this collection of women's writings is more filled with pathos than the manuscript journal of Mary Entwisle. It provides a unique window into the world of an early Methodist woman, the wife of an itinerant preacher. Her life—her spirituality—revolved around a perennial cycle of pregnancy, birth, and death, with a persistent undercurrent of hoping beyond hope that all things would be well. Early in 1793, she enters the final trimester of her first pregnancy. One senses that her anxiety mounts as she comes closer, day by day, to the time of the delivery, despite efforts to resign herself and her child to God's care. "I feel no painful anxiety. I feel power to cast my burden upon the Lord," she observes. "He has promised he will not leave or forsake me. He has said I will strengthen you." Following the birth of her son, Mary lays down her pen for a period of about nine months, only resuming her journal in December of 1793. In retrospect, she praises God for the grace to persevere through the difficulties that ensued but speaks with honesty about the effect of the stress upon her spirit. "I had a very hard time during the time of my pregnancy," she confesses. "I never found liberty to pray for an easy delivery, neither could I join with my dear companion in that petition who was not negligent in laying it before the Lord."

She learns important lessons related to her spiritual well-being through her experiences, and particularly those related to her physical problems following delivery.

> Through mercy I recovered pretty well, but my nipples were bad for some time. I felt great need for patience sometimes when very

> much exercised with pain in my breasts. I was overcome with fretfulness and discouragements which hurt my soul. How needful it is to be looking for fresh supplies of grace continually. Sometimes when we overcome great trials we are overcome by small things not duly considering our helplessness and that the grace we have for the present will not suffice for the next trial.

Moving into a new appointment with their two-year-old son and in the midst of a second pregnancy, she encounters yet another serious challenge. The itinerant preacher succeeded by her husband had left a child sick with smallpox in the house. Since John, her son, had never had the disease, they inoculated him, endangering his life in the process. "I, in a strange place," Mary laments, "my dear husband, true partner of my weal or woe, at a great distance when the child was at the worst. My trials were great, yet praised be the Lord, strength was proportioned to my day. I believed the Lord would spare my child. He did and raised him up again in a few weeks after I was delivered of another fine boy."

With yet another pregnancy approaching delivery, she turns to God in prayer.

> I feel at present especially I have need of a firm trust and unshaken confidence in God. I want power to cast my care upon the Lord and to commit my all to him. Lord, be with me in the hour of nature's sorrow which is fast approaching. Be pleased to bring me safely through and spare me to my friends and family if it be your blessed will. Amen.
>
> Wakefield. March 11th. What shall I render to the Lord for all his benefits. When I look back to the time when I last wrote I see abundant cause for gratitude to my kind preserver and bountiful benefactor. How did he support me in the hour of trial and in answer to prayer bring me safely and easily through? May I trust the Lord at all times. He made me the living mother of a living child.

Not long thereafter, however, agony returns and her lament continues:

> O Lord you have tried us as silver is tried. In the latter end of March I went to my father's for the benefit of the air, but I was sent for back to my dear child who was seized with the small pox.

> O the distress of mind I felt on account of his great sufferings, and the daily prospect of losing my precious boy.
> He died without a struggle and angels no doubt bore his happy spirit away to the realms of light. Lord help me constantly to say thy will be done, knowing you cannot err. You do all things well, however contrary to our feelings. My dear Marmaduke was a sweet, affectionate child nearly two years and seven months old. I trust I shall go to him but he shall not return to me.

One line out of this extended narrative speaks volumes with regard to the experience of women and the nature of their spirituality: "He made me the living mother of a living child." The women faced tragedy with courage and honesty. They offered no simplistic answers to the deep questions related to the mysteries of life, shared their pain with one another and with God, and assimilated the pathos into a theology of suffering in solidarity with the crucified Christ.

A Spirituality of Delight—The Majestic in Life

The motif of delight is manifest in two primary images in the women's writings: that of creation and that of community and companionship. Both reflect a majestic element in life that stands in stark contrast to the tragic dimension just reviewed.

Creation. Mary Hanson writes in a letter to a friend:

> My garden begins to demand my renewed labors. When will you inhale the fragrance of my roses and help me to admire the kindness of our God in providing so much innocent pleasure for the delight of the senses? The study of nature is still my favorite recreation; but to increase in the love and knowledge of God almost swallows up every other desire.

She writes in her journal:

> How delightful is the contemplation of the works of God! My enraptured eye runs over the productions of the earth with a curiosity and interest that never leave me. The passing clouds, the opening flowers, the sweet river, whose constant changes give a variety to the scenes. How successively do these steal on my

imagination, and often how inexpressible is my gratitude for receiving from the hands of God so many outward blessings.

As potent as the image of creation is for Mary—a constant reminder of the majesty that surrounds us in life—she is careful not to fall into a naive sentimentality concerning its wonders. "Nature and all her loveliness," she also writes, "is but transitory in her duration." The greatest wonder of it all, she observes, is the way in which it points to the Creator.

Some of the most powerful expressions of delight related to God's creation are to be found in the poetry of the women. Agnes Bulmer, for example, creates a lyrical portrait of the rainbow:

> Wild the wind, and fierce the flood,
>   Foaming, roaring, raved and rush'd;
> Thunders roll'd—the voice of God:
>   Now the angry storm is hush'd,
> Now the eddying whirlwind sleeps,
> Ocean seeks its barrier deeps.
>
> Beauteous bow! thy arch sublime,
>   Resting on the distant hills,
> Leads me back to earliest time;
>   Hope my pensive spirit fills,
> In thy softest hues I trace
> Gentler, lovelier beams of grace.
>
> Hush! the word of promise breaks,
>   Not in thunders hoarse and loud;
> Lo! the covenant-Saviour speaks
>   Softly from the symboll'd cloud:
> Rise! the storm of wrath is pass'd;
> Judgment shall not always last.
>
> Sun of Righteousness! from thee
>   Soft those lucid rays descend,
> Mildest mercy beams on me;
>   Whispers every storm shall end,
> Now the covenant-sign is given,
> Bright appears the bow in heaven.

INTRODUCTION

The blind preacher, Margaret Davidson, writes about the five senses and finds in each sense a means of understanding more fully the person of Jesus. The reflections of the sightless poet with regard to the miracle of vision are particularly poignant.

> Happy soul, what canst thou learn
>   From all that feeds the eye?
> Only Jesus I discern—
>   He shines thro' earth and sky:
> Radiant orbs, and beauteous flow'rs,
>   Sparkling diamonds seem to say,
> Glory to our glorious source,
>   Who gives eternal day.

Her poem concludes:

> Whate'er I hear, or see, or taste,
>   Whate'er I smell, or feel,
> Christ's my music, light, and feast,
>   My rose, and pillow still:
> In him I always live and move—
>   Exercise thy senses five,
> O my soul, and let thy love,
>   Be fervent, and alive.

Community and Companionship. Community, of course, is a critical component of the relational spirituality we have already explored. But one important aspect of community is the companionship it affords. No theme is more central in the lives of these women than that of spiritual friendship. It is important to remember that many of the women featured in this volume knew one another. Some lived in communities of vital piety and social service together, such as the Leytonstone/Cross Hall circle, in which the women experienced true *koinonia* in a common life centered in Christ. Certainly, one important aspect of these female circles of friendship was the way in which they created space for the women, as J. Raymond has described it, "to create the world as women imagine it could be."[112] Companionship—one woman's sharing of bread with other women—empowered them all to a fuller use of their talents and graces. The women experienced one another in community as gifts.

"My dear friend," writes Mary Hanson in a letter, "I long to see you and shall be impatient till I hear from you." Reflecting upon the support she had received through one of her difficult pregnancies, Mary Entwisle confirms that she can never forget "the kindness of friends during my long confinement. O may I ever feel the good effects of it." "My precious, my invaluable friend," says the dying Mary Fletcher to her faithful companion, Mary Tooth, "I have prayed that light and wisdom may guide you in all, in every difficulty and it will be so. I know it will. My prayer for you is heard, my choice friend." These friends are dear, affectionate, precious, invaluable, long-suffering, patient, kind, intimate, blessed, and the delight of their hearts.

Little wonder that the language of friendship is transferred from the women's experience of female companionship into the description of the way they relate to God. "There is no safety," claims Jane Cooper, "but in his friendship." Attempting to explain her conversion to her mother, Hetty Roe simply confesses that she "had received forgiveness and could call God my Father and my Friend." "The friendship of Jesus, whose love is unspeakable," says Isabella Wilson, "is my joy and crown of rejoicing." Sarah Crosby describes the core of her spirituality: "I know he will be my friend in life and death the same."

A Spirituality of Love—The Miracle in Life

The language of spirituality that is more pervasive than any other in the writings of the early Methodist women is related to their overwhelming sense of God's presence or the gift of overflowing love. It is the language of the heart filled with love. Linked directly in the Methodist mind to holiness, this image often carries with it the overtones of humility, purification, and the miraculous wonder of in-filling love. We conclude this introduction, therefore, where we began. Here is a spirituality of love. In every instance, the experience of love is transformative. Whether received or offered to others, love changes lives. Holiness equals love; love equals holiness; and all is miracle as the faithful live out their lives on the foundation of God's grace.[113]

For the Wesleys, the purpose of the Christian life was the restoration of the image of God in the heart of the believer. "You know that the great end of religion," John would repeat on a number of occasions, "is to renew our hearts in the image of God, to repair that total loss of righteousness and true holiness which we sustained by the sin of our first parent."[114] Mary Hanson provides her own description of true religion. It is "a well of water springing up within me! A holy principle producing joy and peace. A principle which shall make me soar above the world, feel the divine origin of my soul, and be constantly tending towards the source of all true felicity." Elsewhere she prays:

> O, blessed fountain of love! Fill my heart more with [thy] Divine principle. Sink me lower in the depths of humility, and let me sit at the feet of Jesus, and learn of Him. Enlarge my soul, that I may better contemplate Thy glory. And may I prove myself Thy child, by bearing a resemblance to Thee, my heavenly Father![115]

Sarah Ryan, Wesley's faithful correspondent, had a vision of this goal one day and seized upon it as the directing principle of her life:

> [On Sunday] in Spitalfields Church, I saw the Lord Jesus standing, and a little child all in white before him: and he shewed me, he had made me as that child; but that I should grow up to the measure of his full stature. I came home full of light, joy, love, and holiness; and God daily confirmed what he had done for my soul. And, blessed be his name! I now know where my strength lieth, and my soul is continually sinking more and more into God.[116]

Hannah Ball describes the gracious process of sanctification that leads from total reliance on Christ to miraculous liberation into God's love. Holiness is the fullest manifestation of love in our lives.

> I want to feel deeper humility. I want humility enough to bear prosperity, and not to be high minded. I do not feel pride, but I wish to feel lowliness grounded in my heart. On examination, I find more self-contempt, more of the mind of Christ, and more of that love that suffers long and is kind.

> Thee let me now through faith behold,
> And by reflection shine,
> Till nature's dross is turned to gold,
> And I am all divine.

> Happy in the love of Jesus, I long to be with Him my soul loves. My heart is disengaged and free.

"Come, Lord Jesus, come quickly," prays Margaret Davidson, "and cut short your work in righteousness! Burn up, O Spirit of burning, all the dross of my best duties—all the stubble of my inbred sin! O my lovely Jesus, I languish to be all holy, according to my degree, as you are holy."

"A blessed life indeed," writes Isabella Wilson, "to walk in the light of [God's] countenance, and to serve him with a perfect heart and willing mind! This is to have the single eye which fills the body full of light—and love to that adorable Emmanuel who died to redeem, to purify us to himself, and to make us a people zealous of good works." The singular desire of Jane Cooper was the fullness of God's love in her life.

> My soul is broken before my Lord, and desires to follow him as the shadow follows the substance. He has my heart, and reigns the Lord of all my wishes and desires. I need no change of place, person or thing to raise or increase my happiness. The presence of Jesus is sufficient. His will is my resting-place, and his love my delight. But my joy is not every moment full, though in general I can say,
>
>> My full soul doth still require
>> Thy whole eternity of Love.[117]

Mary Entwisle expressed the same earnest desire in her manuscript diary:

> I feel my soul athirst for God, yes, even for the living God. Oh that he would come and take up his lasting abode in my heart, and suffer me no longer to rove, but may I be rooted and grounded in love, and grow up into him who is my living head. Oh, may his love fill my heart, influence my life and conduct so

that all may see I have been with Jesus—I have Christ put on. Oh that my heart were established with grace.

Mary Tatham, a biblical exegete and theologian in her own right, frequently ruminates upon the miracle of God's love, but in the following quotation she discusses the nature of love filling the heart and the ever-processive nature of love's work in the soul:

> Love filling the heart is productive of real holiness, and God being always present with him and his desires going out continually after him, he is kept above the power of temptation and sin. In this state he presses forward to greater degrees of purity and love until the whole soul is changed into the divine image.

* * * *

> Saving faith purifies the heart, converts the soul, sanctifies the affections, and enlarges the desires towards God and man so that, if it were possible, it would embrace the whole world and bring every soul to taste and enjoy the sweetness of that love of which he so freely partakes. O that I may no longer rest satisfied without a full salvation, but seek to be saved even to the uttermost, that I may be filled with all the fulness of God.

Margaret Davidson's "Hymn, in Honour of Jesus" is an amazing vision of the final triumph of God's love in the world and stands as a fitting conclusion to this discussion of the spirituality of early Methodist women.

> I wait till wafted up to thee,
> O thou mysterious One in Three
> By love's encircling arms caress'd,
> And with a view of glory bless'd,
> Now I Abba, Father, cry—
> The same blessing,
> Without ceasing,
> Pour on all below the sky.

Part One
Autobiography as
Theology

INTRODUCTION TO PART ONE

No collection of materials related to early Methodist spirituality would be complete without autobiography. The concept of "enpersonalization" stands at the heart of the Wesleyan understanding of the Christian faith. The social dimension of Wesleyan spirituality is one of its most unique features, but the foundation of it all is the personal realization that "Christ died for *me*." It is the exterior aspect of the Christian life—the imperative to mission and service—that safeguards this fundamental interiority from devolving into an idolatrous form of narcissism. In both corporate settings of worship and intimate circles of Christian fellowship, the followers of the Wesleys told their stories, testified, and bore witness to the grace by which they were saved and in which they continued to grow in their faith. Autobiographical documents both expressed and shaped the spirituality of the movement. We begin our exploration of early Methodist spirituality in this fertile terrain.

In my earlier volume, *Her Own Story: Autobiographical Portraits of Early Methodist Women*, I ring the changes on this theme. In that work I display and examine a wide range of autobiographical materials: accounts of religious experiences, diaries, journals, memoirs, and letters. Without undue repetition, I will offer reminders that are essential to this volume. First, Methodists are somewhat distinctive in their penchant to write, collect, and use autobiographical accounts of faith. The Wesleys, of course, inculcated this passion in their followers. It seems that their primary concern was to see how God works in the lives of faithful disciples, to learn from one another, and to assist fellow pilgrims toward the goal of fully renewed love and witness in the world. Although this seems so simple, it is, in fact, a profound rediscovery; and the gathering of this material into collections was unique.

The repositories of Christian autobiography, such as Wesley's *Arminian Magazine* or Thomas Jackson's *Lives of the Early Methodist Preachers* or Zechariah Taft's *Biographical Sketches of Various Holy Women*, inspired and challenged several generations of devoted Methodist people. Individual memoirs and extended autobiographical works of noteworthy Methodist men and women were common reading and their subjects household names. The early Methodists modeled their lives after the example of these "sainted" figures. This, of course, presents a challenge to today's reader. There is a very slippery slope between biography and hagiography. No figure in Christian history has proven this more, perhaps, than John Wesley himself.[1] Although autobiography does have some inherent safeguards against this devolution, the "dramatis personae" in their own settings in life can quickly take on larger-than-life character and the pattern of their lives prescribe the experience of others. So it is important to keep this in mind.

What is of particular concern to us here is how autobiographical material both reflected and shaped early Methodist spirituality. The first thing to note is the centrality of the way of salvation and the rediscovery of a vibrant, living faith that animated the spiritual lives of these followers of Christ. These narratives articulate a vision of the Christian life in which God acts directly through the presence of the Spirit to convict, convert, renew, heal, and restore. One striking feature of these accounts is the intimacy between the author and God or Jesus. Spiritual liberation is another pervasive theme. Life in the Spirit emancipates the follower of Christ and opens up new vistas of service and witness. Preaching, or other encounters with the Word, immersion in the various means of grace, and interaction with and inspiration from spiritual friends all combine to transform and shape these women's lives. Here is a potently affective form of the Christian faith—a religion in which the heart is warmed, changed, filled, and renewed. But the interior spirituality of these women is made effective in love through exterior movement and action in the world. Those who have been inwardly changed are propelled into ministry and mission as an expression of faith in action.

Introduction to Part One

This autobiographical section begins with an excerpt from Agnes Bulmer's Preface to *Memoirs of Elizabeth Mortimer*. It is the perfect place for us to begin because the author articulates the importance of Christian biography, affords an apology for the Methodist movement, and introduces us to one of the its most celebrated figures. Not unlike the ancient Apologists, she demonstrates the dignity of the Methodist way and applauds the moral elevation part and parcel to the movement. Her vision of a Methodist spirituality of the heart avoids the dangers of enthusiasm or fanaticism, on one hand, and the aridity of intellectualism, on the other hand. The authentic Methodist, like her subject, possesses not only truth, but power in love.

The constellation of women featured here is highly significant. The four excerpts from accounts of religious experience highlight several of the most prominent Methodist women in the history of the movement. Grace Murray, who was as close to being John Wesley's soul mate as any woman would ever come, was the prototype of the early Methodist woman. Her account reveals the importance of critical life events in the unfolding of the spiritual life. Sacred songs shape her faith; the religion of the heart is a faith that sings. Sarah Ryan pioneered with Mary Bosanquet in social service ministries, first in London and then in Yorkshire, providing a primary model of coherence between vital piety and compassionate mission. The Ryan account depicts the ups and downs of real life. She makes no attempt here to dismiss the difficulties, avoid the barriers, or gloss over the challenges in the quest to understand God and live in faith. From her conversion at the Eucharist through her discovery of true peace in ministry among the destitute, her life reflects the perennial need of the faithful to be open to the transforming power of love. Sarah Crosby was the first woman preacher of Methodism. Intellectual struggles dominated Sarah's early life, and her epiphanies came through reading, study, and serious reflection. Her discovery of love in the midst of her quest for knowledge is a profound testimony to the personal dimension of faith. Wesley frequently referred to Jane Cooper as an exemplar of his vision of Christian perfection in this life. Prayer for humility, preaching as the locus of divine/human encounter, and perfect love as the goal of the Christian life dominate her story.

The four women featured through their diaries and journals are no less formidable. Hannah Ball founded the Sunday school movement and pioneered in her work among the children of her community. Her diary is a running commentary on the importance and power of the means of grace in the Christian life. Hester Ann Rogers probably influenced more Methodist people through her husband's publication of her *Experience* after her death than any other woman except Mary Fletcher. Hester's private journals detail the way in which her initial prejudice against the Methodists inevitably melted away as she discovered among them the people of her heart. Devotion to Jesus in her roles as itinerant preacher's wife, mother, and Society leader typify her life. The final two women, Mary Entwisle and Isabella Wilson, are much less known, but no diaries of early Methodism are filled with greater pathos or spiritual wisdom. The Entwisle diary, on the one hand, very brief but very potent, reveals the precarious nature of life for the women of her day. Confronted with life-threatening diseases, the dangers of childbirth, and the inevitable relinquishment of children to God in death, she entrusts her life to God in the midst of personal depression, hardship, and struggle. The diary of Isabella Wilson, on the other hand, soars. Her constant refrain is "Glory be to God": her spirituality is characterized by unfaltering gratitude and thanksgiving. She is the wise spiritual mentor par excellence.

A. Agnes Bulmer's Preface to Memoirs of Elizabeth Mortimer

Editor's Introduction

Agnes Bulmer was born in London on August 31, 1775, and died on the Isle of Wight, August 30, 1836.[2] She was the third daughter of Elizabeth and Edward Collinson, pious Methodist ironmongers and personal friends of John Wesley. Agnes grew up a model child, her favorite study, after the Bible, being Edward Young's *Night Thoughts*. She began reading his religious verse at twelve years of age. After Agnes received her first Methodist class ticket from Wesley's own hand in 1789, Hester Ann Rogers was her first class leader. In 1793, she married Joseph Bulmer, a prosperous merchant who served as one of the stewards of Wesley's City Road Chapel. She contributed much verse to the *Methodist Magazine* and *Youth's Instructor*. Her "Memoir," written by Mrs. Rowley, daughter of Adam Clarke, was published in the *Methodist Magazine* in 1840.[3] In response to inquiries concerning his estimation of her life, Adam Clarke wrote: "That woman astonishes me. She takes in information just as a sponge absorbs water.... Whether it be philosophy, history, or theology, she seizes upon it, and makes it all her own."[4]

Rivingtons published Bulmer's massive *Messiah's Kingdom: A Poem in Twelve Books* in 1833. William M. Bunting, who published her *Select Letters* in 1842, described her as "one of the most intellectual and holy women, probably, whose presence ever adorned this world."[5] In addition to her poetical writings, however, her greatest claim to fame was her editorial work on *Memoirs of Mrs. Elizabeth Mortimer*, published in the year of her subject's death, 1836. This book, greatly enriched by much important Methodist correspondence, introduced this important early Methodist figure, the recorder of John Wesley's death, to a multitude of readers, passing through several editions both in England and America.

Agnes's first noteworthy poem in print is the elegy "On the Death of the Rev. Charles Wesley," written when she was just thirteen years old, and published by John Wesley in the *Arminian Magazine* in 1788.[6] In reference to this important achievement in her life, in his only surviving letter to her, Wesley cautioned: "My dear maiden, Beware of pride, beware of flattery; suffer none to commend you to your face; remember, one good temper is of more value in the sight of God than a thousand good verses. All you want is to have the mind that was in Christ, and to walk as Christ walked."[7]

The following extracts are taken from the preface to her biography of Elizabeth Mortimer and from the summary of her Christian character that concludes the volume. Together, they function as both an apology for the Methodist movement, which she loved so dearly, and as a powerful statement of the centrality of biography in the spirituality of early Methodism.

* * * *

Christian biography is a treasure of no ordinary value. It applies the proper test to principles and calls forth experience to vouch for truth. Nor in this age of infidelity is such a voucher to be lightly estimated. Cold and scornful on the lip of scepticism hangs the taunt of the reviler. He impugns Christianity and affronts its majesty by daring to degrade it to a level with his own cheerless, powerless, heartless unbelief. But from whom receives he license thus boldly to arraign the wisdom and the goodness of high heaven? Not from those who in humility and faith have thankfully embraced the boon of mercy. But from men who have assumed its title merely and adopted its profession from no other motives than those of custom or convenience, beneath its garb but ill concealing worldly-mindedness, indifference, and, too often, flagrant and revolting vice. Men who have never sought acquaintance with its holy principles or proved its power to influence the understanding and the heart.

Before entering on the details of the subject [Elizabeth Mortimer], it may be desirable to notice in what department of the school of Christ the character to be brought forward received that training under which she made so great proficiency as to entitle her to be exhibited as an example to the Christian church. And if the spirit of a pure and universal piety pervading the whole heart and life allows her claim to be adduced as a bright specimen of the efficiency of evangelical religion, must not candor also admit that that species of Christianity whose type she received, by the name of "Methodism," contains within its system those principles of light

A. Agnes Bulmer's Preface

and energy which merit nobler epithets than those which generally assail it from a prejudiced and undiscerning world?

Neither to the philosopher nor the philanthropist can this subject be a matter of indifference or of cold speculation. A machinery of so much moral power as that which, at the commencement of the last century, was put in motion under special instrumentality by the revival of religion which then took place, and which still continues to propel its influence through wider and still widening circles, cannot but invite consideration and excite much interest in reflecting minds.

Methodism had no novelty to present to the world. The doctrines it propounded were the great and leading principles of evangelical truth laid down in the scriptures and contained, not only in the formularies of the universal church, but also in those of the Church of England, of whose communion its distinguished founder, the Rev. John Wesley, was an attached and a conscientious member. It was in spirit rather than in substance that it differed from that established form of Christianity from which it took its rise.

Numerous causes had conspired to check the course of that revival of religion, which the era of the Reformation had seen so gloriously commenced. Supineness and fanaticism contributed each its quota to obscure the truth which then emerged from long-impending night. A new impulse had become essential. The zeal that animated the Reformers required re-kindling from the altar-fires of heaven. To accomplish this important purpose the providence of God selected its own agency, and from the bosom of the Church of England raised up a class of men whose holy zeal and almost apostolic labors roused the dormant and decaying spirit of religion and proclaimed a vital and transforming Christianity in every quarter of the land.

Not without sacrifice were these chosen instruments to be honored as the special messengers of heaven. Earnestness, which in the pursuit of earthly objects men esteem a virtue, when exercised on the important interests of religion was construed to imply the absence of sobriety of mind. Exclusion from their usual sphere of ministerial operation was the consequence of their irregular proceedings; and censure, persecution, and reproach were plenteously awarded in return for sufferings, labors, and privations of no ordinary kind. To these they cheerfully submitted in the meek and animating spirit of that pure philanthropy which is originated only by the love of God.

But while human judgments urged by human passions misinterpreted the zeal and labors of these holy and devoted men, the seal of the divine acceptance attested God's approval of their work. Sinners listened to the voice that warned them of impending danger and awoke from the deceitful dream of false security. The gospel faithfully proclaimed became the power of God to their salvation. And its legitimate effects were manifested in a renovated spirit and a holy life. Thus, by the enlightening and ameliorating influences of a spiritual and vigorous ministry, were thousands rescued from the toils of sin. And on the surface of society, to a considerable extent, especially upon those orders of it most accessible to danger from the peculiar spirit of the age, a healthful and restraining moral power was spread.

But although Methodism has largely participated in the glory of preaching the gospel to the poor, yet has it numbered among its trophies some of the wisest and the best of men, men whose understandings could be subjugated only by the force of truth and who were alike by education and by constitution far removed from the unnatural fervor of a wild fanaticism and from the enthusiastic vanity of expecting to attain an end without the use of means. By minds thus powerful and comprehensive has this revival been regarded as the work of God. Nor have they been ashamed of yielding up their spirits to its influence or of being found cooperators in promoting its extension through the world.

As a member of the Wesleyan Methodist Society, [Elizabeth Mortimer] was one of its brightest and most consistent ornaments, and justified through life the regard with which she had been honored by its venerable and illustrious founder. In those departments of usefulness which the system so extensively presents, she was ever ready to occupy her proper sphere, which she did, not only with unshrinking fidelity, but with great success. Her knowledge and experience of divine truth, together with the liveliness, suavity, and simplicity of her manner, gave her great spiritual influence and access to many hearts.

As a professor of the religion of the heart, Mrs. Mortimer gave proof that spirituality is not necessarily enthusiastic or fanatical;

A. Agnes Bulmer's Preface

but that there is a real, a delightful, a transforming intercourse to which the human spirit is admitted with the ever-blessed God. The deep and mystic promises of the Redeemer on the subject of the union of believers with himself have their fulfilment in some happy hearts. She embraced them thankfully and waited for their full accomplishment. She loved the Savior and yielded to him a willing homage. To her, therefore, he manifested himself as he does not unto the world.

Christianity is a system not only of truth but of power. To this, facts in numberless instances from its first promulgation to the present hour bear indubitable testimony. Nor will it now be questioned but that the honored individual whose course [is here] traced affords an additional demonstration of the efficiency with which it operates in the accomplishment of its important end. The conclusion, then, is manifest; the gospel is, in its origin and in its authority, divine.

What do its mercy and its power effect? What, in the present instance, did that love and power accomplish? In every case it purifies, exalts, and cheers defiled, degraded, miserable man. In this its energy embraced its object in a season of peculiar interest and importance, and introduced a spring into the moral constitution which gave impulse to each faculty and an expansion to the spirit that changed the character and form of life.

Neither for the world, nor for its literature, does Christian biography possess a charm. But to the holy and illuminated mind there is no engagement more instructive or delightful than to mark the period when the first spark of divine light is struck into a human spirit, and to trace its progress as it proceeds to dissipate those clouds of error and of sin which gather round the chaos of the fallen soul. The smile of superciliousness may mark the contempt of the worldling, but angels look down with intense interest on those who have entered the lists and are strenuously pursuing the career of immortality. The exploits of heroes and potentates may engage the breathless attention of the lovers of this world's greatness. Political schemes and national revolutions may engross their interests and speculations. But He who sees in every regenerated spirit the travail of his own soul regards with infinitely greater complacency the arduous and persevering efforts of one immortal being to accomplish the supreme purpose for which life was given. The sympathies of the divine Redeemer are with him who, through the intricacies, toils, and conflicts of this probationary state, urges his course with noble intrepidity, achieving victories in succession over subtle, dark, malignant enemies, bearing meekly various and accumulated trials, consecrating every energy of nature and of grace to the most sublime objects, renouncing both the world and self, and pressing onward to the attainment of an everlasting crown. If, then, the Mediator and the ministries of his invisible and eternal kingdom regard with highest interest the Christian in his course of discipline and duty, can those who have the same perilous path to tread, the same obstacles to surmount, the same enemies to overcome, and the same victories to achieve, be unconcerned to learn from those who have preceded them the lessons which experience teaches to thoughtful and reflecting minds?

SOURCE:

Agnes Bulmer, ed., *Memoirs of Mrs. Elizabeth Mortimer*, 2nd ed. (London: J. Mason, 1836), 4-5, 7-11, 293-95.

B. Accounts of Religious Experience

1. GRACE MURRAY

Editor's Introduction

Grace Murray (1718–1803) was a prototype for female leadership in early Methodism, a spiritual model to whom many women (and men) looked for guidance in the spiritual life. Her *Memoirs,* including the account of her religious experience below, afford a glimpse of early Methodism in its London and Newcastle-upon-Tyne centers. In October 1742, John Wesley appointed her one of the first class leaders of the newly established Society at Newcastle, soon to become the northern center for the Methodist movement, and then housekeeper at his innovative Orphan-House headquarters.[8] She was the principal person employed by Wesley to organize the women's classes in earliest Methodism and traveled with him frequently, assisting in the itinerant supervision of the expanding movement. Wesley highly commended her as a coworker: "I saw the work of God prosper in her hands.... She was to me both a servant and friend, as well as a fellow-labourer in the Gospel."[9]

Grace and John planned to marry, but in 1749, she married one of Wesley's itinerant preachers, John Bennet, owing to the intervention of Charles Wesley.[10] Despite the rift that developed between John Wesley and the couple, Grace's legacy within Methodism was firmly established. Band and class leader, sick visitor, housekeeper, and itinerant "regulator" of women's groups, she functioned, in effect, as a sub-pastor, providing leadership in acts of worship and service throughout the growing network of Societies. Despite her formal departure from the Wesleyan Methodist Societies in the early 1750s, Grace continued conducting prayer and fellowship meetings outside the circle of her former suitor's influence and supervision. Her spirituality was characterized by a constant reliance upon God's grace in the active pursuit of virtue.

* * * *

When we returned to London all places rang with the fame of Mr. Whitefield, who had introduced the practice of field-preaching.[11] I said, poor gentleman! He is out of his mind. So foolish was I, and ignorant! But he continued to blow the gospel trumpet all round London. I found a strong desire to hear him, but my husband would not give his consent. It was not long, however, before Mr. Murray was called away to his occupation. And just after his departure my child sickened, and God was pleased to take her unto himself. When the child was dying I was constrained to kneel down, and having a book with a prayer in it for a departing soul, I read this, and gave up my child into the hands of God. This amazed my sister who had never seen it thus with me before. After the child was interred I was brought into such lowness of spirits that I could rest in no place. I lost my relish for all worldly pleasures, and, though I was taken from place to place to divert me, it was to no purpose. I wanted—but I knew not what.

A young person in our neighborhood, having heard of my distress, sent me word she was going to Blackheath[12] to hear Mr. Whitefield and would be glad of my company. Accordingly I went with her and before we reached the place we heard the people singing hymns. The very sound set all my passions afloat, though I did not know one word they uttered, which plainly shows how the affections may be greatly moved while the understanding is quite dark. At the time appointed Mr. Whitefield came, and young Mr. Delamotte[13] in a chaise with him. When he stood up I was struck with his appearance. I thought there was something in his face I never saw in any human face before. His text was our Lord's address to Nicodemus in John 3:3. "Verily, verily I say unto thee, except a man be born again, he cannot see the kingdom of God." He enlarged on the new birth, but I understood him not and wondered what it was to be born again.[14]

It pleased God to send Mr. John Wesley into England just as Mr. Whitefield sailed for Georgia.[15] The same person who had invited me to go with her to hear Mr. Whitefield sent to inform me that Mr. John Wesley would preach in Moorfields[16] the next morning at five o'clock. I rose and got there with the first before Mr. Wesley came. I do not remember what passage of scripture he preached upon, but in his discourse he said, "Is there any one here that has a true desire to be saved?" My heart replied, "Yes, I have." He added, "My soul for thine, if thou continue laying at the feet of Jesus." On this word I took hold, for I was like a person drowning who would catch hold of anything to save life; but what it was to lay at the feet of Jesus I knew not, for I was as ignorant of the way of salvation by the Son of God as a horse or a mule. I attended all the services. I lost no opportunities. I got acquainted also with many of the people of God, which was a blessing to me. The Lord now showed me that I was a sinner and that I wanted a Savior. I groaned under my burden of sin for some months.

One day, however, as I was reading in the fifth chapter of the epistle to the Romans, I was filled with light and love. I saw my lost estate in Adam and my recovery by Christ Jesus. My soul was overpowered and I cried out to those that were with me, "If all the devils in hell were dancing round me, I fear them not." I was as sensible, when the guilt of sin was removed from my conscience, as a man pressed under a load is sensible when it is taken off his shoulders. Now, therefore, God having set my soul at liberty, he opened my lips to praise him. And all that flow of spirits which I had felt in the vanities of the world was directed towards God. I began to reprove sin in all around me, nor could I suffer it upon my brother in any wise. Now I could say

> All the vain things that charm'd me most,
> I sacrifice them to his cross.[17]

Mr. Charles Wesley, having desired as many as could to write out their experience, I wrote mine and sent it. He requested that I would come and speak with him the next morning, which I did, but shall never forget his piercing look. He examined me very closely. I answered him with simplicity, so far as I knew. When I was coming away, he said, "I will propound you to be a member of our Society." The next meeting therefore I was desired to stay, and a happy meeting we had.

A little after this Mr. Wesley made me a leader of a band.[18] I was afraid of undertaking it, yet could not refuse, lest I should offend God. I was also appointed to be one of the visitors of the sick,[19] which was my pleasant work. And thus was I carried on, all the while Mr. Murray was gone, till I heard of his death at sea, which was about fourteen months after he left me. All the time I scarcely knew whether I was in heaven or on earth, my soul was so filled with the comforts of the Holy Ghost! Whenever I drew near to God in secret prayer (I would with profound humility speak it), he was graciously pleased to commune with me, as it were, face to face. But this was only to prepare me for my great trial! For I would mourn and refused to be comforted on account of my loss.

On my arrival at Newcastle, I found that Mr. Wesley had been preaching both in the town and in the fields, and that the people flocked to hear the gospel, which caused my spirits to revive, when I saw how the arm of the Lord was stretched out to save sinners in my native country [see also Exod. 6:6]. The word was attended with divine power and souls were daily added to the church. Mr. John Wesley being called up to London, his brother Charles came in his room and the work of God increased wonderfully. A society was formed consisting of several hundreds, so that there was ample work for those who knew anything of the work of grace on their own hearts. Soon afterwards Mr. John returned and laid a plan for a preaching house in the town, having purchased a plot of ground for that purpose.[20] This was in the month of December 1742. The Society of Newcastle was divided into classes with their respective leaders, like those in London. Mr. Wesley fixed me in that part of the work which he thought proper, and when the house was finished, I was appointed to be the housekeeper.

Soon also, the people were again divided into bands, or small select societies; women by themselves, and the men in like manner. I had full a hundred in classes, whom I met in two separate meetings and a band for each day of the week. I likewise visited the sick and backsliders, which was my pleasant meat. The work of God was my delight, and when I was not employed in it I seemed out of my element. We had also several Societies in the country, which I regularly visited, meeting the women in the day time and in the evening the whole society. And oh, what pouring out of the Spirit have I seen at those times! It warms my heart now while I relate it. I doubt not but I shall meet some of those precious souls, amongst whom I was so often refreshed in prayer, to sing the high praises of God and the Lamb for ever!

SOURCE:

William Bennet, ed., *Memoirs of Mrs. Grace Bennet* (Macclesfield: E. Bayley, 1803), 4-8, 11-14.

B. Accounts of Religious Experience

2. Sarah Ryan

Editor's Introduction

Sarah Ryan (1724–68) was one of John Wesley's most intimate correspondents. She was converted to Methodism under the preaching of George Whitefield in London sometime during 1741 and 1742. She later heard Wesley preach at the Foundery where she became an active member. Despite the fact that many of Wesley's leaders lacked confidence in Sarah, primarily because of her shaded past and multiple marriages, Wesley appointed her housekeeper of the New Room at Bristol[21] and later at the Kingswood School,[22] in 1757, where she incurred the jealous wrath of his wife. In 1762, Sarah joined Mary Bosanquet in her benevolent activities in London and became her close companion in the years that followed. The two women worked closely together in the development of the Leytonstone orphanage and school in 1763. On June 7, 1768, they moved the entire community to Yorkshire in order to continue their labor of love in that northern setting. Even though they made the move, in part, for the benefit of Sarah's health, unfortunately, she died shortly thereafter at Cross Hall on August 17. She served as a spiritual mentor for this important circle of women and kept Wesley abreast of developments by means of correspondence. It was natural for Wesley to edit and publish account of her spiritual journey that captures the spirit and ethos of the early Methodist movement. Few contemporaries rivaled Sarah in her efforts to combine an interior personal piety with active social service.

* * * *

I was born October 20, 1724 of poor but morally good parents. They brought up their children according to the best light they had in all the outward duties of religion, but inward, vital Christianity I was an utter stranger to. From the earliest time I can remember, the desire of praise was my predominant passion. Nor did I curb it at all, for I thought it right to be admired, and sought after it in all my actions. But my merciful God did not leave me to follow my own imaginations, but often checked me by that thought, "Must all men die? Must all have an end? And must I die?" Sometimes I was so sunk at the thought as to be truly miserable. Not that I had much concern about an after state; death itself was the thing I feared.

As I grew in years my ill tempers gathered strength. I was artful, subtle, cunning, often loved and made lies, and had little regard either to justice, mercy, or truth. And yet something of fear followed me. Hence on Sunday night, I did not dare to sleep without reading a chapter in the Bible. Indeed, I had a great love for reading, and about this time met with an old book which treated of faith. It gave me great pleasure and I was often reading it to see if I could find out what faith was. But it was too hard for me, and the more I read, the more I was confounded.

About this time my mother insisted on my going to church, but I liked better to go to the meeting,[23] thinking I understood what I heard there better and being often affected by the prayers. But my father's circumstances now turning out badly, I was constrained, young as I was, to go out into the world. I soon sunk more deeply than ever into the spirit of the world. And, as I increased in years, so I did in vice, above many of my fellows. The thirst of praise and of pleasure swelled my soul and tossed me about as a bubble on the water.

When I was about seventeen, I heard Mr. Whitefield.[24] He preached upon the prodigal son.[25] I was greatly affected, wept most of the time, and resolved to hear him at all opportunities. Nor did the impressions I then received entirely wear off ever since. Soon after I went to live with some who had much of the form of religion. Here I had several times such drawings of the Father (though I knew not then what they were) as made me seem to be out of the body. And I could scarce cast my eyes on anything, but I saw God in it. Nor had I any fear of his wrath, but always saw him as a loving Father. Hence I went to live with some who truly feared God, where I met with one of Mr. Wesley's Society. She was a great help to me. I cried and prayed and was greatly distressed for God. But soon my unstable mind drove me among a people who had a name to live, but were dead. And my evil heart quickly led me to join with them in great extravagancies. Yet I continued to talk of religion, so that I was now a downright hypocrite.

B. Accounts of Religious Experience

> O God! "I sigh to say, How great thy love!
> All kinds of sinners dost thou save."[26]

God was not yet weary of me, neither left me to the hardness of my heart, but still followed me with secret desires and drawings from above. I now got into a predestinarian[27] family and was quickly deep in their opinions. Here I heard much about faith and easily persuaded myself that I was a believer. And, indeed, "all but the power of faith I had." Yet I was not happy. I sinned and repented, and sinned again, having great desires to be a Christian, but no power.

Being now about twenty and having thoughts of marrying, never did I pray more earnestly for anything than I did, that I might be married to Christ, although I knew not what it meant. And this I continued to do until I was married to the person on whom I had fixed my heart. Then I thought myself happy enough, without Christ. But God said, "This is not thy rest." All my comforts vanished at once, and the man I loved went away and left me once more to the wide world. Destitute and distressed, I went to live in a Jew's family, and soon cast off both the form and power of religion. I sought pleasure and nothing else. Present happiness was the thing I resolved to have.

Mr. Ryan at this time coming from sea, I was exceedingly tried. But I now saw the hand of the Lord in all, till he went to sea again. Having soon after occasion to go to the captain's wife, I found her to be one of the people called Methodists. After some talk she said she was going to the Foundery. I found a desire to go too, which I did. Mr. John Wesley preached. Something said in my heart, "This is the truth. This is the truth I shall live and die by." As soon as the Society began, as I was leaning my head, all attention, I saw by the eye of my mind Jesus standing as he stood before Thomas and saying, "Reach hither thy hand, and thrust it into my side" [John 20:27]. My soul was melted down before him and I longed to be joined with this people. And now I was more earnest to be a Christian than ever. I applied to Mr. Wesley the following week and he received me into the Foundery Society, for which I was very thankful.

I now met in class, not doubting but I had faith, and spoke there as a believer for a whole year. My husband then came home again and tried me exceedingly. But I now bowed down my stubborn neck and said, "It is the Lord." I read my sin in my punishment and was vile in my own eyes. But I still thought myself a believer until I became acquainted with Sarah Crosby[28] who, after talking with me for some time told me that my faith was vain, and I ought to pray that I might know my sins were forgiven. I thought this a very presumptuous way of talking, yet it made a deep impression upon me, so that I began to doubt whether I had faith or not? And the more I considered, the more I was convinced I never had. Soon after I began to feel the necessity of knowing my sins were forgiven. And for a time I continued seeking after it, but then grew as dead and cold as ever.

In April 1754 I had stifled all my desires when by the importunity of Sarah Crosby I went one Sunday, though very unwillingly, to Spitalfields Church.[29] Mr. John Wesley preached on the parable of the sower [Matt. 13:1–9]. As he was describing the stony and thorny ground, I knew all he said belonged to *me*. But when he spoke of the good ground, I could claim no part in it, only I found a wish that I could! When sermon was ended, as I stood in a careless manner, a thought passed through my mind, "O that I may have a blessing!" It was immediately answered in me, "Thou shalt have a blessing." In the same moment I felt my soul all desire, and it was said to me, "Ask, and thou shalt receive" [John 16:24], upon which, clasping my hands on my breast, I said, "I will ask, and I shall receive." But my body was so weak I could hardly stand while I was enabled to say from my inmost soul,

> My soul is on thy promise cast:
> The promise is for *me*![30]

And all the way, as I went up with much difficulty to the table, I was still saying, "For *me* Lord; for *me*." When I came up, my strength being quite gone, I threw my body across the rails, and, being overwhelmed with the power of God, was utterly regardless of outward things. Mr. Wesley offered me the bread, but I was not able to take it. So he passed by me and gave it me when he came back. When he spoke those words, "The blood of the Lord Jesus Christ," they pierced my heart and filled my soul with love to him. Immediately I said, "This is the faith by which the martyrs went to the flames." I felt a change through my whole soul and longed to be alone. As soon as I got home I fell on my knees and cried, "Lord, are my sins forgiven?" I was answered, "There is no condemnation for them that are in Christ Jesus" [Rom 8:1]. But this did not satisfy. I wanted a clear witness that my sins were forgiven and ardently did I wish for the next Sunday, hoping I should receive it at the table. For three weeks I had expected it in every means of grace, when being one night at my class with my sister who was in great distress, I felt the burden of her soul laid upon mine in an inexpressible manner. And while I was exhorting her to believe, the power of God overwhelmed my soul.

[As I went forward to receive the Sacrament on Easter Eve at the West Street[31] service], I still continued to hold the Lord to his promise, and it was to me according to my faith. Just as I came to the rails, God spoke these words to my soul,

> Lift your eyes of faith, and look
> To the signs he did ordain!
> Thus the bread of Life was broke!
> hus the Lamb of God was slain!
> Thus was shed on Calvary,
> His last drop of blood for *thee*![32]

Immediately I was filled with light and joy and love, and said with confidence, "Thou art the resurrection and the life" [John 11:25]. Notwithstanding which, after the service, I began to reason whether it really was of God? But I thought, "I will tell Sarah Crosby and if she believes it, I will take it as a token of the truth of it." I beckoned her to me, but before I spoke she said, "I know what you have to say. You have found the Lord." I fell back in my seat and was quite overwhelmed with the power and love of God.

I find my whole heart and affections entirely fixed on the Lord Jesus. I have no will but what is conformable to his, no happiness but in doing his pleasure. I feel I am capable, yes, very capable, of suffering. And much of this he has been pleased to lay upon me. But through all, my soul sweetly rests on the bosom of my Beloved. I am willing to be offered up as a whole burnt sacrifice to him. And I pray, from my inmost soul, that he would withhold from me no suffering that can work for his glory; only let his will be done [see also Matt. 26:42]. To him I entirely consecrate myself. To him be might, majesty, and dominion, now and for evermore [see also Jude 1:25]!

SOURCE:

"An Account of Mrs. Sarah Ryan," *AM* 2 (1779): 296-302, 304-6, 309-10.

B. ACCOUNTS OF RELIGIOUS EXPERIENCE

3. SARAH CROSBY

Editor's Introduction

Sarah Crosby (1729–1804) was the first woman preacher of Methodism and a formidable influence with regard to early Methodist spirituality.[33] Her intimate connection with the Leytonstone circle of women, and Mary Bosanquet in particular, located her in a strategic center of women's activities in the nascent revival. Although her spirituality was characterized, most certainly, by her preaching above all other activities, like these other women, she was committed to a pattern of life that combined vital piety and social service. Central, as well, was her notion that true religion lies deeper than our ability to articulate our experience of God. The Wesleyan doctrine of Christian perfection dominated her life and preaching. She embodied the understanding of a dynamic goal for the Christian life—holiness of heart and life—which is the fulfillment of God's gracious activity in the believer. Sarah's call to preach the gospel came in 1761 under extraordinary circumstances, and with the approval of John Wesley, she continued in her active ministry for many years.[34] In the summer of 1772, she traveled extensively with Wesley and another woman preacher, Elizabeth Hurrell,[35] throughout Yorkshire. She died at Leeds, the stronghold of the so-called Female Brethren, on October 29, 1804.

A number of manuscript sources related to the life and work of Sarah Crosby have survived. Most important among these are her *Letterbook* and her collected *Papers*, both of which are part of the Perkins Library Collection of Duke University. Composed primarily of copied correspondence, this collection of materials also includes religious accounts, notes, and prayers, making it a rich treasury of early Methodist spiritual writing. Upon the request of John Wesley, Sarah prepared the following account of her religious experience, dated August 17, 1757.

* * * *

From my childhood I had desires to serve God and in particular to love Jesus Christ, and often wished I had lived when he was upon earth, that I might, like Mary, have sat at his feet and followed him wherever he went.

I was twenty years old within a week when God revealed his Son in my heart, and now I thought all my sufferings were at an end. I labored to persuade all with whom I conversed to come to Christ, telling them there was love, joy, peace, etc. for all that came to him.

Soon after this I was persuaded to hear Mr. Whitefield, and many blessings God gave me through him, in particular, while he was showing the marks of one whose sins were forgiven. I found them in myself and this caused me to rejoice more abundantly. For, till then, I had not heard of such a thing, only of having an interest in Christ.

From the time I was justified I had much conversation with a person (who was afterwards my husband) respecting Mr. Wesley and his works, but my prejudices were strong against him. I read his *Appeals to Men of Reason and Religion*,[36] and thereby began to entertain a better opinion of him. Soon after, his sermon on a "Catholic Spirit"[37] was put into my hands. I liked it much and longed to experience all that was there recommended, allowing it to be the truth. But I met with many discouragements and was surrounded with persons who did all they could to keep up my prejudices, and as yet their efforts prevailed.

About eight months after I had found peace with God, one Sunday morning I was awakened by a voice that seemed to come from the clouds and reached my heart, filling it with peace and joy, expressing several times, "I will make with thee an everlasting covenant, even the sure mercies of David" [Isa. 55:3]. This was an hour before preaching at the Tabernacle.[38] I said, I will go to the Foundery first, for I want to see Mr. Wesley. He preached, but, as I thought, with no power. I remembered nothing he said but this—"If it be possible for God to give us a little love, is it not possible for him to fill us with love?"[39] This I have reason to remember, for I answered in my heart, "Yes, it is possible, but he will not do it." Mr. Wesley was just then going to Ireland,[40] and I heard him no more for eight months.

During this time I frequently heard Mr. Charles Wesley and was often much comforted under his ministry. I thought, "It is possible for God to fill a soul with love. And if he will fill me, sure I am willing to receive." But I knew not myself, though I painfully felt my want of purity of heart. I now read Mr. John Wesley's sermon on "Christian Perfection"[41] and was convinced, if this were what he meant by perfection, God could and would make me thus perfect. But I felt much need of that faith and patience which inherit the promises. I was greatly tempted, and often thought what I felt was a judgment from God for speaking against Mr. Wesley, and that the Lord, to humble me, would help me only by him. Soon after he returned from Ireland, I went to speak to him and freely acknowledged all I had said and thought against him. Immediately I joined the society, and it was unto me according to my faith, for I never spoke to him without a peculiar blessing.

I still had thoughts about predestination, until (after a deliverance from great temptation) God applied this verse to my soul by the power of his Spirit—

> Infinite unexhausted love! Jesus and love are one:
> If still to me thy bowels move, They are restrained
>   from none.[42]

Since that time I have had no doubt but grace is free for all.[43] This has been well for me, for in times of great distress, I have doubted. "Could I believe God made one soul to be damned, I should believe I was that soul." But I cannot believe he did.

I know not that, for almost seven years after I knew the Lord, I was ever a day together without being tempted. And the inward conflicts I endured day and night added to outward labors, and constant abstinence weakened my body and hurt my constitution much. But I have often been thankful that, amidst all my temptations, I was scarce ever tempted to doubt of the divinity of Jesus Christ, and one reason is because I have so often found that, when I have been surrounded with an host of foes and could find no other help in earth or heaven, his mighty name has set me free.

Frequently, however, in the midst of my sufferings, when I could find no help from any other quarter, I have found relief in reading and singing Mr. Charles Wesley's hymns[44] which, as well as many of your (John Wesley's) sermons, have been special blessings to me. I was now convinced that I had previously sought knowledge more than the love of God, which error I prayed God to forgive, promising I would now seek his love alone. I often said, not all the creatures on earth, nor all the angels in heaven, can help my soul! None but Jesus Christ can save me. At length, one day while I was sitting at work, the Lord Jesus appeared to the eye of my mind, surrounded with glory, while his love overwhelmed me. I said, this is the power I have waited for, and was

> Constrain'd to cry, by love divine,
> My God! thou art for ever mine.[45]

Soon after I was made a leader of a class, an office which I was tempted to think God did not require me to undertake—I knew not but he could enable me to guide souls aright, and therefore prayed much to know whether I was not doing the will of others or my own, rather than his will, beseeching him to answer me by giving some one a great blessing. I now felt my idol was beneath my feet, and so it has remained ever since. My soul seemed all love and I desired nothing so much as to lay down my life for others that they might feel the same. This was about three and a half years after I was justified, and for the three years following God gave me to walk in the light of his countenance, until "the blood of Jesus Christ, his Son, cleansed me from all sin."[46]

Not long after this, as I was praying, my soul was overwhelmed with the power of God. I seemed to see the Lord Jesus before me and said, "Lord, I am ready to follow thee, not only to prison, but to death, if thou wilt give me strength." And he spoke these words to my heart, "Feed my sheep" [John 21:17]. I answered, "Lord, I will do as thou hast done; I will carry the lambs in my bosom, and gently lead those that are with young" [Isaiah 40:11].

To give an account of all the fiery darts and suggestions I was assaulted with at this time would be impossible.... In the midst of these exercises, however, the Lord lifted up my head and often enabled me to say in faith, "Although the fig-tree do not blossom, and there be no fruit on the vine, or herd in the stall, &c. yet will I rejoice in the Lord, and joy in the God of my salvation [Hab. 3:17-18]; for when he has tried me, I shall come forth as gold" [Job 23:10].

I now felt my soul fully cast on the Lord Jesus and found a rest which before I had not known, while peace and love filled my

B. Accounts of Religious Experience

heart. The day after at church the Lord showed me that many things which I had thought were sins were only temptations, and also what a little thing it was for him to take the root of sin out of my heart. I feared to believe he had done it, but asked a token and prayed he would stamp me with his Spirit's seal and speak to my soul at his table, and was refreshed with these words:

> There, there we shall stand,
> With our harps in our hands,
>   Interrupted no more,
> And eternally sing, and rejoice, and adore! [47]

The next day I could not help believing God had taken full possession of my heart, for though I felt myself weaker than ever, yet the Lord was my strength.

Day and night I was amazed at the blessed change my soul experienced, but I said nothing to any one because I was not as yet sure what the Lord had done for me, though I had always promised if the Lord would but fully save me I would declare his goodness, although I believed it would expose me to various exercises both from ministers and people. A few days after this challenges were suggested to my mind with regard to what I ought to do in order to please God. Immediately I knelt down and besought the Lord, if he were my God, to lift up a standard against the enemy and answer me from his Word, which I then opened on my knees on these words, Isaiah 60:18-20. I then believed God would be a light unto me. Directly he brought to my remembrance how often he had showed me how I ought to walk to please him.

I now prayed much that God might show me if he had taken away the root of sin from my heart, and also if I had been saved from sin in the temptations that were past. And he showed me, as many waters cannot quench love, neither could the floods drown it, so neither had these floods of temptation he had brought me through quenched the love he had given me to himself, for it was the love that never fails.

I was now exceedingly happy, yet I prayed the Lord, if any farther witness was necessary he would give it me. Soon after the glory of the Lord shone around me. I saw, by faith, the glory of God in the face of Jesus Christ [see also 2 Cor. 4:6]. The Holy Spirit had often given me such views of the Savior and of his love and mercy to every upright soul as had filled me with unspeakable consolation, but now I was assured of the Father's love and could not help saying, "They are three, and yet but one God, in glory equal, in majesty co-eternal." I then said in my heart and with my lips, "O! thou holy Triune God!" The Spirit then powerfully spoke to my soul, saying, "I will dwell in thee for ever." I said in my heart, "There is no fear in love; perfect love casts out fear" [1 John 4:18].

From this time I was more established in the truths I had been taught and which I now felt the Lord fulfilling in me. I no longer scrupled to declare the great work he had wrought in me, and after so doing generally felt he afresh shone on my soul. I walked in light and liberty and, blessed be God, continue to do so, but I long for more. Frequently he assures me he will manifest himself more fully than he has yet done. This I am waiting for, and beg leave to subscribe myself,

Dear sir,
Your unworthy child,
Sarah Crosby

SOURCE:

Sarah Crosby, "An Account of Mrs. Crosby, of Leeds," *WMM* 29 (1806): 419-22, 466-73; collated with Zechariah Taft's account of Crosby.[48]

B. ACCOUNTS OF RELIGIOUS EXPERIENCE

4. JANE COOPER

Editor's Introduction

Jane Cooper (1738–62) was an early Methodist saint to whom John Wesley frequently referred as a living and a dying witness of Christian perfection. In response to Lady Maxwell, who had just decided to join the Methodist Society, he advised: "I want you to be all a Christian ... such an one as that saint of God, Jane Cooper, all sweetness, all gentleness, all love."[49] In his attempt to instruct a Methodist neophyte concerning the balance of the affections and the mind in the Christian life, Wesley turned to Jane as a pattern well worth emulation:

> But who has attained this? Who treads the middle path, equally remote from both extremes? I will tell you one that did (although the remembrance of her still brings tears into my eyes), that lovely saint Jane Cooper! There was the due mixture of intellect and passion! I remember one of the last times I saw her, before her last illness, her look, her attitude, her words! My dear friend, be you a follower of her, as she was of Christ.[50]

In 1764, Wesley published *Letters Wrote by Jane Cooper*, giving her high praise in the preface: "Here are no extravagant flights, no mystic reveries, no unscriptural enthusiasm. The sentiments are all just and noble, the result of a fine natural understanding, cultivated by conversation, thinking, reading, and true Christian experience.... This strong genuine sense is expressed in a style simple and artless in the highest degree, but likewise, lively, proper."[51] In his *Plain Account of Christian Perfection* of 1766, Wesley quotes extensively from the account of her death and from one of her letters included in his previous publication of her correspondence, as these writings contained "a plain and artless relation of the manner wherein it pleased God to work that great change in her soul."[52] John Wesley visited her on November 19 and 20 during her fatal battle with smallpox and buried her several days later on November 25, 1762.[53]

Sarah Crosby carefully copied a portion of Jane Cooper's personal diary into her "Letterbook," covering the period January 9 to

March 13, 1762, which reflects important experiences during the final year of Jane's short but eventful life. This record typifies the experience of many Methodist women who became engaged in one way or another in public speaking and sought to live as disciples fully restored in the love of Christ. An excerpt from the Crosby "Manuscript Letterbook," presented here with full expansion and modernization of the original abbreviated text, concludes the selections related to the account of Jane Cooper.

* * * *

A. Letter of February 21, 1761

Your obliging request lays me under a happy necessity of calling to mind the past mercies of God. May every review of them bring trust for future blessings and thankfulness for the present!

Ever since I can remember I was desirous of happiness, but I did not seek it in God. I thought if I was religious I should go to heaven, but I knew not the nature of true religion and I was unwilling to be under the restraint of that I did know. Yet so great a stranger was I to myself that I often thought, if I knew what God required I would perform it.[54] At sixteen I was confirmed and made many resolutions, but they soon wore off. I had a strong impression on my mind that I should die when I was twenty-four.[55] I reflected on those who were put apprentice seven years to learn a trade, and thought I ought to use like application to learn the business of eternity.

I went to the Sacrament the day I was eighteen and found uncommon satisfaction. I exhorted others to do the same, thinking I had now done all that was commanded me and that if I continued in the same way I should be a very profitable servant.

Soon after this I went to London for eight weeks where I heard Mr. Jones[56] (of Southwark) preach and was affected at hearing of the sufferings of Christ, much as I used to be at seeing or reading of a tragedy. I was afterwards asked to hear Mr. Romaine.[57] I did so, but I could not understand him. The night I left London some persons were debating about the millennium. One of them repeated part of the 20th chapter of the Revelation. I was struck at the awful words and thought if Christ was then to come I was not prepared to meet him. I went home very serious and began to search the

B. Accounts of Religious Experience

scriptures and to be more strict than ever. I was often troubled, but knew not the cause, and was ashamed to confess my fears. My friends thought I had a fever on my spirits, and I thought so too. But as I read much, I began to fear that with all my religion I was not converted. I wanted to go to London that I might hear Mr. Romaine.

A year after, I went to London with my father-in-law. At the inn where we lay I saw Mr. Whitefield's *Sermons*. I read what I could and determined to hear him. He was not in town, but I was much affected with Mr. Dyer's preaching. Afterwards I not only went to St. Dunstan's,[58] but to all the Methodist places of worship I knew, and one evening heard Mr. Walsh,[59] at West Street.[60] He preached the necessity of that "holiness without which none can see the Lord" [Heb. 12:14]. His words were as arrows in my heart. I found all my former righteousness deficient. I knew this could not obtain mercy, but I did not feel I deserved hell. I wrote to Mr. Romaine to know what I should do to be saved? He desired to see me and told me two things were necessary, to know my want of Christ and my interest in him.

I went home with great reluctance, for I knew no Christian in the town where I lived. My former acquaintance thought me mad. My mother was greatly alarmed. Not long after I went to Norwich for a few days and found out Mr. Mitchell. He spoke to me of the peace which faith brings to the conscience. I knew myself a stranger to this, but would willingly have suffered the rack so I might attain it. I went home and was, for five or six weeks, in a most unhappy situation. Before, I was not bad enough to come to Christ, now I was too bad for him to receive. Yet the Lord dealt tenderly with me and at different times brought many encouraging scriptures to my mind. But still the stupidity and unbelief I felt caused me to mourn in secret. Still I was constrained to say,

> Scarce I begin my sad complaint,
> When all my warmest wishes faint:
> Hardly I lift my weeping eye,
> When all my kindling ardors die:
> Nor hopes nor fears my bosom move,
> Nor still I cannot, cannot love![61]

I could not rest thus, though I concluded it would always be the case. I expected to be miserable all my life and to perish at the last. I found it as easy to reach heaven with my hand as to believe Jesus died for *me*. I felt, "no one can come to Christ, except the Father draw him" [John 6:44]. Now I knew it was the work of God to believe on him whom he has sent. I prayed he would work faith in *me*, but seemed as distant from God as hell from heaven. I was cut off from all self-dependence. I was a sinner stripped of all.

I was on my knees striving to pray when I heard inwardly a voice say, "Thy sins are forgiven thee." I felt the truth of it in my heart, and in a moment, prayer was lost in praise. I called upon the angels to join with me in blessing him who died for *me*![62] He caused his goodness to pass before me [see also Exod. 33:19] and I rejoiced with joy unspeakable [1 Peter 1:8].

Yet in a few hours after I began to fear I had deceived myself and all was delusion. I was much distressed and had recourse to prayer, and the Lord repeated his mercies and impressed the same words on my mind more strongly than before. I was more assured of his forgiving love and enjoyed much peace in believing. I now thought I could never sin more. My mind was taken up with God, and I conversed with him as a man would with his friend. My confidence in him was unshaken and my hope full of immortality.

I wanted others to rejoice with me. But they were strangers to Jesus, and "intermeddled not with my joy" [Prov. 14:10]. I lamented being alone. My nearest friends thought I carried things too far. My mother was more alarmed, for I could not speak but on religious subjects. A neighboring clergyman advised her to confine me if I offered to hear the Methodists. This I did at all opportunities, though none was nearer than four miles off. Her tenderness gave me much pain. I was sorry to grieve her in anything, and yet, I did not dare to oblige her by acting contrary to my conscience. I could not play at cards nor join in trifling discourse, though my refusal was deemed preciseness.

I was near two years at home after this. Then the Lord fulfilled his promise. He gave me the "bread of adversity and the water of affliction," but my eyes did "see my teachers" [Isa. 30:20]. I was now more desirous than ever to be made conformable to the will of God. But I thought to believe the doctrine of perfection was derogating from the priestly office of Christ.

B. Accounts of Religious Experience

When I first saw you, Sir, at Norwich, notwithstanding my prejudice to your opinions, I found that reverence and esteem for you which have increased ever since.[63] My understanding was then better informed and my desires more fervent for all the grace God had in store for me. I trust my soul is still alive to God and athirst for righteousness. He has borne my manners in the wilderness and sustains me in my utter helplessness. He continues to multiply his pardons and heap his benefits upon me. Every trial is sent in mercy; every temptation is permitted for my good; every cross has proved a blessing in disguise. In his light I see this: I believe he is able to keep me from falling [see also Jude 1:24] and to make me perfect and entire, lacking nothing [see also James 14]. My present situation requires more of every grace than any I have been in before. But I trust he, in whom all fullness dwells, will supply my every want.

I would not have troubled you with so long a letter, but indeed I had not time to make it shorter. And I am desirous to prove by every means that I regard your advice and on all occasions speak with freedom.

SOURCE:

John Wesley, *Letters Wrote by Jane Cooper: To which is Prefixt, some Account of Her Life and Death* (London: [Strahan], 1764), 32-36.

B. Journal, January 16, 1762

I received peace in believing four years ago. For some time after I felt no sin and thought I never should any more. How far it was owing to my own unfaithfulness I cannot tell. But it was not long before I found my inward parts were very wickedness. I was amazed to feel that notwithstanding this, I loved Him who died for *me*, that I still retained my confidence in God and had the witness in myself that I was a child of God. But withal I thought, I should always have a carnal mind which would sometimes be at "enmity with God" [Rom. 8:7].

In this belief I continued, until about two years ago when God brought me to hear the whole gospel. Not long after, those words were continually on my mind, "Once have I heard, yea twice has God spoken, that power belongs unto God" [Psalm 62:11]. And I was deeply convinced that I had in effect denied his power. Even after I had tasted his love I limited the Holy One of Israel. And from this time I began to plead the promises of sanctification. But I still set them at a distance, supposing the accomplishment of them to be far off.

In March following I heard a letter read from one who had entered into the rest of the people of God.[64] It described a happiness in religion which I was a stranger to. I was much stirred up to seek after it and was determined to wrestle with God till I prevailed. One day in prayer that promise was applied, "The Lord whom you seek shall suddenly come to his temple" [Mal. 3:1]. From that time I expected him, in every means I used, to come and destroy the works of the devil. I was agonizing with God in family prayer when he gave me power to venture upon Jesus, as of God "made unto me wisdom, and righteousness, and sanctification and redemption" [1 Cor. 1:30]. He spoke into my heart, "The Lord, even the king of Israel is in the midst of thee; and the enemies thou hast seen this day, thou shalt see them no more for ever" [see also Zeph. 3:14-20]. From this time I have rejoiced indeed, and yet loathed myself in my own sight. I feel no desire but to please him, and know of nothing in me that is not subjected to Jesus. I depend upon him every moment as my advocate with the Father. I daily feel my coming short of what I would be, yet without any condemnation. The blood of sprinkling speaks me clean [see also Heb. 12:24]. Indeed if I could perform the obedience I desire, I should still be ashamed before him.

SOURCE:

Jane Cooper's ms. journal, January 16, 1762, as quoted by Wesley in his "Account of her Life and Death," *Letters by Jane Cooper*, 6-7.

C. Christian Experience

My prayer has been for these fourteen years past that I may be nothing. And I praise God, I have reason to hope, that I come a little nearer to that blessed mark. I well know there is no happiness like that which flows from a constant sense that I am nothing and Jesus is all.[65]

I have, at present, a deep sense of my meanness, poverty, and folly, so that my soul lies in the dust. I am contemptible in my own eyes; yet I feel I am precious in his sight who has paid so dear a price for me. My soul is broken before my Lord and desires to follow him as the shadow follows the substance. He has my heart and reigns the Lord of all my wishes and desires. I need no change of place, person, or thing to raise or increase my happiness. The presence of Jesus is sufficient. His will is my resting place and his love my delight. But my joy is not every moment full, though in general I can say,

> My *full* soul doth still require
> Thy whole eternity of Love.[66]

I see the justice of God in all my trials, and I love him the more because he is just. But I know mercy guides the stroke. I speak feelingly, I know no finite punishment is adequate to my infinite offences. But his merits and mercy exceed them all.

I "rejoice evermore" [1 Thess. 5:16] in a constant union and oneness of spirit with the Lord Jesus and "pray without ceasing" [1 Thess. 5:17], as the desire of my soul is going out after him at all times and in all places. And I, "in every thing give thanks" [1 Thess. 5:18], as I see the hand of God in all I meet with great and small, though at some times in things indifferent I feel dislike, perhaps for a minute, before I advert to it. But when I discover this I immediately embrace the thing I dislike, unless I have a good reason to the contrary. And I am ashamed before the Lord that I can for a moment choose anything after all that he has done for me.

I desire never to feel anything amiss. Yet I desire to spend my whole life in holy shame before him, remembering what I was. I would weep much, and love much, having had much forgiven.

SOURCE:

AM 5 (1782): 408-9.

D. Journal, January 15, 1762

Went to London on Friday to the meeting. Mr. M—d desired any to speak who had not before declared the goodness of God. I was convinced I ought to speak but feared I should bring a reproach upon the cause by my foolishness and was tempted to think I should fall down in a fit if I began and that I knew not how to order my speech aright. But the Lord said, "Take no thought how or what you shall speak, for in that hour it shall be given you" [Luke 12:11-12].

I felt an awful sense of God while speaking and sat down with emotion that spoke to my heart, well done good and faithful servant [see also Matt. 25:21, 23]. My soul was so well satisfied with the approbation of Christ, I neither wished nor feared what man thought of me. I only prayed they might receive the truth in the love of it lest their souls should suffer loss. I am content to be vile,[67] let God be glorified and it suffices.

In going home I heard that Mr. B— said I made an exhortation for half an hour on Friday. What will not prejudice report, my God lay not fully to his charge. You know whose words I spoke and for what cause I did so. All hail my Savior's hallowed cross! Now I begin to be a disciple if all men speak evil of me for your sake [see also Matt. 5:11-12]. Make me steady to stand reproach and give cause for it.

SOURCE:

Sarah Crosby, "Manuscript Letterbook," 111-14.[68]

C. Diaries and Journals

1. MEMOIR OF HANNAH BALL

Editor's Introduction

Hannah Ball (1733–92) was one of the most industrious of the early Methodist women and was founder of one of the earliest Sunday school programs in England in 1769, nearly fourteen years before Robert Raikes began his experimental schools in Gloucester. Converted under the preaching of John Wesley in 1765, she became one of the leading figures in the Methodist Society in High Wycombe, near Oxford. By inference from a letter written by John Wesley to her, Hannah and two other women, Patty Chapman and Nancy Bolton, were the life force of Methodism in their respective communities of High Wycombe, Watlington, and Witney. He acknowledged the absolutely indispensable work of these women in the life of the movement.[69] Unfortunately, she wrote very little about her actual work among the disadvantaged children of her community. Much of that story remains elusive. But her practice was to meet with children who were unable to attend school, "instructing a few of the rising generation," as she said, "in the principles of religion."

Hannah's spirituality was Anglican through and through. It is characterized by daily immersion in scripture, and particularly its use in liturgical settings. References to the means of grace, the duty of public and private prayer, the practice of meditation, and the pattern of fasting and prayer on Fridays pervade her diary. Her diaries reflect an intense interior life, a deep sense of the dreadfulness of sin and the duty of living continually in the presence of God and sanctifying every incident in the day's routine with prayer. Constant interaction with the lonely, the desperate, and the forgotten, such as the prisoners and the sick in her community, punctuates her record. Her memoir, the excerpts of which here span more than twenty years, reflects a life rooted in the means of grace and oriented to the cultivation of a life of virtue and love.

* * * *

I now began to turn my attention to and sought the company of the most serious professors of religion. In these interviews I was much disappointed and entreated the Lord for direction to a people that worshiped him in spirit and in truth. A people, known by the name of Methodist, were brought to my mind. With deep ambivalence I replied, "Lord, I cannot go with them." So great was my aversion to that despised people, I once thought I would as soon go to hell as unite with the followers of John Wesley.

I found prayer, reading, and meditation rendered useful. Observing also that the generality of men were pleasing themselves more than God, I determined my resolutions in favor of a serious life.

About the latter end of the year 1764 I applied closer than ever to reading the Bible. One day, while reading Moses' prayer, divine light was communicated in a greater degree than I had ever known before.

When on a visit to a relation, I first saw Mr. Thomas Walsh's Sermons.[70] They were rendered, indeed, quickening and searching to my soul. From this time I longed to hear a Methodist preacher.

Some time after this, Mr. Wesley came to Wycombe.[71] I had now a conflict between desire and aversion. Desire at length so far prevailed, that though I did not attend the preaching at night, yet I went at five in the morning. I was struck with the venerable appearance of Mr. Wesley, but more deeply affected with the words of his text which were taken from Matt. 15:28: "O woman, great is thy faith: Be it unto thee even as thou wilt."

A few days after, Mr. Hanson[72] preached his farewell sermon. A remark which he made in his discourse on "the knowledge of salvation by the remission of sins" [Luke 1:77], was from that time never erased from my mind. I now clearly saw the necessity of the remission of sins, nor could I ever find rest in my soul till I received that blessing.

Oct. 23 [1768]. My earnest desire is to live to God in deed and in truth. Lord, enable me to search the secret pages of your word, that I may grow in grace and spiritual knowledge, and that I may not err on the right hand or the left.

Nov. 16. How tenderly does my heavenly Father watch over me and proportion strength to my day! When I need much, it is given;

so I have no lack. O may I always be kept in a seeking frame of mind!

Nov. 30. I want to feel deeper humility. I want humility enough to bear prosperity, and not to be high minded. I do not feel pride, but I wish to feel lowliness grounded in my heart. On examination, I find more self-contempt, more of the mind of Christ, and more of that love that suffers long and is kind.

> Thee let me now through faith behold,
> And by reflection shine,
> Till nature's dross is turned to gold,
> And I am all divine.[73]

Dec. 1. Happy in the love of Jesus, I long to be with him my soul loves. My heart is disengaged and free. No creature holds me here. How poor their joys whose hearts are tied to earthly things!

March 2 [1769]. I this day visited three poor sailors in prison, each of them deprived of a limb, apparently ignorant of the scriptures and strangers to the God of their mercies. I pointed them to the Lamb of God which takes away the sins of the world [see also John 1:29].

March 3. My soul was much refreshed by the simple relation a poor woman gave me of her justification. I remembered praying with her and her mother, about eight months before. The purport of my prayer was that Christ would reveal himself to them. Who knows but this was the answer to that prayer? After many days the seed may appear.

March 12. This morning I heard our new curate, the Rev. Mr. Williams, preach. I am of Mr. Wesley's opinion. I pity those who imagine they can receive no benefit in attending the means of grace at church. The Lord has bestowed on Mr. Williams gifts to excite the emotions and engage the attention. I hope he will prove a burning and shining light in the church of Christ and win many souls to worship God in spirit and in truth [see also John 4:24], that he may shine as a star in glory for ever and ever. I frequently pray for him as for my own soul.

April 19. I feel I need the ever blessed Redeemer in all his offices; no less as a King to save, than a Priest to atone, or a Prophet to teach.[74] I need him to continue every blessing he has already bestowed. For more than a year past I have been enabled to give God my whole heart. I still feel the necessity of earnestly seeking the Lord as much as ever, and the more so as I never saw my weakness as I have done since I entered into this liberty of the children of God. Conscious that I come short in my duty, yet I believe it is more from a defect in understanding than in love.

Nov. 15. Mr. W[illiams?] preached last evening from Psalm 119:13 and this morning from Ephesians 6:18-19.[75] He earnestly enforced the duty of public and private prayer. I found much consolation knowing that, through the grace of God imparted to me, I had been enabled to practice this important duty. This day it is my painful lot to accompany the remains of my uncle Harding to the grave. I entreat the presence of the Lord to be with me,

> That, solemn awe that dares not move,
> And all the silent heaven of love,[76]

may possess my soul. O, give me courage to glorify your name that I may enjoy your presence for ever!

Nov. 17. My soul cleaves to my God who can perform all things for me. I desire to be saved from the cares and entanglements of this life. I feel my heart glow with divine love, and that the Lord is teaching me to live unreservedly to him.

Nov. 18. Notwithstanding the rest I enjoy in the love of God, yet I thirst and pant for more. When I awake after your likeness, O Lord, I shall be satisfied. Save me, O Lord, from surrounding foes. In myself I am all weakness, but in the Lord I am strong. I remark, whenever I aim to walk closer with God, Satan is more than ordinarily active in tempting.

Nov. 19. My desire this day is to live close to God by faith, prayer, and holy meditation. I purpose visiting a sick, unawakened woman. I always feel unqualified for the work. Lord, help me, that your name may be glorified! In the evening I heard that dear servant of Christ, Mr. Henderson,[77] preach from these words, "Thou hast a name that thou livest, and art dead" [Rev. 3:1]. My soul was revived on hearing him, for he was the instrument in the hands of God, in helping me to go on to perfection.

Dec. 18. Never was I more conscious that "salvation is not of works, lest any man should boast" [Eph. 2:9]. If I am eternally saved, it will be of mere grace, and I rejoice to be saved in the way of the Lord's appointing. Who can describe the joy arising from faith in Christ and a mind fixed on God? Slights or favors from friends have the same effect. They drive me nearer to the Lord, and I find him to be all in all to my soul.

Dec. 21. This has been a day of weeping and trial. But I trust it shall work together for my good. I want my heart to be filled with love and Christian courage.

Dec. 25. A day of painful and gloomy temptations.

> But love can burst the shades of death,
> And bear me from the clouds beneath,
> To everlasting day.[78]

There is a vast difference between the cautious hypocrite and the genuine Christian. The former is an utter stranger to himself. The latter tries the whole of his inward and outward conduct by the word of truth, as in the presence of Jehovah. "He that doeth truth cometh to the light." John 3:21. The insincere dissolves when tried in the fire of temptation. The truly gracious soul comes forth as burnished gold—the fire befriends him, by refining his dross and loosing his bands. Dan. 3:26.

May 20 [1770]. It has been my privilege this day to be confirmed.[79] I found it a blessing to my soul. May it prove useful to me in time to come! I believe the prayer offered up by the bishop will be answered in my behalf.[80] I am persuaded many members of our Society have quenched the Spirit by not submitting to the order of confirmation. I earnestly pray for a fresh confirmation of the work of God in my heart, that the fruits of the Spirit may be manifested in my life.

[June 3, 1770] I desire to spend the remaining part of my life in a closer walking with God and in labors of love to my fellow-creatures—feeding the hungry, clothing the naked, instructing a few of the rising generation in the principles of religion, and in every possible way I am capable ministering to them that shall be heirs of salvation.

June 3 [1773]. Seven years ago today I found peace with God. And praised be my divine Preserver, to this time I have enjoyed a constant witness of my acceptance, and my soul still hungers Lord for you! It is a source of inexpressible grief to reflect on the apparent distance of some relations from the life and enjoyment of genuine piety.

Feb. 8, 1775. After praying with some children, which I meet every Sabbath day to instruct in the principles of Christianity, I was grievously tempted that I had given my heart to the creature. But upon examination, when or in what, I found it proceeded from the father of lies. My desires are unto God, to be his only, and by divine assistance I feel resolved to believe, till rooted in the knowledge and love of God.

Feb. 17. My soul was much refreshed in visiting a poor woman with five small children and a sixth hourly expected. And yet her only attendant in this situation was her affectionate husband, whose small earnings were the support of the whole family. I found the woman happy and composed in mind, willing to live or die. O, what can equal the support which religion gives to the soul in an hour of affliction?

Feb. 18. I have received, I trust, an increase of patience. My soul rests in God. To the end that I may improve in the knowledge of him, I read, write, and pray, hear the word preached, converse with the people of God, fast, or use abstinence, together with every prudential help as channels only for receiving the grace of God. But private prayer is in general the most strengthening means of all.

April 16. Lord's day morning. Mr. Wolfe[81] preached from these words, "If ye then be risen with Christ, seek those things which are above" [Col. 3:1]. My faith was strengthened and I felt encouragement to press towards the mark for the prize [see also Phil. 3:14], and to believe that Christ would feed his flock. I afterwards commemorated the death of Christ at our parish church[82] and found it good to be there.

I esteem it a privilege to be a member of the Church of England and desire to be kept in her doctrines faithful unto death.

April 17. Yesterday Jesus, according to his promise, fed his flock. My soul seemed to be brought into a wealthy place. I now feel my spirit rests in God and I enjoy a peace passing understanding [see also Phil. 4:7]. Glory be to "Immanuel, God with us," for bringing me into a land of rest and peace! My peace is as a river and my righ-teousness as the waves of the sea [see also Isa. 48:18].

Dec. 31. I earnestly desire an increase of the fruits of the Spirit, and, in ending the year, to lie at the feet of Jesus my Lord, relying on him alone for a renewal of strength. Since I first united with the Wesleyan Methodists, how many happy seasons I have enjoyed! O wondrous grace! O boundless love! May I continue faithful until death. Then shall I receive a crown of life. And, in closing my diary for the year, I would praise my God for all that is past and trust him for all that is to come. Hallelujah! Amen.

Feb. 16 [1776]. Every Friday I set apart as a day of fasting and prayer. This painful task to nature is more than compensated by the divine communications of love to my soul. O transporting thought, to be for ever with the Lord! I long to meditate more on those divine glories which the soul shall be ravished with to all eternity.

Jan. 23, 1779. This day my dear mother went to Abraham's bosom, rejoicing in God her Savior, having lived seventy-nine years and some months in this vale of tears. It was an unspeakable consolation to her surviving children, when standing around her bed, to hear her utter Jacob's dying confession of faith, "I have waited for Thy salvation, O Lord" [Gen. 49:18].

Feb. 18. The little society in this town, having passed through much persecution and great interruption in their public devotions, by a Mr. J—'s frequently beating a drum during the whole hour of meeting, providence has at length pointed out a convenient situation for erecting a chapel. Mr. Batting, after handsomely subscribing to the building, generously undertook the superintending the whole work until it was completed. This labor of love will not be unnoticed by the Lord.

May 18. I have been three weeks confined to the house with the small pox. When I first knew it was that disorder, I felt no fear, but rather a joy in hope it was the Master's call to arise and depart for ever to be with the Lord! Soon after I was permitted to be sorely buffeted by the enemy. In this assault, I said, "Where will this conflict end, in heaven or in hell?" I felt an unshaken peace in my soul and the Lord soon appeared in my behalf. The clouds were scattered and a delightful joy succeeded the tempest.

June 5. Although I have no rival of my heart, yet, unless I am kept by the power of the Lord, I shall presently sink down in desiring some person or thing to make me happy. I have frequently found, after solemn dedication of myself to God, strong temptations have followed to try the sincerity of my love to the Lord.

Nov. 11. The Rev. John Wesley opened our new chapel, by preaching on "We preach Christ crucified; unto the Jews a stumbling-block" [1 Cor. 1:23].[83] On this occasion we had a crowded and genteel audience. My heart's desire and prayer to God is, that this neat and convenient house, erected to Jehovah's glory, may be an everlasting blessing to the town of High Wycombe.

Dec. 5. There is no state of life but needs much grace, and no real happiness but what comes from God. A single life is a self-denying life. One day, meditating on what would constitute a person's happiness that had escaped the incidental allurements of youth, it was powerfully applied to my mind, "The grace of God, and nothing else." I have ever found it true. Jesus is all and in all to the believing soul. And where he is, there is no want of comfort to insure which we must always have this conviction, "that it is by grace we stand" [see also Rom. 5:2].

Dec. 6. I was called to visit a woman whom the Lord had brought, in the furnace of affliction, to a sense of her sins and a clear discovery of his pardoning love. She died rejoicing in God her Savior.

Christ's flock is small compared with the bulk of mankind that know not God. Yet even of these, very few it is to be feared, see and seek fully the good things which God has prepared for them on this side heaven, such as communion with the Father and Son, the divine Spirit as a fountain of living water [see also John 4:10], the pure love of God which casts out slavish fear [see also 1 John 4:18], and for the soul to be kept in perfect peace by a constant reliance on the Lord for fresh supplies of grace.

June 7, 1784. If the Lord renders my feeble attempts in any measure useful to his children or others, I feel a jealous fear lest the least of the praise should attach to dust and ashes, which should redound alone to the Lord. O, to be ever kept so as "that praise may not elate, or frowns depress, my mind!"[84]

Jan. 4, 1785. It is nearly twenty years since I first heard the Methodist preaching. Innumerable are the blessings I have received from a bountiful God. The trials and temptations he has preserved me in and brought me through I cannot recount, but they are all numbered and past. Previously, the Lord has been my help, and the crowning grace of all is a sweet taste of his love.

June 3. Twenty years since I found peace in the favor of God. Ever since that time, through divine mercy and grace, I have been enabled to preserve a good conscience and in some degree have walked with God. To him alone be all the glory, for his own right hand has wrought the work.

> Excluded is my every boast,
> My glory swallow'd up in shame.[85]

Feb. 25. This day I followed to the grave the remains of that faithful friend to truth, Thomas Humphries, who for many years was an ornament to the gospel and the first person that received the Methodist Preachers in Wycombe. He stood by the pious Mr. Walsh amid a shower of stones while he was proclaiming the glad tidings of salvation to a part of the people of the town. His last moments were triumphant. He spoke with the warmest animation of the love of Christ to him, and that his departure hence would be to dwell with angels. His last words were, "Dear Jesus, I am coming."

June 24 [1792]. The Lord has strengthened me a little. I have the use of my hand again which I had lost for a week. I feel much thankfulness to God for this, and the many mercies I enjoy, but above all for that permanent peace of soul which I possess from day to day and a sure trust that, when this poor life shall end, I shall be for ever with the Lord.

July 15. Blessed be my gracious Preserver! He accomplishes his word, wherein he has caused me to hope by keeping me in perfect peace with a mind resting on Jehovah. I am very low but quite resigned to the Lord. O the sweetness of ascribing all glory to the Lord!

SOURCE:

Joseph Cole, ed., *Memorials of Hannah Ball*, 3rd ed., rev. (London: Wesleyan Conference Office, 1880), 4-6, 16-21, 34-35, 39-40, 46-48, 55-57, 91, 97-99, 104-5, 113-21, 127-31, 140-41.

2. Hester Ann Rogers

Editor's Introduction

Hester Ann Rogers (1756–94) was the daughter of a sincere but strident clergyman of the Church of England, the Reverend James Roe, vicar of Macclesfield. After her father's death, the new curate, a clergyman of strong evangelical sympathies, David Simpson, exerted a profound influence on "Hetty." In 1776, she first met John Wesley, who encouraged her to become a devoted class leader within his Methodist system, and who became her personal friend (despite the many years that separated them in age), devoted correspondent, and spiritual mentor.[86] She married James Rogers, one of Wesley's preachers, on August 19, 1784, and shared his itinerant life in both Ireland and England. She died after the birth of her seventh child on October 10, 1794.

Hetty was famous among the Methodists of her day for her eminent holiness, zeal, and Christian influence. Her fame was due in large measure to the publication of extracts from her journal, first appearing in 1796 as *The Experience of Mrs. Hester Ann Rogers*.[87] This work—to which were later added more religious correspondence, Thomas Coke's funeral sermon, and other devotional tracts and religious verse—quickly became one of the most popular devotional publications in early Methodism, on both sides of the Atlantic Ocean. It went through many subsequent printings in the nineteenth century and shaped the lives of Methodists for several generations.

What this account reveals is that despite her religious background and spiritual sensitivities, Hetty felt distant from God and unsatisfied because she had experienced no personal relationship with God. Her journal details the interior tensions and the external obstacles that confronted her daily as she sought earnestly for a more intimate and meaningful encounter with the Divine. The opposition of her parents to the Methodists and their threats to withhold material privileges to which she was entitled wore on her heavily, but nothing was of greater consequence to her than the inward restlessness she felt and her inability to find rest in God. Hers was a profoundly interior spirituality, an understanding of the Christian life identified with the quest, the struggle, and the ultimate satisfaction that comes from abiding in Christ. Her language is sometimes flamboyant and exaggerated, but the joy of being found, and the spiritual emancipation it entails, is the keynote of her life.

* * * *

In the summer of 1773 I was at Adlington with my godmother ... when I heard various accounts of a clergyman whom my uncle Roe had recommended to be curate at Macclesfield,[88] and who was said to be a Methodist, the Rev. David Simpson, author of *A Plea for the Bible*.[89] This conveyed to my mind as unpleasing an idea of him as if he had been called a Romish priest, being fully persuaded that to be a Methodist was to be all that was vile under a mask of piety. These prejudices were owing to the false stories which from time to time I heard repeated to my father, when about seven or eight years old, and also many more which my mother heard after his death, and to the present time.

I believed their teachers were the false prophets spoken of in the scripture, that they deceived the illiterate and were little better than common pickpockets, that they filled some of their hearers with presumption and drove others to despair, that with respect to their doctrines, they enforced chiefly that whosoever embraced their tenets which they called faith might live as they pleased, in all sin, and be sure of salvation, and that all the world besides must be damned without remedy, that they had meetings in the dark and pretended to cast out devils, with many other things equally false and absurd, but all of which I believed. I heard also, that this new clergyman preached against all my favorite diversions.... But I resolved he should not make a convert of me.

[April (Holy Week) 1774] As Mr. Simpson was reading that sentence in the communion service, "If any man sin, we have an advocate with the Father, Jesus Christ the righteous, and he is the propitiation for our sins,"[90] a ray of divine light and comfort was darted on my soul and I cried, "Lord Jesus, let me feel thou art the propitiation for my sins." I was enabled to believe there was mercy for me, and I, even I, should be saved! I felt love to God spring up in my heart, and in a measure could rejoice in him, so that I would have given all the world to have died that moment. But, alas, this was only for a short season!

I had never yet heard the Methodists, nor had I lost all my prejudices against them. But a neighbor who had lately found peace with God advised me strongly to go and assured me they had been the means of great blessings to his soul. I would not promise, but resolved to go privately so that neither the preacher nor any other person would know of it till afterward. I soon after went at five o'clock one morning and got into a private seat. Mr. Samuel Bardsley[91] preached from "Comfort ye, comfort ye, my people, saith your God" [Isa. 40:1]. I thought every word was for me! He spoke to my heart as if he had known all the secret workings there and pointed all such sinners, as I felt myself to be, to Jesus crucified. I was much comforted. My prejudices were now fully removed and I received a full and clear conviction, "These are the people of God, and show," in truth, "the way of salvation."

[November 10, 1774] My cousin, Charles Roe, then much devoted to God, put into my hands a little pamphlet entitled *The Great Duty of Believing on the Son of God*.[92] Jesus was here set forth in all his loveliness of free grace toward a poor returning prodigal, as every way suited to the sinner's wants, and all sufficient to save the vilest of the vile. As willing now, even as willing as when he hung on Calvary, bleeding and dying to save sinners, yes, his very murderers! I was much encouraged in reading this and would gladly have spent the night in prayer. But my mother (with whom I slept) would not suffer it. I therefore went to bed, but could not sleep, and at four in the morning rose again that I might wrestle with the Lord. I prayed, but it seemed in vain. I walked to and fro groaning for mercy, then fell again on my knees. But the heavens appeared as brass and hope seemed almost sunk into despair when suddenly the Lord spoke those words to my heart, "Believe on the Lord Jesus Christ, and thou shalt be saved" [Acts 16:31]. I revived and cried, "Lord, I know this is thy word, and I can depend on it. But what is faith? O show me how to believe. Show me what is the gospel faith or I am yet undone. I desire not deliverance except in thy own way. I desire no happiness but thy favor. What shall I do? O teach me, O help me, or I am lost!" That word came with divine evidence and sweetness to my heart, "Cast all thy care upon him, for he careth for thee."

His power alone can change my rebel heart. My disease is too deep for any other. I can only perish. Nothing can be worse. So there is no hazard. If he is God, he is able and he will save me according to his promise, "Come unto me, all ye that labor and are heavy laden, and I will give you rest" [Matt. 11:28].

Then did he appear to my salvation. In that moment my fetters were broken, my bands were loosed, and my soul set at liberty. The love of God was shed abroad in my heart [see also Rom. 5:5] and I rejoiced with joy unspeakable. Now, if I had possessed ten thousand souls I could have ventured them all with Jesus. I would have given them all to him! I felt a thousand promises all my own, more than a thousand scriptures to confirm my evidence—such as, "He that believeth shall be saved, shall not perish, is not condemned, hath everlasting life, is passed from death unto life, shall never die. There is no condemnation to them that are in Christ Jesus, &c." [Rom. 8:1]. I could now call Jesus Lord, by the Holy Ghost, and the Father my Father. My sins were gone, my soul was happy, and I longed to depart and be with Jesus. I was truly a new creature and seemed to be in a new world! I could do nothing but love and praise my God and could not refrain continually repeating, "Thou art my Father. O God, thou art my God!" while tears of joy ran down my cheeks.

My mother was astonished at the change which appeared in my countenance and whole deportment. And I soon told her the happy cause, that I, a poor sinner, had received forgiveness and could call God my Father and my Friend. Now, said I, "I am repaid a thousand times for all I have suffered. One hour's experience of what I now feel is, itself, rich amends for all! But I see an eternity of bliss before me!" and added, "O that you knew what I feel!" My words and flowing tears made her weep, but she said little, being all wonder. With what joy and gratitude did I now undergo the most servile of all my employments! yes, and it seemed with double strength of body, though I could neither eat nor sleep much for many days and nights. The love of God shed abroad in my heart [see also Rom. 5:5] was now my meat and drink, and the thoughts of the amazing depths of grace which had plucked me as a brand from the burning quite overcame me![93] Me, the most obstinate offender, who had so long and so repeatedly resisted and grieved his Holy Spirit! This love of my God and Savior, so unmerited and free overflowed my soul, nor had I for eight months any interruption to my bliss.

> Not a cloud did arise, to darken my skies,
> Or hide for a moment my Lord from my eyes.[94]

Thursday, January 18th, 1776. I was much comforted by a manifest answer to prayer. Afterward, reading three of Mr. Fletcher's[95] letters to his parishioners was a great blessing. Yet in the evening I found many wanderings and much deadness. I felt dissatisfied with myself and all around me and knew not why. It might in some measure be owing to the indisposition of my body, but I fear it was more owing to the evil of my corrupt heart. O when shall I be holy?

Friday, [January] 19. I have been greatly tried inwardly and outwardly, though I have had some refreshing visits of love. But I feel many evil tempers, much self-will that would not be contradicted, though none saw it but the Lord. Peevishness, pride, and unbelief greatly distressed me. My cry was this evening, "Create in me a clean heart, O God, and renew a right spirit within me" [Psa. 51:10]. And in private prayer I was blessed in a wonderful manner. I lay at the feet of my Lord, as clay in the hands of the potter [see also Jer. 18:6], only beseeching him to stamp me with his lovely image.

Thursday, [January] 25. The Lord shows me more than ever I must be made holy before death. And this day I can say, "As the hart panteth after the water brook, so thirsteth my soul" [Psa. 42:1] for the perfect love of God. O may I never rest until I have received this blessing! Lord, I have in this respect been a trifler. I have been too easy, too lukewarm, while your enemies have had a lurking place in my heart! O forgive me and help me to be more in earnest! Those words were applied while engaged in wrestling prayer, "All I have is thine!" And is not this salvation from sin his gift? It is, and shall be mine.

> O joyful sound of gospel grace,
> Christ shall in me appear;
> I, even I, shall see his face,
> I shall be holy here.[96]

C. Diaries and Journals

Saturday, [January] 27. Mr. Wesley's *Plain Account of Christian Perfection*[97] was this day a greater blessing than before. O how very ignorant, how stupid have I been respecting this great salvation, and even yet I seem to know nothing. Lord, teach me, and save me fully. I find while pressing after entire purity my communion with God increases and I have more power to do his will.

Friday, [February] 23, [1776]. Glory, honor, and eternal praise be to the God of love for ever and ever! His own arm has brought salvation to my feeble, helpless soul. I am now wholly his! I do love the Lord my God with all my heart, and soul, and strength [see also Deut. 6:5]. I am nothing and Jesus is my all. The enemy often suggests, "You will soon lose the blessing. You cannot stand long." But my heart answers, "I will hang upon and trust my God as long as I have any being, and I know he will supply a feeble worm with power!" I have also opened on many sweet promises today. Every moment I find power now to pray and believe. Yea, I live by faith!

Saturday, [Feb.] 24. Last night and this morning I had deep communion with my God. I feel I am indeed one with Christ and Christ is one with me. I dwell in Christ and Christ in me. O blessed union with him my soul loves! And the more I feel of his great love the more I sink at his feet in humbling views of my own nothingness, and here it is I would ever lie. This is my own place. Jesus alone is exalted and I, a poor sinner, saved from sin!

Sunday, [Feb.] 25. Glory be to God for the best Sabbath I ever knew! My body was so very weak and poorly I could not go to preaching. But the Lord was with me and gave me fresh discoveries of my own emptiness and poverty and of his abundant fulness. Those words were also powerfully applied, "Now ye are clean through the words which I have spoken unto you. Abide in me and I in you. As the branch cannot bear fruit of itself except it abide in the vine, no more can ye, except ye abide in me" [John 15:4]. I also feel that gracious promise mine: "If ye abide in me, and my words abide in you, ye shall ask what ye will, and it shall be done unto you" [John 15:7]. O the condescension of God to a poor worm! What a grant is this! My soul draws near and humbly asks,

> Enlarge my faith's capacity,
> Wider and yet wider still
> Then with all that is in thee
> My soul for ever fill.[98]

Thursday, [Feb] 29. I was so happy that I could not sleep in the night. O what deep communion did my soul enjoy with God! It was, indeed, a foretaste of heaven itself. This morning I prayed for a portion of scripture to be impressed on my heart, that should abide with, comfort, and direct me all the day, and I opened on, "Know ye not that your bodies are the temples of the Holy Ghost, which is in you? And ye are not your own, for ye are bought with a price. Therefore glorify God with your body, and with your spirit, which are God's" [1 Cor. 6:20]. Sweet portion! O my blessed Lord, I rejoice that I am your purchased property and not my own and to you I gladly yield body, soul, and spirit.

Thursday, April 4th [1776].[99] On Monday [April 1] the Reverend Mr. Wesley came[100] and I went to see him at old Mr. Ryles'.[101] He received me with a parental tenderness and greatly rejoiced in the Lord's goodness to my soul. He told me I never need to lose the witness of perfect love, but might attain more and more. He preached in the evening from "Many are called but few are chosen" [Matt. 22:13] and met the bands which was a precious time of love. On Tuesday morning his text was "This one thing I do" [Phil. 3:13]. At Mr. Ryles' door in the evening, "He that heareth these sayings of mine and doeth them, &c." [Matt. 7:24]. Dear Mr. Wesley met select band and called upon some who had formerly enjoyed sanctification to speak and exhorted them to see afresh. I believe there was a great revival in many hearts. Several were lost in tears. And a little few testified they loved God with all their heart. May God increase the number. On Wednesday morning I spent an hour with him alone and after breakfast saw him set off for Manchester. What a wonder is that dear saint of God. How above seventy years of age. How healthy and strong? How cheerful in piety? How active and laborious in the work of God? May a tenfold blessing descend this day upon his hoary hairs.

On Sept. 14, 1778, there was a very awful earthquake. The new church in Macclesfield (where I then was) rocked like a cradle and nearly threw some of the people, then kneeling, on their faces. And the noise, for a few moments, was like thunder. The scene that ensued was truly an emblem of that day, "when all faces shall gather paleness, and many shall cry to the rocks and mountains fall on us," [see also Joel 2:6]. Some believed that the church was falling at the steeple end and, therefore, flew in crowds to the opposite doors shrieking and crying for mercy. Some fainted and were trampled nearly to death, others much bruised, and some did not recover the fright. But O, unspeakable grace! My soul was kept calm for I feared not to die. That scripture was brought to my mind: "Yet once more, and I shake not the earth only, but also heaven" [Heb. 12:26]. And I was enabled to exhort those around to be still and look unto the God of grace for salvation which they had too long neglected. Many were deeply awakened by this awful providence and never found rest afterward until they found it in the pardoning love of a blessed Redeemer. And some who may date their conversion from that day will, I believe, be eternal monuments of grace.

[1780?][102] Reading the word of God in private this day was an unspeakable blessing. O! how precious are the promises. What a depth in these words: "For all the promises of God in him are yea, and in him, amen, unto the glory of God" [2 Cor. 1:20]. Yes, my soul, they are so to you! The Father delights to fulfil and the Spirit to seal them on my heart. O that dear invaluable truth!

> Ready art thou to receive;
> Readier is thy God to give.[103]

The Lord poured his love abundantly into my soul while worshiping before him. And I was enabled to renew my covenant to be wholly and for ever his!

Leeds, Aug. 24, 1781. That dear man of God, Mr. Fletcher, came with Miss Bosanquet (now Mrs. Fletcher), to dine at Mr. Smith's in Park Row and also to meet the select society. After dinner I took an opportunity to beg he would explain an expression he once used to Miss Loxdale,[104] in a letter, viz., "That on all who are renewed in love, God bestows the gift of prophecy." He called for the Bible, then read, and sweetly explained the second chapter of the Acts, observing, "To prophesy in the sense he meant, was to magnify God with the new heart of love, and the new tongue of praise, as they did, who, on the day of Pentecost, were filled with the Holy Ghost!" And he insisted that believers are now called to make the same confession, seeing we may all prove the same baptismal fire, showing, that the day of Pentecost was only the opening of the dispensation of the Holy Ghost, the great promise of the Father! And that the latter day glory, which he believed was near at hand, should far exceed the first effusion of the Spirit. And, therefore, seeing they then bore witness to the grace of our Lord, so should we, and like them, spread the flame of love. Then, after singing a hymn, he cried, "O to be filled with the Holy Ghost! I want to be filled O my friends. Let us wrestle for a more abundant outpouring of the Spirit." To me he said, "Come, my sister, will you covenant with me this day to pray for the fulness of the Spirit? Will you be a witness for Jesus?" I answered with flowing tears, "In the strength of Jesus, I will." He cried, "Glory, glory, glory be to God! Lord, strengthen thy handmaid to keep this covenant, even unto death." He then said, "My dear brethren and sisters, God is here. I feel him in this place, but I would hide my face in the dust because I have been ashamed to declare what he hath done for me. For many years I have grieved his Spirit, but I am deeply humbled and he has again restored my soul."

Wed. [March] 27th [1782].[105] I spent this afternoon at Robert Johnson's with Mr. Rogers.[106] He seems much alive to God and I found it a profitable season. Mr. Rogers mentioned an awful circumstance of a clergyman whom I saw at Leeds, and who was since presented to a living, but the morning he was to have taken possession, he put an end to his life, first by cutting his throat and then throwing himself into the river.

Thurs. 28th. Cousin Robert went with me to Robert Johnson's to breakfast with Mr. Rogers, who pressed him to go to Sheffield for a week. Afterwards I went to meet my dear friend Miss Salmon[107] at Mrs. Clewlow's, where also I found John Sellars and the young Mrs. Clewlow from Chester. Mr. Wesley arrived soon after and I drank tea with him at Mr. Ryles.[108] I think he is more alive and full of love to God than ever. Good Friday he preached in the new church in the morning from "Ye know the grace of our Lord Jesus, &c." [2 Cor. 8:9]. In the afternoon [he preached] from "Wherefore laying aside all malice and guile" [1 Pet. 2:1]. At night in our chapel from "I beseech you as strangers and pilgrims, &c." [1 Pet. 2:11]. I spent some time with him alone in the evening and he behaved with fatherly affection. I had never more solid comfort in his company, never found it more truly profitable. He told me of many charges brought against cousin Robert and me, but he suspected from whom they originated, being Joseph Roe, and was quite sat-

C. Diaries and Journals

isfied with the answers I gave him, and he believes the glorious revival is a genuine work of God.

Mon., 30th. Mr. Wesley preached at five from "Blessed are they that hunger and thirst after righteousness, for they shall be filled" [Matt. 5:6]. He addressed it chiefly to believers and offered a free and present salvation from all sin in strong words. One woman was set at full liberty and many were comforted and established. I breakfasted with him and at nine o'clock he took me in his chaise to Leek, where at one o'clock he offered salvation to all from "The Kingdom of heaven is at hand" [Mark 1:15]. He showed first, when the gospel of Christ is preached and received in any nation, city, town, neighborhood, or family, it may be said the kingdom of God is set up there. Or if any individual embraces Christ and the glad tidings of salvation by faith, the kingdom of God is set up in that heart and completed when his kingly power is manifested and all his foes in that heart slain so that he reigns alone. Then second, what it consists in: righteousness, peace, and joy in the holy Christ, all these begun in justification, but without their contraries in sanctification. Then he enforced the text, "*This* kingdom of heaven is at hand." He addressed himself to all sorts of people, states, and conditions—Sabbath-breakers, thieves, liars, and lewd persons—and then told them:

"You may *now* be delivered from the power of your most besetting sins, even this day, this moment. The kingdom of heaven is at hand, crying serve the devil no longer, he is a bad master. Yield now to him who loves you, who died for you, who will love you from all your sins here and from hell hereafter. He loves you all, even you, poor sinner. He bled for you and will you resist him still? Do you feel you are a sinner deserving nothing but hell? Are you willing to know Jesus as your Savior? And are you afraid to come? Fear not. Look up. He is nigh you. Do you want a pardon for all your sins? Shall I tell you, you may have it next year, next month, next week? Nay, I dare not. I am not sure you can. Tomorrow is none of your own. But you may have it *today*. It is at hand. I am sent to offer it. Look up *now*, even this moment. 'Believe on the Lord Jesus Christ and thou shalt be saved' [Acts 16:31]. It is true that in general the work of repentance is carried on by very slow degrees. Most people are a long time after they are convinced of sin before they are justified. But why is it? Even because of unbelief. The word of faith is nigh you. Fear not, only believe.

"Are you a child of God, a believer, and feel his kingdom in a measure set up in your heart? Do you know, 'he has loved *me* and given himself for me' and yet do you feel the remains of anger, pride, self-will, inordinate desires and affections? Then you know the meaning of those words

> 'Tis worse than death my God to love
> And not my God alone.[109]

You are assured 'Without holiness no man shall see the Lord' [Heb. 12:14]. But you are all unholy, all unclean. You are now convinced none but God can bring a clean thing out of an unclean. Hear then his promise to you: 'I will sprinkle clean water upon thee and thou shalt be clean, from all thy filthiness and from all thy idols will I cleanse thee. A new heart also will I give thee, and a new spirit will I put within thee. And I will take away the stony heart out of thy flesh, and I will give thee an heart of flesh, and I will put my Spirit within thee and cause thee to walk in my statutes and thou shalt keep my judgments and do them [see also Ezek. 20:19-20]. I will circumcise thy heart and thou shalt love the Lord thy God with all thy heart' [see also Deut. 30:6].

"'His will is thy sanctification'. But are you to wait a year, a month, a week? Are you to stay till you are more worthy? Not at all. Come just as you are. Come *now,* a helpless sinner to a mighty Savior. But some may say, 'Is not sanctification a gradual as well as an instantaneous work?' Yes, it is both.[110] You may obtain a growing victory over sin from the moment you are justified. But this is not enough. The body of sin—the carnal mind—must be destroyed. The old man must be slain, or we cannot put on the new man which is created after God (or which is the image of God) in righteousness and true holiness. And this is done in a moment. To talk of this work being gradual would be nonsense, as much as if we talked of gradual justification. However, most persons are a long time after they are justified before they are sanctified wholly. But does it need to be so? Not at all. I have known a person justified one month and sanctified the next; justified one week and sanctified the next. Nay, I have known a person justified and sanctified in an hour and glorified the next. A thousand years are with the Lord as one day, and one day as a thousand years [see also 2 Pet. 3:8]. 'He that believeth shalt be saved' [see also Acts 16:31].

"Where are you then? O believer, longing for all that righteousness and peace and joy in the holy Christ, spoken of in my text! This kingdom of heaven is at hand. It is nigh you. It is here. Take it. Now believe. Wait for nothing. Lord Jesus, speak to that heart. Tell it, 'I am God and not man' [Hos. 11:9]. Say unto it, 'I will, be clean' [Mark 1:41]. I am here mighty to save. Behold me, behold me, &c."

Then he prayed for penitents, for backsliders, for the unawakened, and for children, such as could till now break the Sabbath, steal apples, tell lies, disobey parents, etc. In short, I never heard him so particular. He was full of life and love and power, and wept several times while he prayed. All the congregation were in tears and a young man who walked from Macclesfield and came to hear him in great distress of soul was set at liberty and met us praising God who he knew had forgiven all his sins. A young boy about ten years old wept aloud and was crying for mercy, and several more appeared cut to the heart. As we came home in the chaise Mr. W[esley] said, "I never saw a more lovely congregation Hetty. They were like melting wax just fit for divine impressions. But *God* was with us. There's the secret," tears filling his eyes.

At six he preached in our chapel on "God resisteth the proud and giveth grace to the humble. Humble yourselves therefore, &c." [1 Pet. 5:5-6]. His subject was wholly national affairs, yet I found it a profitable season, but not like that at Leek. When I came home my mother was quite kind and affectionate and cousin Robert and I both prayed with her. O my God, you can do all things.

Easter Day, March 31st. Mr. Wesley preached at the new church this morning from "Christ is risen indeed" [see also Luke 24:34]. He showed there is a rational and an experimental evidence of this, but the latter is to be preferred, that as Christ Jesus rose again for our justification, in that instant this experimental evidence begins. He receives the spirit of adoption whereby he can in that moment cry, "Abba Father [Gal. 4:6], *my Lord* and *my God*" [John 20:28]. But this experimental evidence is much stronger when that promise is fulfilled, "I will send the Comforter to abide with you for ever" [see also John 14:16], that this indwelling of God as our sanctifier is the privilege of all believers and is received by faith as well as justification. He then encouraged those who are seeking this and those who have attained. Mrs. Stonehewer[?] was much comforted.

In the afternoon his text was "The wages of sin is death, but the gift of God is eternal life through Jesus Christ our Lord" [Rom. 6:23]. He insisted strongly on this eternal life being the free gift of God, not obtained by works in whole or in part, but alone through Jesus Christ our Lord and through faith in him—that this eternal life is love, begun when being justified by faith we have peace with God and his love is shed abroad in our hearts by the Holy Ghost [see also Rom. 5:5] so that we love him because he has first loved us [see also 1 John 4:19]. But then this love is often mixed with unbelief and wrong tempers, and therefore widely differs from pure love, or that which casts out all fear [see also 1 John 4:18], which rules and fills the whole soul in holiness; that faith is the instrument or receiver of this, but shortly faith shall be swallowed up in light, whereas love never fails but is consummated in glory for ever.

At the preaching house at six he enlarged on "Set your affections on things above not on things on the earth, for ye are dead and your life is hid with Christ in God. When Christ who is our life shall appear, then shall ye also appear with him in glory" [Col. 3:4]. He was very short because of the love feast afterwards which was a season of peculiar grace. About forty made a noble confession and above one half of these testified cousin Robert was made of God the instrument of their blessedness. They also spoke very pointedly on being saved by faith alone and in a moment. Towards the conclusion S. Bradshaw said he had been a Methodist above twenty years and enjoyed a sense of pardon, but he owned he did not experience what he had now heard many profess to do, and yet he believed he should land safe at last.

Mr. Wesley got up and said, "Those who love God with all their heart must expect most opposition from professors who have gone on for twenty years in a lazy, old, beaten track, and fancy they are wiser than all the world. These always oppose the work of sanctification most." He also said many things to encourage the young in years and observed some people accuse us of seeking salvation by works. "They may as well accuse us," he said, "of playing at pushpin." Mr. Wesley kept the meeting till near nine o'clock, being above two hours, which I never knew him do before. But his soul was comforted in hearing so many witness for God.

Monday, April 1st. Mr. Wesley preached at five this morning from Isaiah 66:8-9: "Who hath heard such a thing? Who hath seen such a thing? Shall a nation be born in a day? &c." He showed in a literal sense it could not be, but spiritually understood, it could, no, it has been the case, that it might be said to be fulfilled when on the day of Pentecost three thousand were converted under one sermon [see also Acts 2:41], and soon after five thousand [see also Acts 4:4]. He spoke of the rapid progress of the gospel among all nations in the apostolic days and afterwards and of the work of God within the last century among the Methodists. Then he applied it to the work of grace in the hearts of individuals. "Soon as Zion travailed she brought forth her children. Shall I bring the birth, and not cause to bring forth, saith the Lord. Shall I cause to bring forth and shut the womb? saith thy God" [Isa. 66:8-9]. And here he observed that till the apostles' days, instantaneous salvation was rarely spoken of, that though we have some scripture examples left upon record, yet they were not many, but that the light of grace shines brighter and brighter to the perfect day and is now more clear than in the primitive Church. He told us his own bigotry to the Church of England when at Oxford and how impossible he believed it that any could be justified in a moment by faith—till visiting the prisons—one and another was justified under his prayer. But then he thought these were rare instances, and it was because these were soon to die that God showed them peculiar mercies. But he could not allow even yet that there were living witnesses who knew their sins forgiven. But in a little, some were in deep distress after hearing him and his brother preach, and while he joined with them in prayer, one and other of these also testified the same thing and walked according to the profession made. And then said he, "What was I that I could reply against God?" But twenty years after this time, he had come to believe there was such a thing as instantaneous sanctification. And when Jane Cooper[111] first spoke of having received it thus, he could have hit her in the face. But when he saw Bathsheba Hall and many other witnesses of this in London, he became again silent before the Lord.

He said to me at Mr. Ryles', "We had a lovely meeting last night Hetty. Such evidence cannot be withstood. I hope those in Macclesfield will no longer limit God. I was much pleased with that little maid of ten years old," continued he, "who said, 'When I felt my sins were all forgiven and I could love God, it overjoyed me!' You and Robert Roe must strengthen these young ones. Robert is very simple of heart and very clear, and, while he continues so, will be very useful." We breakfasted at Mr. Simpson's and Mr. Wesley set off from thence for Manchester. John Sellars came home with me and seems a good deal affected with the various witnesses of those who are saved from all sin. He desired me to speak freely with him on the subject which I did, and he appeared sensible that the mystic authors[112] had done him much harm. He was desirous now to become what he saw his privilege, even to love God with all his heart and to seek and preach it as a present salvation. "But," said he, before we parted, "if a person is perfect in love, how can he afterwards grow herein?" I answered him by another question. "How was it that 'Jesus increased in wisdom and stature and in favor with God and man'" [Luke 2:52]? He said, "Your answer is sufficient."

Sun. 8th [June 1793].[113] I was very happy at the new church especially while I viewed in the elements of bread and wine my Savior's body broken and his blood shed for me. Never do I partake of this blessed ordinance in vain. Coming in faith I always prove his flesh is meat indeed and his blood is drink indeed [see also John 6:55], and often do I wonder how any that love the Redeemer can stay away when this table is spread before them.

On August 19, 1784, I was married to Mr. Rogers, in whom the Lord gave me a helpmeet indeed, just such a partner as my weakness needed to strengthen me. He has made us of one heart and one soul, and for above eight years has crowned our union with his constant smile.

We spent a week or ten days after our marriage with my mother, and then hastened to Dublin, where Mr. Rogers was appointed to labor. We were gladly received and the Lord gave us the hearts of the people. Our hands being thus strengthened of the Lord, we agreed solemnly to devote ourselves and our all to him and his work. And glory to his name, we saw a blessed revival. In three years the society increased from about five hundred to eleven hundred and upward and we had good cause to believe above four hundred were converted to God.

C. Diaries and Journals

In August [actually July] 1789 we came over from Dublin to see my mother at Macclesfield. Mr. Wesley and several preachers with families also coming at the same time to England, we took the whole ship.[114] In this passage we were in imminent danger by dashing on a rock called the West Mouse.[115] But prayer was made, the Lord heard, and wonderfully delivered! We landed at Park Gate and traveled with Mr. Wesley to Macclesfield where my mother received us with great affection. After the Manchester conference[116] we returned to Dublin where we had left our little boy. We spent about a week with our very affectionate friends there and then proceeded to Cork.[117]

An intimate friend of mine in the city of Cork [Mary Mahoney] was forced to marry a man for whom she had no affection. He proved a very wicked and bad husband. But the God of wisdom and love, even out of this evil, brought forth good. The trials she daily endured led her to seek rest and happiness in the source of bliss! Beginning frequently, though privately, to hear the Methodists, her mind was drawn out in strong desires after God. But her husband often followed her and dragged her out of the preaching house by the hair of her head. After some time he left her entirely and she saw him no more. She joined our Society about eight years ago and soon found peace with God, which she never lost, and about three years after obtained also a clear witness that her soul was cleansed from all sin. In this salvation she walked without reproach to the day of her death. And though at some seasons she was buffeted with various temptations, yet she always emerged out of them more fully purified. She was called outwardly to follow her heavenly Lord in the way of the cross. But she joyfully took it up and bore it with the meekness of her lamb-like Savior! Like him, her language was, "Not as I will, but as thou wilt" [Matt. 26:39].

Her love of Jesus and her zeal for the glory of God, and for promoting the good of precious souls, were very peculiar. This induced Mr. Rogers to request her to take the charge of a class of young women, over whom she watched faithfully and diligently with tears, fasting, and much prayer. In her last sickness (thought to be a rheumatic fever), her agony of pain in every limb extreme, she told me and others, "When these hands and feet are tortured with pain—yea, such anguish as is almost insupportable—I look to my precious Savior and see by faith his dear hands and feet pierced, and bleeding, and nailed to the accursed tree for my sins! And the view of that mangled body and precious head torn with thorns, and that precious blood streaming for my soul, sweetens all my pain and makes me willing to bear all he pleases to inflict." After she had thus suffered for nine days, and constantly witnessed to all, the goodness of God to her soul, she became delirious. But a few hours before her departure the Lord restored her reason. She was, however, speechless till at last, after struggling some time as in an agony to say something, she cried aloud, "Jesus is precious! Jesus is precious!" and sweetly fell asleep on the tenth of February, 1789, and in the twenty-fifth year of her age.

Here also [i.e., in Cork] the Lord graciously revived his work.[118] His word prospered and prevailed and we had cause to rejoice, not only over a few individuals, but several families who were added to the fold of God. We found three hundred and ninety seven members in society and left six hundred and fifty. In the last year we had some close trials through a few individuals, but our spiritual mercies overbalanced them all. I do not know that I ever enjoyed more of the Lord's presence than at Cork, except during the time of a severe nervous fever, and then the cloud was only for a few days, and that, I believe, was merely owing to the body, for though, in a week afterward, all the feelings of nature were touched, I felt nothing contrary to resignation, patience, or love.

At the time of which I now speak, my own recovery was doubtful. Mr. Rogers (oppressed with grief through my illness, and by his attention to me night and day) was very ill. James had a fever, the maid was confined with sickness, and my little John, six weeks old, in convulsions for three days! Surely, in this scene the Lord magnified his power in supporting my weakness and enabling me then to say, "Good is the will of the Lord." After this season my consolations were abundant and my faith, love, and communion with God much deepened.

I had here some encouraging letters from Mr. Wesley. In the last two he mentioned his intention of removing us to London at the ensuing conference. I trembled at the thought of so important a charge, but committed it to God in much prayer. And notwithstanding our various exercises of body and mind since we came to this city, I am certain divine love has mixed every cup and ordered all things well. To be with that honored and much-loved servant of

God, Mr. Wesley, for five months, and then to be witnesses of his glorious exit was a favor indeed. But O! how awful the scene!—how unspeakable the loss! I peculiarly felt it, being then in a weak state, not quite recovered from my late sickness.

The solemnity of the dying hour of that great and good man, I believe will be ever written on my heart! Well might Dr. Young say, "The chamber where the good man meets his fate, is privileged beyond the common walk of virtuous life, quite in the verge of heaven!"[119] A cloud of the divine presence rested on all! And while he could hardly be said to be an inhabitant of earth, being now speechless, and his eyes fixed, victory and glory were written on his countenance, and quivering, as it were, on his dying lips! O could he then have spoken, methinks it would have been nothing but victory! victory!—grace! grace!—glory! glory! No language can paint what appeared in that face! The more we gazed upon it, the more we saw of heaven unspeakable! Not the least sign of pain, but a weight of bliss. Thus he continued, only his breath growing weaker and weaker, till, without a struggle or a groan, he left the cumbrous clay behind and fled to eternal life in the bosom of his faithful Lord.

Sunday, Nov. 11, 1792. This day it is eighteen years since I received the knowledge of a reconciled God. O that I were in a deeper sense a "mother in Israel"! My Lord has ever been faithful to me. In all my persecutions he comforted me. In the alluring snares of youth, he saved and kept me. It was by his grace I forsook all, denied myself ease, pleasure, friends, and after he had proved me, he gave me easier circumstances and one of the best of earthly friends. He has instructed my ignorance and strengthened my weakness. Through various scenes and in outward perplexities, how often have I received immediate teaching from God! In traveling from city to city, how have I been protected by guardian love and saved from fear and danger on the watery deep! May I never forget the ten thousand proofs of his love in Dublin, in Cork, in London! He has given me favor in the eyes of his children in every place and helped me feebly to serve them. He has given me spiritual children also, some of whom are lodged safely in his bosom, and others in the way to glory.

I have had five lovely children in the flesh, and besides these, my dear Joseph and Benjamin, left with me in charge, and to whom I feel united in all the tenderness of parental love. Nor have they ever been wanting in a due return. One (a fine boy) my Lord has taken to the abodes of bliss, and, for the rest, he assures my heart,

> The children of thy faith and prayer,
> Shall all to thee be given.[120]

SOURCES:

An Account of the Experience of Hester Ann Rogers (New York: Hunt & Eaton, 1893), 15-16, 23-25, 29-32, 40-42, 47-49, 56-57, 70-76, 128, 132-33; Hester Ann Rogers, Manuscript Journals, 1775–84, 3 vols., *Meth. Arch.*

C. Diaries and Journals

3. Mary Entwisle

Editor's Introduction

Mary Pawson (c. 1770–1804) was the second daughter of Marmaduke Pawson, of Thorner, near Leeds, a respectable farmer and Methodist local preacher for more than thirty years. She was also niece of Marmaduke's only brother, the famous itinerant preacher, John Pawson. Mary was converted under the preaching of Joseph Benson in 1780. Her son provides the following portrait:

> Modest, affectionate, and sympathising, she had a heart formed for friendship. A good natural understanding, improved by extensive reading, a sound and discriminating judgment, together with deep, genuine, and growing piety, rendered her a most agreeable and improving companion, and a suitable helpmeet for one who had been called by the great Head of the church to the work of the Christian ministry. [121]

Mary married Joseph Entwisle, yet another important Methodist itinerant preacher, on May 2, 1792, and entered into a life of constant motion and unending transitions. She began a diary in the early second year of her marriage while stationed at Leeds and in it discussed subsequent moves to and ministry in Colne and Wakefield. During this same period, she delivered three sons (John, Marmaduke, and Joseph) and one daughter (Mary) and grieved the death of her second son. Although not recounted in her diary, she delivered twin boys (Thomas and William), the latter of whom died shortly after birth, and yet another son, James, all while stationed at York and Hull, between 1799 and 1802. A seventh son, Samuel, was born late in 1803 in Macclesfield, but Mary never fully recovered from this delivery. She died in March 1804, leaving her husband with six children, the eldest only eleven years of age, the youngest an infant of four months. She was interred at Christ's Church Yard, Macclesfield, and laid in the same grave with Hester Ann Rogers, Ann Cutler, and other noteworthy Methodist leaders.

The thirty-two-page manuscript diary of Mrs. Mary Entwisle, preserved in the Lamplough Collection of the Methodist Archives in Manchester, from which excerpts are taken here, provides a fascinating glimpse into late eighteenth-century Methodism and Wesleyan piety through the eyes of this ardent practitioner. The Entwisle diary portrays the fragile and tragic nature of life for women of that era, including perils of childbirth and threat of disease and the inner strength found in evangelical faith. Covering the brief six-year period, January 27, 1793, to December 23, 1798, this manuscript account provides a realistic, true-to-life portrait of triumphant discipleship in the midst of tragedy and pervasive uncertainty.

* * * *

March 1st [1793]. A day to be remembered with gratitude. When I awoke this morning I felt my heart sweetly drawn out after God. I had some very profitable converse with my dear husband. A review of the Lord's gracious dealings with us melted our hearts and we were enabled to praise him. After we arose we spent some time in reading the scriptures and then joined in offering our humble tribute of prayer and praise, in which we were much refreshed. Surely no people in the world have such cause to praise God as we have. Bless the Lord O my soul and forget not all his benefits [see also Psa. 103:2].

In the forenoon we visited some sick people,[122] and came back much profited. I then retired to pour out my soul to God in secret, and O may I never forget the precious season. Truly the Lord is nigh unto all that call upon him. My soul was like a watered garden. I felt power to cast myself with all my concerns into his hands who had dealt so bountifully with me. As the time of my delivery draws near,[123] I was led particularly to lay this matter before God, and O what sweet consolation I felt. What a sinking into the will of God. I could from my heart say, do with me as seems good in your sight, O my God. I feel no dreadful apprehensions of the trial. I believe the Lord will not leave or forsake me in the trying hour, but will proportion my strength to my day. I feel an increase of faith and confidence in my God. Oh may I praise him as long as he lends me breath to pray or praise.[124] Amen.

March 5th. My mind has been kept calm and composed all day. Blessed be the Lord. Much refreshed in secret in the evening. Very poorly most of the night, but my mind kept in peace.

March 6th. Several symptoms assure me the hour of trial is very near. I feel no painful anxiety. I feel power to cast my burden upon the Lord. He has promised he will not leave or forsake me. He has said I will strengthen you. I will help you, yes, I will uphold you with the right hand of my righteousness [see also Isa. 41:10]. O my God, I rely upon your word. You will be a very present help in the time of trouble [see also Psa. 46:1]. How great and precious are your promises and they all are yea and amen in Christ Jesus to them that believe [see also 2 Cor. 1:20]. O increase my faith, confirm my hope, and may I trust in you and not be confounded.[125] Amen. Even so, Lord Jesus.

December 20th. I have never resumed my diary since I lay in bed, but now I resolve to set my seal to the truth of God's promises for my future comfort. The last I wrote was on the sixth of March. On the eighth I was delivered of a fine boy in the night, a time ever to be remembered with gratitude.[126] Many comfortable portions of God's word had been powerfully applied to my mind within a few weeks before my delivery, all of which I kept fast hold of until the hour of trial, when the Lord in great mercy to my soul applied them with fresh power. Glory be to God for ever for the consolations I felt. My strength was proportioned to my sufferings. I have often thought if it had not been for that divine support which I felt from the Lord raising me above the fear of death or anything else, I should not have got through.

I had a very hard time during the time of my pregnancy. I never found liberty to pray for an easy delivery, neither could I join with my dear companion in that petition who was not negligent in laying it before the Lord. We frequently united in supplicating the throne of grace respecting it in general at those times. I feel an inexpressible sinking into the will of God and can only say do with me, in me, and by me as seems good in your sight, only give me grace to suffer your will. Through mercy I recovered pretty well, but my nipples were bad for some time. I felt great need for patience sometimes when very much exercised with pain in my breasts. I was overcome with fretfulness and discouragements which hurt my soul. How needful it is to be looking for fresh supplies of grace continually. Sometimes when we overcome great trials we are overcome by small things not duly considering our helplessness and that the grace we have for the present will not suffice for the next trial. However, the Lord brought me through all, and now I can testify of his goodness. I have proved him to be a God, hearing and answering prayer. They that trust in him shall never be confounded [see also Psa. 22:5]. Many mercies have I received since then at his bountiful hands, praised be his name. They are repeated daily. May my heart be filled with gratitude and my life show forth his praise who has done so great things for me.

December 21st. This being my birthday, I resolve to begin afresh to write some account of the Lord's dealings with me daily for my own benefit. I have felt gratitude to God this day while I have been looking back upon my past life. I see that goodness and mercy have in a peculiar manner followed ever since I had a being [see also Psa. 23:6]. I trust I have also felt humbled in a measure for the little returns I have made and have resolved by the help of God to be more devoted to him. Without his help I know I can do nothing. For some weeks I have been in heaviness through temptation. I gave up my confidence in God but while I was at the meeting tonight the Lord again shone upon my soul, and I felt a degree of comfort.

Sunday, 22nd. I was much refreshed in private, and at the Society meeting at night felt very dull and heavy under the sermons. Lord, when will you deliver me from this?

23rd. I have felt such eager desires after God as I have not done lately before. Was much blessed in converse and prayer with Miss Rhodes[127] this morning and very much refreshed at preaching this evening.

24th. My mind has been going out after God all day for an increase of every grace.

25th. Christmas Day. This has been a good day. Blessed be the Lord. While my dear husband delivered a discourse in the morning from these words, "For this end was the Son of Man manifested, to destroy the works of the devil" [1 John 3:8], my soul was refreshed. It was indeed glad tidings of great joy [see also Luke 2:10], and I felt a greater determination than ever not to rest till the end of his coming be fully answered in me.

December 26th. My mind has been stayed on God most of the day.

27th. I have not felt much of the divine presence till class time when the Lord was powerfully present with us.

C. Diaries and Journals

January 1st, 1794. I have been poorly all day but my mind has been going out after God. Much harassed at the evening preaching and tempted against the preacher, but got delivered from it before the covenant meeting.[128] It was a solemn time. I felt my heart join in it more sensibly than I ever did before. I felt a fresh giving up of myself to God and desire to do and suffer all his holy will.

Jan. 26th. I have not had an opportunity of writing lately but have reason to think I have got forward a little, though not as I might have done. I have had many times of refreshing from the Lord, but I sensibly feel I want more of the abiding presence of the Lord, a greater establishment in grace. Oh! for a closer walk with God. Lord enable me to set out afresh and serve you with body, soul, and spirit. Amen.

February 2nd. Upon a review of the past week I see cause for humiliation and self-abasement before the Lord. Though I have enjoyed some times of refreshing from the Lord, yet in general, I have not been so alive to God, as in some weeks that are past. At present I am rather indisposed and feel a great weight upon my spirits. Oh! Lord, I beseech you, preserve me from reasoning. Amen. Amen.

March 2nd. My mind has been variously exercised from within and without since I last wrote. Upon examination I find I have suffered loss by several things, first, by looking at others who make a great profession of perfection, and I fear act not as persons who profess such a high degree of grace.[129] Secondly, by reasoning about perfection after hearing people converse differently about it. Thirdly, by suffering my mind to be hurt with the wildness and extravagance of some people in this revival. O Lord enable me to lay aside every weight and every easy besetting sin, that I may run with patience, perseverance, and fortitude the race set before me [see also Heb. 12:1]. I feel my soul athirst for God, yes, even for the living God. Oh that he would come and take up his lasting abode in my heart, and suffer me no longer to rove, but may I be rooted and grounded in love, and grow up into him who is my living head [see also Eph. 3:17]. Oh, may his love fill my heart, influence my life and conduct so that all may see I have been with Jesus—I have Christ put on [see also Gal. 3:17]. Oh that my heart were established with grace.

It is twelve years last month since the Lord brought me to the saving knowledge of himself. Glory be to his adorable name for ever, that he called me so young, blessed me with pious parents, and preserved me from innumerable evils to which youth are exposed, and that though I have most unfaithful been of all whoever his grace received, yet he has borne with me, and I trust my feelings are still in the way to heaven and my soul longing with ardent desire for more of God. Oh! settle and fix my wavering soul with all your weight of love. I desire to offer up myself, my husband, my child, my all, to God's desiring that he may do with us, in us, and by us, what seems good in his sight. Only make and keep us all his own for ever.

I feel exercise for patience at present, being as I have reason to think in a state of pregnancy. The Lord indeed deals favorably with his poor weak creature. I see abundant cause to praise him for his providential dealings with me in this respect. May my heart glow with gratitude and my lips and life ever more show forth his praises. Even so Lord Jesus, grant it. Amen.

July 26th, 1795. It is now above a year since I have noted in writing any thing of God's dealings with me. Innumerable have been the mercies I have experienced. Trials and comforts have been blended. Up to this point the Lord has helped me. Since I wrote last we have removed from Leeds[130] to Colne,[131] from Goshen to the wilderness. Yet I have proved God is here. I met with a very severe trial here. Mr. Harrison's had left a child in the house sick of the small pox. My dear John had not had the small pox and was obliged to be prepared and inoculated immediately. He was severely handled, his life endangered. I, in a strange place, my dear husband, true partner of my weal or woe, at a great distance when the child was at the worst. My trials were great, yet praised be the Lord, strength was proportioned to my day. I believed the Lord would spare my child. He did and raised him up again in a few weeks after I was delivered of another fine boy.[132] And the Lord was with me in the trying hour. He brought me safely through after hard lingering labor. I was enabled in patience to possess my soul. I felt much of the divine presence during my confinement and resolved if the Lord raised me up again to lead a new life, but alas! I have broken my resolutions and I do not yet feel my heart established with grace. I feel my soul humbled before the Lord. I have now spent near a year at Colne and I think I have neither been doing nor getting good.[133]

My dear partner is now gone to conference. I felt concerned on account of the disputes which agitate our Connection.[134] The Lord pour upon your ministers the spirit of wisdom to know what steps to take, and love to submit one to another. O Lord if it be your blessed will grant that liberty of conscience may be granted us with respect to our commemorating your dying love,[135] and that all strife for power or superiority may be done away, and give peace and prosperity to your church.

[July 1796] The Lord has in the course of his providence brought us to this place where we are comfortably situated among a kind and affectionate people, some of them, I think, deeply pious, and where we have every outward comfort which we can desire. I trust I feel a thankful heart and a determination to give myself afresh to God in my new situation. I have been favored with some refreshing seasons both in public and private since I came and, in general, have felt earnest desires to be more deeply devoted to God.

I have had a good deal of outward hurry and my mind too much taken up with the concerns of the family. I want to feel my heart more disentangled from outward things, and to enjoy communion with God. I feel a measure of love to God, and I think a sincere desire to serve him, but I have not lately enjoyed a clear sense of my acceptance with God. Lord, help me to wrestle and pray until I obtain. I feel at present especially I have need of a firm trust and unshaken confidence in God. I want power to cast my care upon the Lord and to commit my all to him. Lord, be with me in the hour of nature's sorrow which is fast approaching.[136] Be pleased to bring me safely through and spare me to my friends and family if it be your blessed will. Amen.

Wakefield.[137] March 11th [1797]. What shall I render to the Lord for all his benefits [see also Psa. 116:12]. When I look back to the time when I last wrote I see abundant cause for gratitude to my kind preserver and bountiful benefactor. How did he support me in the hour of trial and in answer to prayer bring me safely and easily through? May I trust the Lord at all times. He made me the living mother of a living child.[138] Many and great trials indeed I have been exercised with since I came to Wakefield. But up to this point the Lord has helped me. Affliction in my family, a long and tedious nervous fever, with other trying circumstances attending it, but may I never forget the supports from the Lord which I have been favored with and the kindness of friends during my long confinement. O may I ever feel the good effects of it.

O Lord you have tried us as silver is tried. In the latter end of March I went to my father's for the benefit of the air, but I was sent for back to my dear child who was seized with the small pox. O the distress of mind I felt on account of his great sufferings, and the daily prospect of losing my precious boy.

April 7th. He died without a struggle and angels no doubt bore his happy spirit away to the realms of light. Lord help me constantly to say thy will be done, knowing you cannot err. You do all things well, however contrary to our feelings. My dear Marmaduke was a sweet, affectionate child nearly two years and seven months old. I trust I shall go to him but he shall not return to me [see also 2 Sam. 12:23].

September 10th. How manifold are your mercies O God towards them who put their trust in you. Upon a review of your past mercies I see abundant cause for gratitude and thankfulness for temporal and spiritual blessings since I wrote last. First, temporal. In sparing my dear Mary and dealing so tenderly with her in the small pox, and blessing both the children with almost constant health since that time. For freedom from heavy affliction in our family for several months. Secondly, for spiritual mercies. I praise you for the quickening influences of your Holy Spirit with which you have been pleased to favor me lately. For the divine light which has shone upon my mind, discovering to me my hindrances, and the necessity of a closer walking with you. I have seen the necessity of being more dead to outward things, more unlike the world in my outward conduct.

SOURCE:

Mary Entwisle, Manuscript Diary, *Meth. Arch.*

C. DIARIES AND JOURNALS

4. ISABELLA WILSON

Editor's Introduction

The only record of Isabella Wilson's life is preserved in the excerpt of her diary prepared by John Pipe for *The Methodist Magazine* of 1808. We know only that she was born at Sinnethwaite in 1765, was an important instrument of revival in the north of England, and died in 1807. Pipe notes that as Wesley's itinerants preached salvation by means of pulpit and publication, Isabella "strove to cast her mite into the sacred treasury, by meeting classes, holding meetings for prayer, visiting the sick, by epistolary correspondence, and spiritual conversation."[139] She is the unknown woman par excellence apart from this glimpse and those afforded by Mary Taft in her *Memoirs*.

Her diary is a truly remarkable document. The primary characteristic of her life and witness is her total confidence in the presence and power of God. The consistent keynotes of daily entries are gratitude and thanksgiving in all things. The God she worships and adores is a faithful companion whose greatest joy is to do us good and to make us happy. The secret of her life is to be found in her attention to the means of grace, which she describes as "feasts of love to the soul." Her life is transparent to the unbounded love of Jesus and is a powerful testimony to the integral nature of faith and holiness.

* * * *

August 28, [1790]. All glory be to God for grace, free grace, continued to my soul! The friendship of Jesus, whose love is unspeakable, is my joy and crown of rejoicing. Through all the changing scenes of life his love is unchangeable. O Lord, keep my love to you also unchangeable. Then shall I be happy while passing through this foreign land.

January 2, 1797. Glory be to God that another year is gone and, upon recollection, I believe it has been one of the best I have spent since I knew my God. I have had many trials and troubles from quarters I least expected, but it has taught me the truth of this passage of scripture, "In the world ye shall have tribulation, but in me ye shall have peace" [John 16:33]. I can set to my seal that "all things work together for good to them that love God" [Romans 8:28]. My way is plain and pleasant, and my prospect of heaven bright and clear. Though blessed with a good state of health, yet death is the most pleasant reflection to me because it will introduce me to that glory of which I have now such a bright prospect. O Lord, you are cutting down on all hands, and I am in daily expectation of an arrow falling upon me, yet I would patiently wait until my change come. Only let me live or die to glorify you, for

> I am thine by sacred ties,
> —Thy child, thy servant bought with blood.[140]

"O Love divine, what hast thou done"[141] for me, an unworthy worm!

Nov. 8, [1797]. Glory be to my Lord God for his continued favors and blessings. Has he not said, and do I not prove that he is nigh to them that call upon him in sincerity of heart? Yes, he is the same yesterday, today, and for ever [see also Heb. 13:8]. His delight is to do us good and make us happy. He is a God hearing and answering prayer. Ever present and all-sufficient at all times and in all places. It is the privilege of God's children to walk with him from day to day. A blessed life indeed to walk in the light of his countenance, and to serve him with a perfect heart and willing mind! This is to have the single eye which fills the body full of light—and love to that adorable Emmanuel who died to redeem, to purify us to himself, and to make us a people zealous of good works. Hence our daily study should be to glorify God in our bodies and spirits which are his.

April 5, [1798]. This morning I rose with my heart filled with love to my dear Lord. Glory be to his holy name for the means of grace and for hopes of glory! This day I renewed my covenant with God to be wholly his in time, that I may be his when time is no more. Oh! keep me near your bleeding side that I may drink deeper of your Spirit and rise higher in the life of God.

[April] 24. I have been much favored this day with the means of grace which were feasts of love to my soul. I have fed at the table of the Lord on rich grace with thanksgiving. Oh that I may be more united to Jesus, that I may see him in all things who is altogether lovely [see also Sol. 5:16]. Yes, I can say,

> The promis'd land from Pisgah's top,
>   I now exult to see;
> My hope is full, O glorious hope!
>   Of immortality.[142]

Dec. 1, 1798. All glory be to God for persevering grace and more conformity to him in all things. Oh! the unbounded love of Jesus to my soul. His promises are all precious. My peace flows as a river while he teaches me the lessons of his grace, of faith and holiness. My soul is athirst for all the mind that was in him.

> Lord, take my heart and let it be
> For ever clos'd to all but thee:
> Seal thou my breast, and let me wear
> That pledge of love for ever there.[143]

[Feb.] 11, [1802]. Glory be to God for a bright prospect of glory. The sun of righteousness shines on my soul without a cloud between. What delight I feel in all his blessed ways! His service is my reward. I long to live to him as I have never done.

March 3, [1802]. Glory be to God, while passing through time, my prospect for a glorious eternity daily brightens up before me. My faith increases. My love abounds to God and his blessed cause. Surely, Lord, you are preparing me for something I have not passed through, either for death or greater usefulness in your church or suffering. Thy will be done [see also Matt. 26:42]. Thy name adored.[144]

Nov. 1. Glory be to God. My soul is as a watered garden. I feel the graces of his Spirit shoot forth in pious determinations to live as I have never lived. I never saw time so precious, nor was ever so determined to use every power and talent to the glory of God. My heaven here consists in glorifying him. Praised be his name, it is my duty and delight. The power of God was present yesterday at the Love Feast, and souls were justified. My soul rejoices in Zion's prosperity. I am thankful for health to labor for my Lord. My union with him increases. I am rising into a greater glory. O Lord, keep me at your feet and I shall praise you more and more.

Jan. 5, 1807. It is with gratitude of heart I recount the mercies of the last year. Upon the whole it has been one of the best years of my life. Glory be to God for preserving grace. I feel my heart more united to Jesus than ever. With joy I draw water from the wells of salvation [see also Isa. 12:3]. With the new year I feel determined more than ever to speak, and act, and think for God. I see a long field of action before me. O Lord, help me to labor with all my heart. I feel more than ever my insufficiency to any thing of myself acceptable to God without his help.

I think I have learned this lesson more perfectly.[145]

SOURCE:

John Pipe, "Memoir of Miss Isabella Wilson," *WMM* 31 (1808): 516-17, 562-64, 567, 595, 597, 601.

Part Two
Writings in Practical Divinity

Introduction to Part Two

This second major section presents a wide range of material related to the spirituality of early Methodist women. These writings in practical divinity, including selections related to spiritual instruction, religious poetry, prayers, and dreams, will undoubtedly feel more like the "stuff" of Christian spirituality to most readers. We immediately associate such literary works with the spiritual life. Even so, the breadth of the material that follows is noteworthy.

One thing that emerges clearly in these writings is the expectation that the spiritual life requires discipline, effort, stamina, and perseverance. But early Methodist women also recognized that all their efforts were grounded in—and were a response to—God's grace, mercy, and love. Their lives and their writings reflect a dynamic balance of faith and works. Not unlike monastic predecessors in the faith, many of the women designed "rules of life." They lived into habituated patterns of prayer and service. They reflected upon great prayers and themes of the Christian heritage. Those who were more mature in the faith—more experienced in the journey toward holiness of heart and life—took their responsibility to instruct their brothers and sisters very seriously and were given ample opportunity to do so. Their hymns and prayers reflect the full range of religious experience, emotion, and life. They tackled the hard questions in discursive meditations and poetry and stood before God with amazing transparency in their life of prayer. They perceived God's presence not only in the normal round of life, but in the mysterious landscape of dreams and visions as well.

The first block of material below deals with the broad theme of spiritual instruction. The Methodist Societies, it must be remembered, were designed to help disciples of Christ grow in their faith. The goal toward which they all moved was the fullest possible experience of God's love, and the expression of that love toward others through their lives. This quest to love both God and neighbor animated their spirituality.

Given this orientation, spiritual direction was absolutely necessary. No one excelled in this area more than Mary Bosanquet, later Mrs. Fletcher. On the eve of her missionary venture in London,[1] she published a little tract, entitled *Jesus, Altogether Lovely*, that provided instruction to single women in their effort to remain faithful to Christ alone. This unique document draws on the Catholic model of the Beguines to shape a semi-monastic community of vital piety and social service.[2] Another pamphlet, which originated as a letter to a friend, offers advice to Methodist people more generally on how to live out their faith. Here Bosanquet insists that the spirit of true religion is recollecting ourselves in God's presence and offering every thought, word, and act to God. These two documents provide a glimpse of how Bosanquet served as a mentor, providing spiritual direction to those who yearned for companionship along the way.

Another characteristic form of spiritual instruction for Methodists, of course, were rules and regulations. It is not too much to say that the followers of the Wesleys were governed by a "rule of life," much like Benedictine monks and nuns.[3] Indeed, they were labeled "Methodists" in part because of the penchant for organizing both institutional and personal life. A crucial form of this concern are the "General Rules" that Wesley developed as criteria for initial admission and continued fellowship within the movement:

> It is therefore expected of all who continue therein that they should continue to evidence their desire of salvation,
> *First,* By doing no harm, by avoiding evil in every kind—especially that which is most generally practiced
> *Secondly,* By doing good, by being in every kind merciful after their power, as they have opportunity doing good of every possible sort and as far as possible to all men:
> *Thirdly,* By attending upon all the ordinances of God.[4]

Introduction to Part Two

These three overarching rules proved to be wise and powerful guidelines for the spiritual growth of the Methodist people. They also left room for followers to devise more specific additional guidelines, which the Wesley brothers encouraged. Two such "rules of life" written by women are included here. Mary Bosanquet developed regulations for her nascent community at Leytonstone. They provide a clear image of the way this group of women organized itself and fixed its life upon a singular goal. Mary Lyth's "code of life" is much more personal, describing, as it were, the principles that guided her daily walk—her philosophy of life.

Meditation was one of the most important spiritual disciplines for the early Methodist women. Martha Hall, sister to the Wesley brothers, produced a basic guide for this practice, similar in many ways to the tradition linked with the Roman Catholic devotional writer, Francis de Sales. Many other Methodist women recorded their spiritual meditations, which were often published posthumously and read widely within the movement for spiritual instruction. The examples selected for this collection include: the meditations of Mrs. Lefevre, noteworthy for their emphasis upon gratitude and total dependence upon God; Mary Bosanquet's meditative reflections on the Lord's Prayer, which function almost like a case study in meditative technique and practice; and the spiritual "exercises" of Mary Hanson, which discuss themes such as happiness, patience, meekness, prayer, and experimental religion—emphasizing throughout how important cultivation of virtue is in the Christian life.

Although few early Methodist women delved into serious biblical scholarship and commentary on scripture, Mary Tatham is an important exception. She used this form of spiritual instruction often in her role as a class leader. One of her exegetical essays included below addresses the monumental question, "What does the spiritual life have to do with interpersonal relationships?" Other selections include a highly refined theological discussion of the way of salvation, which affirms the Wesleyan, holistic vision of the Christian life, and a most interesting analysis of Jesus' encounter with Mary and Martha.

Early Methodists held hymns and sacred poems in high regard. Religious verse both shaped and expressed their spirituality. The second major block of materials here in part 2 are lyrical writings from a diverse set of early Methodist women. They range from one of the most gifted and published poets of her time to a cryptic Miss T., of whom nothing is known whatsoever. The group includes one of the greatest evangelists of the early nineteenth century, a blind Irish preacher, a Methodist convert to Quakerism, and a woman of African descent. All of the poems in this block were published, but mostly in the nineteenth century, leaving them virtually inaccessible to the modern reader. John Wesley exposed his followers to a wide range of poetic material in the pages of his *Arminian Magazine*. Several of the selections presented here are drawn from this house organ of the Methodist movement. Other early hymns and poems are embedded in the many memoirs, biographies, and journals published prior to the twentieth century. The selections are presented in an essentially chronological framework.

Mary Stokes, a later convert to the Society of Friends and prominent female preacher, extols the mercy and inexpressible nature of God. Several of the poets reflect upon the mystery of death and express their personal grief or critical social commentary through the medium of verse. In fact, the death of children, dangers of childbirth, loss of husbands, and tragic elements of life figure prominently in these writings. But so does the Christian conviction of victory in death, most powerfully expressed in the hymns and spiritual poems of Agnes Bulmer. Her poetry emphasizes the mysteries of God's grace, the majesty of the rainbow promise, the heavenly reward of those who entrust their lives to Christ, and the glory of eternal life with God. The blind preacher and poet, Margaret Davidson, finds God in the sensual, locating Jesus in the beauties of nature that surround us at all times. A central theme in all of this poetic material is the absolute centrality of Jesus and, as Mary Taft demonstrates so clearly, the necessity of absolute commitment to him.

John Wesley described prayer as the foundation of all the means of grace. It is not too much to say that the Christian life begins and ends in prayer. The prayers of thirteen women comprise the third block of material in part 2. These prayers cover the full range of intimate encounters with God, including expressions of adoration, repentance, thanksgiving, and intercession. They model a profound balance of concern for others and for self; they demonstrate the power and peace of lives entrusted to the care of God.

Many of these prayers are extracted from journals and diaries, capturing moments of reflection and introspection when the women naturally break into prayer. These prayers are typically short, pithy, direct, and extemporaneous—lending to the journal a character of ongoing conversation with God. Excerpts from the journals of Susannah Design, Mary Gilbert, and Bathsheba Hall reflect this form of prayer.

Others of the prayers selected are highly refined. Mrs. Lefevre's prayer is dignified, elegant, and learned. Joanna Cook's "covenant prayer" is crafted, highly reflective, even contractual in its feel. A prayer of Ann Cutler ("Praying Nanny") that was also used for covenant renewal reflects the strong trinitarian emphasis of the Methodist heritage. Many of the women "pray the Word," that is, their prayer is shaped by the language of scripture or is often simply a string of scriptural allusions, such as in the prayer of Margaret Davidson.

Sarah Crosby's prayers reflect her deep desire for wholeness in life; Hetty Roe and Isabella Wilson yearn for intimacy with God. No prayer in this collection expresses the passion these women had for the salvation of others more profoundly than the appeal of Elizabeth Evans, the prototype for George Eliot's Dinah Morris in her novel *Adam Bede*. The prayers drawn from Mary Entwisle's manuscript journal are filled with pathos. No easy or persistent growth in grace, Mary's spiritual life is characterized by dark valleys and agonizing cries. Her prayer is real; her expressions of pathos are a testimony both to the integrity of her questions and to her intimacy with God. The final prayer of Mary Hanson reiterates many of the classic Wesleyan themes: the kenotic nature of life in Christ, the necessity of God's in-filling Spirit, the need for growth into the fullest possible restoration, and love as the beginning and end of the journey.

The final block of material in part 2 is devoted to visions and dreams. Early Methodist women believed that God uses visions and dreams to rebuke, confirm, encourage, and guide God's children. These phenomena were an important part of their spirituality, and that of the Methodist men as well. Sarah Ryan, Mary Fletcher, and Sarah Mallet were extremely important women within the life of the movement. They reflect the heart and core of early Methodism, not its fringe.

Sarah Ryan had partnered with Fletcher in her bold missionary endeavors in London, and these two women were extremely close to the Methodist founder. Sarah uses her dreams to interpret what is happening around her and inside her. They provide direction to her and are directly linked to her spiritual growth.

The visions of Mary Fletcher come at critical turning points in her life. They confirm actions and decisions that she is considering. They are also an important source of encouragement as she seeks an entrepreneurial course of action in life. Not only does she record her own dreams and visions, but also she reflects upon the visions of others.

Sarah Mallet, the first woman to receive the full authorization of the Methodist Conference as a woman preacher, provides us with some of the most fascinating material related to the supernatural. What is important about the account of her "fits" is their direct linkage to her call to preach. For many of her Methodist colleagues, her story was a profound vindication of God's call upon the lives of women.

A. Spiritual Instruction

1. MEDITATIONS OF MRS. LEFEVRE

Editor's Introduction

It is unfortunate that we know so little of this remarkable woman. Mrs. Lefevre (1722?–56) exerted an incalculable influence upon a number of prominent early Methodist women, to say nothing of the high esteem in which she was held by the male leadership of the Wesleyan movement. When she died on July 6, 1756, Charles Wesley wrote an elegy, one excerpt of which portrays her character:

> Ah! lovely Christ-like soul, adieu,
> Darling of every heart that knew
> > Thy short-lived excellence!
>
> She was (let all her worth confess,
> Let all her precious memory bless,
> > And after her aspire!)
> A burning and a shining light—
> She was—to gild our land of night,
> > And set our world on fire.
>
> She was (what words can never paint)
> A spotless soul, a sinless saint,
> > In perfect love renew'd;
> A mirror of the Deity,
> A transcript of the One in Three,
> > A temple fill'd with God;
>
> The witness of His hallowing grace,
> Talk'd with her Maker face to face,
> > And, mark'd with His new name,
> His nature visibly express'd,
> While all her even life confess'd
> > The meekness of the Lamb.

> Blest with His lowly, loving mind,
> One with the Friend of human kind,
>   In all His steps she trod;
> In doing good, and bearing ill,
> Fulfill'd her heavenly Father's will,
>   And lived and died to God.[5]

Lefevre's celebrated *Letters upon Sacred Subjects*, published by her husband a year after her death reveals the depth of her piety, the wisdom beyond her years, and her tremendous gifts as a spiritual guide and friend.[6] These letters made her famous within Methodist circles, particularly after John Wesley provided his own edited version of the volume in 1769.[7] She took a strong interest in the spiritual struggles of those who surrounded her. Noteworthy among those within her circle of care was Samuel Furley. A clergyman of the Church of England closely associated with the Methodists, he was appointed perpetual curate of Slaithwaite and subsequently rector at Roche where he joined a group of like-minded evangelical priests in Cornwall.[8] The young and impressionable Mary Bosanquet spent time with Mrs. Lefevre several days before her death and left a record of their conversation:

> In the month of June, 1756, I spent a day with Mrs. Lefevre. It was a profitable time: I found my heart very open, and told her, I believe I could give up even her to the will of God. She replied, "Nothing you could have said would have given me more satisfaction. For a long time I have thought that the thread of my life was nearly spun out. I have no clog upon my chariot wheels; but my greatest pain was for you, who have already so many trials surrounding you." ... three days after ... My mother kindly permitted me to visit her; but I found her on the borders of eternity, into which, after expressing with great difficulty, "I have comforts indeed!" her happy spirit took its flight.[9]

Mary described Mrs. Lefevre as "the greatest comfort" of her life.

At the conclusion of his edition of Mrs. Lefevre's *Letters*, John Wesley appended five of her meditations upon texts of Scripture. One of these is dated 1748. Two brief excerpts from this collection

A. Spiritual Instruction

of meditative writings reveal the deep calm and contentment she felt as she placed her full trust in God.

* * * *

Come unto me all ye that labor and are heavy laden, and I will refresh you [Matt. 11:28].

These, oh compassionate Savior, were your words. This your call, and I obey it. I come unto you, oh light of the world, for rest, peace, and everlasting refreshment. Wearied with treading the paths of folly and vanity, wearied with deceitful hopes and idle fears, and all the gay delusions of this world, I come to you for peace and with full assurance of obtaining it. Assurance founded on your promises. Those promises which are truth itself. Merciful as your own beneficent nature and unalterable as your being. Heaven and earth shall pass away, but your word shall never fail [see also Matt. 24:35]. Encouraged by this word, I come. Not even the reflection of my absolute unworthiness shall keep me from you.

It is to sinners that this heavenly call is addressed. Sinners that labor under the heavy burden of their offence. And such am I. The miserable wretch who is chained to the oar is not more weary of his slavery than I am of my sins. The sins which so easily beset me and so often conquer my best resolutions. Every hour I have new reason to lament my weakness and to confess that your grace is my only refuge. O let that grace, which has kept me from all infamous crimes, be also my preservation against those sins of the mind which, though hid from the short-sighted world, are all open to you and render my soul equally odious to the eye of heaven. Oh save me from myself! I come to you, blessed Jesus, that I may have rest. Oh give me that rest! Then shall all be perfect peace and harmony, and my soul shall feel no emotions but those of joy and gratitude, eternal gratitude for my gracious and almighty benefactor.

O God thou art my God! Early will I seek thee [Psa. 63:1].

When we are deprived of all the joys of life, betrayed by those we trusted, forsaken by our friends, triumphed over by our enemies, and robbed of our dearest hopes, where and to whom must we go for relief? What comfort can be hoped in a condition so desperate—Will reflection on the past give us ease?—Alas! it makes our wounds still deeper, and every remembrance of the treachery of our friends, or the malice of our enemies, draws a new sigh from the oppressed and aching heart, and a fresh tear from the sinking eye.—Shall we look forwards?—All dark and gloomy is the prospect, and the mind, wearied with affliction and wholly depressed by grief and disappointments, shudders at the thought of launching again into the sea of delusions, of again trusting, and being again deceived.

In circumstance so deplorable, nothing can calm our grief, nothing afford us one moment's peace, but seeking early after God. And happy! thrice happy! that soul, which can say with the royal Psalmist, "O God! you are my God, my refuge in all my distresses, my only hope, and everlasting peace!"—A man who can look up to the great author of nature with a confidence like this, who can seek after God with full assurance of finding him, and in him a sure relief for all the troubles and miseries of life, is superior to all events, and may be happy in the most terrible afflictions. Is he deprived of his estate, reduced to a despised and unrelieved poverty? He is still rich in the pleasing hopes that his God will one day bestow on him a glorious and never-failing inheritance. Is he by death robbed of his dearest friends? His grief is immediately calmed by the thoughts of that eternal state to which he is every moment approaching and where he will meet those dear objects of his tenderness, never, never to be parted from them more. Is his reputation made a sacrifice to spite and calumny, and himself condemned, reviled, and hated, by his acquaintance? Still true to his principles and firm in his trust on the Almighty, he braves the storm, and with joy looks forward to that day, when his accusers shall be covered with flame and confusion and his innocence declared in the sight of men and angels. Is he betrayed by those he trusted with an unbounded confidence, by those who were dear to him as himself, and for whose life he would freely have paid his own? Even in this affliction (which is of all others the most grating to human nature) he is still master of himself and possessing his soul in patience and resignation, looks up to that friend who will never deceive him, to that God who is truth itself.

Convinced of the folly of placing his love and trust on creatures, he fixes it wholly on the eternal Creator and acknowledges with

A. Spiritual Instruction

sincerity the mercy of God in thus graciously releasing his heart from those deluding ties which had so often drawn him from the center of the true happiness, the end of his being. Thus blessed is he who can say with faith, gratitude, and humility, "O God, you are my God"!—Grant, oh most adorable and omnipotent Being! grant me this glorious privilege! I have nothing more to ask. That you are my God is a blessing infinitely greater than the whole creation can bestow, infinitely beyond all I can ask or conceive. Possessed of this, I can defy the combined malice of men and devils.

Welcome distress, poverty, disappointment, and affliction of all kinds, even what I have most dreaded! Welcome all, if it is the will of heaven! What hurt are you capable of doing me, while I can say to the rock of ages, "You are my God?" And certainly, oh fountain of life and author of all good, it is your gracious will that I should thus address you, else why this firm reliance on you in all my afflictions? Why this entire confidence on your mercy and goodness, in the midst of my sufferings? How often when my heat has been sinking under a load of sorrow, have I found relief and comfort by applying to you? In troubles which I have thought impossible to be endured, you have been my support.

And when at any time I have been tempted to discontent and dared to murmur and complain, how quickly has your grace inspired me with remorse for my impiety, and enabled me to make a new act of resignation to your providence! Sure and infallible proofs that you are my God! And oh, may I never repay those instances of your compassion and tender mercy with ingratitude! Never more distrust the power which has so often delivered me! But grant, Almighty Father, that in all the trials you have allotted me in this mortal state, I may seek you early, and in seeking you find all the blessings you have promised, peace and perfect tranquility in this life, and everlasting joy and happiness in the next! These favors, these blessings I implore in the name, and for the sake of my merciful Redeemer, Jesus Christ.

Source:

[John Wesley], *An Extract of Letters by Mrs. L**** (Bristol: William Pine, 1769), 101-2, 107-9.

2. Mary Bosanquet's *Spiritual Direction*

Editor's Introduction

Mary Bosanquet [Fletcher] (1739–1815) stands without a rival in the annals of early Methodism.[10] You already know her story and the extent of her influence within the movement from selections in part 1 above. In addition to her multifarious roles as preacher, advisor, counselor, small group leader, minister's wife, and patron, she was a prolific writer. Her *Life*, edited by Henry Moore and composed largely of extracts from her journals and letters, is the most well-known of her writings. But she published many other items that made their way into every corner of British Methodism— including, among others: a narrative history of her work in the Leytonstone foundation (1764); an open letter to the "single women of the Methodist Society," entitled *Jesus, Altogether Lovely* (1766); a catechetical work, *An Aunt's Advice to a Niece* (1780); *Thoughts on Communion with Happy Spirits*; personal reflections on the death of her husband (1785); countless letters published in the *Arminian Magazine* or independently; and her *"Legacy to the People of Madeley,"* revised and published posthumously by Joseph Entwisle.

The four selections that follow are taken from her *Life*; her tract *Jesus, Altogether Lovely*; and a private letter published for public distribution in 1771, "Written to Elizabeth A—ws." The thrust of these writings is spiritual direction. Mary took very serioiusly the practice of aiding other women (and men) in their journey to a more fully developed faith. Like all classical spiritual directors, her primary goal was the formation of the whole person in her or his relation to all aspects of life; but the foundation of her direction was the experience of God in the person of Jesus Christ through the power of the indwelling Spirit. In her instruction to young single women, she elevates self-denial, humility, and entire devotion to God as the central characteristics of the Christian life. Methodical in her approach to all things religious, like her mentor in the faith, she lays down eight regulations for growth toward holiness in her unique "rule of life." Her instructions related to the Lord's Prayer reflect meditative techniques applicable to any age. The concluding letter describes the spiritual life by use of helpful metaphors, such as the mariner's compass; shared experiences, such as hunger and nursing; and powerful analogies, such as those related to our physical senses, all of which point to the promises of God that are deep and wide.

* * * *

Instructions to Single Women

My desire and prayer to God for you is that you may every moment behold Jesus as altogether lovely [see also Sol. 5:16]! The infinite consequence this is of to your soul has often been the subject of our conversation. That there is but one way of beholding him now and that this way is by faith we all know. But how to keep this eye of the soul always clear and unsullied, like the finest glass, free from every speck and flaw, is the point we want to be instructed in.

It is by a life of self-denial alone that the eye of our faith can be kept clear. I was not a little blessed the other day with the words of a good man, expressing his desire of being devoted to God in a solemn observance of chastity, poverty, and obedience.[11] The words struck me much and appeared to contain the whole of a Christian life. The Lord was pleased to apply them close to my soul. And I will endeavor simply to relate what then occurred on each head.

We should consider our souls as the image of God, and our bodies as the temples of the Lord [see also 1 Cor. 6:19], both pure and consecrated to his service, and our hearts as an altar on which the love of Jesus as a pure flame should continually burn, and that the fuel we are to cast into this fire is every earthly object that presents itself, whether to the eye, the ear, or any other of our senses, casting them in as soon as perceived, feeling the force of that expression, "All the vain things that charm me most, I sacrifice to Jesu's love!"[12]

To you who are able to receive this saying I will speak the inmost sentiments of my heart. Whatever others are, you are called to the glorious privileges of a single life. O cast them not behind you. Nor having beheld the beauties of the lovely Jesus now forget that he is fairer than the sons of men. I shall not attempt to enumerate the particular advantages of your situation. I am not persuading you to it. I need not. All your soul stretches itself out after that entire devotion to him whom having seen you love.

O beware of judging. For God is love and every wound to love may therefore, in some sense, be said to be a wound to God. May he who came not to judge but to save the world [see also John 3:17] preserve you from this most pernicious of all evils. Never then consider yourself as secure, but hang every moment on Jesus as if on the very brink of falling. And let your reading, meditation, and prayer turn as much as may be on the advantages of a single life. And may a holy ambition to know nothing but Jesus fire your spirits while you are made deeply sensible that no grace can be guarded but by humility.

In short, we should see God in everything and make it our sole business inwardly to listen to that still small voice, which none but silent souls can hear, and outwardly to meet him in the order of his providence, remembering we are all his own, and lying before him as soft wax ready to be formed into any shape he pleases. And this simple recollecting ourselves in the presence of God, receiving every occurrence as from him and offering up every action to him, is the spirit and life of true religion.

Cry for an obedient, humble, peaceable spirit. O were we all but penetrated with true humility.... The earnest desire of my soul for you is that you may abide in the faith and endure unto the end [see also Matt. 24:13], that you may covet to walk in the most excellent way and be found continually standing on your guard and watching unto prayer. Then will the eternal God be your refuge and underneath you the everlasting arms [see also Deut. 33:27]. He will set your sins far from you [see also Psa. 103:12] and cause you to dwell in purity of heart and in safety. You shall be a people saved of the Lord, who shall himself become your guide and your exceeding great reward.

SOURCE:

Mary Bosanquet, *Jesus, Altogether Lovely; or A Letter to Some of the Single Women in the Methodist Society*, 2nd ed. (Bristol: s.n., 1766), 2-6, 9-12.

A. Spiritual Instruction

A Rule of Life

As you have expressed a desire that I would give you on paper the few observations I have sometimes made on Wednesday nights, I will endeavor so to do, as far as I can recollect. And if my dear Lord is pleased to help you through so weak an instrument, he shall have the more abundant praise.

First, I would recommend you to be very careful whom you admit into your meeting.[13] Consider no one as member thereof who is not steadily seeking after Christian perfection; that is, a heart simplified by love divine, and kept each moment by faith from the pollution of sin. Whosoever agrees not with you on this point will greatly interrupt your design.

Secondly, see that you fix on your minds—We come together to get our faith increased and expect as much that our souls should be refreshed by our meeting as we do our bodies to be refreshed by our food. Come with a lively expectation. And that your expectation may not be cut off, keep your spirit all the time in continual prayer. United prayer can never go unanswered.

Thirdly, bear with each other's mistakes or infirmities in love. Consider the members as if they were your own children. How much will a man bear with in "his own son that serveth him [Mal. 3:17]? A threefold cord cannot be easily broken" [Eccl. 4:12]. Satan will leave no stone unturned to disunite you. But O, remember the characteristic of the evangelical dispensation is,

> The love that turns the other cheek;
> The love inviolably meek
> which bears, but conquers all.[14]

tFourthly, be well aware of that deadly poison so frequent among professors,[15] I mean evil speaking. It will cover itself under a thousand forms. And, alas! how many sincere hearts swallow this gilded bait before they know what they are about. Never repeat the fault of an absent person unless it is absolutely needful. In particular, speak not evil of dignities, neither of our king, on whose account we have the greatest reason to be thankful, nor yet of any in authority under him. Neither those whom God has set over us as spiritual teachers. If any of these do not speak just as we could have wished, never forget that one may have his gift after this manner, another after that. The exhortation not so immediately useful to your state may nevertheless be put into their mouth at that time for another person then present. Known unto God are all his ways. And as he has said, "A cup of cold water given to a prophet" [see also John 4:10] shall not be forgotten. How pleasing will it be in his sight if by faith and prayer we hold up the hands of his praying servants [see also Exod. 17:12].

Fifthly, hold fast the truth in a pure conscience [see also Acts 24:16].[16] Let not one spark of your light be put out. Though all your teachers, brethren, friends, yes, the whole Church, were to turn against the truth, let nothing make you forget "The blood of Jesus cleanseth from all sin" [1 John 1:7], and that he keeps that soul for ever clean who day and night hangs on him by simple faith.

Sixthly, be always ready to give an account to those that ask you a reason of the hope that is in you [see also 1 Pet. 3:15]. In order to this, let us pray for clear ideas of what we seek and what we possess. Bear in mind that to "perfect holiness in the fear of the Lord" [2 Cor. 7:1] is no more than you have already promised. First, by your sponsors in baptism;[17] secondly, in your own person when you made those vows your own by confirmation; and, thirdly, whenever you renew that covenant by coming to the Lord's table. "You have engaged to renounce the devil and all his works, the pomps and vanities of this wicked world, and all the sinful lusts of the flesh; to believe all the articles of the Christian faith; to keep God's holy will and commandments, and to walk in the same all the days of your life."[18] And is not this vowing to "perfect holiness in the fear of God" [2 Cor. 7:1]? Does the first part of this sacred engagement, to renounce the devil and all his works, leave any room for the least agreement with the devil, the world, or the flesh? Does the second, to believe all the articles of the Christian faith, make the least allowance for one doubt with respect to any one article of the Christian faith? Or does the third allow the wilful breach of any one of God's commandments? Again, do we not all profess to believe it to be our duty "to love God with all our hearts, and our neighbour as ourselves" [Luke 10:27]? Weigh the depth of those two expressions. Do they not imply love made perfect, or in other words, Christian perfection?

Seventhly, remember that saying of Solomon, "The wise man's eyes are in his head" [Eccl. 2:14]. Let your eye of faith be steadily fixed on your living head, deeply conscious of that word,

> Having done all, by faith I stand,
> And give the praise, O Lord, to thee![19]

... So true is that saying of our Lord, "Without me ye can do nothing" [John 15:5].

Eighthly, consider yourselves as united by a holy covenant to God and to each other, aiming to advance the glory of God all you possibly can.

> Ye for Christ your Master stand
> Lights in a benighted land.[20]

Beware then that your light become not darkness. Let no one be discouraged from seeking Christian holiness by anything they see in your life and conversation. We must become a whole burned sacrifice [see also Gen. 22:2]. The soldier enlisted under the banner of his king may neither leave his post nor choose his employment. We have covenanted to be the Lord's and may not draw back one power, no, nor one thought from his service. Be it then engraved on our hearts, as with a diamond pen, "Thy vows, O God, are upon me; I have opened my mouth unto the Lord, and cannot go back" [Judges 11:35].

SOURCE:

Henry Moore, *The Life of Mrs. Mary Fletcher, Consort and Relict of the Rev. John Fletcher, Vicar of Madeley, Salop: Compiled from her Journal and Other Authentic Documents*, 2 vols. (Birmingham: J. Peart, 1817), 1:87-91.

Reflections on the Lord's Prayer

January 5, 1776. I find it very hard to be recollected in private prayer. Today I tried the following plan with some advantage. I placed my watch on the bed that I might know when the hour was out. I first strove to consider myself as in the presence of God, as before the throne, worshiping with the heavenly host. Then I strove with recollection to repeat the Lord's Prayer [see also Matt. 6:9-13], giving each sentence full scope in my mind. In the words, "Our Father," I felt a powerful remembrance of him "after whom the whole family in heaven and earth is named [Eph. 3:15]," and with delight I then repeated, "Hallowed be thy name!" That sentence, "Thy kingdom come," was much opened to my soul. I see that kingdom is the great promise of the Father which Christ said he would send upon his children. That indeed is "the kingdom which suffers violence, and the violent take it by force" [Matt. 11:12]. As I repeated, "Thy will be done on earth as it is in heaven," I felt

> The will of God my sure defense,
> Nor earth nor hell can pluck me thence.[21]

"Give us this day our daily bread." Is he not our own Father? Is he not engaged to provide for his babes? Well then, thought I, freedom from debt is more to me than bread, and will he not preserve me from this? It was then brought to my mind, "The Lord is my shepherd, I shall not want" [Psa. 23:1]. In the next petition, "Forgive me as I forgive," O! what a cry did I feel for more love! Lord, must I say,

> That mercy I to others show,
> That mercy show to me?[22]
>
> Ah, no! I will rather cry out,
> Mercy, good Lord! Mercy I ask,
>   It is the total sum;
> For mercy, Lord, is all my plea,
>   O let thy mercy come![23]

"With what measure ye mete, it shall be measured to you again" [Matt. 7:2]! O how would that cut me off from all hope were it not for those words, "The blood of Jesus cleanseth from all sin" [1 John 1:7]! "Lead us not into temptation." How has this prayer been answered to me! How would I have run into ruin, but you did not suffer the temptation to approach. You kept my powers as "with bit and bridle" [Psa. 32:9] and conquered for me, and that when I did not strive or even know my danger. "But deliver me from evil." Lord, I am a desolate woman who has no helper but you. O keep me from evil of every kind. "Thoroughly purge away my dross, and take away all my tin" [Isa. 1:25]. "For all is thine for ever and ever." This I am assured of when the soul turns inward to seek the Lord. That moment he turns to it and smiles upon it. And if it abide with him, it will always grow. But as of a healthy child, one does not see it grow, and yet it does. So the soul, surrounded by temptation, may not discover its growth. Nevertheless, the sun does not more freely give its light and warmth to the earth, than the beams of the immaterial Sun meet the seeking soul.

SOURCE:

Moore, *Life of Mary Fletcher*, 1:130-31.

On Living by Faith

To live by faith is to eye the loving Savior as your wisdom, righteousness, sanctification, and redemption, and to maintain a loving sense of the immediate presence of God, or a walking in a constant remembrance of him who is the fountain of all your mercies. Neither is a bare remembrance the thing I mean. For if the mariner was only to remember his compass, it would do him little good. No, he must look on it, and be guided by it too, or he will never reach the desired haven. To live by faith is to feed every moment on the bread of life [see also John 6:35ff]. Therefore, if you would grow strong, see that you feed continually on this heavenly manna. Do you complain of your weakness and inward decay? Is it with difficulty you conquer one of the feeblest of your enemies? The reason is plain. You do not eat. You have lost your appetite. Your soul is starving. No wonder, then, it is not strong. But if this moment you will begin to live by faith on Jesus, this moment shall you begin to prove all the promises of God, "Yea and Amen in him" [2 Cor. 1:20].

Do you understand what I mean by feeding on Jesus? I am not speaking of any outward ordinance, but of that inward and spiritual act of the soul by which it casts its whole self into the arms of its beloved, and sweetly abiding there in tranquility of spirit draws every moment divine life from that inexhaustible fountain, as the fair and flourishing branch draws sap from the vine. Or, like the tender infant hanging on its mother's breast, though it only receives the milk by its mouth, yet does the nourishment thereof spread through the whole body till it becomes the very substance of it, and by degrees the child grows up to its full stature. So let your soul desire and draw in the sincere milk of the word [see also 1 Pet. 2:2] by simply acting faith on Jesus, exercising all your senses on that only amiable object. As you have five outward senses by which you comprehend the visible creation, so does faith open in the soul spiritual senses analogous thereto. Fix, therefore, the eye of your soul on Jesus as those of a servant are to the hand of his master, sweetly expecting each moment his approving smile or a fresh discovery in the clamor of nature. It is that voice which only silent souls can hear. Taste the sweetness of the fruit that grows under his shadow, that bower for weary spirits made by the celestial vine. Taste them with delight, feed thereon, and let your heart be comforted with that love which is better than wine [see also Sol. 1:2]. Feel his love shed abroad in your heart [see also Rom. 5:5] by constantly abiding under the droppings of his sanctuary. So shall the stone be removed and your heart, still feeling my beloved is mine [cf. Sol. 2:16] and his desire is towards me, shall be refreshed with the odors of his rich perfumes.

But do you still say, "Alas! I know not how to do this, for darkness has covered the earth and a gross darkness my soul." Well, I will endeavor to speak in the plainest and most simple manner I can. And may my adorable Savior give you to feel what, till then, you can never understand.[24] I mean, lift up your heart as you are able this moment to God and remember his eye is over you just now. He is now looking upon you. He now hears your prayer, passes by you, and stopping asks, "What do you want me to do for you?" Now let your heart reply, "Lord, that I may fear, believe, and love, and for ever dwell in your presence." Then abide in that heavenly frame of mind, often speaking to him with a loving familiarity, as a dear child to its tender parent, believing that word, "My God shall richly supply your want." Believe, ask, and persevere in asking. So shall you bring forth much fruit and be his disciple indeed [cf. John 15:16]. Hear him saying,

A. Spiritual Instruction

> Beneath my Love's almighty shade,
> O, Israel, sit and rest secure;
> On me thy quiet soul be stay'd;
> Till pure as I, thy God, am pure.[25]

Endeavor to keep your spirit free from all hurry and confusion, for he peculiarly works in a composed and quiet mind. Abide in the full expectation of his love. Believe that "he will do for you exceeding abundantly above all that you can either ask or think" [Eph. 3:20]. For I tell you, in the name of my great Lord and Master, he has purchased holiness for you. Yes, for you. And if you abide in the constant exercise of faith you shall soon learn the meaning of that word, "He saveth his people from their sins" [Matt. 1:21]. Entreat him to take all your will and affections and fix them on himself, to give you to live in Jesus as you have died in Adam, experiencing as complete a life in Jesus as you have experienced a death in sin, bearing the image of the heavenly, as you have borne that of the earthly.

Be not straightened in yourself, for God's promises are wide and deep. Yes, he is as a place of broad rivers and streams. Dare to believe. There is nothing so puts the crown on Christ's head as to believe his readiness to save, to venture on his free salvation. Hear him saying, "Come, lose thyself from the bands of thy neck, O captive daughter of Zion" [Isa. 52:2]. As the neck joins the head and the body together, so does living faith join Christ the head to his body the church. And as a person whose neck is bound down to the earth can neither enjoy nor act, so is the soul while fettered with the bands of unbelief. No, your head is bound also, for he has also declared, "He could not do many mighty works, because of their unbelief" [Matt. 13:58]. Come, then, believe as you are able. Stretch out the withered hand [see also Mark 3:1-3]. Let your faith reach out towards him. Walk as in his presence and behold him every moment as beholding you. So shall you experience in your own soul, "This is the victory that overcometh the world, even your faith" [1 John 5:4].

SOURCE:

Mary Bosanquet, *A Letter, Written to Elizabeth A—ws, On Her Removal from England* (Leeds: James Bowling, 1771), 5-9.

3. Martha Hall's Discourse on Meditation

Editor's Introduction

Martha ("Patty") Hall (1706–91), thought by most of the family to be the favorite of Susanna Wesley, was one of the younger girls in the Wesley family. Like most of her sisters, tragic circumstances stalked her throughout life. Living under the patronage of her uncle Matthew in London, she was secretly courted and informally engaged to one of her brothers' close associates from the Oxford "Holy Club," Westley Hall. During a visit to Epworth, Rev. Hall became infatuated with Kezziah Wesley, Martha's sister. He jilted Martha, only to return to her with a public offer of marriage in 1735. This turn of events unjustly alienated Martha from many within this tightly knit family who, unaware of her previous relationship with Hall, blamed her for stealing Kezziah's lover. In the course of their disastrous marriage, Hall inflicted his long-suffering wife with a string of mistresses, continuously shameless behavior, and ultimate abandonment. The support and care Martha provided to one of her husband's mistresses at the time she delivered Hall's illegitimate child is just one manifestation of her magnanimous nature.

Of the ten children born to Martha while living near Salisbury, nine died in infancy. The Wesley brothers took the one surviving son, demanding that he be educated away from home, given the shocking infidelity of his father. A potential source of consolation and strength to his mother, he died from smallpox at fourteen years of age. One of the sustaining diversions from her unhappy life was through her London connections with one of the central cultural circles of the age. She delighted in the company of Dr. Samuel Johnson, in particular. Perhaps her difficult domestic circumstances pressed Martha to find comfort and resolution most particularly in prayer. After Hall abandoned her, the Charles Wesley family "adopted" her, and she maintained a close connection with the Methodist movement, particularly in London after the family moved there in 1771. Her interest in meditation seems to have developed early in her life.

A. Spiritual Instruction

The following outline of Hall's notes on meditation are undated. They are reminiscent of the spirituality associated with Francis de Sales (1567–1622), who described a particular form of meditation in his classic work, *Introduction to a Devout Life* (1608). His greatest gift was his ability to make the loftiest goals of the practical mystical tradition accessible to ordinary men and women. Salesian meditation, sometimes referred to simply as "Anglican meditation" because of its pervasive influence within English Christianity, consists in several key elements. There is attentive apprehension of God and invocation at the beginning, which may also include the use of the imagination. The element of "consideration," or what might be described as the substance of the meditation, strengthens faith and gives rise during the prayer to affections, petitions, and resolutions. The purpose of this devotional practice is neither abstract nor mystical; rather, this form of meditation seeks to activate love, move resolution to action, and offer thanksgiving to God. One particularly characteristic feature of Salesian technique is the "spiritual nosegay," the act of carrying a word, phrase, or thought out of the meditation for guidance and encouragement throughout the day.

Unfortunately, we know virtually nothing with regard to the origins of Martha Wesley's discourse. Speculation about when it might have been composed—in earlier life or in the midst of an unfortunate marriage—offers little reward. Of still greater interest, yet equally unanswerable, are questions about the way in which such meditative practices may have sustained her through unrelenting periods of suffering and personal agony. This terse guide, however, locates Martha squarely within the Anglican heritage of her birth and demonstrates the importance she placed upon the practice of faith.

* * * *

1. Meditation impresses the sense of our duty upon our minds.
2. It keeps our conscience tender, afraid to offend.
3. It habituates our minds to spiritual objects.

To make our meditation useful to the best purposes, we must observe the method.

1. Prepare your minds for the purpose of imploring God's assistance.

2. Choose the subject of your meditation.

3. Fix your minds upon such considerations as are proper to your subject.

4. The understanding. Be convinced by consideration, excite your will and affections to love, desire, or to hate.

5. The considerations that relate to a subject, the affections that are excited thereby, must be followed by your resolutions.

6. Conclude your meditation with a particular address to God.

SOURCE:

[Martha Hall], "A Discourse on Meditation," Martha Hall Manuscripts, pp. 23-37; *Meth. Arch.*

A. SPIRITUAL INSTRUCTION

4. MARY TATHAM'S *MEMOIRS* AND BIBLICAL COMMENTARY

Editor's Introduction

Mary Strickland (1764–1837) was born into a family of strict Calvinist Dissenters. When she was five or six years old, while reading the Bible, she was powerfully struck by the description of the new heaven and the new earth in the Revelation of St. John, her first religious impression. Perhaps it was this primal experience that gave her a lifelong passion for the study of scripture. Distressed by a lack of intimacy with God, she closely examined the collects, catechism, baptismal, and confirmation services, as well as the eucharistic liturgy of the *Book of Common Prayer*. About the same time, John Wesley's abbreviated publication of Thomas à Kempis's *Imitation of Christ* fell into her hands, as well as a number of Wesley's other publications, including the *Plain Account of Christian Perfection*. She was greatly influenced by her study of these texts and received her first Methodist class ticket in 1784. Her meticulous examination of John Fletcher's anti-Calvinist writings convinced her of the antinomian dangers of her original theological heritage, and she became a convinced Arminian Christian.

On February 6, 1787, she married John Tatham at the Old Church in Leeds, a historic center of Methodist women's activities. Nearly immediately, however, she and her new husband moved to Nottingham, and later to Halifax. Over the course of more than forty years, she had the charge of at least three classes. To prepare herself properly for the spiritual direction of those under her care, she provided commentary on biblical texts, thirteen of which expositions were published in her *Memoirs*.[26] She also provided tightly argued expositions of critical doctrines such as justification by grace through faith and sanctification. Able to speak with authority and precision with regard to matters of theological concern, she also possessed the ability to communicate effectively with the common person. Mary was just as much at ease offering practical advice regarding reconciliation in the context of strained relationships as she was defending the Wesleyan concept of salvation against a Calvinist critic. Her biographer provides a detailed analysis of her spirituality, characterized by the pious fear of God, active and generous benevolence, strong faith and prevailing prayer, a contemplative frame of mind coupled with an insatiable thirst for knowledge, and the prayerful study of scripture.[27] The selections below demonstrate her intellectual abilities and her sincere desire to direct others in ways that lead to fullness of life and love.

* * * *

On Receiving Injury

I have been considering what is best to be done on receiving an injury from any one, either by word or deed, whether designedly or undesignedly, openly or secretly, from professors or profane, from friend or foe.

Is it good to resent an injury? No. Our Lord says, "Resist not evil; but whosoever shall smite thee on thy right cheek, turn to him the other also" [Matt. 5:39]. Is it well to speak of an injury? It is not well to reproach the person from whom we have received the injury. But it is very good to suffer patiently and to be silent under provocations, though sometimes there may be a necessity to make mention of an injury, to a wise person, if we stand in need of redress, or advice how to act for the glory of God and our own good without doing any hurt to the offending party. Is it good to think of an injury? It is not good to aggravate it by dwelling upon its baseness. But it is very good to forget it, to rend it from our minds, and freely to forgive the offender. But this is not agreeable to nature. Flesh and blood cannot bear such discipline. Yet it is made easy by the grace of God to all those who seek him fully for power to act thus. How, then, are we to seek? By prayer, and that instantly, upon every occasion of injury offered. What should be the purport or manner of our prayers? This depends upon the nature of the injury and the person by whom it is offered. But we should always lay the case simply before God, and then our own feelings under it.

2. We ought patiently to resign ourselves to God and seek only that his will may be done and his gracious designs answered.

3. We ought to pray earnestly for the offenders, and beg of God to forgive them, to turn their hearts and not lay their sin to their charge [see also Acts 7:60]. If they are professors we should be more

importunate still with God in their behalf, that if they have acted unadvisedly, ignorantly, through the force of temptation or loss of grace, they may take heed for the future, be delivered from the temptation, or strengthened against it, and raised from their fall. By so doing we shall be supported under every trial from man, be kept from rash judgment, rash words, and rash actions. And thus overcoming evil with good [see also Rom. 12:21], we shall deliver our own souls and may be made instrumental of the conversion or recovery of others through the perseverance of our prayers, the patience of our souls, the prudence of our actions, and the kindness of our behavior towards them. But if our conduct has not this blessed effect, it will cut off all evil on our part and shame them who continue contentious and rebellious, putting to silence all evil doers. So shall God be glorified and we ourselves have cause of rejoicing, inasmuch as we have overcome evil with good.

SOURCE:

Joseph Beaumont, ed., *Memoirs of Mrs. Mary Tatham, Late of Nottingham* (London: Simpkin & Marshall, sold by John Mason, 1838), 66-67.

On Justification

Therefore, by the deeds of the law there shall no flesh be justified in his sight. Rom. 3:10.

Justification is a free act of God's mercy and love to fallen man whereby he is freely acquitted from all the guilt and punishment due to his sins, from which he could not be acquitted by the deeds of the law, but is so by the righteousness of another, even of him whom God has set forth to be a propitiation through faith in his blood [see also Rom. 3:25], to declare his righteousness for the remission of sins that are past. For if there had been a law that would have given life, then righteousness had come by that law, and Christ would have died in vain. But God has imprisoned all in unbelief, that he might have mercy upon all [see also Rom. 11:42].

For the promise is not to him who works, but to him who without works trusts, is his faith accounted for righteousness [see also Rom. 4:5]. And herein God is both just and the justifier of him who believes in Jesus. Therefore, the apostle says, we conclude that a man is justified by faith, without the deeds of the law [see also Rom. 3:28], for by the law is the knowledge of sin [see also Rom. 3:20] (without any efficient means to deliver from its condemning power), and whosoever will not submit himself to God's righteousness (God's righteous method of justifying the ungodly), but will go about to establish his own righteousness, such a one rejects the counsel of God against himself and refuses the only remedy God has appointed or could appoint for the salvation of a ruined world. Let not any man say, therefore, that he is not a debtor to the law, but rather let him accept the terms of reconciliation and acknowledge that in point of justification before God, his best righteousness is as filthy rags [see also Isa. 64:6], and will not cover him in that day when the secrets of all hearts shall be revealed and when every work shall be brought into judgment, whether it be good or evil.

Now a justified man is a saved man, and as long as he retains the blessing of justification he lives the life of faith. A man, therefore, must be made or constituted just before he can live the life of faith, for the just man is a justified man (otherwise his uprightness does not repose upon the foundation which God has laid). He is one that is made just by faith, who has submitted himself to the righteousness of God and been made partaker of a new nature by faith which is in Christ Jesus. No man, however uniform or exact his outward deportment may be, or however sincere or upright in intention of his mind, or however desirous he may be to approve himself to God, can by his utmost efforts and all his duties render himself just before God. All that he has done cannot justify him. He is still unjust in the eye of the law until he accepts the terms of reconciliation and submits to be saved by mercy alone, through faith in him who died, the Just for the unjust, to bring him to God [see also 1 Pet. 3:18]. Every man is a sinner by nature and by practice and must be a recipient of God's mercy by faith or he cannot be saved either from the guilt and condemnation of sin or from the power and indwelling of it. His righteousness, therefore, must be derived from another source than himself. He must be made just by faith before he can live to God, work the works of God [see also John 6:28], and live eternally with God.

A. Spiritual Instruction

What is justifying faith? It is a gracious act, whereby a soul under conviction of sin apprehends Christ as his redeemer and lays hold upon him for pardon and reconciliation before God.

What effect does this justifying faith have upon the heart of every true believer? It fills him with love and with astonishment at the greatness of God's mercy. It works an utter abhorrence of all sin and casts out slavish fear [see also 1 John 4:18]. It opens a way of access between God and the believing soul and imparts unto him the spirit of adoption, whereby he cries, "Abba, Father" [Rom. 8:15]. Thus delivered, the language of his heart is no longer, "O wretched man that I am, who shall deliver me from the body of this death" [Rom. 7:24]? but, "Thou art my God [Psa. 118:28], and my Deliverer [see also Psa. 40:17], the Holy One of Israel! whom have I in heaven but thee? and there is none upon earth that I desire in comparison of thee" [see also Psa. 73:25]. Being thus freed from the guilt and dominion of sin and initiated into the family and favour of God, he becomes a servant of righteousness, has his fruit unto holiness, and his end everlasting life [see also Rom. 6:22]. Love filling the heart is productive of real holiness, and God being always present with him and his desires going out continually after him, he is kept above the power of temptation and sin. In this state he presses forward to greater degrees of purity and love until the whole soul is changed into the divine image.

It may be objected that what is here stated relates to sanctification. It does so inasmuch as justification leads immediately to sanctification, although many who receive justification are never fully sanctified and some who are justified draw back and finally perish because they do not "stand fast in the liberty wherewith Christ hath made them free, but again entangle themselves in a yoke of bondage" [Gal. 5:1].

Not abiding in the love of Christ, by keeping his commandments, taking up their cross daily, and seeking his glory above all things, they grow cold in their affections and languid in their desires. Their spiritual life insensibly declines and their desires after God become so faint that they can live whole days, weeks, months, and years, without a comfortable sense of his presence or ever bemoaning their loss, and seeking for a fresh manifestation of his favor, unless God awakens them again to a sense of their sin and danger. Whereas the true believer delights in God continually and beholds by faith the glory of the Lord in the revelation of Jesus Christ, who is become unto him wisdom, righteousness, sanctification, and redemption [see also 1 Cor. 1:30]. Every thing in comparison of his Savior is esteemed only as dung and dross [see also Phil. 3:8]. He cannot live without a sense of his love and he is willing to part with all rather than lose one mite of his glorious treasure. Such a one, by insensible and slow degrees, may lose the life of God and become dead in trespasses and sins [see also Eph. 2:1]. While another, by adding grace to grace, and keeping his eye steadily fixed upon his divine Lord, is changed into the same image, even as by the Spirit of the Lord.

SOURCE:

Beaumont, *Memoirs of Mary Tatham*, 69-75.

On Sanctification

If, then, we are justified by faith, by what means are we sanctified? Doubtless, by continuing to believe. If a deliverance from the guilt and dominion of sin, peace with God, and joy in the Holy Ghost follow justification, what is implied in sanctification? Sanctification is a freedom from all sin, love purifying the affections, influencing every action, and filling the heart with a still more abundant measure of peace and joy in the Holy Ghost. How must we continue to believe? By continuing in the love of God. How may we continue in the love of God? By keeping his commandments, and his commandments are not grievous. What are his commandments? "Thou shalt love the Lord thy God with all thy heart, with all thy mind, with all thy soul, and with all thy strength, and thy neighbour as thyself. On these two commandments hang all the law and the prophets" [Matt. 22:40]. How are we to keep these commandments? By cleaving close to Jesus. By being united to him as the branch is to the living vine, continually receiving life, nourishment, and strength from him, as the branch does from the vine [see also John 15].

It is the privilege of the faithful believer to experience, moment by moment, that peace of God which passes all understanding,

A. Spiritual Instruction

which does continually keep his heart and mind in the knowledge and love of God [Phil. 4:7]. And, instead of being overwhelmed by the power of temptation, he is enabled to quench all the fiery darts of the wicked one [see also Eph. 6:16], and to resist manfully his every attack under the most trying dispensations, whether from the world, the flesh, or the devil.

Is a person sanctified by faith without works? Justification being a free gift and wrought in the soul by the operation of the Spirit of God, so also is sanctification begun, carried on, and perfected by the same Spirit.[28]

But how may a believer know when he is sanctified? By the change which he finds effected in him, his entire re-creation in the divine image and full renewal in righteousness and true holiness, in his liberty from sin, his heart being cleansed from all unrighteousness [see also 1 John 1:9]. Filled with divine love, his desires and affections are holy, inasmuch as they spring, not from himself, but from the Spirit of Christ dwelling in him. The body of sin being destroyed [see also Rom. 6:6], the spirit of life, liberty, and love possess his soul. Not that one thus saved is beyond the reach of temptation or can be so long as he sojourns in a tabernacle of clay. But while he dwells in God, and God in him, that wicked one touches him not [see also 1 John 5:18]. The tempter may violently assault from without, but he never can prevail against the believer so long as he keeps himself, because all is peace within. The whole heart being given to God, Jesus reigns alone, and every power and faculty of the soul are brought into subjection to the obedience of Christ. Hence there is no inward war or tumult, but peace flows as a river and righ-teousness as the waves of the sea [see also Isa. 48:18].

As all sin emanates in pride and self-will, so real holiness takes its rise in humility and self-abasement. When a soul is truly humbled and brought to see its own ignorance and utter inability to do anything of itself that is good or acceptable to a holy God, it becomes willing to be taught the lessons of his grace and gives itself up simply to the teachings of his Holy Spirit, and is thereby led into all truth [see also John 16:13]. But if the soul is not truly humbled and divested of its own wisdom, simplified, and brought low before God, it will seek out many ways and means to overturn and invalidate some of the plainest and most express truths in the word of God and raise many objections against particular doctrines and parts of the analogy of faith.[29] And because it cannot comprehend by natural reason how such and such things can be, it will wrest Scripture, if not to its own destruction, yet to the great injury and prevention of its own spiritual progress. Whereas a simple, humble mind, ever aspiring after the best things, seeks more to sink into the will of God than to rise into esteem with the men of the world. For his delight is in the Lord alone, and his favor the joy of his heart.

Until the love of God becomes the ruling principle of the soul, no work is acceptable unto him. For whatsoever is not of faith working by love [see also Gal. 5:6] has in it of the nature of sin, not flowing from a pure principle within. But saving faith purifies the heart, converts the soul, sanctifies the affections, and enlarges the desires towards God and man so that, if it were possible, it would embrace the whole world and bring every soul to taste and enjoy the sweetness of that love of which he so freely partakes. O that I may no longer rest satisfied without a full salvation, but seek to be saved even to the uttermost, that I may be filled with all the fulness of God [see also Eph. 3:19].

SOURCE:

Beaumont, *Memoirs of Mary Tatham*, 75-81.

Martha, Martha, thou art careful and troubled about many things; but one thing is needful. *Luke X.41.*

Martha was very careful to entertain Christ and his followers who had called at her house. Perhaps she was making great provision for their entertainment, her intention being pure and her love without dissimulation, but her apprehensions of Christ and her views of his character and offices and of the end of his mission were incorrect and an obstacle in the way of her faith and real holiness. Had she understood the divine character of her guest, she would, with Mary, have been more solicitous to be served by him than in encumbering herself with so many things to recreate and please her heavenly visitor.

A. Spiritual Instruction

It is not improbable that our Lord had brought a large company of his disciples with him to Martha's house, so that the number and unexpected arrival of so many visitors had thrown her mind into some degree of perplexity how to administer to their respective wants so promptly as she apprehended they stood in need of, without more assistance. Her love to Jesus and his followers cannot be doubted and her affection toward his disciples was not less than Mary's. Her desire to serve them with all her power and to make suitable provision for their wants, by paying them every possible attention, is fully manifested. It appears that Mary, in her anxiety to hear the words of Christ had left Martha with the whole weight of things upon her hands to serve alone. This led her to refer her complaint to Christ who was more pleased with Mary's attention to his word than with Martha's great assiduity to make suitable provision for their refreshment. Her solicitude to accomplish the business she had in hand in a proper manner encumbered her mind and agitated her spirits. The burden of everything rested upon her at the very time when she needed more than ordinary assistance, and when she desired the company of Christ as much as Mary did. But this she could not have because she was left to serve alone, Mary being too deeply engaged to attend to secular affairs. Martha's patience at last began to fail, and her tongue complained of Christ's disregard to her perplexity and embarrassment and of his inconsideration in keeping up Mary's attention to his discourse, at a time when she could so ill be spared.

Mary was so taken up with her divine teacher that she entirely lost sight of her sister's encumbrance and the situation wherein she was placed, and was more desirous to be fed with living bread by him than to administer unto him. Her happy spirit was drawing in the vital stream of heavenly life from her living Head, and while she partook of his bounty she was taken off from every other thing and neither remembered her sister's anxious situation nor the common calls of nature in any of her guests. Poor Martha! had you rightly known him whom you were so careful to entertain, you would with Mary have desired to be first entertained by him and would have chosen your sister's part.

Some persons, like Martha, are anxious always to do the thing that is right and would not be negligent in any duty or in any good work. But, at the same time, they are so solicitous to have everything go on in their own order that they would not suffer one thing to be neglected or out of its place. When circumstances cross each other and they are thwarted in their designs or retarded in their work, they become fretful and impatient and are full of complaints and murmurings. Like Martha, they are ready to charge God and man foolishly. Christ saw the spirit by which this good woman was actuated under the circumstances in which she was placed and with meekness reproves her impatient and murmuring spirit. He points out to her the need she had of learning of him to be meek and lowly in heart, that she might find rest unto her soul. Mary is justified by Christ for her attention to his ministry and is detained by him from entering into the cumber and hurry of worldly employments, which ought to be followed only with moderation and composure of mind.

Numbers, like Martha, are more anxious to serve the Lord Jesus than to be served by him. Like her they lose sight of the divinity in the humanity of the Son of God. They, indeed, love the Savior and are ready to support his interests and minister to his followers, but their dependance is more upon their own efforts and exertions than on the power of Christ. They are apt to lose sight of the need they have of partaking first of his fulness before they can give and work themselves. Martha's hospitality and her desire to serve Christ are highly commendable, as also is her attention to the wants of his disciples. Her diligence in making provision for them discovers a character of sterling worth. But her anxiety and fretfulness under trial show the ignorance and weakness of human nature still predominating and bringing the nobler powers of the soul into captivity.

SOURCE:

Beaumont, *Memoirs of Mary Tatham*, 276-78.

A. SPIRITUAL INSTRUCTION

5. MARY LYTH'S CODE OF LIFE

Editor's Introduction

When Mary Burdsall married a young farmer near York at Holy Trinity Church and recorded the events of the day in her journal—"I gave my hand to John Lyth at Hymen's altar. I endeavoured to do it by faith, as well as I could."—one could hardly imagine from her words that the occasion was radiantly joyful. Her journal, in fact, is written in a stiff and formal style that hardly ever betrays the vitality and winsome personality that others admired in her. The reader only catches glimpses of her more vivacious side, such as that reflected in the outburst of a thirteen-year-old girl: "O that I had a voice that would reach to all the world, I would tell them how happy I am."[30] Whether an idealized memory or not, the same woman, reflecting back on her childhood, could write:

> The Spirit of God strove with me when but a little child. One time, I remember, while repeating my prayers to my aunt, the grace of God shone so sweetly upon me, I was melted down into tenderness before the Lord; and it seemed as if the glory of the Lord shone round about me, while I repeated the well-known hymn: "Glory to Thee, my God, this night."[31]

The following personal memorandum, articulating a basic code of life, and first published by her son in his biographical study, reflects the more direct and typical, no-nonsense aspect of Mary's spirituality. These are very simple regulations, reminiscent of John Wesley's own lists of resolutions and rules, devised for both personal use and for use by the Societies.[32] Without question, Mary emphasized those actions that assist in moving toward the goal of godliness in life. Simplicity and resolution were the dominant characteristics of her life, reflected even in the simplicity and neatness of her dress, modeled after the style of the Quakers.

* * * *

1. Let me rise early.[33]
2. Never let me trifle with a book with which I have no present concern. In applying myself to any book, let me endeavor to recollect what I may learn by it, and then beg suitable assistance from God.
3. Never let me lose one minute of time, nor incur any unnecessary expense, that I may have the more to spend for God. When I am abroad let me be desirous of doing good. Let me have in readiness some subject of contemplation and endeavor to improve my time as I go along.
4. Let me endeavor to render myself agreeable and useful to all around me by a tender, compassionate, friendly behavior, avoiding all trifling and impertinent stories, remembering that impudence is sin.
5. Never let me not delay anything, unless I can prove that another time will be more fit than the present, or that some more importune duty requires my immediate attention.
6. O may I never enter into any long schemes about future events, but in general refer myself to God's care.
7. O that I may be delivered from the least inclination to judge my neighbors, and that henceforth I may find fault with none so much as myself.

SOURCE:

John Lyth, *The Blessedness of Religion in Earnest: A Memorial of Mrs. Mary Lyth* (London: The Book Society, 1861), 30-31.

A. Spiritual Instruction

6. Mary Hanson's Meditations

Editor's Introduction

Little is known about Mary Hanson (1786–1812) beyond the biographical details provided by the eminent Methodist biblical scholar, Adam Clarke, who exerted a significant influence upon her life. In the year 1806, at twenty years of age, she began to compose "religious meditations." The eldest daughter of John Hanson, esq., Mary was born in London on September 16, 1786, but was not introduced in a serious way to Methodists until 1809, the same year that, under the Methodists' influence, she began to maintain a regular spiritual diary. Inspired by the preaching of Thomas Coke and Adam Clarke, she became a regular member of the Methodist Society in 1810. Through these new connections she was introduced to John Cooper, whom she married on August 27, 1811. On June 16, 1812, she gave birth to a son but died in less than a week due to complications related to the delivery.

The following selections from her personal meditations reflect a depth of spirituality beyond her years. Mary provided titles for each of her meditations, the themes of which resonate in significant ways with the Methodist tradition she was soon to embrace. Mary articulates a vision of the Christian life that is transformational at its core. It is integral in the sense of emphasizing both heart and mind, the experiential and contemplative. The portrait of redeemed humanity that she paints is an image of nobility, joy, dignity, and value. True happiness or blessedness is the ultimate goal toward which the child of God is compelled to move, not out of self-interest but for the glory of God.

* * * *

On Happiness, July 20th, 1806

Happiness is the universal object of pursuit.[34] But how various are the ways which men propose to themselves for its attainment! When the desired object is possessed, alas! it also has inscribed upon it "vanity and vexation of spirit" [Eccl. 1:14]. The hope still remains that the next attempt will prove more successful. But, alas!

it is not in the power of finite creatures to impart it. God in his wisdom has made us dependent on himself for happiness. He has given us a free will to choose this world for our portion, or himself from whom flow pleasures for evermore. Sin has so bewildered, so darkened the faculties of our souls, that everything beyond what is finite is enveloped in a mist. Revelation, the best gift of God to man, unfolds the glories of an invisible world. The solitude I have so long enjoyed, and yet alas! so little improved, has often led me to retire into my own mind and converse with my heart. I have discovered a jewel, little prized because little known. This treasure, bestowed on all God's creatures, when improved may become a source of consolation and felicity that will make them superior to the contempt of men and the agitations of disquietude. I feel convinced that to improve my intellectual powers is to have in store a constant spring of delights. It may prevent me from running into those snares which are held out as baits to the vacant, listless mind. But let me not forget that inward monitor, that soul bestowed upon me, that it is immortal and will return to God who gave it, and that it is made capable of happiness or misery beyond this visible state. The thread of life, so very slender, so soon broken, is in the hand of God. O! Searcher of hearts, cold and senseless, as I am to spiritual things, let not a consideration at once so awful and impressive pass over my mind without its due weight.

On Patience and Meekness, August 10th, 1806

The cultivation of patience and meekness, both personally and relatively, is of the utmost social importance. If meekness in the sight of God is of great price, how must the possession and exercise of that spirit promote the peace of the possessor and diffuse the charms of kindness around.... I desire to live and act as in the sight of God, of him who gave an example of what his followers should be. Professors of religion, while they study to preserve outward decency and circumspection of deportment, too often stop there. This is a stumbling block to many. Is this all Christianity has effected? Was it for this only the great sacrifice was made? Blush, Christian! and be not called by that holy name while you indulge dispositions and propensities which are in direct opposition to the lovely spirit of the gospel. It breathes love and benevolence. The old nature of passion, revenge, malice, and envy, is to pass away,

A. SPIRITUAL INSTRUCTION

and the new nature of meekness, gentleness, and easiness to be entreated to take its place. It requires both holiness of heart and life. Hence the serenity of the Christian is secured and he is made capable of tasting that peace which passes all understanding [see also Phil. 4:7].

On Prayer, Fast Day, February 17th, 1808

Prayer, by which only that mysterious communication between the Creator and his creatures can be maintained; prayer, which has sometimes introduced a very heaven into the soul; the most exalted and blissful employment of finite creatures; that which angels behold with delight and devils tremble to view. Alas! alas! how often has a stupid indifference been substituted for this. I have entered my closet, have shut the door, and strangely forgotten that the eyes of the Lord see upon a stupid senseless creature. Little did the humble posture of my body then accord with a rebellious stubborn heart, alive to every thing but its eternal interests!

Prayer, formally, carelessly performed. O my God! I confess with shame and confusion of face that from this I trace pride, self-sufficiency, worldly-mindedness, and an indifference to those ordinances which once filled my soul with calm delight.

Sometimes, indeed, when I have asked my own heart on entering upon my devotions, "What is it you need? God knows and beholds you." Then have I been enabled to pour out my soul in confessing my sins and have found lively impressions of the presence of God and have arisen determined to be more diligent in obtaining an acquaintance with my own heart. But a few days have shown me the treachery of my intentions, and the impossibility, without the assistance of God's Spirit, of maintaining anything like the life and power of religion within me. The grace of God, like a spark in the ocean, can only be kept alive by a miracle.

Trust in the Lord, Sunday, February 21st, 1808

Blessed is the man that trusts in the Lord [see also Jer. 17:7], that makes the Lord his portion, who, with eyes filled with tears of gratitude can say, "The Lord is my Shepherd" [Psa. 23:1]. Blessings beyond mortal calculation are included in this personal appropriation.

Thus to regard that God of whose approach thunder and lightning were the symbols when about to dispense his laws to his creatures, to call him by that endearing epithet—what a mysterious privilege! My soul, diligently seek to be included in the number of that blessed flock. He who said, "Let there be light, and there was light" [Gen. 1:3], who, by an act of his will, created man and, but for infinite love, might have destroyed him when he broke the only command imposed on him. He who takes up the isles as a very little thing, who counts the nations as a drop of a bucket [see also Isa. 40:15]—even this God proposes himself for your portion, O my soul!

Lost in the contemplation of your attributes, teach me, O Lord, to comprehend how it is, so intimate a relation as a father and child can subsist between you, who are infinitely great, and a rebellious lost child of Adam? It is enough. That holy word inscribed by the pen of mercy exhibits it to my understanding. I would wonder and adore!

On Religion, January 22nd, 1809

Religion! What does it effect unless the heart be transformed. Meekness should take place of anger. Kindness of revenge. Love of hatred. To be decided in this momentous contest, to wage a constant warfare with the natural corruptions of the heart—this habitual decision alone can give that peace which the gospel proclaims to be the portion of the upright. The heart must be devoted to God. The breathing of the soul must be after him. Conformity to him must be the predominant principle of the soul.

On the Works of God, April 30th, 1809

How delightful is the contemplation of the works of God! My enraptured eye runs over the productions of the earth with a curiosity and interest that never leave me. The passing clouds, the opening flowers, the sweet river, whose constant changes give a variety to the scenes. How successively do these steal on my imagination, and often how inexpressible is my gratitude for receiving from the hands of God so many outward blessings, and a mind capable of drawing the truest delight to view will fade and die. Nature and all her loveliness is but transitory in her duration. Time with me has a destined period. But time is a loan.... Revelation takes me up where reason leaves me.[35] It has drawn aside the veil and made manifest a mode of access whereby the deity receives into the arms of his love the creature who had revolted from his government, but who returns with penitential tears and asks for mercy through the atoning sacrifice.

Oh! my soul, press forward with more alacrity in the heavenly road. Much is to be done. A corrupt heart must be renewed. The motives of your conduct must be traced to the love of God. Every attainment in knowledge must be consecrated to God, must be subservient to the end of your being. And humility must mark every part of this deportment. How much is to be done?

On Experimental Religion, **February 20th, 1810**

O for simplicity of heart to receive the kingdom of God as a little child [see also Mark 10:15]! Away with caviling and skeptical reasoning. When did these ever produce joy and peace in believing [Rom. 15:13]? Experimental religion is not a subject which a natural man can reason upon. It is foolishness to him. It can only be spiritually discerned. O may the religion I profess be a well of water springing up within me [see also John 4:14]! A holy principle producing joy and peace. A principle which shall make me soar above the world, feel the divine origin of my soul, and be constantly tending towards the source of all true felicity.

SOURCE:

Adam Clarke, *Memoirs of the Late Eminent Mrs. Mary Cooper, of London*, New Edition (Halifax: William Nicholson and Sons, [1910s]), 16-18, 20-25, 33-36, 42.

B. Hymns and Sacred Poems

1. HYMN OF MARY STOKES

Editor's Introduction

Mary Stokes (1750–1823) was a trusted leader within the earliest Methodist Society in Bristol, one of the greatest and most influential women preachers of the eighteenth century, and later a convert to the Society of Friends after her marriage to the Quaker Robert Dudley of Clonmel, Ireland. Zechariah Taft published but two of her poetic works in his anthology *Holy Women*. Her poem is a testimony to the mercy of God, a hymn of praise concerning the triumph of grace in the life of the redeemed.

* * * *

A Hymn, Written in the Twenty-first Year of Her Age

How shall I tune a trembling lay,
    How touch the soften'd string?
Fain would I heav'nly love display—
    The god of mercy sing.

I would,—but Oh! how faint each power,
    How far too high the theme;
Come, blessed spirit, aid, restore,
    And raise the languid flame!

What wonderous grace! what boundless love!
    What soft compassion this,
That calls my rebel heart to prove
    A never fading bliss!

Long have I sought the pleasing sound,
    But sought, alas! in vain,

B. Hymns and Sacred Poems

Explor'd in pleasure's mazy ground,
        In nature's desert plain.

What grace that I am not consum'd,
        Not hurl'd to endless night;
Mercy has all her pow'r assum'd,
        And yields a cheering light.

'Tis mercy bids me seek the Lord;
        'Tis mercy bids me fly;
'Tis mercy speaks the balmy word,
        "Repent, thy God is nigh."

'Tis mercy fills my trembling heart,
        With agonizing pain,
With keen distress and poignant smart,
        Nor heave these sighs in vain.

The tears that now in torrents flow,
        This mercy will repress;
Remove the load, a pardon show,
        And speak a healing peace.

Then let me humbly wait the hour,
        The hour of sweet release;
Incessant, saving grace implore,
        Incessant, pant for peace.

At thy blest feet my Lord and King,
        Resigned let me lie.
Till the glad peals of triumph sing,
        And faith behold thee nigh.

Then shall the stammerer's tongue proclaim
        The goodness of the Lord;
In grateful strains rehearse his flame,
        In hymns his love record.

> I'll warble to each list'ning ear,
> The feeble song of praise;
> My sweet employ while trav'ling here,
> To lisp redeeming grace!

SOURCE:

Taft, *Holy Women*, 2:152-53.

B. Hymns and Sacred Poems

2. Religious Verse of Miss T—

Editor's Introduction

The poetical writings of the next three women are all drawn from early issues of the *Arminian Magazine*, between 1779 and 1784. In her first hymn, Miss T., whose identity remains elusive, sings of the restoration of perfect love in the life of the believer. Employing one of the favorite meters of Charles Wesley (8.8.8.8.88),[36] her poem is a profound lyrical expression of the Wesleyan doctrine of Christian perfection with all of its attendant features: the centrality of grace, the goal of restoration, and the urgency of the quest. She employs a "romance meter" (88.6.88.6), Charles Wesley's next most prolific form, for her "Hymn to Christ," a hymn that loses in sturdiness what it gains in speed.

* * * *

The Wish

Nor let a wish for earth remain,
    Nor let me grovel here below,
When heav'nly honors I may gain,
    When joys immortal I may know;
When freed from woe, and endless pain,

My soul in heav'n with Christ may reign!
Nor earth, nor sense, nor sin, shall find
    A resting-place within my soul;
All, all for Jesus is resign'd:
    O! come, my Lord, possess me whole!
My soul, my body's pow'rs possess,
And sanctify me through thy grace!

I long for this, for this I pray,
    To know that perfect love of thine,
When sin shall all be done away,
    When in thine image I shall shine,

When I shall feel continual peace,
And all the fruits of righteousness!

Ah! come, and move in me, and live,
    And triumph o'er my willing breast;
I would thy fulness now receive;
    I would partake thy people's rest;
Thine utmost goodness fain would prove,
And antedate the joys above.

Jesus, my Savior, now fulfil
    Thy great design, thy grand decrees;
In me be done thy righteous will,
    Accomplish'd all thy promises;
Let grace renew and cleanse my heart;
The mind which was in thee impart.

Not only, Lord, my sins forgive,
    But spread the sanctifying leav'n;
O! make me meet with God to live,
    With all the perfect saints in heav'n;
With them, before thy glorious throne
May I adore, and cast my crown!

Then will I praise thine holy name,
    And bless thee for thy wond'rous grace;
Thy matchless glories then proclaim;
    Thy wisdom, pow'r, and faithfulness;
I'll emulate the hosts above,
And sing the riches of thy love.

From my own works NOW bid me cease,
    And own the strength of thy right-hand;
Now perfect me in holiness,
    Let all submit to love's command;
Subject me to thy wise control;
New model, thou, my ransom'd soul.

B. Hymns and Sacred Poems

Father, my wand'ring footsteps guide,
      Make me with Christ in spirit one,
And call thy favorite to thy side,
      And seat me on thy glorious throne,
And let me there securely dwell,
Beyond the reach of death and hell.

To God, who reigns enthron'd on high,
      The Father of eternal days,
To Christ, th'incarnate Majesty,
      And to the Spirit of his grace,
Be honor, praise, and glory giv'n,
By sons of earth, and hosts of heav'n.

SOURCE:

AM 2 (1779): 268-70.

Hymn to Christ

Before Jehovah's awful throne
My spirit bow: his Godhead own;
      Adore him for his grace:
Let praise as fragrant incense rise,
Let air, and ocean, earth and skies,
      Resound his lofty praise!

Worship with reverence at his feet,
And still thy grateful thanks repeat,
      My much-indebted soul:
Sun, moon, and stars his love display,
As swift ye tread the lucid way,
      And through the ether roll.

Revolving seasons still declare,
The God whose wisdom guide the year,
      Who winter gives and spring:

Summer, thy rich profusion pour;
And autumn, with thy golden store,
    Your annual tribute bring.

Flocks, herds, and every meaner thing
Extol the universal King,
    The God who rules the whole:
Let all beneath, above, combine,
Let seraphim, and cherubs join;
    With every human soul.

Let all exalt the Savior's name;
And sing the honors of the Lamb,
    Whose presence fills all space:
Jehovah! Jove! divinely good,
"Thou great First-Cause, least understood!"
    The source of love and grace.

Fall prostrate, but in wonder fall!
Our God resigns his breath for all,
    For all our Jesus dies!
I sink beneath thy powerful hand:
No more thy weight of love withstand,
    Thou bleeding sacrifice.

Oh! make me as the passive clay,
While humbled at thy feet I pray,
    Renew, and change my heart:
Form all my mind averse from sin,
In judgment reign, dear Lord within,
    And bid it all depart.

Then shall my soul record thy love,
The church below, the church above
    Unitedly shall sing.
The blood-redeemed shall raise their voice,
And saints and angels shall rejoice,
    To Thee the eternal King.

SOURCE:

AM 3 (1780): 285-87.

3. Lament of Phillis Wheatley

Editor's Introduction

Phillis Wheatley is noteworthy in being a poet of African descent. In 1781, John Wesley published her poetic lament on an experience all too common to the age, the death of a young child. Her rhymed couplets contrast the dark and broken nature of life in this world with the blessing and light of the heavenly realm. In an effort to comfort those who mourn she gives voice to the departed child, Nancy, who extols the wonder of the angelic choir.

* * * *

On the Death of a Child, Five Years of Age

From dark abodes, to fair ethereal light,
The enraptured innocent has winged her flight;
On the kind bosom of eternal love
She finds unknown beatitudes above.
This know, ye parents, nor her loss deplore,
She feels the iron hand of pain no more;
The dispensations of unerring grace,
Should turn your sorrows into grateful praise;
Let then no tears for her henceforward flow,
No more distressed in our dark vale below.

Her morning sun, which rose divinely bright,
Was quickly mantled with the gloom of night;
But hear in heaven's blest bowers your Nancy fair,
And learn to imitate her language there.

"Thou, Lord, whom I behold with glory crowned,
By what sweet name, and in what tuneful sound
Wilt thou be praised? Seraphic powers are faint
Infinite Love and Majesty to paint.
To thee let all their grateful voices raise,
And Saints and Angels join their songs of praise."

SOURCE:

AM 4 (1781): 676.[37]

4. Lament of Portia Young

Editor's Introduction

In conventional iambic pentameter, Portia Young speculates about the tragic circumstances and despair that led a young woman to take her own life. What is particularly impressive about her poetry is the compassion and empathetic spirit of this early Methodist woman. She is clearly a deeply caring Christian who is moved by the loss of one fallen sister and expresses her grief in such a way as to inspire others to caring service and love. Her poetry speaks not only of unfulfilled dreams and broken hearts—and alludes to the oppression and abuse of the innocent—but also of the worth and value of every human creature.

* * * *

On a Young Woman, found dead in St. George's Fields

Unhappy daughter of distress and woe,
    Whate'er thy sorrows, and whoe'er thou art;
For thee the tear of sympathy shall flow,
    Warm from the purest fountain of the heart!

Perhaps though now neglected and unknown,
    A parent once beheld thee with delight;
The darling of a Father's heart alone,
    Or the loved idol of a Mother's sight!

For thee, perhaps, they toiled, they watched, they prayed:
    O'er thy sweet innocence with rapture hung;
And w ell they thought their tenderest care repaid
    To hear the artless music of thy tongue.

When dawning Reason shed her ray benign,
    And all thy excellence became revealed;
Charmed did they see thy opening beauties shine,
    And heard thy praise with transport, ill concealed.

For who alas! can tell thy secret worth,
  What soft angelic virtues might appear;
The bosom laid defenseless on the earth,
  Might once be grateful, generous, and sincere.

The lips that knew no friend to bid farewell,
  Might once the noblest sentiments express:
The stretched head that unsupported fell,
  Might once be turned to stories of distress.

Some bare deceiver, practiced to betray,
  Might win thy easy faith, destroy thy fame;
Then cast thee like a loathsome weed away,
  The sport of fortune and the child of shame!

Poor wanderer! perhaps thou couldest not find
  One liberal hand the slender gift to spare,
Insatiate Avarice the soul confined,
  And timid Prudence disbelieved thy prayer.

Then from the world despairing, and forlorn,
  Careless of life, and hopeless of relief;
Thy agonizing heart retired to mourn,
  And breathe its last in unmolested grief.

Whate'er thy lot has been, unhappy shade,
  From sin, at length, and sorrow, thou art free;
Thy debt to Virtue,—it is amply paid,
  And weeping Pity pays her debt to thee.

SOURCE:

AM 7 (1784): 283-84.

5. Poems of Agnes Bulmer

Editor's Introduction

Agnes Bulmer (1775–1836), introduced in part 1 of this collection, was a poet with few equals in her day. The first two selections below reflect the esteem of a teenage girl for the founders of the movement of which she was so central a part. Her first noteworthy poem in print is the elegy "On the Death of the Rev. Charles Wesley," which the older brother published in his *Arminian Magazine*; the second poem is for John, dated February 6, 1790. The elderly Wesley endorsed the original with the inscription, "Agnes Collinson, aged 14."[38] Agnes wrote the next hymn during the fatal illness of her husband, Joseph Bulmer, who died in 1822. Her prayer is for her husband to experience a joy unknown, a sight of faith, a hallowing fear that is the gift to all who entrust their lives to Christ.

It is noteworthy that much of her poetry was inspired by experiences with death, hardly surprising given the tenor of the age and the lasting influence of Edward Young's *Night Thoughts* on her poetic ambiance and style. Agnes turned attention to her poetic *magnum opus*, *Messiah's Kingdom*, following the death of her mother in 1825. James Montgomery, the great hymn-writer and critic, described this work as:

> The longest poem by a lady in any language that I am acquainted with. It seems to embrace the sum of the lessons which an immortal spirit has learned of itself, of its fellow-creatures, and of God, on its progress to glory and felicity, through a world fallen and miserable. The versification is distinguished by remarkable freedom and fluency. It is a volume from which hundreds of happy quotations might be made.[39]

The first excerpt below from *Messiah's Kingdom* focuses on the work of the Spirit and features her fine paraphrase of Jesus' words in John 3:8: "The wind blows where it chooses, and you hear the sound of it, but you do not know where it comes from or where it goes. So it is with everyone who is born of the Spirit." This poem is remarkable for the variations of its grandeur and beauty; its texture

B. HYMNS AND SACRED POEMS

is rich and harmonious. The selection on the Holy Scriptures reveals a deep reverence for the Word of God.

Two hymns follow. Agnes's hymn on the rainbow covenant is written in a more unusual but galloping six sevens (7.7.7.7.77), with a rhyme scheme like that of Charles Wesley's favorite six eights (ABABCC) metre, but trochaic in form. The most noteworthy aspect of this hymn is the way in which the poet connects the ancient covenant with Noah to that new covenant between God and humanity secured through the sacrifice of the cross. The second hymn selection she wrote for the laying of the foundation stone of Oxford Road Wesleyan Chapel in Manchester, otherwise known as Ancoats' Chapel. This hymn illustrates her ability to experiment with seldom-used meters, this one in particular hardly to be found in any hymnal today. Written in a rather robust 7.6.7.6.7.8.7.6 and cross-rhymed throughout with an alternating trochaic-iambic sequence, the hymn is majestic and awesome. But it also reminds the singer that the true temple of God is the human heart.

The death of Hester Ann Rogers in October 1794 provided the impetus for Bulmer's lengthy elegy, *Thoughts on a Future State*, a substantial portion of which is presented here. Her poem is essentially a lyrical exploration of Paul's allusion to the prophet Isaiah in 1 Corinthians 2:9: " 'What no eye has seen, nor ear heard, nor the human heart conceived, what God has prepared for those who love him'—these things God has revealed to us through the Spirit." She contrasts the world to come with that which is known in this life. All that is partial here is brought into complete fruition in the life to come. She describes the reunion of Hester and her son who died in infancy, as well as the fulfilment of God's promises in the fuller revelation of God's love. She even offers interesting speculation about other worlds and galaxies unknown—of God's creatures throughout the universe all brought into essential harmony as they contemplate the goodness and holiness of God.

* * * *

On the Death of Charles Wesley

Ah happy man! thy griefs are passed away;
    Thy struggling soul to heaven has took its flight:

To bliss eternal winged its wondrous way,
> And safely lodged in realms of pure delight.

Summoned by God to join the heavenly band,
> And dwell with Him in everlasting rest,

Thou now art happy in Immanuel's land,
> Where grief and pain shall never more molest.

But ah! how many will thy loss deplore?
> Unmindful that 'tis thy eternal gain;

They mourn their Friend so quickly gone before,
> Forgetting he is gone from toil and pain:

Forgetting he is gone to joys on high,
> And join the angelic hosts in heavenly lays

Far, far above yon bright ethereal sky
> To aid the concert of eternal praise.

And now for every pang he felt below,
> His soul receives a full, and sure reward;

While heavenly joys in streams of glory flow,
> And Jesus crowns him with divine regard.

Then why should Death appear so great a foe?
> Why with such terror is the subject fraught?

Since he relieves the just from every woe,
> And brings them bliss, beyond the reach of thought!

SOURCE:

"Verses on the Death of the Rev. Charles Wesley," *AM* 11 (1788): 557.

A Poem for the Rev. Mr. John Wesley

Dear Honored Sir, your kind regards I claim,
> While I in artless strains my thanks rehearse,

Tho' many are the errors, spare to blame
    The faulty writer of this humble verse.

For properly my thanks for to express,
    Might well require a far more able pen,
In words well formed, adapted to address,
    So great a person and so good a man.

Your sage advice, so needful unto youth,
    I'll ever strive with ardour to pursue,
Ever look forward to the ways of truth,
    And with fresh vigor still the chase renew.

The pardon, Honored Sir, all faults in this,
    Since to do well the youthful writer strove,
And let the motive plead for what's amiss,
    And show my duty, reverence, and love.

SOURCE:

Transcription by B. F. Fielding. Wesley Historical Society Library Collection. Wesley and Methodist Studies Centre, Westminster Institute, Oxford Brookes University, Oxford.

[In Sickness]

High on Thy heavenly seat,
    Jesus, to Thee I pray!
O see the sinner at Thy feet,
    Nor turn Thine ear away.
Embolden'd by Thy word,
    By want and weakness pressed,
To Thy Divine compassions, Lord,
    I pour my full request.

I ask thy joy unknown
    That from Thy presence springs

When, prostrate at Thy awful throne,
    Thy mercy's shadowing sings
Temper the light which breaks
    Resplendent from Thine eye;
When soft the whisp'ring Spirit speaks,
    "The Lord is passing by!"

I ask that sight of faith
    To humblest mourners given,
That view of Thy mysterious death,
    Thy pleading pow'r in heaven,
Which calms the troubled breast
    When guilty fears invade,
And bids the trembling spirit rest
    In Thy perpetual aid.

I ask that hallowing fear,
    That heaven of humble love,
Which joins a saint in worship here
    To saints redeem'd above,
E'en now the veil withdrawn,
    In fellowship with Thee,
Oh, might the day of glory dawn
    The twilight shadows flee!

On me, Thy suppliant child,
    Be all Thy form impressed,
Thy nature pure, Thy spirit mild;
    That, meet for heavenly rest,
I may that call attend
    Which shall my soul remove,
And from Thy footstool here ascend
    To share Thy throne above.

SOURCE:

S. W. Christophers, *The Poets of Methodism* (London: Hodder and Stoughton, 1877), 269.

B. Hymns and Sacred Poems

Excerpts from *Messiah's Kingdom*

As through mid-air the sweeping current blows,
Or, gently gliding, sinks to soft repose,
All uncontrol'd by man, who knows not where
Fierce hyperborean storms their shafts prepare,
Or whence, descending mild, on balmy wing,
Soft zephyr comes to fan the flowers of spring;
So works, by human counsels undefined,
The teaching Spirit on the pliant mind;
Nor to the world His secret course declares,
But unperceived His instrument prepares;
Then in the finish'd work unfolds His skill,
And bends His agent to His perfect will.

Hail, Holy Record of supernal love!
Thy living lines even seraphs search above,
And saints below with holy wonder trace,
Intent to learn thy mysteries of grace.
Stupendous register of truth sublime,
'Tis thine to chase the darkling mists of time;
To cheer the mariner with friendly light,
Through shelving rocks to guide his course aright:
To show beyond the deep, that peaceful shore,
Where waves subside, and tempests rage no more;
But heaven's unsetting splendors radiant glow,
Nor seasons change, nor night of sorrow know.
Eternal Oracle of Truth, thy voice
Bids misery hope, and holy Faith rejoice;
The wayward step of thoughtless youth restrains;
Soothes hoary age, amidst its cares and pains;
Pours heavenly music on the raptur'd ear,
When Death's dread angel draws in stillness near;
Proclaims beside the grave, that destin'd hour,
When strangely quicken'd by all-conquering power,
Each captive, from its dark recesses brought,
Shall share the victory by Messiah wrought,
Emerge from Hades' deep sepulchral gloom,
And wave his palm of triumph o'er the tomb.

SOURCE:

Christophers, *Poets of Methodism*, 270-72.

[The Rainbow Covenant]

Gloomy cloud, that, low'ring low,
    Shadowest nature's lovely light,
Wide thy deepening darkness throw,
    Catch the sunbeam bursting bright;
Gently on thy humid breast,
Bid its soften'd splendors rest.

Wild the wind, and fierce the flood,
    Foaming, roaring, raved and rush'd;
Thunders roll'd—the voice of God:
    Now the angry storm is hush'd,
Now the eddying whirlwind sleeps,
Ocean seeks its barrier deeps.

Beauteous bow! thy arch sublime,
    Resting on the distant hills,
Leads me back to earliest time;
    Hope my pensive spirit fills,
In thy softest hues I trace
Gentler, lovelier beams of grace.

Lo! the tempest's rage is o'er,
    Flashing fires no longer gleam;
Solemn thunders cease to roar,
    Silvery clouds resplendent stream;
Bright the bursting sun appears,
Ararat its summit rears.

From his floating home released,
    Noah on the mountain stands,
Spreads the sacrificial feast,
    Lifts to Heaven his praying hands,
Listens to the Voice Divine,
Looks on thee, peace-speaking sign.

B. Hymns and Sacred Poems

Hush! the word of promise breaks,
    Not in thunders hoarse and loud;
Lo! the covenant-Savior speaks
    Softly from the symbol'd cloud:
Rise! the storm of wrath is pass'd;
Judgment shall not always last.

So upon the anxious heart,
    Chased with sorrow's wild alarm,
When the troubled clouds dispart,
    When the rough wind sinks to calm,
Breaks the light from distant spheres,
Falling on a mist of tears.

Sun of Righteousness! from thee
    Soft those lucid rays descend,
Mildest mercy beams on me;
    Whispers every storm shall end,
Now the covenant-sign is given,
Bright appears the bow in heaven.

Resting on th' eternal hills,
    Arching high the emerald throne,
Heaven with hallow'd light it fills,
    Sends its soft effulgence down.
Holy light! I hail thee now,
Circling, mild, Emmanuel's brow.

Yes, that meek, resplendent sign
    Presages a cloudless sky;
Heaven's eternal light shall shine,
    Truth and mercy meet on high,
Righteousness and Peace unite,[40]
Mingling beams divinely bright.

Hush, my sorrow! from a storm,
    Fierce, and terrible, and wild,
Sprang that bow whose splendrous form,
    Radiant, round the Reconciled;

Glory's fountain set in shade,
Earthly lights retired dismay'd.

From the Cross, where darkness shrouds
    Him who suffered there for me,
In the fearful tempest clouds,
    Resting dread on Calvary,
Mercy's beaming sign appears,
See, believe, and dry thy tears!

SOURCE:

Christophers, *Poets of Methodism*, 273-74.

Hymn for the Ancoat's Methodist Chapel

Thou who hast in Sion laid
    The true Foundation-stone,
And with those a covenant made,
    Who build on that alone:
Hear us, Architect divine!
    Great builder of Thy Church below;
Now upon Thy servants shine,
    Who seek Thy praise to show.

Earth is Thine; her thousand hills
    Thy mighty hand sustains;
Heaven Thy awful presence fills,
    O'er all Thy glory reigns:
Yet the place of old prepared
    By regal David's favor'd son,
Thy peculiar blessing shared,
    And stood Thy chosen throne.

We, like Jesse's son, would raise
    A temple to the Lord;
Sound throughout its courts His praise,
    His saving name record;

B. Hymns and Sacred Poems

   Dedicate a house to Him,
       Who, once, in mortal weakness shrined,
   Sorrow'd, suffer'd, to redeem,
       To rescue all mankind.

Father, Son, and Spirit, send
       The consecrating flame;
Now in majesty descend,
       Inscribe the living Name—
That great Name, by which we live,
       Now write on this accepted stone;
Us into Thy hands receive,
       Our temple make Thy throne.

SOURCE:

Christophers, *Poets of Methodism*, 275-76.

Thoughts on a Future State

Oh, had we seen thee when the vale undrew,
And thy free'd spirit from its prison flew!
What floods of glory burst upon thy sight,
What sounds melodious rung the ether bright,
As heav'nly spirits led thee through the sky,
Midst blazing suns, and rolling worlds on high;
While joyful friends throng'd thick the heav'nly way,
And hail'd thee to the bright abodes of day;
Then joining in their songs of triumph high,
The loud hosannas echo'd thro' the sky.
    And now what mighty joys thy pow'rs surprise,
Stretch'd out from mortal to immortal size;
Surrounded, fill'd, absorp'd in Godhead's sea,
And wrapt in visions of the Deity.
Yet not o'erwhelm'd, bewilder'd, or confus'd,
Thy nature so with the divine infus'd,
So fitted to thy state, so pure and high,

That heav'ns profounds suit thy capacity.
    Thy glow-worm knowledge here by faith begun,
In open vision bursts into a sun;
Thro' organs weak no longer dribbled in,
Nor labors purblind Reason scraps to win:
But senses large, congenial with the skies,
'Wake to new life, and into action rise:
By intuition now, all ear, all sight,
Perception all, and piercing as the light,
Thou need'st no medium to convey delight.
With open face thou view'st the Eternal Three
In union join'd, a glorious Trinity!
And at the view increasing raptures flow,
While proving, "'tis eternal life to know."[41]
Thou view'st unveil'd the attributes divine,
Which in unrivall'd beauty round thee shine,
Adoring the transcendent harmony,
Which joins them all in man's redemption free.
    Alike by thee his government's survey'd,
Where'er his all-creative pow'r's display'd,
Allow'd his circling providence to trace
From heav'ns first order to the reptile race:
Here wonders new create sublime delight,
And holy praise breaks forth at ev'ry sight.
    Nor less his grace thy searching mind employs,
Since "Angels o'er a penitent rejoice;"[42]
Here thou discover'st mercies richest store,
And endless cause to wonder and adore.
Now thou well know'st the secret works of grace,
Which first attracted thee to seek his face,
From hence pursuing all the steps divine,
Which thro' thy life in ceaseless mercies shine;
The end discov'ring of each grief and pain,
Why they were sent, and what thy endless gain:
Alike survey'd is ev'ry hidden snare,
Esca'd by thee thro' providential care;
A thousand blessings now to thee are known,

B. Hymns and Sacred Poems

O'er which on earth a pierceless vail was thrown.
What funds of pleasure must such views supply,
And themes for praise throughout eternity!
      Creation's works are open to thy sight,
From lifeless matter to the seraph bright:
What wonders in the world of spirits shine,
Expressive of their origin divine!
Here beings high, and things inanimate,
Which still retain their pure primeval state,
Are understood by thee, whose piercing eye
Can into beings' inmost essence pry:
And if revisiting this nether sphere
How differently each object must appear!
No longer can the surface bound thy sight,
But nature's secret springs are brought to light,
And God appears diffus'd throughout the whole,
The source of life—creation's living soul.
      Is such thy knowledge of thy glorious Lord?
Then sure thy love in measure must accord;
Possessing now the end thy soul pursu'd,
In near fruition of its perfect good:
No more (as here) frail nature sinks opprest,
When with peculiar revelation blest;
Then words were lost in love's immense abyss,
And silence best express'd th' unutter'd bliss.
(What proof that love is heav'ns commencement here,
Since mortal language sinks beneath its sphere,
Praise aims in vain to set its glories forth,
And only songs celestial gave it birth):
But now at large, uncircumscrib'd and free,
Thy vast affections feed on Deity:
Exstatic love in holy rapture flows,
Increasing ever as thy knowledge grows;
In full enjoyment and immediate sight,
Of him whose beauties are thy sole delight,
Thy praise unwearied, must forever flow,
And pleasures no embarrassment can know;

Renew'd by having his continual smile,
No doubt intruding thy delights to spoil,
But large returns for ever flow to thee,
Of mutual love and sweet complacency.
    And Joy (Love's first-born offspring) live to prove
And celebrate the jubilee above;
Immediate draughts receiving from the throne,
While thy lov'd Saviour makes his joy thy own;
Thou shar'st in all his glorious victories,
Exulting o'er its vanquish'd enemies,
Ascribing endless glories to his name,
And ever crying "Worthy is the Lamb
"Who wash'd our robes and conquer'd all our foes,
"And now on us eternal life bestows:"[43]
And fresh discov'ries of unfathm'd love
Will thro' eternity thy joys improve.
    Are such the glories of thy perfect state?
Then thy employments must alike be great;
(For spirit is to action ever bent
And torpid rest is not its element.)
Art thou engag'd in acts to us unknown
Of solemn worship 'fore th' eternal throne,
Which all thy mighty faculties employ,
And give full scope to wonder, love, and joy?

* * * *

Now fellowship is perfect and complete,
Where thought communes with thought and notions meet,
And swift as light'ning distant souls can reach,
With clear expression far surpassing speech;
Thus fitted for sublime society,
With beings of consummate purity,
Thou hold'st high converse with angelic choirs,
Cherub, and seraph, and with human sires,
With all the glorious hosts around the throne,
Perhaps with beings yet to us unknown,
Gather'd from num'rous worlds remote from ours,

And form'd with various faculties and pow'rs;
While each the victories of grace declare,
And countless acts of providential care:
Then joining in melodious strains of praise,
To mercies center, and the source of grace,
Each happy soul takes in large draughts of joy,
And unconceiv'd delights thy pow'rs employ.
    Say does some spirit (perhaps thy infant son,[44]
For sure by them he's still belov'd and known)
Direct thy flight along th' etherial way
Where suns unnumber'd burn, and comets stray
To some new workmanship of pow'r divine,
Where beings in Adamic glory shine,
And uncurs'd nature all harmonious glows,
And shining fair its Maker's glory shows.
Here wonders rise on wonders to thy view,
In objects fair, immaculate and new;
And seem with thee in concert sweet to join,
In one delightful hymn of praise divine.
    Are such as these thy blest employs on high?
While God is all in all and ever nigh;
For wide extended space is full of him,
Nor ought thy ever-waking sight can dim;
Hence, tho' engag'd at natures utmost bound,
Thy heav'n,—Thy God must still thy soul surround.

Source:

Thoughts on a future State, Occasioned by the Death of Mrs. Hester Ann Rogers (Birmingham: J. Belcher, 1795), 2.37-151, 181-216. The poem is dated May 15, 1795.

6. Poems of Margaret Davidson

Editor's Introduction

Margaret Davidson (fl. c. 1760–80), the first Methodist woman preacher in Ireland, was born into a poor family near Ballybredagh in Killinchy and was blinded by an attack of smallpox at two years of age. She appears to have been introduced to Methodism by the preaching of James Oddie around 1758. Her blindness impeded Margaret's initial efforts to join her new community of faith. Despite a difficult journey of some seven miles, she determined to find her way to the Society meeting in Comber. After two failed attempts to locate the meeting, she eventually found her way. Reverend Hudson welcomed her warmly into the fellowship of the small band of Methodists. On May 1, 1765, she heard John Wesley preach at Newtownards and retained a vivid memory of the experience. "While he was speaking my heart was inflamed with love to God and man; and as I was placed near him, I could just observe the waving of his hand between me and the light. After preaching," she continued, "he took me gently by the hand and said, 'Faint not, go on, and you shall see in glory!' These words left a lasting impression on my mind."[45]

She later moved to Lisburn, where she was held in high esteem because of her ministry of prayer. In the winter of 1769–70, she was instrumental in the great revival that took place in Ballinderry. She caught the attention of Rev. and Mrs. Edward Smyth, who took her under their wing and supported her ministry generously over the years. In fact, Rev. Smyth, an ordained priest of the Church of England, invited her to engage in cottage preaching and launched her public ministry at Dunsford. Her keen intellect, retentive memory, fluency and fervency of speech, and simple witness combined to shape a powerful style of preaching. According to Margaret, her general approach to preaching was "to draw inferences from their own catechism and from the hymns with which they were affected."[46] Her reference to these materials, in particular, reflects the unique nature of her spirituality, holding the Anglican prayer book and the Methodist hymnbook, as it were, in either hand. She received many invitations to preach, and the combination of her blindness and intense emotion, as well as her gender, proved to be novel and effective.

The two hymns presented here demonstrate some of the more interesting aspects of Davidson's spirituality. Her first hymn, in honor of Jesus, contains potent images of intimacy, transformation, and mystical flight. The central theme is love for Jesus and its ability to restore and renew. The meter is extremely unique, opening with a typical long meter verse, but concluding with the galloping 7.4.4.7 refrain. Her hymn on the five senses is truly exceptional as well, but even more owing to the imagery Margaret employs.[47] Her blindness, of course, must have heightened her awareness of and sensitivity to the other senses. Here is a wide-ranging hymn of gratitude for the created order. The poem is almost a lyrical expression of a "practice the presence of God" motif. Both hymns point to the fact that in her vision of the spiritual life, all things point to Jesus, if we have eyes to see and senses to experience the goodness of God.

* * * *

A Hymn, in Honor of Jesus

Jesus, thou odorif'rous name!
The ravish'd Choirs transporting theme!
Thou object, worthy of all love,
In and by whom the Cherubs move,
> Grant propitious smiles, while I,
> > Struck with glory,
> > Fall before thee,
> Holy, Holy, Holy, cry.

My Lord, my sin-atoning God,
Apply thy efficacious blood—
Extirpate now indwelling sin,
And make me glorious all within:
> Change the crimson white as snow—
> > All thy merit
> > Grasps my spirit,
> Only thee resolv'd to know.

Constrain'd by energy divine
To call my Jesus ever mine,
I languish to be all like thee,
Till lost in thy immensity:
    Struggling into thy dear breast,
        Lord, I enter,
        And there center,
    Happy in thy glorious rest.

I wait till wafted up to thee,
O thou mysterious One in Three
By love's encircling arms caress'd,
And with a view of glory bless'd,
    Now I Abba, Father, cry—
        The same blessing,
        Without ceasing,
    Pour on all below the sky.

In each the carnal mind transform—
Suspend the will's impetuous storm;
Let our extinguish'd passions feel
Thy pow'r, and hear thee say, "Be still:"
    Let the nations own thy sway—
        Reign victorious,
        Jesus glorious,
    Let thy subjects all obey.

Each bosom secretly inspire
With hallow'd, sin-consuming fire:
Dissolve each adamantine heart—
Diffuse thy life thro' ev'ry part;
    Till our nature's pow'rs shall own
        Only Jesus
        Truly precious,
    Who has chang'd the heart of stone.

Then hallelujahs shall we raise
Superior to Angelic lays,
Whilst we adore a bleeding God,
Who bought, and cleans'd us with his blood—

B. Hymns and Sacred Poems

>   Cast our crown before his feet,
>   Self-abasing—
>   Jesus praising—
>   Lost in transport, endless, sweet.

SOURCE:

Edward Smyth, ed., *The Extraordinary Life and Christian Experience of Margaret Davidson, as Dictated by Herself* (Dublin: Dugdale, 1782), 160-62.

On the Five Senses

> Happy soul, what canst thou hear
>   Midst all these various sounds?
> Jesus charms my list'ning ear—
>   With joy my heart abounds.
> Thunder, hail, and tempests roar—
>   Trumpet forth Immanuel's name;
> Drawn by Mercy's sweeter lure,
>   I know no other theme.
>
> Happy soul, what canst thou learn
>   From all that feeds the eye?
> Only Jesus I discern—
>   He shines thro' earth and sky:
> Radiant orbs, and beauteous flow'rs,
>   Sparkling diamonds seem to say,
> Glory to our glorious source,
>   Who gives eternal day.
>
> Jesus, thou art all in all—
>   Thy love surpasses wine;
> In hone y, vinegar, and gall,
>   I taste thy love divine;
> Seas'ning all our earthly food,
>   The curse incurr'd by sin departs—
> Ev'ry creature leads to God,
>   Who banquets in our hearts.

Cassia, myrrh, and frankincense,
    Their spicy odors breathe—
Rich perfumes they all dispense—
    But oh! how far beneath
Christ, the lilly of the vale!
    In fragrant fields, and gardens gay
Sharon's rose, well pleas'd, I smell,
    More sweet by far than they.

What delights my feeling sense
    Doth Jesu's goodness prove;
Still I feel his love immense,
    Where'er I rest, or rove:
In downy bed, or balmy air,
    The scorching sun, or cooling tide,
Faith can find its object there—
    My Jesus crucified.

Whate'er I hear, or see, or taste,
    Whate'er I smell, or feel,
Christ's my music, light, and feast,
    My rose, and pillow still:
In him I always live and move—
    Exercise thy senses five,
O my soul, and let thy love,
    Be fervent, and alive.

Omnipresent Lord, my God,
    I can no longer doubt;
Now I feel thy precious blood,
    And loud Hosannahs shout:
Glory, honor, thanks and praise
    Be render'd to the sacred Three!
Praise employ my happy days,
    And bless'd eternity!

SOURCE:

Smyth, *Life of Margaret Davidson*, 162-64.

B. Hymns and Sacred Poems

7. Poem by Mary Barritt

Editor's Introduction

Mary Barritt (1772–1851) was one of the most famous evangelists of the early nineteenth century. Born near Colne in the Lancashire village of Hay, she published an extensive autobiographical account of her work as a revivalist in 1827. As had been the case among her female predecessors, prayer in class meetings, testimony, and exhortation at Society gatherings led to preaching. In spite of her actions arousing immediate hostility, invitations for her to preach were many and came from some of the most prominent ministers of Methodism. Revival erupted wherever she spoke. Her brand of evangelism combined powerful preaching and meticulous aftercare for her converts, exhibiting her strong desire to make genuine disciples for Christ. Eyewitnesses to Mary Barritt's preaching are unequivocal in their praise of her theological depth and balance. In 1802, she married Zechariah Taft and soon became the most published of the women protagonists. Both Mary and Zechariah plunged headlong into a storm center of controversy over the role of women in the expanding Wesleyan Methodist Church.[48]

In her journal, dated June 1, 1798, Mary describes the circumstances that gave rise to the poem that follows: "Hearing, by letter, that my kind friends, Mr. Wade of Sturton Grange, and Mr. Allen of Church Fenton, were disappointed in coming to see me at Sheffield, as they had purposed to do, I sat down and made the following lines." The poem reflects a woman of resolute commitment. Hers is an active spirituality, ever progressing, ever pressing forward toward the mark for the prize of the high calling of God in Christ Jesus (Phil. 3:14).

* * * *

> Let all my heart for ever be,
> Constrain'd, my Lord, to follow thee;
>   Through all my way to death;
> Resolv'd to travel on the road,

That leads through all on earth to
God;
    Till I resign my breath.

I seem denied of earthly friends,
But thou hast wise, and gracious ends
    In all thou dost to me;
Lord I resign myself, and say,
Thy holy law I will obey,
    And give my heart to thee.

For ever keep this heart of mine
Thou Lord of all! Thou love divine!
    From all created things;
That I may know thy heav'nly will,
And all thy work on earth fulfil;
    As Jesus' priests and kings.

Like them I would thy will perform,
And live for thee in ev'ry storm;
    Till this short life be past:
With blessings crown my life, if spar'd,
I'd live on earth, to be prepar'd
    To live with God at last.

SOURCE:

Mary Taft, *Memoirs of the Life of Mrs. Mary Taft; Formerly Miss Barritt*, Part I, 2nd ed. (York: Printed for and sold by the author, 1828), 89.

C. Prayers

1. SUSANNAH DESIGN

Editor's Introduction

All that is known of Susannah Design must be culled from the manuscript journal, parts of which are presented in this volume, from the manuscript narrative account of her religious experience prepared for Charles Wesley at his request, and from the few letters to John Wesley that he preserved. She was a leader in one of the Bristol bands during the formative decade of the 1740s and was acutely concerned about her spiritual well-being. She noted in one of her letters to Wesley, "When I meet my bands I neither want words to speak nor power to pray for them.... Blessed be the Lord, my little girl is very much awakened."[49]

Her manuscript journal, from which the following verbatim prayers are drawn, consists of forty-three pages, dated June 10, 1741 to May 8, 1742. It is simply headed "Mrs. Design's Journal 1742." Much of the narrative is punctuated with brief prayers, such as those below. Scripture permeates these prayers; indeed, many of her prayers are simply reiterations of classic petitions of the faithful from the Psalms to the Gospels. The desire for purity of intention, however, dominates these pithy expressions of the earnest longing of her heart.

* * * *

June 1741

O Lord, where does this yearning and thirsting come from? Are they not from you? Will you give me desires after holiness and not fulfill them? O Lord, you are able to do more for me than I can desire or ask [see also Eph. 3:20]. You have said, be perfect [see also Matt. 5:8]. Be it unto me according to thy word [see also Luke 1:38].

Tuesday, June 23, 1741

O Lord, grant that they and all that seek you may all be made perfect in one, you in us and we in you [see also John 17:21]. O Lord, it is your own prayer, your own desire. Fulfill it in all our souls. Amen.

Friday, June 26, 1741

O Lord, grant that you may be the rock that shall cover me in that great day. In your wounds may I find sanctuary.... Except the kingdom of heaven was first set up in my heart, I could never enter into the kingdom of glory.

Saturday, June 27, 1741

O my dear Savior, hasten that time when I shall taste and see you [see also Psa. 34:8], and in everything whatsoever thing my hand is employed in, my heart may be with you. O that I had a heart after your will.

Sunday, June 28, 1741

O Lord, I am not worthy that the least of your servants should come under my roof [see also Matt. 8:8], and yet you send your faithful ministers unto me. O teach me to praise you for all your mercies and send forth more such laborers into your harvest [see also Matt. 9:38], and make us a faithful people. O make Jerusalem a praise in the earth [see also Isa. 62:7]. O preserve your ministers which you have already called to declare your truth to every creature. Let them turn many souls to righteousness and shine as the stars in the firmament for evermore [see also Dan. 12:3]. Amen.

Friday, July 10, 1741

O my Savior, let me weep much and love much because I have been much forgiven. O let me sit at your feet [see also Luke 10:39] and wait till you shall fully heal my soul which has sinned against you.

Sunday, July 13, 1741

O Lord, whatever I suffer, let me not turn back into Egypt. O may I not receive your grace in vain. Be glorified in my salvation and not in my destruction.

August 18, 1741

O Lord, open my eyes that I may see the footsteps of Jesus and tread in all his righteous ways, turning neither to the right hand or the left [see also Deut. 5:32], but keep in that path which ends in everlasting life. Amen.

Monday, September 8, 1741

O Lord, prosper my handy work. O give me a simple eye to your glory and a heart free from selfishness. Let your spirit direct me to guide the children and do give them hearts to understanding and to receive instruction. O Lord, grant that they may remember their creator in the days of their youth and as they grow in years may they grow in grace and in the knowledge of the Lord [see also 2 Pet. 3:18].

December 6, 1741

O Lord, not unto me, but unto your great name be the glory. I am less than the least of your children and yet you make me a witness of your everlasting truth. O humble my soul and keep it low. Let not the foot of pride come against me. Give me a single eye and a clean heart that I may set you always before me. So shall I not greatly fall.

SOURCE:

Manuscript Journal of Susannah Design, *Meth. Arch.*

2. MRS. LEFEVRE

Editor's Introduction

For an introduction to the life and work of Mrs. Lefevre, see part 2, selection 1. The prayers of Mrs. Lefevre are refined and elegant. Characterized by neither spontaneity nor immediacy, these prayers are highly reflective and meditative acts of worship. While focused to some extent upon the fallen nature of humanity and the possibilities of restoration in Christ, her concern is also for the health of the church as well as her own well-being. She seeks growth in grace and movement toward the fullest realization of God's love in life for both herself and the whole community of faith.

* * * *

Oh gracious and adorable Being! ... look with compassion on a soul which pants for grace and forgiveness! A soul sensible of her weak and polluted state, and entirely relying on your mercy. Oh speak peace to this troubled sea and all shall be calm [see also Mark 4:39]! Give me strength to resist those temptations I so often sink under! But above all, change this wicked and deceitful heart, and give me a new heart and a new spirit. Mortify in me all proud thoughts and vain opinions of myself, and let not the blessings you have bestowed upon me increase my condemnation by being made motive for pride and vain glory. Hear and grant my requests, Oh ever-merciful God, for the sake of Jesus Christ, our only Mediator and Redeemer. Amen.

O merciful God! I adore you past all expression and the notions I have of your divine attributes inspire me with an unbounded confidence. Unworthy as I am of the least of all your mercies, I cannot but hope for the greatest, and in the midst of my continual offences, I look up to you as my friend, my only refuge and constant benefactor. When I grieve for my sins, it is not for fear of punishment, but from the cutting reflection of my black ingratitude, in offending my Creator and preserver, the God in whom I live, and move, and have my being, the God to whom I owe infinitely more than I can conceive, to whom I owe the glorious and the assured hopes of incorruption and immortality. And here again, O my soul, take wing, again lose yourself in the blissful prospect! Think on the joy you will feel when this corruptible shall have put on incorruption [see also 1 Cor. 15:53-4], when this companion (which in spite of the miseries it betrays you into, is still dear and still too tenderly beloved) shall become (instead of a clog or a prison) a vehicle pure and ethereal, perfectly fitted for all the purposes of your enlarged faculties, and the completion of your glory and happiness. O blessed and desirable re-union! State of permanent delight and never fading joy! With what rapture does your idea inspire my soul! Amen.

Oh blessed and ever merciful God! Look down with compassion on the deplorable state of the Christian world! See how your church is laid waste and rent asunder by the fraud, malice, or blind zeal of particular men. In one place overrun by superstition, in another undermined by scepticism, and everywhere robbed of her primitive peace and purity. Oh restore that purity! Restore that peace! Heal her breaches, reform her superstitions, and grant that we may, with one heart and one mind, with universal love and unbounded charity to our fellow creatures, and a firm and lively faith in our blessed Redeemer, adore you the only true God; and, after a life of piety and virtue, attain one of unalterable glory and happiness. Amen.

Oh sweetest and most compassionate Jesus! How do your tender mercies follow and support my soul, and still I am ungrateful, and still I am not as you would have me to be! Oh when will you make a full end of sin and bring in your perfect righteousness? All things are possible to you [see also Matt. 19:26], and do I not know, do I not taste that you are gracious! Oh my sun, my shield, life of my life, look into my heart. I dare appeal to your all-searching eye, that there is nothing so dear to it but I would this moment part with it for you!

And why then, dearest Lord, will you not form your whole blessed image in my soul? My unworthiness I know is greater than that of any other creature in the universe. But this unworthiness will the more magnify your mercy. I have only my unworthiness to plead, and I have no hope but in your atoning blood. Oh let this blood, which has bought my peace, cleanse me also from every sin. And let that blessed Spirit, who has sealed and witnessed this peace to my soul, be now a spirit of burning to consume all my dross and to purify me even as—Oh glorious prospect, heart-enlivening hopes, let me sink into the dust before you!

God of glory, God of purity, I am lost in self-abasement! But have you not promised? And will you not fulfil your own gracious word? Oh give me then perfect sanctification of body, soul, and spirit. And let this heavy cross which seems now coming upon me be, by your all-powerful grace, turned into a means of forwarding your blessed work in my soul. Let every bitter cup which you permit to be given me be joyfully received, as serving in some degree to conform me to your sufferings. And let me in all things, though ever so contrary to my corrupt nature, give thanks and say continually, Lord not my will, but yours be done [see also Luke 22:42]. Amen.

SOURCE:

[John Wesley], *An Extract of Letters by Mrs. L**** (Bristol: William Pine, 1769), 101, 103-4, 106-7, 110-11.

C. Prayers

3. Joanna Cook

Editor's Introduction

Joanna Turner, née Cook (1732–84), heard the evangelical preachers on a visit to London and was introduced to the Methodist Societies by her cousin, Elizabeth Johnson, the devout class leader in Bristol, who was reckoned one of the most pious women among the Methodists in the west of England.[50] Joanna associated herself with the Calvinistic Methodists under the direction of George Whitefield and, in 1766, built a tabernacle for use by his connection in Trowbridge. Though she never moved into the Arminian camp of the evangelical revival, she wrote a letter to John Wesley in 1772, expressing her sympathies for his ministry.[51] Wesley preached at her chapel on September 12, 1780, at her invitation, and her connections with Methodism remained intimate throughout her life.[52] At the time of her death in 1784, Wesley prepared (but did not publish) an abridgment of her husband's account of her life and death.[53] Her niece, Mary Cook, married the noted biblical scholar and Methodist leader, Adam Clarke. Her connections with and influence upon Methodism, and upon the Methodist women in particular, therefore, merit the inclusion of the following prayer that she used on the occasion of her covenant renewal with God in 1751. Deeply rooted in the Puritan heritage of English Christianity, this practice was a central aspect of early Methodist spirituality. It marks the need for recurrent acts of dedication to God and the way of Christ throughout life.

* * * *

O Lord God! the Maker of heaven and earth! by whose word and for whose glory I and all creatures were made! I am now come to acknowledge you as the author of my being, the preserver of my life, and the giver of every good thing I enjoy; and do therefore submit myself to you as my rightful owner, and sovereign Lord and Father. I have sinned against heaven and in your sight, and am no more worthy to be called your child. I shall think myself highly honored and very happy if you will receive me as one of your meanest servants [see also Luke 15:18-21].

I bring you a creature of your own that has been straying from you. This soul and body, now prostrate at your footstool, I humbly offer unto you that you may go over your work again and create me anew after your own image; and so will I be your faithful servant as long as I live. O blessed Jesus, if you will now take my part and plead my cause with your Father, I am ready to profess myself your disciple upon your own terms and to follow you, if my heart do not deceive me, whatsoever you do. I do sincerely give up myself to your teaching and instruction. O give me understanding that I may know the truth as it is in Jesus. I do unfeignedly consent to your government, and with a mind willing to obey you, I can now say, "Lord, what will you have me to do?"

I will ascribe all the honor of my salvation to your meritorious death and powerful intercession. In you alone will I repose my trust; and now, if my Lord will undertake that his grace shall be sufficient for me, there is nothing too difficult to attempt, or too much to suffer for you! I do enlist myself under your banner, as the great Captain of my salvation, frightened to think that I have been so long under the power and tyranny of the devil, whom I shall from this moment resist to the uttermost.

I am persuaded that this world is nothing but vanity and vexation of spirit, and therefore shall set myself by your help, according to your example, to conquer it and bring it into subjection. I have found my own heart corrupt, wicked, and deceitful, and therefore shall no longer manage for myself, but shall rejoice to give up every thought, will, and affection, entirely to you. I am now desirous to be yours, O Lord, so as not to be another's; yours and not the world's; yours and not my own.

To you, O Holy Spirit, do I acknowledge myself indebted for these and all other good inclinations, and that I may be enabled to hold my present purposes and to improve in a holy, heavenly disposition of mind, I now cast myself upon you for all that direction and assistance which my circumstances may require. Henceforth I shall yield up myself to your conduct and influences, and shall make it my care to attend to all your motions and convictions, both in performing my duty, and abstaining from sin; and so do those things that may be well pleasing to you, O Father, Son, and Spirit, with my whole heart!

I desire freely and fully to devote myself to you for my everlasting portion, and purposing to serve you as my supreme Lord and Master while I have a being. And as a proof of my sincerity and of my ardent desire to make good such a profession, I am willing to bind myself, by setting my hand to all this, that it may be a witness for or against me, as I behave myself agreeably or disagreeably to what I now do.

Joanna Cook

SOURCE:

[Mary Wells], *The Triumph of Faith ... Exemplified in the Life, Death, and Spiritual Experience of ... Mrs. Joanna Turner* (Bristol: Religious Tract Society, 1787), 11-13.

4. MARY GILBERT

Editor's Introduction

The Gilbert family name is famous in the annals of early Methodist mission. Nathaniel Gilbert (c. 1721–74) was called to the bar in 1746, took his father's seat in the Antiguan House of Assembly, was appointed to the Governor's Council in 1750, and later served as Speaker of the House. Converted through his study of John Wesley's *Appeals to Men of Reason and Religion*, under the influence of his younger brother Francis, he resigned his House seat in 1757, returned to England after the baptism of his fourth daughter, and settled in Wandsworth, south of London. At the beginning of 1758, Wesley preached in his house, and on December 29 of that year, he baptized two of Gilbert's African-West Indian slaves. Nathaniel and Francis returned to Antigua early in 1759, pioneered Methodist work in the West Indies, and established a racially mixed Society. Upon their father's death in 1761, they inherited his large plantation. Although Wesley urged him unsuccessfully to emancipate the hundreds of slaves now in his possession and under his care, Nathaniel instructed them in the Christian faith and led them in Methodist worship, assisted by a young Methodist widow, Mary Leadbetter, who later married Francis.[54]

This is the family and circumstances into which Mary (1751–68), eldest of the five daughters of Nathaniel and Elizabeth Gilbert, was born. At eight years of age, after two years in England, Mary returned to the West Indies with her family. In 1764, her parents sent her back to England to complete her education. The grief she experienced in this separation from her parents and siblings was eased only by the promise of an early reunion. On January 1, 1765, she began to keep a diary, which consisted primarily of the account of her spiritual development. In Wesley's introduction to his extract of her journal, he observes that she "applied her heart unto true wisdom."[55] Mary met Wesley in March when the Gilbert family accommodated him at their home in Kendal and she attended his preaching services.[56] In August 1765, after she moved to Chester, Mary records Wesley's visit to the new Octagon Chapel. He returned in March 1766.

Throughout this period, Mary devoted herself diligently to her studies and to a deepening relationship with God through Christ. She also continued to place her hopes in an imminent return of her family, whom she missed very much. In early January 1768, however, she contrasted to an illness that would take her life before the end of the month. John Wesley's only direct statements about Mary come from his prefatory comments in the extract of her journal, which he published upon her death and described as "a masterpiece in its kind."[57] His comment concerning her life is both cryptic and profound: "What a prodigy of a child! Soon ripe, and soon gone!" She was only sixteen years old when she died, just a month from her seventeenth birthday.

* * * *

January 9, 1765

God of Love, quicken my drooping powers! Stir up and waken my insensible soul, and give me to seek your face with my whole heart! And O be found in me!

January 16, 1765

Lord, give me power over a trifling spirit! Give me a continual sense of your presence! Then I shall not easily yield to this or any other temptations.

January 20, 1765

O God, give me grace that I may not prove a forgetful hearer, but a doer of the Word, that so I may be blessed in my deed [see also James 1:23]!

January 23, 1765

O my God give me yourself. Then shall this wilderness become like a watered garden which you have planted [see also Jer. 31:12].

February 2, 1765

O God, who searches and tries the reins of the children of men! give me to see more and more of the sinfulness of it, and wash and cleanse it in the blood of Jesus!

September 11, 1765

O! what must the full enjoyment be! Lord as you have given me this desire, O fulfil it! Let me never rest till I am made a joyful partaker of the inheritance of the saints in light [see also Col. 1:12]!

October 30, 1765

Dearest Jesus! how long will it be before you will manifest yourself to me, as you do not unto the world! O come and take up your abode in my longing heart, and live and reign in me without a rival!

October 31, 1765

O Son of God, do now impart to me this great and inestimable blessing, and make me truly happy in your love! Do now arise upon my poor soul with healing in your wings [see also Mal. 4:2], and keep me continually!

January 21, 1766

I am willing, yea Lord, I am desirous, to forsake all my sins and to return unto you. O my God, make me in earnest, and take me for your child! Keep me! Keep me, gracious Lord, and never let me go!

February 28, 1766

Jesus, Lord, lend me your aid, and I will devote myself to you, body, soul, and spirit, a living sacrifice! Lend me your aid, and I will take you for my prophet to teach me; my priest to atone for my sins; and my king to reign over me![58] Come, dear Lord, and take me for your own! Yours in time, and yours to eternity!

April 27, 1766

O Lord help me this day to take your sweet yoke upon me and learn of you [see also Matt. 11:29], for I am truly convinced that till then I shall never find rest to my poor soul. I have no objections to make. Take me as I am and let me be yours for ever!

April 29, 1766

Lord, help me so to put on the whole armor of God that I may be able to withstand in the evil day, and having done all, to stand [see also Eph. 6:11]!

SOURCE:

[John Wesley, ed.], *An Extract of Miss Mary Gilbert's Journal*, 2nd ed. (London: Henry Cock, 1768), 13-17, 32-35, 41-48.

5. Margaret Davidson

Editor's Introduction

For an introduction to the life and work of Margaret Davidson, see the section of poetry and hymns above. Margaret's prayers express the deepest possible longing to be conformed to the image of Christ in love. The second prayer comes in the context of a letter written to a minister's wife who was experiencing difficulty under the strain of her many responsibilities. Margaret's is an earnest appeal for God to act, to bring God's promises to fruition.

* * * *

I cannot cease magnifying and adoring the wonders of unbounded love and unmerited pity towards me. O compassionate lover of my soul, take the whole matter into your hands—the sole management of my most important and minute concerns! Oh that I could in every condition of life, say, "Your will be done" [Matt. 26:42]! I think I can—but am afraid of being deceived through the deceitfulness of my back-sliding heart. Trier of the reins of the children of men, reveal to me what I am. Let me not have a name to live, if I am dead before you. You only know that no other evidence can suffice than your Holy Spirit, together with the testimony of a good conscience [see also 2 Cor. 1:12]. These and these only, can comfort me in every place and state, and afford me ground of rejoicing in prospect of everlasting bliss—which bliss I humbly beg may be the portion of all my enemies, and the glorious reward of all my benefactors, through the merits of the suffering Son of God! Amen! and amen!

Come, Lord Jesus, come quickly [see also Rev. 22:20], and cut short your work in righteousness! Burn up, O Spirit of burning, all the dross of my best duties [see also Isa. 1:25]—all the stubble of my inbred sin! O my lovely Jesus, I languish to be all holy, according to my degree, as you are holy. I beseech you, delay not to destroy the very in-being of sin, which is interwoven with my nature, so that I cannot love nor praise my God as I ardently long to do! When, O my dear Redeemer, when shall I enjoy that heaven of loving you alone? I pant for more of the divine life—I thirst for a full salvation from sin. Oh when shall I find it utterly extirpated? For this my soul is on the stretch—Nothing less can quench the sacred spark which glows in my longing breast—Nothing in earth or heaven, O my beloved, but the copious flagons of your soul-transporting love.

> Thy only love to me be giv'n —
> Lord, I ask no other heav'n.[59]

SOURCE:

Edward Smyth, ed., *The Extraordinary Life and Christian Experience of Margaret Davidson, as Dictated by Herself* (Dublin: Dugdale, 1782), 119-20, 138-39.

6. Sarah Crosby

Editor's Introduction

For an introduction to the life and work of Sarah Crosby, see part 1 above. It is important to note that Sarah's prayers are expressions of faith in the context of journaling. Like other Methodist women, she found this discipline extremely helpful in her desire to grow in grace toward the goal of perfect love. She praises God by rehearsing the ways in which she has perceived God to be active in her life. Her plea is for God to make her "pure, spiritual, holy." The keynotes of her life of prayer are gratitude and thanksgiving.

* * * *

August 8, 1763

Gracious Lord, how shall your poor creature praise you? Help me to "take the cup of salvation and call on the name of the Lord" [Psa. 116:13]. What great mercy have you shown me this month past! You have often taken me into your banqueting house, and your banner over me has been love [see also Sol. 2:4]. Now I sit under your shadow with great delight. O blessed Jesus! you have also greatly humbled me before you, giving me to remember my past sins and follies.

> May I this life improve
> To mourn for follies past;
> And live this short revolving day,
> As if it were my last.[60]

This you know is the one desire of my heart. O what have you done for me! What a great deliverance have you wrought! Lord, make me pure, spiritual, holy. Mold as you will the passive clay [see also Isa. 64:8]. Sweetly and quietly to live in your will and prove that God, my God is love, is my request. Will you not grant it? Lord, increase my faith, for "Whatever I ask in faith I have, as sure as God is true" [John 14:13].

C. Prayers

January 1, 1774

Glory be unto you, my Almighty Father, my eyes are again blest with the sight of a new year! With this new year, O! my good God, let me begin afresh to praise you! I freely offer myself up unto you. Guide me by your eye, instruct me by your providence and your Spirit, for I am yours. You have accepted me, although the most unworthy of all whoever your grace received. Keep me at your feet till you shall take me up to cast my crown before you, O! holy, triune God!

January 27, 1800

I thank my God, I have no desire but to devote myself to him. I am surrounded with mercies. Lord, help me to improve them to your glory. I long to possess a greater fulness of your Spirit, free from enthusiasm, on the one hand, and lukewarmness and formality, on the other; and producing a calm acquiescence in your will. Let all my pains be sanctified, that you may be glorified by my patient suffering.

SOURCE:

WMM 29 (1806): 521, 565, 612.

7. Bathsheba Hall

Editor's Introduction

Bathsheba Hall (1745–80) was converted at the age of eighteen while residing in London as part of the Foundery community. Upon return to her native Bristol, she became a conscientious member of the Methodist Society there and married John Hall, about whom nothing is known. Despite recurrent illnesses, Bathsheba proved extremely influential through her prayers and private exhortations among her Methodist friends. John Wesley published seven extracts from her diary in the *Arminian Magazine* in 1781 after her death.[61] The extant portion of her diary covers the period between December 12, 1765, and April 24, 1775, crucial years with regard to theological development in the history of early Methodism. Hall's diary, essentially a narrative account of her spiritual journey, provides an indelible portrait of a soul renewed in love and wholly devoted to God. Moreover, it often expresses the tensions that women felt at this period, torn between a sense of duty in discipleship and a fear of condemnation, especially from male counterparts in the movement. Wesley described her as a "blessed saint ... a pattern for many years of zealously doing and patiently suffering the will of God."[62]

* * * *

But still, O Lord, you are the one thing which I desire in earth or heaven! O that you would invigorate my soul! All my strength is derived from you! I long that all within me should be holiness unto the Lord. I am sunk at the foot [of] Jesus' cross!

All hail rising Savior! My soul adores you in blessed poverty of spirit. What a ceasing do I find from my own works! Yea, let me be divested of all things, so I am not divested of Christ in me, the hope of glory [see also Col. 1:27]!

SOURCE:

AM 4 (1781): 40, 149.

C. PRAYERS

8. HESTER ANN ROE

Editor's Introduction

For an introduction to the life and work of Hester Ann (Roe) Rogers, see part 1 above. Hester's prayers are characterized by an amazing directness. She is free and open before God, relying completely on the gracious nature of the relationship. A sense of total dependence upon God who delights to make us happy and holy pervades these prayers.

* * * *

Lord, do you care for me? And is this faith, to cast all my care, even all my sins (for I have no other care) upon you? May I? Do you bid me? a poor hell-deserving sinner, a sinner against light and conviction and repeated vows? Can such love dwell in you? Is it not too easy a way? May I, even I, be saved, if I only cast my soul on Jesus? My burden of sin, my load of guilt, my every crime? What, saved from all this guilt? Saved into the favor of God! the holy God! and become his child, and that now, this moment! O it is too great! Lord Jesus, I will, I do believe. I now venture my whole salvation upon you as God! I put my guilty soul into your hands; your blood is sufficient! I cast my soul upon you for time and eternity.

O how precious are your ways to my soul, suited to my weakness, worthy of a God! I am nothing! You are all. I live moment by moment upon your smiles and dwell under the shadow of your wings [see also Psa. 17:8]. I desire nothing but to please you, to grow in inward conformity to your will and sink deeper into humble love, to let the light of what your grace has bestowed shine on all around, and to live and die proclaiming God is love.[63]

SOURCE:

An Account of the Experience of Hester Ann Rogers (New York: Hunt & Eaton, 1893), 30, 128-29.

9. ANN CUTLER ("PRAYING NANNY")

Editor's Introduction

Ann Cutler (1759–94), affectionately known as "Praying Nanny," was born in Thornley, near Preston, in Lancashire and died in the Methodist stronghold of Macclesfield. She was famous among all the Methodists of her day for her life of prayer. Apparently a very serious and spiritually sensitive girl, she converted to the Wesleyan Methodists when they first visited her area. Despite opposition primarily from male leaders in the Methodist Societies, she started to pray in public and was in constant demand to pray with people who found themselves in trouble. Upon the insistence of her later biographer, William Bramwell, the great Methodist revivalist, she began to travel further afield and to join in prayer meetings specifically for the revival of genuine Christianity. In the advertisement to Bramwell's account of her life, Zechariah Taft observed that "her peculiar call from Heaven appears to have been chiefly the exercise of *importunate believing prayer*."[64] According to Bramwell, she would frequently say:

> I think I must pray. I cannot be happy unless I cry for sinners. I do not want any praise: I want nothing but souls to be brought to God. I am reproached by most. I cannot do it to be seen or heard of men. I see the world going to destruction, and I am burdened till I pour out my soul to God for them.[65]

Although her public prayers were generally very short, the extent and intensity of her personal devotional life was unparalleled. It was characterized by frequent and often lengthy periods of private prayer. It was not uncommon for her to set aside as many as twelve to fourteen times for prayer each day in addition to frequent night vigils. Bramwell testified that he never expected to see her equal again. She was instrumental in the revival of Methodism in Dewsbury in 1792 and traveled extensively throughout the north of England on evangelistic missions with Bramwell until her death. A letter to a friend provides a glimpse of her work:

> I have seen many souls convinced and converted to God. I was above a week in Oldham circuit. We believed there were near a hundred souls brought to God. I have been above a fortnight at Manchester ... in Leek circuit ... in Derby circuit. In this week above forty souls were set at liberty: some cleansed of sin.... I am going for Macclesfield. They have sent for me. I have had a very happy time in my own soul.[66]

Ann died in Macclesfield and was buried at Christ Church in the company of other sainted Methodist women. Her epitaph reads:

> Underneath lies the remains of Ann Cutler, Whose simple manners, solid piety, and extraordinary power of prayer, distinguished and rendered her eminently useful in promoting a religious revival wherever she came.

The following prayers reflect Ann's heartfelt desire to be an instrument of the Triune God, nothing less and nothing more. Hers is a spirituality of total surrender, total dedication to the service of God. According to Bramwell, and on the basis of notations he discovered among her papers, it was Ann's practice to renew her covenant with God every day using the words of the second prayer.

* * * *

I am yours blessed Jesus. I am wholly yours. I will have none but you. Preserve my soul and body pure in your sight. Give me strength to shun every appearance of evil. In my looks keep me pure, in my words pure—a chaste virgin to Christ for ever. I promise you, upon my bended knees, that if you will be mine, I will be yours and cleave to none other in this world.

Blessed Father, loving Jesus, holy Spirit! I give my body and soul into your hands. Have your whole will on me, use me for your glory, and never let me grieve your spirit. I will be yours every moment; and all that you are is mine. We are fully united. We are ONE. And I pray that we may be one for ever. I give myself again to you. Give yourself again to me!

Father! I reverence your majesty and sink before you. You are a holy God. I submit my all to you. I live under your inspection and wonder at your glory every moment. Blessed Jesus! You are my constant friend and companion. You are always with me. We talk together in the nearest union. I can talk with you as my mediator. You show me the Father and I am lost in beholding His glory. You take me out and bring me in. You are with me wherever I go. My eyes are upon you as my pattern and continual help.

Holy Spirit! You are my comforter. I feel from you a constant burning love. My heart is set on fire by your blessed influence. I pray by your power. It is through you that I am brought to Jesus; through Jesus I am brought to the Father; and in the Father I am swallowed up in what I call glory. And I can say, Glory be to the Father, glory be to the Son, and glory be to the Holy Spirit!

SOURCE:

William Bramwell, *A Short Account of the Life and Death of Ann Cutler; A Pious Character, and Useful Instrument in the Work of God* (York: Printed by John Hill, 1827), 12, 13-14.

10. Isabella Wilson

Editor's Introduction

For an introduction to the life and work of Isabella Wilson, see part 1 above. The opening prayer reflects the annual practice of most Methodists to renew their commitment to God at the beginning of the year, more often than not using the well-established Service of Covenant Renewal.[67] Urged upon all of Wesley's followers as early as 1747, such a service was held formally for the first time at French Church in Spitalfields on August 11, 1755. Many of the Methodists, such as Isabella, formulated their own prayers as well. Isabella seeks full union with Jesus. Her prayers express a desire for full conformity to the image of Christ.

* * * *

[January 1793?]

O Almighty Lord and Savior, it is with heart-felt joy that I renew my covenant with you, to be wholly yours for evermore. With the greatest humility I further implore your heavenly grace and Holy Spirit to be my guide through this my pilgrimage to the heavenly Canaan. O my Lord, with what delight do I pass through the wilderness of this world! The light of your countenance daily shines upon me. O my God, it is enough. I have mused, and the fire burns; but, oh! in what language shall the flame break forth? What can I say but this, that my heart admires you, adores you, and loves you? My little vessel is as full as it can hold, and I would pour out all that fullness before you, that my heart may become capable of receiving more and more. You are my hope, and help, and salvation. When I set myself under the influence of your good Spirit to converse with you, a thousand delightful thoughts spring up—a thousand sources of pleasure are unsealed and flow in upon my soul, with such refreshment and joy that I am, as it were, wrapped up into the third heaven [see also 2 Cor. 12:2].[68]

I bless you for this soul of mine which you have created. I bless you for the knowledge with which you have endued it. I bless you for that grace with which I trust I may, not without humble wonder, say, You have sanctified it; though, alas! the celestial plant is fixed in too barren a soil, and does not flourish as I could wish it. But, O blessed Lord, let the dew of your heavenly grace fall upon it, then will it not fail to flourish as willows by the water courses. Unless your heavenly grace distill on the Christian's soul, it will wither, droop, and die. Oh then let us live dependent on you, our merciful God, for the supply of every want. Oh! how humble ought we to be, who, of ourselves can do nothing, and who find in the friend of sinners we can do all things. May I walk humbly with you, my God, all the days of my life, that I may at last rise to the life immortal.

February 11, 1802

O establish me, and then use me for your glory! I feel willing to do and suffer all your will. The language of my heart is,

> Or life, or death, is equal; neither weighs:
> All weight is this,—O let me live to Thee![69]

O Jesus, impart yourself to me. I covet the best gifts. I long for the closest union with you. My delight is in your law; therein do I exercise myself day and night [see also Psa. 1:2]. I feel the Spirit's seal, the stamp divine.

March 3, 1802

I am yours altogether. Do with me as seems good to you, only give me grace to glorify you in all, and I shall not complain. The daily cry of my heart is for all the mind that was in you [see also Phil. 2:5]. As you, Lord, have given me this desire, you will fulfil the same. Your promise never fails to those who love and serve you.

SOURCE:

John Pipe, "Memoir of Miss Isabella Wilson," *WMM* 31 (1808): 468, 567, 595.

11. MARY ENTWISLE

Editor's Introduction

For an introduction to the life and work of Mary Entwisle, see part 1 above. Mary Entwisle's prayers express a diversity of feelings and concerns. She prays for forgiveness; she commits those she loves to God's care; she yearns for consistency in the interior and exterior aspects of her spiritual life. Her prayers are ejaculatory, honest, and open.

* * * *

Lord be merciful to me and forgive my coldness, lukewarmness, and indifference. I have no might, no power, no strength. O Lord help me, for vain is the help of man. O quicken me and lead me in the right way. Manifest your love that I may praise you.

I feel my mind in a barren, uncomfortable frame. Lord, quicken me to preserve me from anxiety respecting my dear Mary. Help me to commit her into your hands and to say your will be done [see also Matt. 26:42]. If it pleases you, O Lord, bring her safely through the small pox and may no evil remain from them.

Lord, make me more like you in the inward dispositions of my heart,[70] then shall my outward conduct be agreeable to your word and will. O for more true humility of heart. Lord, help me to strive to live more in the exercises of this grace.

SOURCE:

Mary Entwisle, Manuscript Diary, *Meth. Arch.*, dated July 26, 1795, May 14, 1797, and September 10, 1797.

12. ELIZABETH EVANS

Editor's Introduction

Elizabeth Evans (1776–1849) was the niece of the famous novelist George Eliot (also known as Mary Ann Evans). Her biography and the story of Eliot's fictional Dinah Morris, heroine of *Adam Bede*, are so inextricably tied together that it is virtually impossible to separate them. Elizabeth Tomlinson, born to Methodist parents in Newbold, Leicestershire, was converted in her early twenties while listening to a sermon by George Smith of Newfoundland, the spiritual upheaval of which threw her into extreme asceticism. The account of her spiritual journey[71] chronicles her struggle to be faithful to the call of God upon her life. Exhortations in prayer meetings held in Derby eventually led to a renowned preaching ministry. When Samuel Evans heard her preach in Ashbourne, he not only was impressed, but also fell immediately in love. "Simplicity, love, and sweetness," he observed, "are blended in her. Her whole heart is in the work. She is made instrumental in the conversion of many sinners."[72] The two were married in 1804 at Wirksworth, which remained their family home for years.

Despite the restrictions placed upon women preachers at the Wesleyan Conference of 1803, Samuel and Elizabeth continued to conduct joint evangelistic tours as Methodist local preachers until 1832. They associated for a while with the Primitive Methodists and then became active among the Arminian Methodists (also known as the Derby Faith Folk). This latter group, noted for their enthusiastic revivalism and employment of women preachers, welcomed the Evans couple warmly. Eventually, however, both Elizabeth and Samuel returned to the Wesleyan Methodist tradition, in which they both died.

Although Elizabeth Evans's sermons have been lost, this one prayer was passed on carefully through her husband and found its way into *Adam Bede*, on the lips of Dinah Morris. Church, in *Early Methodist People*, has made the comment: "[This prayer] is not the careful creation of the novelist, nor the cool and balanced petition of the priest, but it has a certain torrential appeal and passionate sincerity which survives the years."[73] This prayer was purportedly

C. Prayers

used frequently in conjunction with her preaching. It is characterized by an extreme sense of urgency.

* * * *

Savior of sinners! when a poor woman laden with sins went out to the well to draw water, she found you sitting at the well [see also John 4:6-15]. She had not sought you. Her mind was dark. Her life was unholy. But you were ready to give her that blessing which she had never sought. Jesus, you are in the midst of us and you know all men. If there are any here like that poor woman, if their minds are dark, their lives unholy, if they had come out not seeking you, not desiring to be taught, to deal with them according to the free mercy which you did show to her. Speak to them Lord. Open their ears to my message. Bring their sins to their minds and make them thirst for that salvation which you are ready to give.

Lord, You are with your people still. They see you in the night watches and their hearts burn within them as you talk with them by the way [see also Luke 24:32], and you are near to those that have not known you. Open their eyes that they may see you weeping over them, and saying, "You will not come unto me, that you might have life" [John 5:40]; see you hanging on the cross and saying, "Father forgive them, for they know not what they do" [Luke 23:34]; see you as you will come again in your glory to judge them at the last. Amen.

Source:

George Eliot, *Adam Bede* (London: Tallant, 1859), 17-18.

13. Mary Hanson

Editor's Introduction

For an introduction to the life and work of Mary Hanson, see the section "Spiritual Instruction" above. Her simple prayer is a profound expression of the integrated life, characterized by a rhythm of emptiness and fullness, negation and affirmation. She draws on potent biblical images here, including divine in-filling and radical reversal in the reign of God.

****

O, blessed fountain of love! Fill my heart more with your divine principle. Sink me lower in the depths of humility and let me sit at the feet of Jesus and learn of Him [see also Luke 10:39-42]. Enlarge my soul that I may better contemplate your glory. And may I prove myself your child by bearing a resemblance to you, my heavenly Father!

SOURCE:

Clarke, *Memoirs of Mary Cooper,* 170-71.

D. Dreams and Visions

1. The "Account" of Sarah Ryan

Editor's Introduction

For an introduction to the life and work of Sarah Ryan, see part 1 above. In her diary, Sarah Ryan records several dreams and visions that she considered to be instrumental in her spiritual life. The dreams are often accompanied by a sense of divine forgiveness and presence, of solace and well-being. One, however, is quite disturbing and involves the destruction of "venomous creatures" that threaten her life with God. Interestingly, Sarah more often than not interprets her dreams in the context of her own narrative reflections. Plants represent God's graces in her life; a riverbank signifies her heart; the creatures of terror are "inbred corruptions," the two most difficult of which are pride and unbelief. Jesus appears to Sarah repeatedly. The final vision, in which she pictures herself as a child in the presence of Jesus, is an amazing testimony to the depth of her relationship with God through Christ and her desire to grow in the grace she experienced in her life.

* * * *

I went to live in the Jewish family again where, in a little while, I fell sick. They were exceeding kind and sent for my mother to nurse me. But I had no thought of God till one night I dreamed I was in Mr. Wesley's society room and saw an angel, who quickly disappeared, and I awoke. Falling asleep again I thought I was in the same place and saw a beautiful garden and the angel walking with me, till he laid his hand upon my arm, and said three times, "Come out from these Jews, or you will be damned." I turned and said, "If I live, I will amend my life." It disappeared, and I awoke.

I fell back in my chair and my eyesight was taken from me. But in the same moment the Lord Jesus appeared to my inward sight and I cried out three times, "O the beauty of the lovely Jesus. Behold him in his vesture dipped in blood!" A little after my leader asked me, "Do you now believe?" I faintly answered, "Yes." But I felt something of a doubt still and wanted a stronger witness. The next morning these words were applied with power. "Thy sins are cast as a stone into the deep waters." I answered, "Now I do believe. Now I know my sins are forgiven me."

I came home rejoicing and continued for about six weeks full of light, happiness, and heaven. I then dreamed I saw a bank full of green plants just coming up. While I was admiring them, one came and began to dig it up, when to my great surprise, as he turned up the shovel, there appeared a large body of all venomous creatures joined in one. Lifting up my hands and eyes, I said, "How could these plants grow with such creatures at the root?" Then he laid them down on the ground and they were spread almost all over the place. Afterwards a company of people, coming from the Foundery, began to kill them, in which I likewise was employed. But two clung about me for a long time. At last they also were killed, and I awoke. Reflecting on this I thought the bank was my heart; the plants, the graces God had sown therein; the man was the preacher; the venomous creatures were my inbred corruptions, the two last of which were pride and unbelief.

I felt a cold sweat and a trembling come over me. I knew it to be the power of God, but said nothing to those with me. After a few minutes, attempting to take up my work which had fallen out of my hands, I felt my strength quite taken away and fell out of my chair. In the moment I saw (not with my bodily eyes) the Lord Jesus standing before me and saying, "This day is salvation come to this house" [Luke 19:9]. I saw all my works and attainments laid at his feet as nothing worth. And I saw my soul as it were taken up and plunged into God. Recovering myself a little, I began, as I was able, to tell what I had seen, when S[arah] C[rosby] cried out, "Let us pray." And while she was at prayer my body was in such an agony as it is not possible to repeat. I said, "Pray for me, pray for me" and would have said, "Pray in those words,

> Empty her of self and pride,
> With all thy fulness fill."[74]

But I could not get out the words. However, though I could not speak them, she used nearly the same words. While she spoke them, God said to my soul, "I will sweep away thy sins with the besom of destruction" [Isa. 14:23]. Immediately I felt the Spirit of God as it were go through my whole soul. My agony ceased and

D. Dreams and Visions

the love of Jesus was again represented to my mind, only he now seemed above me, and as I looked up, I said, "Lord, John leaned on thy breast [see also John 21:20], but I am in thy bosom." To which my Lord replied, "Neither heights, nor depths, nor things present, nor things to come, nor any other creature, shall for one moment separate thy soul from me," in time or eternity [see also Rom. 8:39]. Quickly after, those words were spoken into my inmost soul,

> Fill'd with abiding peace divine,
> With Israel's blessing blest,
> Thou, thou the church above shalt join,
> And gain the heav'nly rest.[75]

After I had sat silent before God some time longer, he further spoke to me in the following words,

> Well-pleas'd on thee thy God looks down,
> And calls his rebel to a crown.[76]

And with these words, I saw the Lord Jesus present my soul to God the Father.

I continued sitting in the same manner and waiting what the Lord would speak, only crying out between whiles, "O, the power of God! O, the power of God!" Sometime after it came into my mind, "Would it not be better for me to retire to prayer?" But I thought, "What can I pray for? What more have I to ask for? The whole eternity of God is mine. How has he fulfilled his word, Give me thy will, and I will give thee all that I have?" And my soul continued lost in praise, in astonishment, and love.

[On Sunday] in Spitalfields Church,[77] I saw the Lord Jesus standing and a little child all in white before him. And he showed me he had made me as that child, but that I should grow up to the measure of his full stature. I came home full of light, joy, love, and holiness; and God daily confirmed what he had done for my soul. And blessed be his name! I now know where my strength lies, and my soul is continually sinking more and more into God.

SOURCE:

"Account of Mrs. Sarah Ryan," *AM* 2 (1779): 299, 302, 307-10.

2. Mary Fletcher's *Journal*

Editor's Introduction

For an introduction to the life and work of Mary (Bosanquet) Fletcher, see the section "Spiritual Instruction" above. The four visions presented here span nearly half a century in time. The first three are Mary Fletcher's own experiences, the fourth, the vision of another recorded in her journal. Mary's dreams and visions tend to provide instruction or confirm a course of action. She clearly understands that God works through these means to provide insight and guidance in her journey through life. The first dream, set in the context of a church, is a divine reproof, establishing anew a keen sense of total reliance upon God. In 1763, Mary was facing one of the most critical decisions of her life. She was contemplating her move to Leytonstone and the establishment of her orphan house there for the poor children of London. Mary is overwhelmed in her vision of Jesus' majesty, purity, and holiness and is strengthened to move forward with her revolutionary scheme. Confirmation comes again in the context of a vision, not long after the death of her husband, accompanied by a passion to entrust her life fully to God. The final vision in this collection comes from an S. Colley. It is an interesting manifestation of God as "the great eye," a strengthening presence and power in times of uncertainty.

* * * *

1755?

I dreamed one night I was in a church and saw written on the wall, in letter of gold, these words: "Thou shalt have no other gods but me" [Exod. 20:3]. While I was looking on it, I saw the name of Mrs. Lefevre[78] wrote under it. I was surprised and presently beheld the following line, If this is your god, then what am I? I awakened with a deep conviction that I had placed too much confidence on an arm of flesh. I knew it was the voice of God by this mark—a great sweetness accompanied the reproof. This was the method the Lord has always used toward me. He held me up with one hand while he smote me with the other.

D. Dreams and Visions

1763

About this time a house of my own at Leytonstone became untenanted. My friend as well as myself saw many reasons for our removing to that place. We prayed much about it and I asked the Lord to show us clearly his will. At length I felt from the Lord, first, a liberty to believe that if my father did absolutely forbid my coming, I was not required to do it. Secondly, I knew God did not require impossibilities. I had not yet an income sufficient for living in that place. I asked, therefore, as a farther mark, the settling an affair which kept me out of part of my fortune occasioned by a flaw in the making of my grandmother's will. I had taken some pains about this affair before, but to no purpose. However, I slightly mentioned it again, and it was settled directly. Then I made known to my father my thought about living at Leytonstone. I used no deception, but told him plainly the end I proposed in so doing, my mother being present. He made not the least objection, only added with a smile, "If a mob should pull down your house about your ears, I cannot hinder them." We waited before the Lord, believing it was his call, and held ourselves in readiness for immediate obedience.

One night I dreamed I was in one of my houses there, in company with all kinds of people, rich and poor, most of whom appeared very ungodly. It was strongly impressed on my mind to speak to them, but I started from the thought and said with emotion, "Lord, what am I doing here among this people? For they are not your people, and what am I to do with them?" I then beheld the Lord Jesus stand as just before me. The awful majesty of his presence had such an effect on me as I cannot express! It seemed to me I sunk down before him as if I were sweetly melting into nothing. I saw no shining brightness or anything dazzling to the eye. He appeared only as a man clothed in white. Yet to my mind there was what I cannot put into words. It was a sense of his purity! It was the glory of holiness which so overcame me! There seemed but about one yard distance between my Savior and me—when he spoke with a voice clear and distinct, these words: "I will send you to a people that are not a people [see also 1 Pet. 2:10], and I will go with you. Bring them unto me, for I will lay my hand upon them and heal them [see also Matt. 19:13]. Fear not, only believe" [see also Luke 8:50]!

1785

I dreamed I was in a room with Sally [Lawrence][79] and saw a picture, or rather the ground work for a picture, on which was only painted one small sheep lying down. The rest was all plain. I said to her, "Sally, look on that picture and what the Lord says, your dear master will draw it out for me to read?" I then saw letter by letter come out, as if wrote (though without any hand or pen) as follows: "She that dwelleth in the secret place of the Most High shall abide under the shadow on the Almighty" [Psa. 91:1]. I felt it a confirmation of my faith and said, "There is no better path than to repose the soul in God and to go on in quiet resignation, whatever we may feel." As I was making that reflection, I heard, though yet asleep, my dear husband's voice, as if close to my face, speaking these words:

> Shout, all ye people of the sky!
> And all ye saints of the Most High:
> Our God, who thus his right obtains,
> For ever and for ever reigns![80]

The beginning I heard in my sleep, but as it woke me, the rest was heard afterward. And I could have known his voice among a thousand. I saw from it we never render to God his right till we abandon, by a perfect resignation, all our concerns, spiritual as well as temporal, into his hand and learn to lie still before him, in the posture of a little child, hanging each moment by faith on his mercy.

January 25, 1790

A dream which was told me the other day by S. Colley[81] was blessed to me. She thought she was surrounded by dangers, but looking up she saw a large eye always fixed on her, which much encouraged her faith in an overruling providence. Then she thought she got into a river and began to sink. It was very deep and clear, and she was much afraid. But looking down she saw this great eye underneath her, which caused such a faith to spring up in her soul that she laid herself down on the water with as much comfort and ease as if upon her bed. She felt she could not sink with the power of the Almighty underneath her [see also Deut. 33:27].

SOURCE:

Moore, *Life of Mary Fletcher*, 1:16, 1:45-46, 2:48-49, 2:105.

D. DREAMS AND VISIONS

3. THE "ACCOUNT" OF SARAH MALLET

Editor's Introduction

One of the most celebrated of the female preachers, Sarah Mallet (1764–?) is noteworthy because of the formal authorization she received from John Wesley and the Manchester Conference of 1787.[82] Born on February 18, 1764, in Norfolk, she received her first Methodist ticket in 1780 and experienced a call to preach in 1785, against which she resisted vehemently, only to succumb in 1786 by preaching in her uncle's house and the Methodist chapel in Long Stratton. Unfortunately, very little is known about her life and work subsequent to her marriage to a local preacher by the name of Boyce, in spite of the fact that she was included with him in the listing of the preachers for many years. She carried on a lengthy correspondence with John Wesley; but whereas a number of his letters to her have survived, apparently none of hers remains extant. Zechariah Taft possessed a number of important manuscripts related to her, some of which he published in *Holy Women*.

The account of Mallet's "fits," provided by her uncle and interspersed with her own reflections, is one of the most fascinating documents of early Methodism, published by John Wesley in his *Arminian Magazine* in 1788. Wesley visited Long Stratton on December 4, 1786, and was captivated by Sarah's testimony concerning her experience. His record of their conversation is worth quoting at length:

> Of the following relation which she gave me, there are numberless witnesses.
>
> Some years since, it was strongly impressed upon her, that she ought to call sinners to repentance. This impression she vehemently resisted, believing herself quite unqualified both by her sin and her ignorance, till it was suggested, "If you do it not willingly, you shall do it whether you will or no." She fell into a fit and, while utterly senseless, thought she was in the preaching house at Lowestoft, where she prayed and preached for near an hour to a numerous congregation.... she had eighteen of these fits, in every one of which she imagined herself to be preaching in one or another congregation. She then cried out, "Lord, I *will* obey

thee, I *will* call sinners to repentance." She has done so occasionally from that time. And her fits returned no more.[83]

John Wesley was influential in winning for her the full support and approval of the Manchester Conference of 1787. The document of authorization was delivered to her by Joseph Harper and reads: "We give the right hand of fellowship to Sarah Mallet, and have no objection to her being a preacher in our connexion, so long as she preaches the Methodist doctrines, and attends to our discipline."[84] William Mallitt's account of her experience is presented in reduced type, followed by Sarah's own reflections on her experience.

* * * *

[May 28, 1780] The next morning at breakfast she was suddenly struck, went into another room and lay down on the bed. She immediately lost her senses and lay as dead till three in the afternoon. When she came to herself she said she had seen two angels who took her where she had a full view of the torments of the damned. And afterwards, of the happiness of the blessed, into which she asked if she might not enter? But was answered, "Not yet, she had work to do upon earth."

She grew weaker and weaker till the 15th of December [1785], when she was seized with an uncommon fit. From that time all her other complaints ceased. But her fits returned every twenty-four hours, and often continued four hours at a time.

They began thus. While we were talking together, she leaned back in her chair and lost her senses. Her eyes were wide open, her face like that of a corpse, her hands quite cold, all her limbs stiff and immoveable. On the 18th we concluded she was dying. But then something ulcerated broke within her and her fits took a quite different turn. She began to speak in the fit. The first words I heard her speak were, "Father, turn to God," with several other words to the same effect. In another fit she earnestly exhorted her sisters to seek God in their youth. In the following fits her voice grew stronger and stronger.

On the 25th Mr. Byron[85] came to my house, who entering the room, and seeing her sitting in her chair, and looking like one dead, he was so struck that he thought he

D. Dreams and Visions

should not be able to preach. Meantime she thought herself to be in the preaching house at Lowestoft,[86] before a large congregation, and that she took her text from Rev. 3:20. "Behold, I stand at the door and knock." This discourse she preached in Mr. Byron's hearing. The next day she preached again in Mr. Byron's hearing on John 7:37. She continued to preach in every following fit, speaking clear and loud, though she was utterly senseless.

From December 29, her fits came every second day. From Jan. 15, every third day. I then called in some of the Society to hear her. She spoke on Mark 16:16. More of them came to hear her on the 18th day, and still more on the 21st. The thing being now known abroad, many were desirous of hearing her, and did so on the 24th, when a mixed company being present, she spoke from Isaiah 57:1. I then permitted all that would to come in, particularly on the 27th, when she preached an hour on 1 Pet. 4:18. "If the righteous, &c." On the 30th she preached from Isaiah 55:1 to about two hundred persons. From that time her fits left her, and she spoke no more. She had one fit more on the tenth of April, but did not speak one word.

In September [1785] the Lord visited me again with affliction, the particulars of which my uncle has given you better than I can do. For during my fits I was utterly senseless. But when I came to myself I could well remember the place where I had been preaching and the words I had been speaking from. I grew weaker and weaker and expected to die soon. But death was a welcome messenger, and the foretaste of those joys to which I thought I was just going took off the edge of my pains. In my sharpest pains I thought, what is all this to what I should have suffered had not the Son of God suffered for me? And I continually said, "Lord, give me yourself, and then deal with me as you please!" In this affliction he weaned me from the creature, from all created good, so that the world was utterly dead to me and I unto the world.

And in this affliction God made known, notwithstanding all my resistance, the work he had called me to do. And not me only, but to all that were round about me, by opening my mouth whether I would or no. While every sense was locked up, the Lord prepared me for the work which he had prepared for me. And I thought, if he should restore me, I would spend my latest breath in declaring his dying love to sinners. From this time my strength continually increasing, my uncle asked, "Have you any objection to speaking in public?" I answered, "Whatever is in your mind concerning me, I consider as appointed by God." So in the beginning of February 1786, he desired me to speak in his preaching house. Fear and shame caused me to tremble at first. But the Lord gave me strength and loosed my tongue.

I was now appointed to speak in my uncle's house every other Sunday evening. The Lord gave me light and liberty, and I had great peace in my soul, and more nearness to God than ever. I walked continually in the light of his countenance. And sometimes meditating on the dying love of Jesus to a guilty world, I have had such manifestations of his love to my soul as were more than my body could bear.

SOURCE:

[William Mallitt], "An Account of S[arah]. Mallitt," *AM* 11 (1788): 91-93, 238-39.

Part Three
The Art of Living and Dying

INTRODUCTION TO PART THREE

The final section of this anthology includes twenty pieces of correspondence and material related to a unique genre of literature known as the *ars moriendi,* or "art of dying." The juxtaposition of these materials demonstrates how the spirituality of the early Methodist women was profoundly teleological. The women define every aspect of the Christian journey from the vantage point of the goal. Having discovered the true meaning of life in Jesus Christ, and having experienced the witness of many to his love and grace in death, they write this revelation back into life, as it were. The journey itself can be understood only with reference to its goal. The Methodist people lived well, so they would say, because they had learned how to die well. They viewed the Christian life as an unfolding revelation of the meaning of life, understood most profoundly in coming to terms with the reality of death. The art of living and the art of dying, therefore, were inextricably bound together.

In *Her Own Story,* I examined a smaller selection of letters in reference to the portrait of life they paint.[1] I demonstrated there how the correspondence of Methodist women provides immediate and often striking insight into the human situations and experiences that were part and parcel of the Wesleyan revival. The slightly larger sampling of twenty letters here has been selected to reflect some of the more critical issues related to spirituality that recur in women's writings or that offer a unique articulation of persistent themes.

Three of these letters come from collections of correspondence published by John Wesley and Zechariah Taft.[2] One of the most important sources of Methodist correspondence is the *Arminian Magazine* (and its successor publications), from which three additional letters are drawn. While the majority of the letters (nine) have been extracted from published memoirs of early Methodist women, five are transcribed directly from the original holographs. Thirteen different authors are represented in the collection, and they reflect quite a wide range of voices within the movement. Mary Bosanquet Fletcher authored four of the featured letters. Two letters each are drawn from the memoirs of four other prominent early Methodist women: Hannah Ball, Sarah Crosby, Hester Ann Roe Rogers, and Elizabeth Ritchie Mortimer. All of the recipients are women, except in the case of two very important pieces of correspondence directed to John Wesley from Sarah Crosby and Elizabeth Ritchie. Regardless of sender or circumstance, I have attempted to preserve the original spontaneity and emotive power of each letter, reprinting them here, for the most part, in their entirety. The letters are organized chronologically.

I believe that the letters I have selected for this section are representative and reflect with a high degree of authenticity the spirituality of the early Methodist women. In culling through hundreds of letters to frame this collection I made one observation that I believe is of particular note and for which I have, as of yet, no satisfactory explanation. As we have seen by its frequent appearance in journals and published memoirs, the spirituality of the early Methodist women was characterized by a holistic balance of works of piety and works of mercy. For some reason this holism is less evident in the correspondence. For example, although Mary Fletcher's published biography reflects an amazing conjunction of vital personal piety and active social service, her letters provide much less sense of the centrality of works of mercy in her life. Reading these silences requires particular care since it is easy to read either too much or too little into the text.[3] We must take into account the author, epistolary genre, context, and spiritual intent. It seems most likely that the absence of much discussion about her engagement in works of mercy reflects Mary's concern to guard against the sin of self-pride.

INTRODUCTION TO PART THREE

However these silences are construed, there is no question that the correspondence of all these women is characterized primarily by what might be called "personal religion." To some extent all of these letters are pastoral. They are variations upon the pervasive theme of religion as a vital, dynamic, personal relationship with God through Jesus Christ. They are contemplations of the spiritual life and guidance concerning it.

The letters reflect central themes of Wesleyan spirituality: foundations in grace, spiritual narrative, accountable discipleship, works of piety, works of mercy, and the gift of song. They also point to the foundational nature of prayer, the need to entrust one's life completely to Christ, the goal of holiness of heart and life, and the importance of faith activated by love in Christian vocation. Mrs. Lefevre's letter consists almost entirely of advice with regard to the life of prayer. To a very dear friend and close colleague in ministry, Hannah Ball describes how the Lord deals with her soul, and to another she reflects upon the nature of assurance in the Christian life. Jane Cooper and Hester Rogers expatiate on the meaning of justification by grace through faith and its foundation in the redemptive work of Christ. Several discuss, defend, or simply contemplate the nature of Christian perfection. Mary Fletcher, in particular, recasts this Wesleyan vision in the language of a holiness most fully experienced in private prayer. Many of the letters involve encouragement of one form or another: for a daughter at the outset of a new chapter in her life, for a preacher in quest of security in her call, for a friend in search of hope. Some of the women share insights with regard to their ministry as preachers and evangelists and the way they seek to make disciples through the gifts with which God has blessed them. Included among their letters of spiritual guidance are issues ranging widely from political developments within the Methodist movement to the plight of the suffering and vulnerable widow. But central to them all is the closeness of God they feel, the all-sufficiency of God's grace, and the intimacy with Christ that they share so freely with everyone in their circle of life.

This volume concludes with eight items that reflect the early Methodist preoccupation with the art and craft of dying well.[4] *Ars moriendi* refers in general to texts that deal with preparation for the moment of death. A genre of practical, devotional literature, these guides or instruction booklets first appeared in the fifteenth century in Europe and remained popular up to the nineteenth century in England.[5] Although the key assumption of the earliest tracts was that one's eternal fate was determined at the moment of death, later Protestant and humanistic influences shifted attention to the way in which these guides could show the Christian how to live the good life in the present moment, prior to death.[6] John Wesley was strongly attracted to this literary tradition in Britain, where it tended to flourish, especially as burgeoning urban centers made life increasingly tenuous for the masses.

In the face of disease, unsanitary living and working conditions, the ravages of war, and high infant mortality, death pervaded life. Those who survived into their fortieth year were exceptions to the rule, even by the close of the eighteenth century when smallpox vaccinations were available. Childbirth was one of the leading causes of death among women. Death functioned as a pervasive reminder of the fragility, if not futility, of life and the helplessness of women at the hand of forces beyond their control.

Significantly, attitudes about death that had remained rather constant over hundreds of years in European history changed radically by the eighteenth century. Whereas the earlier period interpreted death as an experience within the context of community, according to French historian Phillipe Ariès, the Western discovery of the individual led to emphasis on death as the termination of one's own life. "My death" represented the last act of a personal drama.[7] The development of the Protestant *ars moriendi* genre in England reflects this shift in attitude. "The Protestant *ars* writers aim, then, to mitigate man's fear of death and the spiritual paralysis it causes," observes David Atkinson. "In keeping with man's need for hope in the face of death they generally stress the rewards of preparing for death rather than the punishments of hell or the awfulness of God's judgment."[8] Instruction for and accounts of death also dwell increasingly on the glories of heaven.

John Wesley's very first sermon, "Death and Deliverance," in which he celebrates death as a passport to a happier life than this world affords, reflects his interest in the art of dying.[9] In another early sermon, "On Love," he includes two accounts of death and defines the "comfortable death" as "a calm passage out of life, full of even, rational peace and joy."[10] He had come to know the *ars moriendi* tradition most directly through Jeremy Taylor's *The Rule and Exercises of Holy Dying* (1651), but it had also been popularized by contemporary poets such as Edward Young in his *Night Thoughts* (1742) and James Hervey through his *Meditations Among the Tombs* (1745–46).[11] All of these devotional writers wielded tremendous influence, not only upon the Wesley brothers, but also among the rank and file of the Methodist movement.

The assumption of the Wesleys and their followers was that it took a lifetime of living to learn what it meant to die and that death, conversely, was the greatest schoolmaster of life. The fact that Methodists died well, they all believed, pointed to the ultimate triumph of love and of God's power to defeat all those forces that seek to separate us from that love. Despite their differing nuances related to the doctrine of Christian perfection, both Wesley brothers believed that the gift of perfect love—the goal of the Christian life—was usually deferred until the moment of death. This theological concern alone explains in large measure the widespread Methodist interest in accounts of triumphant death of all sorts.[12] End of life issues and the quest for perfect love merged in obvious and predictable ways. The witness of those who died in faith, glorifying God, cannot be underestimated with regard to the continuing growth of the Methodist movement throughout the eighteenth century and the continued stress on Christian perfection. Deathbed testimonies reinforced Wesley's concern that inordinate attachment to this world was the one great hindrance to saving faith in Christ and also confirmed the liberation—both in life and in death—that a God-centered existence affords. If the Christian ideal in both life and death was courage to face whatever providence might bring, then the miracles of justifying faith and growth toward the fullest possible love were twin gifts enabling "the assurance of things hoped for, the conviction of things not seen" (Heb. 11:1). The Methodist accounts of death, as a peculiar expression of the *ars moriendi*, helped inculcate the vision of holy living as a life emptied of spiritual pride and filled with the serenities of holy love of God and neighbor and helped shape the spirituality of early Methodist women and men alike.

All of the literary works in this section were written by women and are about women. Hester Ann Rogers contrasts the dying bed of the saint and the sinner in a brief devotional tract appended to virtually every edition of her *Experience* and *Letters*. Used most certainly as an evangelistic tool and as a word of encouragement to the believer, this document also demonstrates the centrality of the hymn in the spirituality of the women. Of the seven remaining accounts, the first three record the deaths of lesser-known women. The final selections provide a concluding portrait of four women who have figured very prominently in this volume. Although little is known about Ann Highfield, her subject, Ann Cutler, was noted as one of the greatest praying women of the Methodist movement. Mary Fletcher remembers her much-beloved "adopted daughter" in the faith, Sally Lawrence. The death of the first woman preacher, Sarah Crosby, is reported by her faithful companion, Ann Tripp. This collection of early Methodist women's spiritual writings is brought to a close, most appropriately, with the account of the death of Mary Fletcher, who bore faithful witness to the Pauline confession: "living is Christ and dying is gain" (Phil. 1:21).

A. *Ars Vivendi:* The Spiritual Life in Letters

1. MRS. LEFEVRE TO MRS. ***

Editor's Introduction

For an introduction to the life and work of Mrs. Lefevre, see part 2 above. In this excerpt from a letter to a friend, Mrs. Lefevre offers words of encouragement to someone who has been negligent in prayer. She describes the great peace of heart and mind that prayer affords and emphasizes the importance of placing one's trust in God. Acknowledging her own "wilderness states," she describes the faithfulness of God and the inexpressible joy of finding Christ anew.

* * * *

My dear friend,

I praise God with my whole heart for your happiness and strength, and I pray him to increase it every moment. Oh may that blessed peace never leave your soul. It is eternal life begun, and ten thousands laid in the balance with this peace would be all lighter than vanity. It is a glorious sign that in outward troubles or inward temptations, you can leave the means of your deliverance entirely to God, without suffering your imagination to run out after the manner in which you probably may be delivered. Oh that we could always venture ourselves upon the mercies of our God! Then would he indeed work wonders for us—wonders which we now can scarce believe, though the God of truth himself declares them unto us. And this God will surely keep you in the dangers to which you are going to be exposed if you will be watchful to keep the eye of your mind constantly turned towards him, and wait and hang upon him as a little child on its fond parent, drawing all your help, all your comfort from him, and him alone ... shut more closely the door of your heart, and there in its inmost recesses commune with your God and redeemer. There be continually crying unto him, "Lord you know all things, you know that I love you [see also John 21:17]; you know, O life and joy of my soul, that I desire nothing but to do your perfect will and to be conformed to the likeness of your sufferings, as well as to the likeness of your resurrection. Oh crucify in me the whole body of sin! Give me an humble, a mortified, and child-like spirit, and in your own good time perfect the work you have begun in my soul."

Still steadfastly fixed on the rock which cannot be moved [see also Psa. 62], we will endure, nay joyfully take up the reproach for his sake who hid not his blessed face from shame and spitting for our sakes [see also Isa. 50:6], to make us (accursed and lost creatures) heirs of eternal glory [see also Titus 3:7]. Oh that his strength may but accompany us, and the light of his countenance continually abide with us [see also Psa. 4:6]; and then we shall not fail to go on conquering and to conquer. Amen.

Oh cry to God every moment from the bottom of your heart and he will do more for you than you can either ask or think [see also Eph. 3:20]. I am a witness of his free and boundless mercy. For some days past I have been in the wilderness, my soul weary, faint, and desolate. No rejoicing in God. Not one ray from the sun of righteousness. But this morning, this blessed morning, my beloved returned to my soul and I rejoiced with joy unspeakable [see also 1 Pet. 1:8], and could say with the fullest assurance, "My sins are done away. Christ is mine. God the Father is my reconciled father. God the Holy Ghost is my comforter and guide." Oh my friend, my heart is now so overwhelmed I can scarce write. I could repeat a thousand and a thousand times over—Christ is mine. My soul is ready to spring out of its prison, and I could at this moment face death in all its utmost horrible prospects to go to my Redeemer. "Oh death, where is thy sting? Oh grave, where is thy victory" [1 Cor. 15:55]? My dear love, you know not what you lose by your negligence. Oh seek, strive, agonize. Could you suffer the utmost tortures in body or mind, they would be all as nothing to gain one moment of this sweetness. And oh pray for me, that I may not by sinning grieve the blessed comforter and lose my present peace. God be with you my dear friend. God bless you both now and for ever.

SOURCE:

[John Wesley], *An Extract of Letters by Mrs. L**** (Bristol: William Pine, 1769), 21-24.

A. *Ars Vivendi*: The Spiritual Life in Letters

2. Jane Cooper to Mrs. M. M.

Editor's Introduction

For an introduction to the life and work of Jane Cooper, see part 1 above. This brief note from Jane Cooper to a close friend contains a simple but potent articulation of her view of salvation by grace through faith. She affirms the centrality of true self-understanding and the enpersonalization of faith, wooing her recipient into a faith-based relationship with God through Christ.

* * * *

August 29, 1757

I sincerely rejoice to find you are convinced of a most important but self-abasing truth, that you are yourself utterly unable to work out your own salvation, or to form so much as one good thought, or one desire towards it. Rest not in this conviction, but seek, ask, knock [see also Matt. 7:7], and you shall assuredly obtain that faith which is the gift of God. Give me leave to repeat, that religion consists, first, in a true knowledge of our want of Christ. Secondly, in knowing him to be not only the Savior of the world, but *our* Savior in particular; in knowing him to have died for us that we might live through him. There is a great difference between this scheme of religion and that we form to ourselves when we begin to desire eternal happiness. I then thought I must refrain from evil words and be constant at church, and I should doubtless go to heaven, though I walked not in a narrow, but much frequented way. I saw not that Christ alone was the way to heaven. But though I could not but see my works were insufficient, yet I hoped God would accept this patchwork obedience and supply what was wanting. Beware of building your hopes on this sandy foundation. See, but seek forgiveness and acceptance with God through him who is the rock of ages. Let him not go until he bless you. For there is no safety but in his friendship, and no peace, but in his favor.

May every blessing attend my dear friend. Wherever her abode is, she has a place in my heart.

[Jane Cooper]

Source:

Wesley, *Letters Wrote by Jane Cooper*, 13-14.

3. [Mary] B.[osanquet] to a Friend

Editor's Introduction

For an introduction to the life and work of Mary Bosanquet [Fletcher], see part 2 above. Mary instructs a friend who struggles with an impediment that stands between her and full fellowship with God. One aspect of her message of encouragement is the confession that she has encountered similar difficulties in her life as well. Creating a sense of solidarity with her friend, she reminds her that little things can sometimes become great obstacles in relationships but that Jesus provides the antidote to all spiritual ailments.

* * * *

May 25, 1762

Dear Friend,

My desire and faith for you are greatly increased. There is no danger of my being wearied out. He that has laid the burden upon me will bear it for me, though I believe I feel it heavier than you do yourself. You cannot conceive what a weight it is to my soul! But I always find a blessing in praying for you.

My soul does exceedingly plead with the Lord that he would show you whatever hinders. Does not his Spirit point out something which it would be more excellent to do or to leave undone? Before he clearly showed me my way I had at times many secret warnings. Several little satisfactions I was, as it were, invited to sacrifice to Jesus. If I was faithful (but I seldom was) then more light broke in. But if not, the spirit of conviction was quenched and it was some time before I found it again. I found also that the sins I had long since committed might still be visited till I was deeply convinced of the guilt of them and carried them to the atoning blood. I likewise saw that I needed much searching and earnestly cried to God to discover to me those little foxes that still spoiled the vines [see also Sol. 2:15]. For by little things, especially if they touch the affections, we are often kept low.

Suffer not such a thought to approach as if the most excellent way was now shut up from you. I know Satan would gladly persuade you to think so. But regard him not. If you now desire to walk in the narrowest part of the narrow way, what should hinder you? Nothing is wanting on your Savior's part. Witness you streaming blood!

I exceedingly feel for you. I know what a cleaving temper is; and a grievous task it is to subdue it. But fear not! The greater the conflict, the more glorious shall your conquest be. True it is, nothing but a stroke of omnipotence can do you any good. But this you surely shall experience when once you earnestly wrestle with the angel of the covenant. O cry to the strong for strength! Redouble your cries! You have need of Jesus! No power in earth or heaven but his can do you any good. All other help is vain!

Bear with me a little further. While you are thus crying to Jesus, put away with all your might every thing that can in the least degree draw you to any creature. Even what is good for one in health may be poison in a dangerous fit of sickness. And what may be lawful to another, to your temper is absolutely unlawful. I feel for you in this. It is indeed tearing out a right eye and cutting off a right hand [see also Matt. 5:29]. But shrink not, neither be afraid. Stand firm as a beaten anvil to the stroke! Give up all for him who gave up all for you. And while you are resisting with your might, in one moment, Jesus, your Almighty Captain, will take out of your affections every thing displeasing to his pure eyes and make you holy as he is holy [see also 1 Pet. 1:16].

God has a peculiar favor for you and calls you to rest wholly on himself. Let not therefore Satan paint to your mind any other happiness.

Suffice for this the season past![13]

Now let you and I renounce from the ground of our heart, and keep at the utmost distance from the very appearance of idolatry.

The Lord guide and keep you!\
I am, dear Friend, your real well-wisher.\
M[ary]. B[osanquet].

SOURCE:

AM 4 (1781): 660-62.

4. Hannah Ball to Miss Bedford

Editor's Introduction

For an introduction to the life and work of Hannah Ball, see part 1 above. Hannah offers words of advice to her cousin with regard to the doctrine of assurance as linked with the experience of justification by grace through faith. Drawing upon the theological resources that John Wesley made available to his membership, she demonstrates her ability to deal effectively with serious theological questions.

* * * *

March 12, 1770

My Dear Cousin,

I suppose you think it long since I wrote to you. It has not been for the want of love, but of knowing what would be useful to you. Of this I am sensible that nothing will be useful without the blessing of God.

The Scripture says that "His Spirit bears witness with our spirits, that we are the children of God" [Rom. 8:17]. See what the Assembly's Catechism says on justification: "Justification is an act of God's free grace, wherein he pardoneth all our sins, and accepteth us as righteous in his sight, only for the righteousness of Christ imputed to us, and received by faith alone."[14] And can we believe anything and not know it?[15] Suppose a poor sinner under a deep sense of his guilt crying to God for forgiveness, and Jehovah speaks peace to his soul—would he not be sensible of it? Yes; and so much so that he could sing the song of Isaiah, as recorded in the 12th chapter of his prophecies: "O Lord, I will praise Thee: though Thou wast angry with me Thine anger is turned away, and Thou comfortest me. Behold, God is my salvation; I will trust and not be afraid, for the Lord Jehovah is my strength and my song. He also is become my salvation. Therefore with joy shall ye draw water out of the wells of salvation. And in that day shall ye say, Praise the Lord, call upon His name, declare His doings among the people, make mention that His name is exalted. Sing unto the Lord; for He hath done excellent things. This is known in all the earth. Cry out and shout, thou inhabitant of Zion, for great is the Holy One of Israel in the midst of thee" [Isa. 12:1-6]. Observe, my cousin, "in the midst of thee." Christ within you, the hope of glory [see also Col. 1:27]. Except we have the spirit of Christ, we are none of his. The Lord be with you, and give you a spiritual understanding in all things, is the prayer of, my dear cousin,

Yours affectionately,
H[annah]. Ball

SOURCE:

Joseph Cole, ed., *Memorials of Hannah Ball*, 3rd ed., revised (London: Wesleyan Conference Office, 1880), 47-49.

5. HANNAH BALL TO ANN BOLTON

Editor's Introduction

For an introduction to the life and work of Hannah Ball, see part 1 above. This letter is addressed to Ann ("Nancy") Bolton (1743?–1822) of Witney, one of Hannah's closest friends and a coworker in the Methodist movement.[16] John Wesley described Ann, one of his most valued correspondents, as "the sister of my choice" and linked her very closely with the pioneering work of Hannah and of other Methodist women. Writing to Francis Wolfe in 1775, he confessed:

> Ever since that madman took away her office in Witney from Nancy Bolton, Witney Society has dropped; such as Wycombe Society would do if you took away Hannah Ball from them. She has all Hannah's grace, with more sense. See that she be fully employed. You have not such another flower in all your gardens.[17]

Hannah Ball's letter to Ann opens with some discussion of the doctrine of assurance. Hannah then moves quickly to respond to Ann's request that she describe the way the Lord deals with her soul. The letter is filled with images of nourishment and the continual need to be fed.

* * * *

May 28, 1770

My Dear Sister,

I should be exceedingly glad to hear whether you have a clear witness that you are born of God.[18] If not, never let him go until he blesses you, for he surely will come, and will not tarry [see also Heb. 10:37]. Be assured you cannot seek in vain. The Lord bless you and keep you [see also Num. 6:24] is my earnest prayer.

Agreeably to your request, I joyfully proceed to acquaint you with the Lord's dealings with my soul, who am a tempted follower of the blessed Jesus. Glory be to him! I am not overcome. No, through various storms he gently clears my way and feeds my soul with food of which the world knows nothing. All is sweet that comes from my Jesus. I cannot be displeased with his choice. Ease or pain, life or death, all are sweet with Jesu's love, which, glory be to his name, I daily taste. If he sends me religious friends, I rejoice. If he withholds them from me, I am content. For I am well satisfied he knows what is best for me and most for his glory. And if he is glorified, I rejoice.

I feel I daily stand in need of fresh grace. And I often think the Lord feeds my soul in a spiritual sense, with the manna of his love as he did the children of Israel in the wilderness, day by day [see also Exod. 16]. For he gives me my daily bread [see also Matt. 6:11], and at night I have nothing over. In the morning I am as poor as a beggar. I arise and petition for fresh grace and strength. And I find if I have strong trials I have strength and grace granted me to encounter them. And if I ever fail, it is for want of looking to the strong for strength. I never feel satisfied but as I find my soul on the full stretch for eternal glory. I want to possess a bright crown. The way that leads to it is a suffering way. Up to this point I have not shrunk from the cross when I have clearly seen it was the will of the Lord I should take it up [see also Luke 9:23]. I have often erred through ignorance, but the desire of my heart is to be all the Lord's.

I need your prayers, for there is no one more frail than myself. Blessed be God, although surrounded with temptations, I am free from all entanglements of body and mind. I often long to depart and to be with Christ, which is far better, but my will is swallowed up in the will of God. O, may many be the living witnesses of God's power to save to the uttermost [see also Heb. 7:25]! I have three nieces and a nephew living with me who are about to enter on the stage of life to act their parts.[19] O, may they have grace to choose that good part that shall not be taken from them! Pray for them. My love to all Christian friends.

Your affectionate sister,
H[annah] Ball

SOURCE:

Cole, *Memorials of Hannah Ball*, 54-56.

6. Sarah Crosby to John Wesley

Editor's Introduction

For an introduction to the life and work of Sarah Crosby, see part 1 above. The letter presented here is one of only two letters in this collection addressed to John Wesley. Sarah writes to her spiritual mentor in response to a letter, hitherto unpublished, which she had copied in her "Manuscript Letterbook," the pertinent portion of which reads: "Do you see Christian Perfection now in the same light you did Twenty or Ten Years ago? In the same that it is describ'd in the 'Thts. upon perfection, or in the Plain Account'? And do you experience now what you did then?"[20] John Wesley examined his settled opinions in matters of theology in relation to the lived experiences of his followers. Given Sarah's stature within the movement, Wesley's esteem, and her profession of Christian perfection, he was concerned about the issue of perseverance in perfect love. Of particular concern to her was Wesley's own definition of "sin properly so-called," that is, "voluntary transgressions of a known law," and her desire to move away from language that seemed to imply "sinless perfection." Sarah provides a protracted discussion of this most central of Wesleyan themes.

* * * *

Cross Hall, Jan. 26, 1773

I own I have been long silent to your important questions, though not for want of regard, but traveling and many engagements prevented my having the quiet, undisturbed time for reading over the *Plain Account of Perfection*,[21] which I thought was quite needful in order to answer you justly and particularly.

But now I can assure you with a pleasing satisfaction that I was blessed in reading it, finding it solid food for my soul. But when that tract was first published, I did not altogether see with my own eyes, so did not fully approve.

Though there is one word which I have heard many express their dislike of, nor can I say that I like it. You say, "The most perfect have continual need of the merits of Christ, even for their *actual transgressions*."[22] Would it not have been less exceptionable in some other words? As, "for their transgressions through ignorance," which I humbly presume, dear Sir, is your meaning? Pardon the liberty I have taken in thus writing to my truly honored father.

I think I can likewise assure you, my judgment is the same now that it was ten years ago or more, unless for that space of time wherein I preferred S[arah] R[yan]'s[23] judgment to my own, and to speak simply, I preferred it to everybody's. But I believe there is some difference in my judgment now from what it was twenty years past.

It is now twenty-three years since I felt a want of something more than I had, having been justified near six months. But the predestinarians[24] made perfection to appear such a bugbear, I was affrighted at the thought of it, yet continued to be very uneasy at times. When reading your sermon on perfection[25] I said, provided this is what Mr. Wesley means by perfection, this is what I want, and I believe God can and that he will make me thus perfect. And I can never rest until I attain it. After this time, I often thought of the only words I remembered in your sermon, the first time I heard you, which were, "If it is possible for God to give us a little love, is it not possible for him to fill us with love?"[26] I then answered in my heart, "Yes; it is possible, but he won't do it." But now my language was changed, and I often said, Lord it is possible, O! that you would fill my soul with love.

Soon after this I told you my case. You gave me a ticket. O blessed time never to be forgotten by me. I now expected soon to be filled with pure love. And I felt great need of it, for my evil nature raged more than ever and I was very inexperienced in the knowledge of God or myself. I had constant need of saying,

> Force my violence to be still.
> Captivate my every thought,
> Charm, & melt, & change my will,
> And bring me down to naught.[27]

As I was now very simple, I freely and frequently expressed my desire and expectation and was willing to part with whatever could hinder my being closely united to Jesus. For my one desire was to love him perfectly. But I was often told I must have more knowledge of myself first, till I believed so too, and have sometimes thought myself better for knowing more of my evil nature than those that were happy in Jesus, whom I thought did not know themselves.

And now my judgment was changed for near five years to come, wherein I labored and prayed for a deeper and deeper knowledge of myself and a perfection that would save me from every natural infirmity and every deviation (though through ignorance) from the perfect law of God. At length the keen sense of want of constant union and communion with him, who was indeed the beloved of my soul, constrained me to cry mightily to him for help. For though I was favored with much nearness to and communion with him at times, I knew not how any longer to bear the feeling of anything that I knew displeased him, though in a less degree than ever. And my prayers and tears were not in vain. For Jesus showed me that as he had answered for my actual transgressions in his own body on the tree, so he had answered for my original sin and for every deviation from the perfect law. He then gave my heart a power to believe him thus my whole Savior, which I never could do before. And now I felt a peace come into my soul, superior to all I had ever known and which I could not tell how to explain, till it came as though someone had spoken. It is the peace that ruled the heart of Christ in the days of his flesh. There were many more particulars, which I haven't room for, and have acquainted you with many years ago. O may my every breath be praise.

And now my Lord instructed me as a little child, daily showing me how wrong my former judgment had been, from feeling myself still surrounded with various infirmities, and yet a sweet, constant union with him, which these did not interrupt nor would they have interrupted before but through want of faith. So that I now saw every failure in obedience was for want of more faith. And as I received freely, so I freely gave [see also Matt. 10:8], laboring to show all with whom I conversed the way of faith more perfectly.

And thus I now believe and endeavor to practice, and have so believed from the time above mentioned. (Only when I observed the wrong use some made of what they called faith, and how likely many more were thus to err, I spoke more of the necessity and blessing of self-knowledge. And doubtless a blessing it is to know much of our own helplessness and natural tendencies to depart from the living God, which faith only, as the instrument, saves us from.)

But in answer to your question, dear Sir, whether I now experience what I did then? I freely acknowledge I have not uninterruptedly enjoyed so great a degree of the glorious liberty wherewith Christ made me free sixteen years past, as I did then. For although I have been kept in many a close and sore trial and temptation, yet in others I think I have sunk below my privilege. And I have sometimes been drawn in some degree from my center, by preferring others' lights to my own. But gratefully do I praise my heavenly Father that I could never find my rest below this blessed mark. That is, loving God with all my redeemed powers and aiming to serve him the best I could.

And glory be to his ever adorable name, I now find him as precious and present with me as ever. He is the center of all my hopes, the end of my enlarged desires. I have no pursuits nor wishes but to please him and no fears but to offend him. I would live to do his will, or I would die to see him. He knows I love him with a measure of the same love wherewith he has and does love me. And I know he will be my friend in life and death the same.

All my good comes from him. He is the life and strength of my soul and without him I can do nothing [see also John 15:5]. Yea I am nothing. A poor, weak worm, helpless as infancy, and surrounded with numerous infirmities. Lord, help and humble me.

As one entirely unworthy your notice, dear Sir, I commend myself to your prayers, wishing you all the blessings of the new covenant, with long life and life everlasting.

I remain with all due respect, in divine bonds,

Your Affectionately obedient
child and servant,
S[arah]. Crosby

SOURCE:

Holograph at Duke University[28]

7. Hester Ann Roe to a Family Friend

Editor's Introduction

For an introduction to the life and work of Hester Ann Roe [Rogers], see part 1 above. The following letter appeared as letter 1 in all the editions of Hester's *Spiritual Letters*, originally published separately, but subsequently appended to her popular *Experience*. The author finds herself in a position of having to defend her new-found faith to her family and their wealthy circle of friends who consider themselves faithful to the institutional church and believe Hester to be apostate in her views. She presents one of the most thoughtful apologies for Wesleyan theology and bases her position on scripture (the letter is little more than a string of scriptural passages, drawing particularly on Romans), the Articles of Religion, and Homilies of the Church of England. She marshals her sources, integrating her view of the atonement with a Pauline understanding of justification by grace through faith. Salvation, in her view, is composed of three basic aspects: (1) obedience to God's law, (2) satisfaction owed by fallen humanity to God, and (3) restoration of the moral image of God to the soul. This holistic vision of the Christian life is a profound articulation of the Wesleyan synthesis of the forensic and therapeutic understandings of salvation.

* * * *

Macclesfield, Nov. 12, 1775

Dear and Honored Madam,

I beg leave to return you my most sincere and humble thanks for your kind letter and advice, and as you are so kind as to express a concern on my account, I hope you will pardon the liberty and allow me to say what is my opinion and belief, and on what alone I can build any hopes of heaven and happiness.

Man, as he came out of the hands of the Creator, was perfectly holy and happy. In him shone all those amiable and lovely attributes of the deity—goodness, truth, justice, mercy, and love. But by disobeying the divine command he entailed upon himself and his whole posterity (for he acted as the parent or head of all mankind) the sure wages of sin, which is death—death temporal, spiritual, and eternal [see also Rom. 6:23]. The body of man became that day mortal, his soul spiritually dead, and he was every moment liable to death eternal. The guilt of Adam and the depravity of soul which he contracted by the fall immediately devolved upon his unhappy offspring. And, we are told, when he begat a son, it was "in his own likeness, after his image" [Gen. 5:3], so that now man is born in sin and under the wrath of God, and if he die in that state will stand exposed to the sentence of eternal death. And what can a lost man do in this case? Atonement for himself, or offering meet, he does not have to bring. And to pardon sinners without a satisfaction would not be what is commonly called mercy, but it would be giving up the essential glory of the Godhead.[29] What must be done then? Why, God of his free grace and unlimited bounty has provided a ransom [see also Mark 10:45], an all-sufficient ransom, even his well-beloved Son! He who is the brightness of his Father's glory, and the express image of his person [see also Heb. 1:3] became man to die that man might live.

All that was necessary to be done to complete our salvation consisted chiefly in these three things. First, a perfect obedience to the divine law. Secondly, an infinitely meritorious satisfaction to the law and government of God for the dishonor brought upon them by the sin of man. Thirdly, a restoration of the moral image of God to the soul, which image was lost by the fall of man. The first of these was completed by the life of our Redeemer, the second by his death, and the third is effected by the Holy Ghost. This provision (ample provision) is made for the salvation of man, so that God can preserve untainted his adorable perfections, or, as St. Paul declares, he can now be just and yet justify and save penitent, believing man [see also Rom 3:26].

That Christ suffered in the place of sinners is expressed by St. Peter in these words, "Who, his own self, bare our sins in his own body on the tree" [1 Pet. 2:24]. Also, Isaiah says, "Surely he hath borne our griefs, and carried our sorrows. He was wounded for our transgressions, he was bruised for our iniquities. All we like sheep have gone astray; we have turned every one to his own way, and the Lord hath laid on him the iniquity of us all" [Isa. 53:4-6]. St. Paul says, "He hath made him to be sin for us, who knew no sin, that we might be made the righteousness of God in him"

[2 Cor. 5:21]. And again, in the third chapter of the Romans, he says, "There is none righteous, no, not one. There is none that understandeth. There is none that seeketh after God. They are all gone out of the way. They are together become unprofitable. There is none that doeth good, no, not one" [Rom. 3:10-12]. Therefore, he adds, "By the deeds of the law there shall no flesh be justified in his sight. But now the righteousness which is without the law is manifest, being witnessed by the law and the prophets, even the righteousness of God, which is by faith in Jesus Christ, unto all, and upon all them that believe. For there is no difference, for all have sinned and come short of the glory of God. Being justified freely by his grace, through the redemption that is in Christ Jesus, whom God hath set forth to be a propitiation through faith in his blood, to declare his righteousness for the remission of sins that are past, through the forbearance of God. To declare, I say, at this time his righteousness, that he might be just, and the justifier of him that believeth in Jesus" [20-26].

With St. Paul, then, I would go on and ask, "Where is boasting then? It is excluded. By what law? Of works? Nay; but by the law of faith. Therefore, we conclude, that a man is justified by faith, without the deeds of the law [27-29]. For, to him that worketh is the reward not reckoned of grace, but of debt. But to him that worketh not, but believeth on him that justifieth the ungodly, his faith is counted for righteousness. Even as David also described the blessedness of the man unto whom God imputeth righteousness without works, saying, Blessed are they whose iniquities are forgiven, and whose sins are covered. Blessed is the man unto whom the Lord will not impute sin [Rom. 4:4-8]. Abraham believed God, and it was imputed to him for righteousness [Rom. 4:3]. Now it was not written for his sake alone what it was imputed to him, but for us also, to whom it shall be imputed, if we believe on him that raised up Jesus our Lord from the dead, who was delivered for our offences and was raised again for our justification" [Rom. 4:23-25]. Now from all these and many more texts of Holy Scripture which might be named, I believe and am sure that works are not the meritorious cause of our salvation, yet I believe they are absolutely necessary, and will follow as the sure and inseparable fruits of a true faith.[30] If you will be kind enough to read the Eleventh, Twelfth, and Thirteenth Articles of the Church of England, they will further explain my meaning.[31]

But there is a third thing also necessary to our salvation, which is that the image of God be restored to the soul. Now, this is done in regeneration. Our Savior assures us, "Except a man be born again, he cannot see the kingdom of God" [John 3:3]. And again, "Except ye be converted, and become as little children, ye shall not enter into the kingdom of heaven" [Matt. 18:3]. Nor indeed are we fit for it, till renewed by the Spirit of God. For, were it possible to be admitted there, we could not enjoy the pure and spiritual delight of the saints above. Their joy consists in an entire freedom from all sin and corruption, and in serving, adoring, praising the Father of all their mercies, the Son of his love, and Spirit of holiness. And they are so far from being weary of this that they think eternity too short to utter all his praise! How irksome would be an eternity spent in this manner to a person who never had his affections spiritualized and his will brought into a conformity to the will of God? This is a change which must be wrought in this world. For there is no repentance in the grave. As death leaves us, judgment will find us. Then, "He that is unjust shall be unjust still. He that is filthy shall be filthy still. And he that is righteous shall be righteous still. And he that is holy shall be holy still" [see also Rev. 22:11]. The Holy Ghost is the author of this conversion or new birth. For no man hath quickened his own soul. It is he that must begin, carry on, and complete it.

Now, if any man have not the spirit of Christ, he is none of his. And the fruits of this Spirit are "love, joy, peace, long-suffering, gentleness, goodness, faith, meekness, temperance, against such there is no law. And they that are Christ's have crucified the flesh with its affections and lusts" [Gal. 5:22-24]. "If any man be in Christ he is a new creature; old things are passed away; behold, all things are become new" [2 Cor. 5:17]. And Jesus Christ is made of God unto us "wisdom, righteousness, sanctification, and redemption, that according as it is written, he that glorieth, let him glory in the Lord" [1 Cor. 1:30-31]. "God forbid that I should glory, save in the cross of our Lord Jesus Christ, by whom the world is crucified unto me, and I unto the world" [Gal. 6:14].

This, dear madam, is what I believe, and this, I think, is agreeable to the word of God and to the Articles and Homilies of the

Church of England, and no schism of the church of Christ. Forfeiting your love and friendship is a great trial. But believe me, when I think of seeking salvation in any other way it seems as a sword piercing my very heart! And seeing my dear mother so very unhappy on my account gives me more grief than I can express. And the thought of my being detrimental to her in worldly things, and that my conduct should make you less her friend, seems strange, and is to me very afflicting. But I think these things ought not to be urged too far, especially when the soul is concerned.

I am afraid I have tired your patience, so will hasten to subscribe myself, honored madam, your most obliged and dutiful daughter,

H. A. Roe

SOURCE:

An Account of the Experience of Hester Ann Rogers (New York: Hunt & Eaton, 1893), 180-86.

A. *Ars Vivendi*: The Spiritual Life in Letters

8. Hester Ann Roe to [Ann] Loxdale

Editor's Introduction

For an introduction to the life and work of Hester Ann Roe [Rogers], see part 1 above. In 1811, Ann Loxdale married Dr. Thomas Coke, an Anglican priest, Methodist bishop in America, and pioneer in mission.

Hester opens her letter in a strongly mystical vein. Her language is that of bathing, plunging, sinking into the love of the trinitarian God. But her mystical flight shifts rather immediately into a more cerebral explication of the Wesleyan doctrine of Christian perfection. Critical to her discourse is the employment of Wesley's classic definition of sin as a willful transgression of God's law.[32] Christian perfection, she is clear to point out, is freedom from "sin properly so-called." It is the power not to sin willfully and its concomitant freedom from the tyranny of evil. She attempts to describe, explain, and defend Wesley's doctrine so that her recipient will have the proper evidence to launch her own apologetic.

* * * *

Nantwich, June 30, 1779

Dear Sister,

My dear friend's letter was indeed a pleasure and a blessing to me. And my Lord's great goodness to you is a fresh motive to love and praise him. But fresh motives of this kind are no new things to me. I am ever discovering instances of his goodness that fill me with wonder and astonishment and cause me to exclaim with holy David, "Lord, what is man, that thou art mindful of him" [Psa. 8:4]? Great things, indeed, my dear sister, has the Lord done for you, and for your unworthy friend. And yet, O stupendous grace! we have only received a drop from the ocean of his love. An endless prospect, and a maze of bliss, lie yet before us! opening beauties, and such lengths, and breadths, and depths, and heights, as thought cannot reach or mind of man conceive! It is, my friend, the fulness of the triune God, in which we may bathe, and plunge, and sink, till lost and swallowed up in the ever-increasing, overflowing ocean of delights. His fulness. O what is it! Shall we ever fathom it? ever know a ten thousandth part? Ah no! A ten thousandth part of that effulgence we could not bear to know and live! Nay, and when disembodied through the revolving ages of eternity, I am persuaded we shall only seem beginning to know his fulness of love.

What thoughts are these! When I enter into them, as into a labyrinth, they almost overcome my natural powers. O how very little of his revealed glory can this earthen vessel contain! But a time is hastening on (and I eagerly wait for its approach) when, no longer imprisoned in clay, our eyes shall be strengthened to see him as he is, see him for ourselves, and bask for ever in his smiles. Yes, we shall be with Jesus and behold his glory. He will reveal to us also, as much as we can bear, of the fulness of the Father's glory. And we shall be with Father, Son, and Spirit, filled to all eternity! But I have been led further than I intended. I must return.

Permit me to ask, my dear friend, what are your ideas, what is your opinion, or what your experience of inward, instantaneous sanctification, whereby the root, the in-being of sin is destroyed? I do not mean or allude to a state of angelic or Adamic, but a Christian perfection, a destruction of every temper contrary to love, a state consistent with many temptations of the devil, if our hearts repel those temptations, and our will do not embrace or yield to them. For that cannot be sin, in which our will has no part.[33] Thus it was with Jesus. "In him was not sin, yet he was tempted in all points as we are" [Heb. 4:15]. Before his pure eyes did that enemy display all the kingdoms of the world and the glory of them [see also Matt. 4:8]. To his spotless soul he suggested disturbing doubts and presumptuous expectations. But in the Son of God they found no place. Again, what I mean is a state consistent with a growth in grace. For Jesus, though always pure, "increased in wisdom and stature, and in favour with God and man" [Luke 2:52]. Is not such a state expressed and described in the thirteenth of the first book of Corinthians? And is it not commanded in these gracious words, "Rejoice evermore, pray without ceasing, and in every thing give thanks" [1 Thess. 5:17]? Does the apostle add, "This is the will of God concerning you" [5:18]? And after praying, "Now the God of peace sanctify you wholly," does he not pray that "your whole spirit, soul, and body, (after they are so sanctified,) may be preserved blameless to the coming of our Lord Jesus

Christ" [5:23]? Then follows the glorious promise, "Faithful is he that calleth you, who also will do it" [5:24]. And is not the same thing promised in the sweet passage you named: "I will sprinkle clean water upon you, and you shall be clean. From all your filthiness, and from all your idols will I cleanse you" [Ezek. 36:25]? And again, did he not "swear to our father Abraham, that he would grant unto us, that we, being delivered out of the hands of our enemies, might serve him without fear, in holiness and righteousness before him all the days of our life" [Luke 1:73-75]? By the state I weakly attempt to describe I mean that degree of humble love which excludes every temper contrary thereto, and faith that excludes the remains of unbelief and every tormenting fear. "For he that feareth is not made perfect in love" [1 John 4:18]. It is "fellowship with the Father, and with his Son Jesus Christ" [1 John 1:3], through the Spirit, by whose abiding witness we can say, "Abba, Father [Rom. 8:15]—my Lord and my God" [John 20:28] with an unwavering tongue.

I know this precious gospel salvation is even derided by some and exploded by many. Perhaps you may have conversed with some of these, and not have met with many who have dared to speak for God in this respect. Some of my expressions may therefore appear odd or unusual, but compare them with scripture and mention with freedom any of them you wish me to explain. As I know your situation, you will excuse the liberty I take in advising you not to meddle with opinions. This will insensibly eat out of the soul the precious life of God. Dispute not with any, or, if they seek doubtful disputations, it is a good way to propose prayer. But it may be well, as much as can be, to avoid the company of those who love vain controversy. Endeavor to possess a calm, recollected spirit—a heartfelt union with a holy God. Sweet truth—God is love, and love is the Christian's all. Love in us is his nature imparted. It is the fulfilling of the law [see also Rom. 13:10], the perfect law of liberty [see also James 1:25]. Whosoever "loveth his brother" hath fulfilled the law to his neighbor [see also 1 John 4:21]. And he who "loveth the Lord his God with all his heart, and soul, and mind, and strength," hath fulfilled the law to him also [see also Mark 12:30]. To such "his commandments are not grievous" [1 John 5:3], not a task, a wearisome burden, but a delight. "They are ways of pleasantness—they are paths of peace" [Prov. 3:17]. And as we are under a law of love to God, so God, our God in Christ, is under a covenant of love in which is made over to us all he is and all he has to give. His every attribute. His wisdom to guide and teach. His power to protect, and help, and strengthen. His faithfulness, his truth, his mercy, all sealed over and secured by covenant promises and covenant blood.

O my dear sister, what a blessed portion is ours! Let us determine to prove it all. We may, I trust we shall, and together praise in endless day the great Three One. I am ever yours in him,

H[ester]. A[nn]. Roe

SOURCE:

Account of the Experience of Hester Ann Rogers, 223-27.

A. *Ars Vivendi:* The Spiritual Life in Letters

9. Elizabeth Ritchie to John Wesley

Editor's Introduction

This is the first of two letters by Elizabeth Ritchie (1754–1835), later Mrs. Mortimer, included in this collection. Her published life and her spiritual letters, like those of Hester Ann Rogers, were well-known in the circles of early Methodism and functioned as important instructional documents. A native of Edinburgh, Elizabeth's father had served as a naval surgeon before his retirement to the Yorkshire Dales and then, after her older brother's birth, to Otley, near York. Despite being raised in affluent and cultured circumstances, her family sympathized strongly with religious reform. Through an interesting chain of events, including Wesley's visit to her parents' home in 1770, Elizabeth experienced God's grace in her life and committed herself to the Wesleyan way. On July 3, 1771, at eighteen years of age, she began to keep a spiritual journal that documents the dynamic nature of her life of faith.[34]

Elizabeth carried on a lively correspondence with John Wesley from 1774 to 1788, during which time she frequently apprized him of Methodist activities throughout the north of England, keeping her finger on the spiritual pulse of the movement. Contrary to his general rule to write only in reply to letters he received, he initiated much correspondence with her related to "spiritual advice." She cared for the elderly Wesley in his dying days and, at the request of Dr. John Whitehead, prepared a narrative account of his death.[35] In the following letter she provides some indication of her busy schedule and evangelistic activities, involving extended travel throughout the northern shires.

* * * *

Otley, November 11th, 1782

Will my Reverend and dear father excuse my seeming negligence? While I was from home the multiplicity of my engagements among the people wherever I went left me no time for writing. But, now that I am again settled in my peaceful dwelling I will endeavour to give a little account of the many mercies bestowed on me and others during my late journey.

I found, as you observed, at Liverpool, a new scene opened to me.[36] For some years my lot has not been cast so much among worldly people as at that place. But, blessed be God, he kept me separate in spirit from those that knew him not! Never did I feel more love and pity for those who were entangled in the allurements of this vain world, or more thankfulness to that God whose gracious love had set my spirit free. As to our own people there, they are very friendly and kind.

At Macclesfield I found a happy, lively people, and was greatly refreshed among them. I spent a few days with our dear friends, Mr. and Mrs. Mayer,[37] at Portwood, where I was much humbled and richly comforted. The Stockport society love the whole truth, but, as yet, few of them enjoy the full liberty of the gospel. At Bolton I had a good time. The Lord blessed me in my own soul, and gave his blessing to the people.

O that the love which is the fulfilling of the law may everywhere prevail! I rejoice in the prosperity of others; and, blessed be God, I daily rejoice in him whose love is without measure or end. Never was my spirit more disengaged from all beneath. And though, at times, I deeply feel how much more fully I might have improved all my mercies, yet I am kept from discouragement by the reviving presence of my Lord, who by his Spirit points out and discovers this to me with inexpressible tenderness. I see such wisdom, such love in all his dealings with me as sinks me into the dust and fills my heart with grateful praise.

May all blessings be poured from on high upon my dear and much-loved father! I am, my dear Sir,

Your truly affectionate, though
unworthy child,
E[lizabeth]. Ritchie

SOURCE:

Agnes Bulmer, ed., *Memoirs of Mrs. Elizabeth Mortimer*, 2nd ed. (London: J. Mason, 1836), 106-8.

A. *Ars Vivendi*: The Spiritual Life in Letters

10. Sarah Crosby to Mary Holder

Editor's Introduction

For an introduction to the life and work of Sarah Crosby, see part 1 above. The first woman preacher of Methodism, Sarah Crosby, wrote the following letter of encouragement to an aspiring preacher and potential colleague, describing the central conviction that had sustained her life and ministry. The recipient, Mary [Woodhouse] Holder (1751–1836), was born in Whitby and was admitted as a teenager to the Methodist Society by William Brammah in 1767.[38] During the 1770s, she linked herself with the important circle of women, including Mary Bosanquet and Elizabeth Ritchie as well as with her correspondent here. All of these women held important positions of leadership within the Methodist movement and engaged in preaching ministries of tremendous influence. After her marriage to a Methodist preacher, George Holder, she assisted her husband in his various circuits.

* * * *

Kirkstall-Forge, June 20, 1790

My Dear Sister,

How thankful I was and am to know that you not only stand fast in the Lord, but are taking up your cross that you may follow the Lamb wherever he goes. "One cross, one glory, and one crown." Our reverend and dear father's direction to me used to be, "Do all you can for God."[39] I believe it would be the same to you, because Moses like Mr. Wesley, would say, "Oh that all the Lord's people were Prophets" [Num. 11:29].

Where we know we have the Lord's approbation, we should stand like the beaten anvil to the stroke, or lie in his hands as clay in the hands of the potter [Jer. 18:6]. Through evil report and good we pass, but all things work together for good to them that love God [Rom. 8:28].

I trust my dear that your dear husband and you will steadily press forward in the narrow path into which our dear Lord has brought you, remembering his blessed word, "One of you shall chase a thousand, and two of you shall put ten thousand to flight" [see also Deut. 32:30]. Fear not, only believe [see also Luke 8:50].

Speak and act as the spirit gives liberty and utterance. Fear not the face of man, but with humble confidence trust in the Lord, looking unto him who is able and willing to save to the uttermost all that come unto God by him [see also Heb. 7:25].

In waiting upon the Lord, we renew our strength [see also Isa. 40:31]. How sweetly fulfilled was this by the blessed manifestation given you, although you understood not the Manx language. Oh, how great is his goodness and how great is his beauty. If we should not love and adore the great and glorious Jehovah, surely the very stones would cry out against us [see also Luke 19:40]. Yea, but we will, we do love the altogether lovely and cry "sinner you may love him too." Lord in mercy look upon them.

I also my dear friend hope for an interview with you when God so orders it and believe it will be for good. Tell them we rest in his providential order, feeling the blessing of being disposed of by our Lord and not left in our own hands, for our greatest crosses (which we should not choose) are designed for our greatest good. My dear friend [Ann] Tripp[40] unites with me in the best love to you both. She is but in a weak state of health, but has been much worse, yet sweetly resigned and earnestly desiring a greater meetness for the glory which shall shortly be revealed. As to myself, I have often much pain to labor with, the consequence of increasing years, and much labor too in constantly meeting three classes and bands, visiting the sick and well, and other employments. And glory be to my Lord, I can say he makes my duty my delight. I can now praise him for all that is past and trust him for all that's to come.

I am often very thankful on reflection how I was enabled to go on in past years. And although I cannot do much now, my master is not hard with me, but accepts according to that which I have and gives me a feeling sense that he is love to my soul. I walk in his light and stand in his might. Glory be to his name for his goodness to such an unworthy worm. Oh! how faithful is our God! "even unto hoary hairs will I carry you" [Isa. 46:4]. Yea, he will show himself beyond the grave, our everlasting friend.

Our three preachers are, I believe, much united, and the people in general united to them all. We have had a good increase and many conversions for which I unfeignedly praise our dear Lord.

A. *Ars Vivendi:* The Spiritual Life in Letters

> When brethren all in one agree,
> Who knows the joy of unity.⁴¹

Pray for us, as we for you, my dear friends. Farewell in him we love, in whom

I am, Your's with much
affection,
S[arah] Crosby

Source:

Zechariah Taft, *Original Letters* (Whitby: George Clark, 1821), 66-67.

11. Mary Fletcher to Mrs. Dalby

Editor's Introduction

For an introduction to the life and work of Mary [Bosanquet] Fletcher, see part 2 above. Two of Mary Fletcher's letters to a Mrs. Dalby of Castle-Donnington in Leicestershire, of whom little is known, were published in the 1818 issue of the *Methodist Magazine*. The first (of which an excerpt is presented here) is dated December 26, 1792; the second (presented here in its entirety) is dated August 27, 1793. The first letter is a response to Mrs. Dalby's request for guidance concerning the quest for holiness. The second letter is a lengthy exposition of the prayer of Jabez in 1 Chronicles 4. Both letters demonstrate the importance of spiritual direction and guidance among the Methodist women.

* * * *

Do you ask what is the surest and shortest way to holiness? Alas, how shall I answer the important question! I can only tell you what way agrees best with my soul. First, as the ground work of my expectation, I look for all in and through Jesus alone. I see it all free gift, therefore may expect as well to receive it this moment as another. And if I have been a sinner of the most scarlet die, then, having much forgiven I am encouraged to believe I shall love the more.

As to the manner of seeking, I have always found private prayer the truest touchstone. I do not mean it was never well with me when prayer was difficult. No, that is not the mark. But when I labor most in prayer, I get best forward. When I am very conversant with the throne of grace, I soon discern there is a passage from that to the holy of holies, and a continual look brings a continual power. For while we abide in Jesus, he stands as walls and bulwarks of salvation round the believing soul. In that spot may you and I for ever dwell!

If any thing I can write may be of use or comfort to you, I am ready to comply with your desire. I am sensible our heavenly Father does speak by whom or what he pleases. And now, Lord, what shall I say to your handmaid?

It comes on my mind to recommend to your imitation the prayer of Jabez; "And Jabez called on the God of Israel, saying, Oh that thou would bless me indeed, and enlarge my coast; and that thine hand might be with me, and that thou wouldest keep me from evil, that it may not grieve me! And God granted him that which he requested" (1 Chron. 4:10).

You complain, my dear sister, that your soul is not fixed and settled but prone to wander from your good shepherd's side. Then cry to the God of Israel to enlarge your coast, to bring you into that rest which remains for the people of God, that being rooted and grounded in love [Eph. 3:17], you may abide in the good land of which it is said, "The eyes of the Lord are upon it, from the beginning of the year to the end of the year" [Deut. 11:12]. Then, in order to facilitate your entrance, may you not ask, Lord, enlarge my coast of *prayer*. Drive out those spirits of unbelief or distraction which so interrupt my approaches to the throne of grace. Pour out upon me the spirit of grace and supplication. Prayer is, indeed, the key to heaven. But if by neglect and sloth we let it grow rusty, the hand of faith will find it very hard to turn it. Oh, let us then plead for the power to pray without ceasing [see also 1 Thess. 5:17].

Secondly, may we not ask, Lord enlarge my coast of *understanding*. You say your "heart is full of corruption; your mind of darkness and error." Well then, join me in this prayer. Enlarge my soul's capacity for spiritual things. Make me comprehend the length, the breadth, the height, the depth, of your incomprehensible love, according to my measure [see also Eph. 3:18]. Let me feel that this is eternal life to "know thee," and "Jesus Christ whom thou hast sent" [John 17:3]. Show me the wonders of your word. Let my eye be single and my whole body full of light [see also Matt. 6:22]. Yes, let me be filled with "all wisdom" and "spiritual understanding" [Col. 1:9].

Thirdly, let us plead for an enlargement of our *spiritual affections*. You know it is love that casts out fear [see also 1 John 4:18]. You tell me, "I often fear (or rather Satan suggests it) that it is impossible for me to escape eternal vengeance." Well then, let us lift up our voice and cry mightily for an enlargement of this part of our coast. Give us, O Lord, the ardent flaming love. Let every idol fall before you, and the Lord alone be exalted in our souls! Grant us love to you with our whole hearts. For whatever we have besides, or without this love, we are but as sounding brass or a tinkling cymbal [see also 1 Cor. 13:1].

Fourthly, St. Paul advises, "Covet earnestly the best gifts" [1 Cor. 12:31]. May we then not ask an enlargement of coast, so far in this particular as shall tend to lead ourselves or others to the more excellent way? May we not ask a tongue touched with a living coal from the altar that may enjoy the honor of being God's advocate, may plead his cause with man, and sound forth with heavenly wisdom the Redeemer's praise? And as the child of God knows no interest but his, may we not add, enlarge the coast of Zion which is mine because it is yours—let me behold the prosperity of Jerusalem and fulfil that word, "Thy sons shall be brought from far, and thy daughters shall be nursed at thy side" [Isa. 60:4].

Fifthly, but above all let us cry, "Enlarge my coast of *faith*, since God has chosen this grace to be the measure of all the rest." If you can believe, all things are possible. Be it unto you according to your faith [see also Matt. 9:29]. Faith is the uniting principle which, as the neck, joins to our sacred head, his body, the church.

Again, Jabez asks, "Let thine hand be with me" [1 Chron. 4:10]. It is the presence of God that brings all good and preserves from all evil. "If thou art but with me all shall be well," says the Enoch-like soul who longs to walk with God. You observe, "I want that faith by which the soul discerns a present Savior in every time of need." Ah! this is the point. Then let us ask it in faith. Jesus, give us the power to abide in your presence! One says, "Recollection is faith and silence in the presence of God."[42] Faith which relies on the "full, perfect, all-sufficient sacrifice,"[43] and whether in darkness or light still labors to hold fast confidence and keep its grasp of the shield, well knowing "this is the victory that overcometh, even our faith" [1 John 5:4].

This presence of God (or rather, the recollection of it) implies a silence of spirit, cutting off useless thoughts and waiting, as Mary, at the Master's feet [see also Luke 10:39], sweetly sinking under every cross and making it our one business never to turn away our eye from the Savior, which is indeed a transforming look.

"And that thou wouldest keep me from evil, that it may not grieve me." I think this part of Jabez's prayer will never be answered but by the accomplishment of that promise, "I will sprinkle clean water upon thee, and thou shalt be clean" [Ezek. 36:25]. For the soul that loves will be always grieved with any departure from the Lord. But he has promised to cleanse us from all our idols, and self being the grand Baal, I will most heartily join you when you say, "ask for me genuine poverty of spirit." Yes, my friend, let us "ask, seek, and knock" [Matt. 7:7], for when we have learned of him to be "meek and lowly" [Matt. 11:29], we shall possess an heaven in our souls. "And God granted him that which he requested." Let us try what prayer can do. Let us keep in the faith and silence of true recollection, and "pray without ceasing" [1 Thess. 5:17], till we can rejoice evermore and in every thing give thanks, "in a more abundant manner" [see also Phil. 1:26] than we have yet experienced.

I think it is time to bid you farewell, for you know not in how much pain I write. It at present so affects my head to look steadily on anything. However, lame hand and lame head has striven for once to obey the dictates of my heart, which desires your spiritual enlargement, and that of those you mention. May the rich love of Jesus be made known to you all, prays your sincere friend and servant in Christ,

M. Fletcher

SOURCE:

WMM 41 (1818): 687-90.

12. ELIZABETH HURRELL TO FRANCES PAWSON

Editor's Introduction

Awakened under the preaching of the Reverend J. Berridge, Elizabeth Hurrell (1740–98) became one of the most noteworthy women preachers of the north, traveling extensively throughout Yorkshire, Lancashire, and Derbyshire. Zechariah Taft observed that her preaching "often manifested such a strength of thought, and felicity of expression, as were irresistibly impressive."[44] For unknown reasons, but perhaps owing to pressure put upon her by influential Methodist leaders who opposed her work, Elizabeth discontinued preaching in 1780, died in London on March 13, 1798, and was interred at the City Road Chapel. In retrospect, she deeply lamented her decision to abandon her call. Shortly before her death she is purported to have said: "I am going to die.... O that I had my time to live again, I would not bury my talent as I have done."[45]

Her recipient, Frances [Mortimer] Pawson (1736–1809), was one of the most well-known early Methodist women at the beginning of the nineteenth century by virtue of her *Experience*, published after her death by Joseph Sutcliffe and widely read in Methodist circles.[46] Her own spiritual journey, that led eventually to great depth and maturity of faith, had been a crucible of doubt and searching. Through it all she had developed an intense loyalty to the Methodist movement, its leaders, and particularly the important circle of women preachers in Yorkshire, including the author. In the following letter, Elizabeth expresses her concerns to Frances about the changes she has observed in Methodism subsequent to the death of John Wesley. Of primary concern are the divisive forces, here related in particular to the agitation of Alexander Kilham, who did, in fact, lead the first schism of Wesleyan Methodism in his foundation of the Methodist New Connexion just two years after this letter was written.[47] Her commitment to the unity of the church was an important aspect of her Wesleyan spirituality.

* * * *

A. *Ars Vivendi:* The Spiritual Life in Letters

No. 3, Winkworth Buildings
City Road, April 21, 1795

My very dear Friend,

Neither distance or time has erased you from my affection, and although I have been silent, I've often reflected with pleasure on the agreeable moments spent in your company. And though we have been called to pass through various trials, yet I trust we have seen the hand of God therein, and join the book in saying, "Thy every act pure blessing is; Thy path unsullied Light."[48]

Permit me, at length, to congratulate you on your union with our valuable and esteemed friend whom I have held in the highest estimation, believing him an Israelite indeed in whom there was no allowed guile [see also John 1:47].[49]

> May you mutually help each other on
> 'Til both receive the starry crown.[50]

May you never seek your own but the Lord's glory and the salvation of precious souls, how need such daily cry,

> The bondage of corruption break,
> For this my spirit groan;
> Thy only will I feign would seek,
> Oh! save me from my own.[51]

The Methodist Church[52] at this critical juncture calls for much of that wisdom that comes from above, to rest on her sons in the gospel.[53] May our dear friend be one that, humbly bold, will nobly stand in the gap and piously oppose the growing evil of innovations, that evil spirit of liberty and equality having crept into religion as well as the state, and grows predominant. Oh! how is our gold become dim, our wine mixed with water [see also Isa. 1:22]. Men loving preeminence have leaped the bound of meek modesty and as much as in them lies, in luciferian pride, are setting themselves on the sides of the worthy and crying, "who is Lord over us" [Psa. 12:4]? Thus answering to the character given by St. Peter and Jude, "Speaking evil of dignities" [see also 2 Pet. 2:10; Jude 1:8]. Oh! my dear friend, how is my soul grieved at our unhappy, shameful divisions? How does the enemy of souls triumph? How will infidels scoff and precious souls get essential hurt, the same turned out of the way? And we give the enemy cause to blaspheme? Those who are now grasping after power, by aspiring to something similar to church honors will, I fear, like others on pinnacles find their heads dizzy and forget the rock from whence they were hewn and the hole of the pit from which they were dug [see also Isa. 51:1], and give cause to the Most High again to say, "When Israel was a little child I loved him" [Hos. 11:1]. "When Ephraim spoke, trembling, he exalted himself in Israel, but when he offended, in Baal, he died" [Hos. 13:1].

May this never be the case with our beloved old preachers, whatever may happen to the young. For if it is, I believe the language of many of the most sensible and pious among the Methodists will be, "Every man to your tents, Oh! Israel" [2 Chron. 10:16]. Newfangled ways may please New Methodists,[54] but those who have from principal followed God through our Reverend Father's instrumentality will not like the new wine, but will say "the old is better" [Luke 5:39], on all accounts, as individuals and as a Society and because by separating from the Church they will effectually shut the door God has, by Mr. Wesley, opened for the benefit of the members of the Church of England and by which an innumerable multitude has been brought into marvelous light. This seems one of the many grand reasons why we should abide by the old plan.

Excuse my dear friend, the freedom I have taken, but I think our aspiring brethren grieve God, injure his cause, and stumble precious souls. I know the wives have some influence, some a great deal over their husbands, therefore beg my very dear friend would endeavor to bias the mind of her beloved partner on the side of old Methodism. May every blessing of the new covenant be possessed and enjoyed by you and Mr. Pawson, and may you mutually promote God's glory in the salvation of precious souls, is the servant desire of, my dear friend,

Your affectionate Friend
in the Best Bonds,
Eliza Hurrell

P.S. I shall esteem a letter; a favor, and as soon as possible.

SOURCE:

Holograph in *Meth. Arch.*; see also Davies, et al., *History*, 4:291-92.

13. Isabella Wilson to Mr. and Mrs. Wilson

Editor's Introduction

For an introduction to the life and work of Isabella Wilson, see part 1 above. Isabella's letter below reflects the continuing centrality of evangelism in some quarters of Wesleyan Methodism following the Wesleys' deaths. Although developments were underfoot to move the autonomous Societies in the direction of "respectability," there was still a strong revivalist spirit manifest in figures such as William Bramwell and Mary Barritt [Taft]. Antagonists who stood against such revivalism placed a high value on social conformity in their effort to establish a legitimate place for the Methodists in the new order of the nineteenth century. Isabella was concerned about the encroachment of formality and a loss of focus upon the empowerment of the Holy Spirit.

* * * *

Nottingham, Jan. 2, 1800

Dear Brother and Sister,

Bless God, I am well and happy. The work of God prospers throughout this circuit. It is three weeks today since sister [Mary] Barritt came here. She is well received and the Lord owns her labors. I was with her at Ratcliffe, about six miles from this place, from Friday until Monday. We had blessed times, especially at a class on Friday evening when seven or eight persons obtained purity of heart. Glory be to God, his people here are rising daily! We often wish for you to come among us to help us in the blessed work. Sister Barritt intends stopping here until about March. So I hope you will come to see us before long. I am sorry to say that Mrs. Tatham[55] is in a poor state of health. She is very weak and low. She seems ripe for glory, though she can be ill spared. The church will find a great loss in her. When, however, I see a soul fit for heaven, I think, how much better it is to be there than in an afflicted body. The Lord help us to praise him for every dispensation of his providence towards us, for he is wise in all his ways. Mr. Bramwell[56] is better of his lameness so he is driving about again.

We have blessed news from all quarters of the work of God spreading. Oh, for more faith in God, that formality may come to the ground. I see clearly how we have lost ground in our circuit, by yielding to man. I hope we shall learn something by what we have suffered. The Lord help us!

I have often thought of you and the circuit. It has powerfully struck me that if those who are alive to God and have the spirit of prayer and of faith in God would meet together and plead for a revival, I believe the Lord would answer them. I think we do not sufficiently feel for the souls of those who are not happy in God. I hope you will unite with me in caring for souls more than ever. When I look back, I am ashamed of myself before God, but at present he blesses me abundantly. Oh, for a closer walk with him! This I feel determined on with the new year. We shall soon have done with all below. Let us aim at the crown and we shall seize it as our due. We had two souls brought into Christian liberty last night and one obtained full salvation.

Your loving Sister,
Isabella Wilson

Source:

Mary Taft, *Memoirs of the Life of Mrs. Mary Taft; Formerly Miss Barritt*, Part I, 2nd ed. (York: Printed for and sold by the author, 1828), 110-11.

A. *Ars Vivendi:* The Spiritual Life in Letters

14. Mary Taft to Mary Fletcher

Editor's Introduction

For an introduction to the life and work of Mary [Barritt] Taft, see part 2 above. This letter is the first known exchange between two of the greatest women preachers of the Methodist movement. While aware of each other's activities for some years, the impetus for this letter was Taft's concern about misogynist attitudes among the male preachers that seemed to be on the ascendant and about specific actions taken at the Conference of 1803 that restricted the ministry of women. After Wesley's death in 1791, controversy erupted over the preaching activities of women throughout the Methodist movement, both in Ireland and in England. When the question whether women should be permitted to preach among the Methodists was posed at the Manchester Conference of 1803, the assembly approved a restrictive resolution. Previously, in Ireland, women were prohibited from functioning as public exhorters, and now, in England, they were seriously restricted in terms of a preaching role as well.[57] Mary Taft had become the storm center of this controversy, in fact, and the erosion of the status of women was a serious blow to her egalitarian spirituality.

* * * *

[Oct./Nov.? 1803]

My Dear Sister in Christ Jesus,

For some years I have felt a great desire to see or hear or be some way acquainted with you, but when I have looked at my own unworthiness and little improvement in the things of God have as often declined it.

But I am moved to do it now on this ground. I once heard an account of your maid's[58] public labor that much rejoiced my heart, for I do rejoice if any one is made useful to the awakening and conversion of never dying souls. But I felt grieved to find in reading the account of her in the Magazine that nothing was said of her speaking for God or of her sowing the seed of eternal life and I particularly wished to know if you left out that part of her life so precious to me or the Editor had thought proper to omit that part.[59] I labored a little for the Lord while my name was Barritt and dare not give it up now for my own soul's sake and have some reason to believe my labors have not been in vain in the Lord, though I am very unworthy of such a master and still more to be employed in such a work.

Shall also be glad to know if you still labor for the Lord and in what way. Numbers of your friends and many of the preachers think the minute of last Conference goes too far on that subject.[60] I have been much blessed in reading Mr. Fletcher's works and have read your letters with pleasure and profit and hope your goodness will favor unworthy me with a few lines which I shall ever esteem as a great favor consigned on an unworthy worm. And may our good Lord bless you with all spiritual blessings in Christ Jesus and though we may not be permitted personally to see, know, convince, and be acquainted with each other in this vale of tears, yet I trust our kindred spirits will shortly meet where the wicked cease from troubling and the weary are at rest [see also Job 3:17].

My Dear Mr. Taft unites in kindest love to you wishing you every blessing.

I am Dear Sister,
Yours affectionately,
Mary Taft

P.S. I shall esteem it a great favor if you will write me the first opportunity—and please to direct for me at the Methodist Chapel
Epworth
Lincolnshire

SOURCE:

Holograph in *Meth. Arch.*

A. ARS VIVENDI: THE SPIRITUAL LIFE IN LETTERS

15. MARY FLETCHER TO MARY TAFT

Editor's Introduction

For an introduction to the life and work of Mary [Bosanquet] Fletcher, see part 2 above. Fletcher's response to the preceding letter includes a brief narrative of her call to and experience in preaching the gospel. While she defined her ministry very carefully as an "extraordinary" call or dispensation of God's work, her preaching practice filled the hours of her days and quickly became the ordinary round of her life. Mary's spirituality was shaped by the practice of evangelistic preaching and the gathering of communities in which Christian disciples were formed through her leadership.

* * * *

Madeley, Nov. 28, 1803

Your labors, my dear Sister, for the cause of our adorable Jesus, I have heard of with pleasure and wish you the blessing of the Almighty in all your undertakings. I scarcely know how to answer your question concerning my manner of acting in the work of God. When about twelve years old, I used to read and pray with some poor neighbors (before my parents were up), in one of the little cottages near our garden. At eighteen I began to meet some classes when I could get out where Mr. Wesley appointed me. But when at twenty-one I was put out of my father's family, I was soon after called to settle at a place (Leytonstone) where there was no gospel. I then held public meetings, and a society was formed, a way being made for the preachers. When I was in Yorkshire, for near fourteen years, I went about a good deal and had many meetings, both there and in other parts. The same also after I came here. But now my breath is very short, and many complaints render me unable to travel. I therefore feel the Lord leads me to apply to what little I can do in my own preaching room where the congregation increases and many come from far, and I am, through mercy, at present carried through six or seven meetings in a week, of different sorts. For some years, I was often led to speak from a text. Of late I feel greater approbation in what we call expounding, taking a part or whole of a chapter, and speaking on it. We have lately found the Lord very present, and many souls have been blessed. My Sally's [Lawrence] usual way was to read some pious author and stop and apply it as the Lord gave her utterance. But everyone must follow their own order and the Lord has promised, "I will instruct thee in the way thou shalt go" [Psa. 32:8]. I do look on the call of women as an extra—not an ordinary call.[61] Therefore I strove, and do strive now so to act, not out of custom but only when I have a clear leading thereto, and this leading may and will differ at different parts of our lives. But to follow the cloud is the thing I aim at, and the soul feels a peace and comfort in so doing, for "where the spirit of the Lord is, there is liberty" [2 Cor. 3:17]. Some of our dear people have just entered glory. Oh, that we may be ready to stand in blood-washed robes before the throne. I must break off as writing so affects my head, though I have much of it on my hands. But it cannot be for long, as I am in my sixty-fifth year, and still I beg our Lord, let me begin to live to and for Him.

With Christian love to your partner, I remain,

Your affectionate Sister in the Lord,
Mary Fletcher

SOURCE:

Taft, *Holy Women*, 1:19-21.

A. *Ars Vivendi:* The Spiritual Life in Letters

16. Ann Tripp to Frances Pawson

Editor's Introduction

Ann Tripp (1745–1823) was a devoted member of the Fletcher/Ryan/Crosby nucleus, nearly from the foundation of the Leytonstone community in 1763. She had been awakened under the preaching of Wesley's first lay preacher, Thomas Maxfield, in London. She moved to Yorkshire with the Leytonstone family in 1768 and continued there as governess of the Cross Hall School. Following Mary Bosanquet's marriage to John Fletcher in 1781, Ann helped Sarah Crosby transplant the community to Leeds where they formed the "Female Brethren" at the Old Boggard House, the mother chapel of the Methodists there.[62] She died on September 16, 1823, and is buried with a number of other significant Methodist women at the Old Parish Church, Leeds. On the recipient, Frances Pawson, see letter 13 above.

Ann's letter to Frances demonstrates the way in which Methodist women cared for one another. Frances's husband, John Pawson, died on March 19, 1806. Much of this letter has to do with logistical matters related to the widow's resettlement. She is still in the deep throes of her grief, and Ann immediately sets her network of connections with other women in motion. So intimate were the connections among these various women that few details of one another's lives slipped their attention. Every aspect of life fell into their arena of compassion and care. The text of the manuscript letter has not been modernized.

* * * *

April 23, 1806

My very dear friend,

I just snatch a few moments to say I am always glad to hear from you and shall be happy to see you when providence makes the way plain to Leeds. I was in hopes before this time to have had the pleasure of informing you of a suitable habitation, but have hitherto been disappointed. But trust before you want; something will be handed out. Should a likely house fall out, it will not do for me to write you word and wait the answer. I shall be forced to engage it directly, houses about that [. . .] are so soon caught up.

Mrs. Harrison and I actually took one for you in St. Peter's Square[63] to enter in the latter end of May, of the people who said they had the letting of it; but some persons who saw us go to look at it went immediately to the [. . .] landlord and got his promise, so we was forced to relinquish it. Mrs. Proctor says they could like to remove if they could hear of a likely house near their business, but there is a friend of theirs has been waiting their memorials near two years. The house Br. [Scar—] mentioned is let though it is not yet finished, and I think would not have been very suitable. We may rest secure in that blessed promise, "If we acknowledge him in all our ways, he will direct our paths" [Prov. 3:6]. He can make ways where none appear, and I believe he will.

Dear Mrs. [Elizabeth] Mortimer's[64] advice is good. Your feelings I am persuaded are, and will for some time be deeply exercised. But your gracious Lord has said, "As thy day, thy strength shall be" [see also Matt. 6:34]. You are now peculiarly called to the exercise of patient resignation to the will of God, and faith in him as a God of providence, whose tender care I believe you will more than ever prove. May he who has promised to be with you night and day so divinely support you that you may upon the mournful occasion be raised above those painful feelings and depressions, your weakness of body, etc., may expose you to. Yet a little while and I trust we shall join our dear friend in the realms of light and glory. They are still near in spirit, how near, who can tell.[65]

How any one could make such a mistake about Mrs. Hardon I know not? Though she has, as you know, suffered a good deal of loss by her brother's failure, she is still in the same house she was when Mrs. Mortimer was here, and for anything I know likely to continue there. Through mercy her circumstances are better than they have been since the dividend was paid. She has a sister that is house-keeper to a widow lady, somewhere beyond London.

Dear Mrs. Mortimer talks of being down this summer; she hopes at the Conference.[66] When you write to her, I shall be obliged to you to give my love. Tell her I forgot to recommend poor Mrs. Wood (Mrs. Hodgson's son's wife) to her notice. She is in London and I expect in [. . .] call upon her, if she can be of use to her soul, or in commending her to a suitable situation. I believe this will be a labor of love pleasing to God. She is an object of pity, and I hope will tell her simply the course that has brought her into those painful circumstances. She was once very happy and met class with Mrs. [Sarah] Crosby.

I must now conclude with respects to Mr. and Mrs. Pawson, and begging any interest in your prayers,

I remain, my dear friend,
Yours affectionately,
Ann Tripp

Prissy joins me in love to Esther. She is very poorly in a rheumatic complaint. Shall hope to hear when I may expect you.

SOURCE:

Holograph in *Meth. Arch.*

17. Mary Fletcher to Elizabeth Collet

Editor's Introduction

For an introduction to the life and work of Mary [Bosanquet] Fletcher, see part 2 above. Elizabeth [Tonkin] Collet (1762–1825) was one of the most remarkable figures of Cornish Methodism.[67] After joining the Wesleyan Society of her native Gwinear, she came under the influence of the first Cornish woman preacher, Ann Gilbert. She pressed into preaching herself in 1782 and was involved in a regularized ministry under the superintendency of Joseph Taylor. She married a Mr. Collett in 1785, was the mother of eleven children, and preached in Roseland and Veryan for some years before resettlement in St. Erme where she preached her final sermon in 1804 in a chapel built by her husband. This letter comes some years after she had retired from her preaching career and was enduring a period of great suffering. Mary attempts to console, encourage, and support her during a time of trial.

* * * *

Madeley, March 18, 1807

My dear Sister in affection, and in the patience of the Lord Jesus.

I perceive you are in the Lord's furnace. Well, fear not. You shall come forth as pure gold. When I see some, who like you, are for years together kept in the fire, I think it is because they are intended for a closer union with the blessed Savior. Remember we are now "heirs of God, and joint heirs with Jesus Christ, if so be that we suffer with Him, that we may be glorified together" [Rom. 8:17].

The one thing our Lord aims at in all our many trials is to bring us perfectly to lose our wills in his. Therefore if you strive by acts of resignation to lie as clay before the potter [see also Jer. 18:6], your soul shall grow as the lily, and cast out its root like Lebanon [see also Hos. 14:5]. It is true your bodily sufferings may keep you sometimes from feeling that degree of joy which some may feel who have less faith and love. But you must observe, our part is to believe and God's part is to give the joy of believing, when and as he sees good. Do not measure your state of grace by your degree of joy, but by a power to hang on the word of the Lord, with a continual cry in your heart, "Thy will be done" [Matt. 26:42]. Let it comfort you to remember that our bodies are, as St. Paul says, members of Jesus Christ [see also 1 Cor. 6:15], and the body is for the Lord, and the Lord for the body [see also 1 Cor. 6:13]. Will he not then take care of his own? If you say, "My trial is not so much for my body as for my soul," I answer, that is still nearer to him. For they who are joined unto him are one Spirit. Oh then sweetly sing,

> I'll trust my great Physician's skill,
> What He prescribes cannot be ill![68]

I will mention a death we have had this way. (Indeed we have had seven happy deaths here in the two first months of the year.) It was a boy not quite twelve years old. He had endured a most painful illness near three years and was drawn to God in that time. A short time before his death he had a wonderful manifestation of the love of God, insomuch that he was quite overcome. When he could speak, he begged his father and mother to be more in earnest, assuring them it was well worth their while. "For Father," said he, "if that chest of drawers were full of gold, I would not take it for what I see and feel. O, what a ransom! Lord, shall I come now? Lord, let me come now!" He lay silent for some time, and then said, "No; I must suffer a little longer." At another time he was again overwhelmed with the power of God and cried out, "O how pretty! how grand! how glorious!" He then expressed his love to the Savior in the most striking words. "The faith of the martyrs," cried he, "I do not wonder at father! If they were to come and cut me all in little bits for the sake of Jesus, I would not mind it! But when I think of those who once loved Jesus and are drawn back, O, this makes my heart bleed!" One day as he was sitting in his chair (for he could not lay down for want of breath), and the maid was putting the room to rights, he said, "Mother, don't let there be a noise, it disturbs me. I am very busy. Jesus and I are making a sweet bargain. He shows me if I am willing to suffer a little longer, it shall be a thousand, nay, a million times better for me in glory than if I die now." A few days after he told them he was very bad, but very happy, and said, "put a pillow and I will try to lean back." He did so, and soon after cried out, "Triumph! Triumph!" and then fell into a sweet sleep and waked in eternity!

I seldom write such a long letter. My sight by old age is much impaired. But I trust that through eternity your happiness will be much increased in glory by your sufferings. And may this convey some comfort to your mind. Farewell, my dear friend. May the Lord put his arms of love underneath you [see also Deut. 33:27]. Pray for,

Your sister in the Lord,
Mary Fletcher

SOURCE:

AM (BC) 2.8 (August 1823): 286-88.

A. *Ars Vivendi:* The Spiritual Life in Letters

18. Mary Hanson to a Friend

Editor's Introduction

For an introduction to the life and work of Mary Hanson [Cooper], see part 2 above. Mary faithfully exchanged correspondence with a friend identified simply as Mary Ann. Adam Clarke published quite a number of their letters in his *Memoirs of Mary Cooper*. Mary's Methodist *apologia* is extracted here from a letter dated about one year after her first introduction to the people called Methodists through the preaching of Thomas Coke and Adam Clarke. In answer to the questions of her friend, Mary defends a holistic understanding of the gospel in which a life devoted to love is based upon the firm foundation of justification by grace through faith. For her, faith and works must be held together in a dynamic tension. She articulates these views with an irenic spirit and an ecumenical vision that are part and parcel of her spirituality.

* * * *

[March 30, 1810]

Your last letter, my dearest friend, so long in coming, marks me out rather a more controversial course than I am disposed to take. Independent of the true affection we have borne each other, I should not particularly object to a paper controversy with you, as I believe you to be more candid and reasonable than the generality of those who are of your sentiments. But we are friends, nor do either of us wish to feel less attachment. I believe so—but rather to have it on the increase. We must not close our eyes to the many sad examples of Christians losing for a while their charity, who, instead of loving their enemies, have hated the friends of Christ who differed from them in some points of doctrine. Let us avoid approaching the rock on which many, more stable than ourselves, have split. That the doctrines of the Wesleyans are those of the Bible, I am more and more convinced. And after an examination of them for twelve months, and of the discipline and people, I have the pleasure of telling you I have joined the Society. To keep me from it I have had every earthly motive; to unite me to it every spiritual one.

When we see each other, Mary Ann, I will, if you desire it, enter fully into the points wherein we differ. For your present satisfaction I will, however, answer your questions. Had you been acquainted with the sentiments of that great and good man Mr. Wesley you would not have asked them: You ask me, "If I place any dependence on my own performances, as being at all able to recommend me to the favor of God?" Not in the least. Justified freely by his grace [see also Rom. 3:24], I must come just as I am, poor, blind, and naked, or he will never receive me. But, observe, I believe that sanctification follows; the tree is known by its fruits. "If a man love me He will keep my commandments" [John 14:15]. Faith works by love [see also Gal. 5:6]; this is the wedding garment [see also Matt. 22:12].[69] By the fruits of faith I believe you and I shall be judged at the last day. Read Matthew chapter 25. There is no merit in all this. We are first justified by the righteousness of another, and all the good we do is owing to the influence of the Spirit freely offered and received, but which we might have grieved, and quenched, and resisted.

As to your second question, "Whether God can regard you with fatherly affection today and the next cast you from Him," I answer, the decrees of God respect men as believers and unbelievers. The righteous shall be saved and the wicked condemned, whoever they be. These are the sovereign decrees.[70] But as it respects individuals, personally considered, there is this condition implied, such persons must become righteous, continue in righteousness (by the grace of God) or if they fall from it, return again in order to be saved. But as God is unchangeable and does not love and again hate the same person while he continues in the same state, but as he is found doing his will or the contrary, so he loves and blesses the righteous and hates all workers of iniquity. Should we change a thousand times from bad to good, God is the same in his love to us, or the contrary, as we are found doing or not doing that which he requires of us. While we continue in the grace of God freely imparted, watching and praying, loving God with all our hearts, none shall pluck us out of the Redeemer's hands [see also John 10:28-29]; nothing shall separate us from his love [see also Rom. 8:39]. But if we grow careless, neglectful of prayer and reading the word of

God, count his service weariness, and hold communion with the world instead of the Creator, can you think such persons meet for the kingdom of heaven?

These instances, my dearest friend, are not uncommon. I do believe that if you and I have once received the grace of God, it is our own fault, and chargeable alone upon ourselves, that we ever lose it. God deals with us as with reasonable creatures, and certain conditions are prescribed to us. We are to ask, seek, and knock for the Holy Spirit [see also Matt. 7:7]; having received it, we are to watch and pray [see also Matt. 26:41], deny ourselves [see also Luke 9:23], abstain from all appearance of evil [see also 1 Thess. 5:22]. The power is from above, and through Christ we can do all these things [see also Phil 4:13]. I have said three times as much as I intended; forgive me, my friend.

Through the divine influence, I enjoy, with little interruption, great peace of mind. I never was so truly happy. I feel that I love God, his ways, and his will. And my happiest moments are employed in imploring his continual aid and holding communion with him. Indeed, my dear friend, I find the advantage of associating but little with that bane of piety, lukewarm professors. The true spirit of religion I find diffused among our Society, a nonconformity to the world and a loving spirit among its members, helping each other in the paths of religion, just what I needed to quicken my poor dead soul, sunk as it was in spiritual sloth and destitute of that sacred peace the Spirit has promised to bestow.

Well, dearest Mary Ann, do not let these sentiments and enjoyments, if contrary to your own, diminish the love you have borne me. Mine for you glows with the same fervor. And I shall have just reason to reproach myself if I suffer the entrance of indifference. All will meet in heaven who love God, by whatever name they are called. The more we get of this divine principle, the more we shall love each other. O! how altogether supernatural is the life of God in the soul. How utterly incapable are we of ourselves to maintain it one instant. As our wants are moment by moment, so must our supplies be. Blessed be God, for all this is promised!

My dear friend, I long to see you and shall be impatient till I hear from you. My garden begins to demand my renewed labors. When will you inhale the fragrance of my roses and help me to admire the kindness of our God in providing so much innocent pleasure for the delight of the senses? The study of nature is still my favorite recreation; but to increase in the love and knowledge of God almost swallows up every other desire. And no reading but what tends to it satisfies me. Brother William and I have entered into an engagement to rise at six every morning, or forfeit one shilling, the fruit of our laziness to be put into a poor box, of which I have the disposal.

Adieu, my dear friend. Be assured you are very near the heart of
Your most affectionate
Mary

SOURCE:

Clarke, *Memoirs of Mary Cooper*, 56-57.

A. ARS VIVENDI: THE SPIRITUAL LIFE IN LETTERS

19. MARY ANDERSON TO MARY TAFT

Editor's Introduction

Little is known about the author of this letter directed to the famous evangelist at Horncastle. An abbreviated form of the letter appears in Mary's *Memoirs* (2:80-81). The practice of spiritual direction and the relationship of mentor-to-disciple forged particularly strong bonds of friendship among the women. This letter reflects the familial nature of community, especially that most intimate *koinonia* formed between spiritual mother and daughter.

* * * *

Alford, Oct. 13, 1811

Dear Mother in Christ,

I take the liberty of addressing a few lines to you as you will always be dear to me. For you were the blessed instrument in the hand of the Lord of bringing me out of darkness into marvelous light [see also 1 Pet. 2:9]. I think you will recollect me when I say I was brought in under your preaching at Tedford where we then lived. It was on the sixth of June, nine years back, and it was Whitsunday, and you preached from the second chapter of the Acts of the Apostles.[71] I was then convinced of sin, and in a fellowship meeting after preaching found peace with you. I used to come to Mrs. Sutton's to you and was there the last morning you left us which was in August the same year. I must confess with shame that I have many times been unfaithful to the grace given, but never left the people, but alas like Peter followed my Lord at too great a distance [see also Luke 22:54]. However, I can truly say that at present I feel and know myself to be a child of God. Glory be to his name. I was much disappointed in not seeing you when you were this way. Shall esteem it a great favor to have a few lines from you when Mr. Taft comes. Love to you and permit me to subscribe myself your affectionate daughter in the gospel.

Mary Anderson

SOURCE:

Holograph in *Meth. Arch.*

20. Elizabeth Mortimer to Mary Holland

Editor's Introduction

For an introduction to the life and work of Elizabeth Mortimer [Ritchie], see letter 9 above. While the letter immediately above (the letter from Mary Anderson to Mary Taft) reflects the importance placed upon spiritual parentage among the early Methodist women, the letter below reveals the important spiritual connection between a Methodist mother and her biological daughter. A singular example in this collection, it demonstrates a special bond of affection and care. Here is the seasoned advice of a wise spiritual director, words of encouragement and counsel as a child embarks on a new life's journey. This brief letter contains many pithy statements and many potent images related to the spiritual life and the means of grace. It is a distinctive expression of the Methodist concern to cultivate a life in Jesus, to find in him and in his way the key to the abundant life. It provides unique insight into the role of Methodist mothers in the spiritual nurture of their children.

* * * *

July 24th, 1817

My Dear Mary,

Your welcome letter not only reached my hands, but drew from my heart grateful acknowledgments to the God of all our mercies. I rejoice in your comfort and pray him, who alone can do it, to bless all your blessings and sanctify every creature enjoyment.

I can scarcely tell you what we all felt after you left us. We saw the hand of God in your removal and felt resignation to the divine will, but Mr. Holland had made a chasm in our social circle which we deeply felt. Though poor Eliza needed comforting herself, she strove to comfort her parents. The day after you left River-Terrace,[72] she told me, in a kind and affectionate manner, "Mother, I can never be to my father and you what Mary has been, but I will try to do what I can to fill her place." And she has fulfilled her promise, beyond our expectations. Blessed be God, we live in peace and love, and the God of love and peace is with us!

A. ARS VIVENDI: THE SPIRITUAL LIFE IN LETTERS

You are often in our minds, and we are thankful that we can meet before our Father's throne. He is our center, and the nearer we live to him, the nearer we shall feel to each other. You remember the simile of the circles drawn round the hill. On whatever side we ascend, if we keep ascending we shall get nearer to each other as we get nearer to the top. I am glad that Mr. Holland and you feel agreed to seek a closer walk with God. Lady Maxwell,[73] in one of her letters, says, "In secret prayer and meditation I get enlarged views of the salvation of God; and what is thus discovered to me faith goes out after, and according to its strength are its returns." This, my dear Mary, is the way. May the God of love help you to walk in it! Cultivate a life of faith. Think much of it and talk often between yourselves of the objects of faith. Use all the power you now feel to embrace revealed truth. Love and heavenly-mindedness will follow. The Christian only shines by reflection, and therefore, if he would fulfil the character which St. Paul ascribes to him, he must live under the direct influence of the Sun of Righteousness.

Wherever you are, and whatever you feel, endeavor to learn the happy art of coming to Jesus. He is always waiting and always willing to receive you. For with him is no variableness, neither shadow of turning [see also James 1:17]. His one will towards his creatures is to save them from their sins and to raise them out of the ruins of their fall. I am glad that you give us so particular an account of the means of grace which Raithby[74] affords. Use them in faith and you will prosper.

We may live to God wherever his providence places us if it be not our own fault. Large towns have their advantages—popular preachers and multiplicity of means; but when too much depended upon, they rather stand in the way of communion with God than help the souls that are favored with them in the spirit of simple, humble love. In the country, to a reflecting mind, every thing becomes a preacher. We may learn

> From birds, and fruits, and plants, and flow'rs,
> How to employ the happy hours.[75]

The few and homely means of grace afforded, if used in the right spirit, will send the soul to God in secret. And the lessons learned from the Holy Spirit upon our knees are often blessed ones.

May my dear Mary, and the partner of her days, learn many of them, daily feeling the truth of that promise, "All thy children shall be taught of the Lord, and great shall be the peace of thy children" [Isa. 54:13]!

Your father and Eliza join me in kindest love to you both. That the best of blessings may rest on you, my dear Mary, is the prayer of

Your affectionate mother,
E. Mortimer

SOURCE:

Bulmer, *Memoirs of Elizabeth Mortimer*, 222-24.

B. *Ars Moriendi:* Accounts of Triumphant Death

1. Hester Ann Rogers

"The Dying Bed of a Saint and Sinner Contrasted"

Editor's Introduction

For an introduction to the life and work of Hester Ann [Roe] Rogers, see part 1 above. In this fascinating account, Hester contrasts the deaths of two imaginary people, one who has lived life apart from God, and the other whose companionship with Christ through life has led to the ultimate experience of a good death. This imaginative apology for the Christian life was most frequently inserted between Hester's *Experience* or *Life* and her *Spiritual Letters*, along with other materials related to her life, all bound together in a single volume.[76] Given this location, it served as a literary exhortation to the reader, an evangelistic appeal that called for conversion of heart and life. Multiple references to well-known and unidentifiable poetic material punctuate her account. It is a unique explication of the Methodist *ars moriendi*.

* * * *

Dust we are, and unto dust we shall return [see also Gen. 3:19]. A few more rolling years, a few more months or weeks, no, perhaps a few more setting suns or fleeting moments and we are gone. Gone where? O! that awful, dreadful, blissful thought! Awful to all, dreadful to the unholy, to sinners, and blissful to the saints of God. See a man approaching the verge of eternity. How are all his views changed! How trifling to such a one appears all below the sun! How important the things of God and the salvation of his never-dying soul! Let us consider one ignorant of God through life, immersed in pleasure, lost in pride, careless, secure, surrounded and beloved by his carnal friends, and possessed of a moderate share of wealth, such a one in the bloom of life. Some fatal distemper seizes his mortal frame. He is racked with torturing pain, surrounded by weeping friends whose help is all in vain. The physician gives no hope of his recovery, and he perceives he is before long to launch into a boundless eternity! What are his views in such a state? Such a scene have my eyes beheld and therefore with greater certainty I may describe it.

"Wretched man that I am [see also Rom. 7:24] (I think I still hear him cry), where are my pleasures now? What has pride profited me, or what good have riches, with all my vaunting, done me? These are passed away as a cloud, and now, O horrible, to think!

>   Now leaving all I love below,
>   To God's tribunal I must go,
>   Must hear the Judge pronounce my fate,
>   And fix my everlasting state.[77]

But can I hope to dwell with God? Ah! no, it cannot be. He is holy; I am vile. He is just and will punish the guilty. He called and I refused. He stretched forth his hand and I would not regard. And now he laughs at my calamity and shuts his ear to my cry. Then I would not, now I cannot pray. He often knocked at the door of my heart saying, by an inward whisper, 'Thou art wrong; repent, and turn to God. Seek the Lord while he may be found, call upon him while he is near [Isa. 55:6]. Turn ye, turn ye, why will ye die' [Ezek. 33:11]? But I heeded none of his counsel and turned away my ear from his reproof. I refused the yoke of Jesus, despised his ministers, and neglected that salvation which was long offered to me. But now I feel the dire effects! Me miserable! which way shall I flee infinite wrath and infinite despair? O eternity! eternity! eternity! Fall, fall rocks, and hide my guilty head. Hide me from him that sits upon the throne and from the wrath of the Lamb! But O! even this cannot be. I must endure his indignation. I must suffer the vengeance of eternal fire! My damnation is sealed! Who can dwell with devouring fire? Who can endure everlasting burnings? Take warning, O my careless friends! A gaping hell awaits me! My soul is going! Friends are waiting to receive it; they encircle me round. O horror, and eternity!"

B. *Ars Moriendi*: Accounts of Triumphant Death

The person described above was afterward reprieved for a short season from the jaws of death, but he did not manifest any genuine repentance. And, in about six months after, died in raging despair.

Let us next see the child of God! the heir of glory (pleasing contrast), how different his prospect! He longs to reach his Father's house and kisses the kind rod of his afflicting hand. The welcome news that he shall soon be there elevates his soul with rapturous joy. He has a foretaste of those pleasures which are at God's right hand for evermore and the language of his heart is,

> Haste, my Beloved, fetch my soul
>   Up to thy blest abode:
> Fly, for my spirit longs to see
>   My Saviour and my God.[78]

O yes, blessed Savior, and this you know is also the language of my heart while I now bid adieu to earth and all terrestrial scenes.

"Farewell, my dearly beloved children, I leave you, but your parents' God has promised to care for you. Choose him for your portion and then if we both leave you exposed to the waves of a dangerous world, the faithfulness of an unchanging Jehovah is engaged to pilot you safe into that haven where we shall meet you all again [see also Psa. 107:30], being bound up together in the bundle of life with the Lord our God.

"Farewell, in particular, my ever dear husband. How was our friendship ripened almost to the maturity of heaven! How tenderly and closely are our hearts still knit together! Nor shall the sweet union be dissolved by death, but being one in Christ, we shall be one for ever. Mourn not that I go to him first. He saw it best for my weakness. My feeble frame might not have supported your absence! A very little while and you will follow me, and O with what joy shall I welcome your arrival on the eternal shore and conduct you to him whom our souls love! Until then, adieu, my dearest companion in heaven's road, whom God in the greatest mercy gave to me. I leave you with the most grateful sensations for all the kind tokens of affection which I have ever had from you. For all your care, your love, your prayers, I bless my God and thank you. But I now go to Jesus who is yet infinitely dearer to me. With him I leave you, nor doubt his care who has loved and given himself for you. It is but a short separation. Our spirits shall soon reunite, and then never, never know separation more!

"Farewell to all my dear friends. Weep not for me, but love my God. O make your peace with him and you shall follow me to glory. He is worthy of your hearts, and only he! O give them wholly to him! I have not served my God for naught. I have lived a heaven below in Jesus' love, and now eternally shall praise the glories of his grace! And you who know my God, O love him more and never leave him. So will he be to you what he is now to me. Continue 'steadfast and immoveable, always abounding in the work of the Lord' [1 Cor. 15:58a]. For I can testify to his glory. 'Your labor shall not be in vain' [1 Cor. 15:58b]. Be faithful unto death and he will give you a crown of life which I am now hastening to receive. 'The chariots of Israel, and the horsemen thereof' (2 Kings ii, 12), are all in waiting to carry me home!

> See the guardian angels nigh,
> Wait to waft my soul on high!
> See the golden gates display'd,
> See the crown to grace my head!
> See a flood of sacred light
> Which shall yield no more to night;
> Transitory world, farewell,
> Jesus calls with Him to dwell![79]

"He cries, 'Arise, my love, my fair one, and come away' [Sol. 2:13]. 'Amen,' says my willing, joyful soul, 'even so, come Lord Jesus' [Rev. 22:20]. My soul is on the wing. Burst asunder you bonds of clay which hold me from my love! How welcome the stroke that shall break down these separating walls, knock off my fetters, throw open my prison doors, and set me at liberty! This corruptible body, this tottering house of clay, which now cannot sustain this weight of love, shall soon be made a glorious body incorruptible:

> Shall the stars and sun outshine,
> Shout among the sons of glory;
> All immortal, all divine![80]

B. *Ars Moriendi*: Accounts of Triumphant Death

And able then to enjoy the full fruition of my God. Yes, I shall soon see him as he is, not through a glass darkly, but face to face [see also 1 Cor. 13:12]. The beatific sight

> Shall fill the heavenly courts with praise,
> And wide diffuse the golden blaze
> Of everlasting light.[81]

> Waiting to receive my spirit,
>   Lo, my Saviour stands above;
> Shows the purchase of his merit;
>   Reaches out the crown of love.[82]

"Angels surround my bed to carry me away. I come, I come, blessed messengers of my God! Haste and convey me to his loved embrace! My faith already beholds the crucified Redeemer. I think I see him smile, while around him stand the heavenly host exulting! O glorious train of blood-bought souls! What an innumerable company! And I shall join the choir,

> Shall shout by turns the bursting joy;
> And all eternity employ,
>   In songs around the throne."[83]

How delightful the theme! It has set my soul on fire. Yet I cannot express a thousandth part of my ideas or the prospect that lies before me. But I shall prove the unutterable bliss! The inheritance is mine! A foretaste now I feel! No, so am I filled with glory and with God that more I could not bear and live! O may I ever feel the sacred flame and through eternity proclaim the depth of Jesus' love! Amen and amen.

SOURCE:

Account of the Experience of Hester Ann Rogers, 165-71.

2. SARAH COLSTON

"SOME ACCOUNT OF THE DEATH OF MARY THOMAS"

Editor's Introduction

The next three selections should be viewed as a unit. All three are brief publications that appeared in *Arminian Magazine* in the first decade of its existence, recording the deaths of three women between 1745 and 1784. None of these women were well-known throughout the movement, nor were those who provided these accounts, excepting the first writer, Sarah Colston (17??–1763?), featured in my earlier volume.[84] Colston was apparently an active member of the nascent Methodist Societies in Bristol. Although little is known about her life, the account of her religious experience, prepared for Charles Wesley in 1742, provides insight into her journey of faith. Her own spirituality was formed by immersion in the class meeting, in an environment intended to foster dynamic growth and spiritual vitality. John Wesley printed the Colston account of Molly Thomas's death in his published *Journal* as well as in the *Magazine*.[85] All three of these accounts bear witness to the value placed upon the good deaths of ordinary women devoted to God. The means of grace, centrality of hymns, serenity of spirit, and resting in the grace of God figure prominently in them all. The accounts function as exhortations to living lives rooted in Jesus.

* * * *

Bristol, June 6, 1745

On Saturday night Mary Thomas was taken home. She was always constant in the use of all the means of grace and behaved well both at home and abroad. After she was taken ill she was distressed, indeed, between the pain of her body and the anguish of her soul. But where is all pain gone when Jesus comes? When he manifests himself to the heart? In that hour she cried out, "Christ is mine! I know my sins are forgiven me." Then she sung praise to him that loved her and bought her with his own blood. The fear of death was gone and she longed to leave her father, her mother, and all her friends. She said, "I am almost at the top of the ladder. Now I see the towers before me and a large company coming up behind me. I shall soon go. Only let Christ speak the word and I am gone. I only wait for that word, 'Rise up, my love, and come away'" [Sol. 2:10].

When they thought her strength was gone, she broke out again,

> Christ hath the foundation laid,
>   And Christ shall build me up:
> Sure I shall soon be made
>   Partaker of my hope,
> Author of my faith he is;
>   He its finisher shall be:
> Perfect love shall seal me his
>   To all eternity.[86]

So she fell asleep. O Lord, my God! glory be to you for all things. I feel such desires in my soul after God that my strength goes away. I feel there is not a moment's time to spare, and yet how many do I lose? Lord Jesus, give me to be more and more diligent in all things. It is no matter to me how I was an hour ago. Is my soul now waiting upon God? O that I may in all things, and through all things, see nothing but Christ! O that when he comes he may find me watching!

Sarah Colston

SOURCE:

AM 5 (1782): 21-22.

3. Mary James

"An Account of the Death of Mrs. Doyle"

****

Mrs. Doyle was delivered of a daughter the twenty-eighth of July and continued to appearance as well as anyone could be, until the tenth of this month when she was seized with a bilious cholic which carried her off on Wednesday the twelfth. For some time before her delivery she had an impression upon her mind that she would die soon. To a friend that was conversing with her a few days before, she said, "I have been asking for wisdom to act in my family and he tells me the time of my departure is at hand." At the time of her travail she bore her pain with remarkable patience. To one that observed this, she said, "I bless the Lord, I am not afraid of the strongest pain." When I went to see her on the night she was delivered, she said, "My dear, I was so supported and my soul was kept so joyous that I could have sung in the midst of my pain." The day before she was taken for death we conversed freely on Christian experience. She said, "When the Lord first set my soul at liberty, I thought there was nothing to do. Since then he has showed me every grace is to be called forth to exercise. I long," said she, "to be that Christian spoken of in the thirteenth of the Corinthians." Her pain was violent, but she bore it with great composure, frequently saying, "Lord, I know that in one moment you can remove it if it is for your glory. But I ask neither ease nor pain, neither life nor death. Your will be done, and your name be glorified." About an hour before her death I was by her bedside when she showed marks of grief. She said, "Molly, the Lord cannot err in his dispensations, though they may be painful." Soon after this she sweetly fell asleep.

Mary James
Bristol, Aug. 20, 1767

Source:

AM 2 (1779): 642-43.

B. *Ars Moriendi*: Accounts of Triumphant Death

4. Elizabeth Henson

"Account of the Death of Her Mother"

* * * *

My dear mother was released from the body on the twenty-sixth instant, about nine o'clock in the evening.

The last five days she lived, she said, "The enemy is constrained to withdraw, for the Lord knows my weakness and does not suffer me to be tempted." She had a great desire to see Mr. Wesley, but when he came, she could speak but little to him.[87] However his words and prayers were a great comfort to her. One day when I thought she was dying, I asked her if she had any doubt of her acceptance with God? On which she answered, "No. I feel no doubt. Christ is precious to me." Afterwards she said, "Perfect love casteth out all fear that hath torment [see also John 4:18]. I have nothing to do now but to fear offending my good and gracious God. He is the good shepherd and cares for his sheep [see also John 10:11]. What a good shepherd have I? But O, how little have I labored for him! But the precious blood of Christ is all my dependance now. O, what a Savior is he! Why are you cast down, O my soul! And why are you disquieted within me? Trust in God, for I shall yet praise him" [Psa. 42:5].

Some friends coming to see her, she told them she had no doubt. She then said to me, "O, my dear child! I long to be with him whom my soul loves." The rest of the day she was frequently heard to say, "O, precious Christ! O, blessed Jesus! O, what a Savior have I!" Her last words were, "God is love, and he that dwelleth in love, dwelleth in God, and God in him" [1 John 4:16].

E. Henson
Whittlebury, Nov. 30, 1784

Source:

AM 8 (1785): 249.

5. ANN HIGHFIELD

"ACCOUNT OF ANN CUTLER"

Editor's Introduction

Ann Highfield prepared the following account of the death of Ann Cutler in the form of a letter to Dr. Aspen of Backburn, written from Macclesfield on January 12, 1795. William Bramwell appended this account to his *Short Account of the Life and Death of Ann Cutler*. John Hill subsequently published a revised edition of the account, including an appendix by Zechariah Taft, an account of the life of Elizabeth Dickinson, and various letters, in 1827. This is a remarkable account, noteworthy for the meticulous detail concerning the final days of her life and the portrait of devotion it provides. Ann engaged in works of mercy and works of piety up to the day of her death. Her concern for others, the centrality of prayer to her life, and her constant communion and intimacy with Jesus are transparent throughout. Bramwell preached her funeral sermon on February 11, 1795, at Kirkstall Forge from 1 Corinthians 1:27-29.

* * * *

She came to Macclesfield, on December 15 [1794], very poorly of a cold, being our preaching night. She had an earnest desire to have a prayer meeting, but I told her preaching beginning so late as eight o'clock, and classes to meet after, it would not be convenient. But she was very importunate and said she could not be happy without one, adding, "I shall not be long here, and I would buy up every opportunity of doing something for God, for time is short." Knowing she had an uncommon talent for pleading for such souls as were coming to God, we got a few together to whom she was made a blessing.

Tuesday the sixteenth she was poorly, but used no less exercise in prayer, and would frequently say, "I want to redeem time better, for I believe I shall not be in this world much longer." She would lift her eyes to heaven and say, "O, blessed Jesus! teach me to

B. *Ars Moriendi:* Accounts of Triumphant Death

redeem time better, that I may live more to you than I have ever done, that I may walk as you also walked here below." At night we had our prayer meeting in which she was very earnest in wrestling with the Lord for a present blessing for every soul. Indeed, it was a blessed time to very many, a time in which much of the power of God came down. I believe it was a season that will never be forgotten. After this meeting concluded we went to another where she exercised several times. I think it may be truly said that she prayed with all prayer and lived constantly in this spirit.

On Wednesday the seventeenth she complained of a soreness at her breast, and, for all this, did not abate of her usual exercise in prayer. The morning she employed in visiting sick persons and many times prayed with and sweetly for them. The afternoon she spent in praying with several friends. In the evening we had a public prayer meeting in the chapel. She then stood upon one of the forms and gave us an exhortation which was well approved. She was uncommonly earnest for precious souls. The zeal she had for them seemed to be unparalleled. There were many singularly blessed of God. The meeting continued until one o'clock in the morning. After this she took a little refreshment, and after our family devotion she desired us to retire and leave her, for she wished to pray awhile by herself. I said, "Nanny, you have had a long meeting, go to bed." She said, "Bless the Lord! My soul is quite happy. I feel a nearer union with Jesus than I did yesterday." In the forenoon she said, "I want us to pray together that we may obtain a blessing. Come, let us go to the Lord Jesus, and let us go empty that we may be filled." When we were sat down to dinner, she praised God and said, "Glory be to God. I find he is quite willing to give grace and glory! I feel he does not withhold any good thing from me." She seemed quite in a rapture, saying, "O Jesus! I long to be with you that I may give you greater praise." She now retired and spent the greatest part of the afternoon in prayer, as usual. A friend invited her to drink tea. The time being come, she came to me and said, "Did I promise?" I told her I did not know. To which she replied, "I am so feeble in body, I think I had better stay." A person calling upon her, she went and came back exceeding poorly, but thankful to God, saying, "Last Christmas I went to see my mother, but now she is in glory, and I wish much to see her ... and I know not but I shall, for I feel as if I expected it." This was not the only time she talked so, for she frequently made use of some such language.

This evening we went to a meeting a little out of town, and in the meeting she prayed several times and repeatedly blessed God for condescending to bless both her body and soul. About the middle of the meeting she gave out, "This, this is the God we adore,"[88] evidently feeling every word she spoke, at which time she sung with all her might, though singing was very unusual with her. It was a blessed time to many and also to herself. Much of the divine presence was with us and I bless the Lord she was well received. As we were returning home she said, "The Lord has wonderfully blessed me, not only in my soul but my body, for I feel quite well." Soon after we got home she began to cough very much, but soon, being better, she resumed her conversation which was always about heaven or heavenly things. She said, "Friends, I shall be in heaven before you, and then how glad shall I be to welcome you there! I long to see Abraham, Isaac, and Jacob; Wesley, Fletcher, and some other dear friends that I have known on earth."

Friday the nineteenth her cough began to be exceedingly troublesome, yet she was not less fervent in spirit. She spent all the day in retirement and, I doubt not, had she been seen, it was the greater part of the time upon her knees, pouring out her soul before God in prayer and praise. At night her cough still increasing prevented her being at the preaching.

Saturday the twentieth she was worse and could not exercise in prayer without great difficulty. She came into the prayer meeting, and it may be said, she prayed as Christ did in the garden, which well became a dying person.

Sunday the twenty-first she had great difficulty in breathing and often said, "Jesus is going to take me home. I think I shall soon have done with this body of clay. And oh, how happy shall I then be when I cast my crown before him, 'lost in wonder, love, and praise.'"[89]

Monday the twenty-second she was much the same in body, but in sweet frame of mind, perfectly resigned to the will of God, saying, "Welcome life, or death, or sickness, just as seems good in the sight of the Lord."

Tuesday the twenty-third she was much worse. It was with much pain that she could talk. After dinner she was obliged to go to bed and did but say little. In the evening she came into the prayer meeting, but was obliged to leave us as soon as she had prayed once. She had but little rest this evening.

Wednesday the twenty-fourth she sat up as usual and spent most of the morning in prayer. After dinner she went to bed again, and the little she could say was seasoned with salt, administering grace to the hearers.

Thursday the twenty-fifth she came down for the last time, but, by the advice of the doctor, she went to bed. Her affliction became very heavy, yet she continued instant in prayer and praise to God, often saying, "All I have and am, I will give to you, my God! Make me live every moment in the Spirit. Dear Jesus, take me for your bride, and walk in me every moment! Oh, how I long to be with you in heaven!" She had a very restless night.

Friday the twenty-sixth she was desired to say if there was any person that she would have sent to. She answered, "No, except to ———," who was immediately written to. At five o'clock in the evening she began to be so ill that we thought her departure was at hand. About seven o'clock she said, "I think I have the pains of death upon me; but what a blessing it is I am going to Jesus! For I am sure he is mine, and I am his." As she was able she repeated these words: "I am sure he is mine, and I am his," at least twenty times. At nine o'clock she was easier and had a comfortable night.

She was much better in the morning and continued to be so all the day. Her soul seemed very much engaged with God. In the afternoon I asked her the state of her mind. Her answer was, "Quite happy in the love of God."

About half-past twelve o'clock on Sunday morning a friend and I joined in prayer with her. When we had concluded she sat up in bed and prayed with such exertion of voice as astonished us. She prayed most earnestly that God would revive his work in Macclesfield. The preachers and leaders seemed much impressed upon her mind. She was uncommonly drawn out in prayer for them.

Sunday the twenty-eighth she was a little better and was desirous of getting up, and did while the bed was made, but wished to lie down again immediately. After dinner she was worse and complained of a pain in her breast. I asked her if I might send for the doctor. She said, I might, but added, "He has done all he can. Let us both be perfectly resigned to the will of God." In the evening she was very restless with a degree of delirium.

About three o'clock on Monday morning she began to ascribe glory to the ever blessed Trinity, and continued saying, "Glory be to the Father, glory be to the Son, and glory to the Holy Ghost," for a considerable time. Afterwards she altered much for death. About seven o'clock the doctor, with those about her, thought she was just gone, but to our great surprise she continued in this state till between ten and eleven o'clock in the forenoon. She then lifted herself up, and looked about her, and spoke just to be heard, and was very sensible. She seemed perfectly composed, but her strength nearly gone. About three o'clock she looked at her friends and said, "I am going to die," and added, "Glory be to God and the Lamb for ever," so loud as to be heard in any part of the house, till she was quite exhausted. About six o'clock I said, "Nanny, how are you?" With a faint voice she said, "I am very ill." I replied, "You are, but I trust your soul is perfectly happy." She said, "Yes it is, but I cannot so fully rejoice because of the weight of my affliction." I said, "Well, the Lord does not require it, or he would give strength." "Yes," she said, "He would. Glory be to God and the Lamb for ever!" These were her last words. Soon afterwards the spirit left this vale of misery. So died our dear and much valued friend, Ann Cutler.[90]

SOURCE:

William Bramwell, *A Short Account of the Life and Death of Ann Cutler; A Pious Character, and Useful Instrument in the Work of God* (York: Printed by John Hill, 1827), 20-26.

B. *Ars Moriendi*: Accounts of Triumphant Death

6. Mary Fletcher

Account of Sarah Lawrence

Editor's Introduction

For an introduction to the life and work of Mary [Bosanquet] Fletcher, see part 2 above. Sarah Lawrence (1759?–1800) was the niece of Mary Fletcher's devoted friend, Sarah Ryan.[91] Sarah, known affectionately as Sally, grew up in the most important community of early Methodist women, the Leytonstone circle, having been incorporated into this little family when she was orphaned at four years of age. After the death of her aunt and namesake, she remained in the home and was a faithful companion of Mrs. Fletcher throughout the course of her life. Raised in the context of a community of vital piety and active, social service, she joined the Methodist Society as a teenager and was confirmed as a devoted Anglican at the Old Parish Church in Leeds. Mrs. Fletcher cultivated the unique talents that her adopted daughter possessed, grooming her as a designated successor. Mary would survive her, however, by some fifteen years.

After Mary's marriage to the Reverend John Fletcher in 1781, Sally moved with them to Madeley and continued in a vigorous ministry in her new surroundings. She went to the most destitute in the parish and visited the poor door to door, extending a ministry of evangelism and care throughout the community. In the account that follows, Mary describes the expansion of her ministry at that time. When mining operations were opened at Carport, a small neighboring village, she established a Methodist community there and preached every other Sunday evening for several years. She assisted Mary regularly, and the two women developed a legendary ministry of Christian discipleship in the region.

In addition to the account of her death, Fletcher provides a fascinating glimpse of Sally's ascetic practices, especially those associated with her childhood and youth, her experience of sanctification, her interpretation of God's guidance received through dreams, her methods of evangelism, and her compelling love for all people. As is the case with many of these accounts, the hymns of the tradition figure prominently in the account of her death as well as the perennial inquiry into the state of her soul.

* * * *

Sarah Lawrence was the niece of my friend Sarah Ryan. Providence cast her into our hands when a little child. As she increased in reason we observed a remarkably upright, obedient spirit in her, and a great attachment to us. When very young she would often cry to the Lord with great earnestness that she might never be separated from me. Before she was eight years old, she was often under strong convictions of sin. When she was about ten years of age, she found a strong desire to be devoted to God, and when she heard us read in the family of the sufferings of our Lord or of the martyrs, it would kindle in her breast an intense desire to suffer something for him who had borne so much for her. And she used to do many actions, according to her childish idea, to satisfy that desire—such as tying her hands behind her all night, and lying in the most uneasy posture she could. When about sixteen, conviction of sin was fastened more deeply on her mind. And I have heard her tell with what earnest cries and tears she used to wrestle with the Lord, that he would make her a Christian indeed, and join her to his people here and hereafter.

When near eighteen she was taken into the Society and the June following she went to Leeds Old Church to be confirmed. She walked home again alone (about five miles) and all the way was pleading with the Lord that she might never grow slack. When she got near home, the word came to her with much power, "I will keep thee as the apple of mine eye" [Psa. 17:8]. This filled her so with delight and consolation, now firmly believing she should be made a true child of God. Soon after she obtained a clear sense of the forgiveness of her sins. And soon after saw it her privilege to be cleansed from all sin. The way she obtained this shall be given in her own words:

> One Wednesday night, in that blessed meeting we used to have once a fortnight at Cross Hall, where so many were blessed, while I was waiting on the Lord, and saw myself as lying at the pool side, longing for the Lord to say, "Be clean" [Matt. 8:3], my soul

B. *Ars Moriendi:* Accounts of Triumphant Death

was engaged in fervent prayer that I might that night be brought into clear liberty. And while my dear mistress was praying, several promises were applied to my mind such as "Thou art clean through the word I have spoken unto thee" [John 15:3]. I now felt unbelief give way and enabled to cast my soul on the perfect atonement, and felt the divine efficacy of that blood which cleanseth from all sin [see also 1 John 1:7]. (This was December 30, 1778.) From that night I felt a very great change and began to walk much more closely with God than I had done before. That which I enjoyed in justification was precious, but this far exceeded. Now I could begin the new year with a new heart. And so powerfully did the love of God fill and enlarge my soul that I was constrained many times to cry out in the fulness thereof, "Whom have I in heaven but thee, and there is none upon earth I desire in comparison with thee" [Psa. 73:25]. I could truly say, "All slavish fear is gone. I have but one fear, to displease that gracious God who hath done so much for me." Now I could rejoice in tribulation, crosses, and provocations. I felt the love which never fails and a delight in the thought that I had anything to bear for God. I found a continual watchfulness and such an invariable sense of the Lord's approval that I was every moment, as it were, afresh accepted in the Beloved.

I would here observe, some time after my dear Mr. Fletcher's death, as I was one day pleading with the Lord to raise up more helpers in the work, the word came to me, "the spirit of Elijah shall rest on Alice" [2 Kings 2:15]. I thought it meant her, and soon after a visible concern arose in her mind, more forcible than ever, for the souls of the people and in particular of the rising generation. And such a gift was then given her for children as I have hardly seen in any one, and a love like that of a parent. Next, the sick were laid on her heart, and she ran far and near to seek and relieve them, both in soul and body, insomuch that it greatly broke her little strength, which was always but small.

One night she dreamed she was looking out at our chamber window on a parcel of fowls of all sorts and sizes in the yard, when she saw a very little bird flying to and fro over them, and as each put up its head the little bird put a bit into its mouth. After looking on them for some time she thought she called me and said, "Only look how that little creature feeds those great fowls." She then saw a most beautiful pillar in the sky. It appeared like gold exceedingly bright. She was solemnly affected at the sight, and awoke with the application of these words to her heart, "I have made thee as this little bird. Follow me, and I will make thee a pillar." This brought to her mind a promise given her many years back. "I will make thee a pillar in my house to go out no more" (Rev. 3:12).

I have been humbled to the dust at the ardent zeal and diligent application wherewith she sought after the good of her fellow creatures. For reproving sin and inviting to the means of grace, few could equal her. Here I did indeed see the spirit of my dear Mr. Fletcher seem to rest on her. And like him, she began a meeting in a very hardened part of the parish with a bell in her hand.

Madeley Town is a hardened spot. I do not know that I ever found more discouragement in speaking anywhere than there. And she was brought to shed tears over them many times, when going from door to door she entreated them to come, and in return met with only reproach and rudeness. But that was nothing to her who sought no honor but from God. Sometimes Satan would represent how ridiculous she appeared in their eyes, and when carnal strangers passed by in carriages, that they would think her mad. But as these means she knew had been instrumental in calling some and had been blest to many, as well as prevented much sin, she rejoiced to have the honor of being thought a fool for Christ. And such an intense love did she feel towards them at the very time they were ridiculing her that she has told me it seemed she could with pleasure submit to be bound to a stake and burned, if it might but draw these souls to choose the way of life.

One night passing by a public house where they were dancing, she looked to the Lord for power, and going in among them began to plead for them, and in a very moving tender manner to express the love and concern she felt for their souls. And glory be to God, we have some in heaven who dated their first conviction from that hour. Indeed her whole soul seemed to be drawn out after the salvation of all around her. She began meetings in different places on which numbers attended. Her method was, after singing and prayer, to read some life, experience, or some awakened author, stopping now and then, to explain and apply it as the Lord gave her utterance. And several, who are now lively believers in our connexion, were brought in through that means. But in every step she inquired of the Lord, fearing much to take one out of his order.

B. *Ars Moriendi:* Accounts of Triumphant Death

She has mentioned to me that [in a dream] she thought she was informed her father (who died in the Lord many years ago) was in a certain place and desired to see her, and that she and I went together for that purpose. But ... in the way, I asked her to go and look at a dial and tell me what hour it was. She went down a step stone walk and saw it was just eleven and came to a place which struck her with a solemn impression that God had work to do there, and having a dish of corn in her hand, she stopped and said, "I will throw some of this corn about, in token the Lord will sometime sow his gospel in this place." As she went, a woman came out of her door and abused her much. But in her return the same woman bestowed many blessings upon her. She thought we went on until we came to a house where we found her father. He showed her much affection and said, "My dear child, I could not rest till I saw you." (A little before his death he had a promise of salvation for all his children.) After this she awoke. The dream made a strong impression on her mind, and often has she told me she did believe she was to be called to some place she had never seen. But as it had a resemblance to some we passed through in Wales, she rather thought it would be in that country.

When the mining works commenced in Carport and the inhabitants began to increase, she was strongly invited to go and hold a meeting there and found her mind drawn to accept this offer. But how was she struck when the very stone walk and all the place where she had sown the corn was as plain to her natural eye, as before she had seen it represented in her dream. On her return she said, "The houses and every part is as exact as if I had had it drawn in a picture." Here she continued to attend every other Sunday night for four years and much of the power of God was felt there. The sinners would scoff, but her word was amazingly received by numbers and deeply did they lament when she could no longer meet with them as usual. And many an earnest prayer did they put up that she might be restored to them again.

I could never discern in her any spirit but that of the most perfect deadness to earth and such a submission to crosses of every kind.... Her will was entirely lost in that of God.

My dear friend, Sarah Lawrence, was many years weak and infirm, but her ardent desire for the salvation of souls carried her frequently beyond her strength, and many times, when she was speaking to sinners with a view to bring them to repentance, her poor body was fitter for bed than any other place. It might be truly said that the zeal of the Lord did eat her up. And after she was quite confined, what tears and prayers did she offer for souls in and about this parish.

When I was going a few Sabbaths ago to meet the people at Coalport-House, she said to me, "You may give them my loving remembrance. If ever I was called anywhere, I surely was to that place. It seemed at times as if my whole soul were drawn out in their behalf, and when I think of the dear children, and grown persons too, who used to come through such deep roads to meet me, I cannot help turning my eyes with tears and prayers many times towards that spot. Well, I have strong confidence I shall meet many of them at God's right hand. When I have been coming home in a dark night over Sutton-Common, I have found such a sense of the heavenly host being round about me, and such communion with them as I cannot describe."

She told me, "It seems as if the Lord had bound the enemy. He cannot afflict me as formerly. And if he suggest an accusation, these words passed through me in an instant,

> Myself, with all my sins, I cast
> On the atoning blood.[92]

"Then Jesus shows me he takes them all away and the temptation is conquered."

When in much pain from continual coughing, with spasms all over her body, she sometimes cried out,

> Corruption, earth, and worms,
> but refine this flesh,
> Till my triumphant spirit comes
> To put it on afresh.[93]

Nov. 8. The complaint so affected her throat that she could neither swallow nor speak without great pain. She said, "I seldom wake but with these words in my heart, 'Ask what thou wilt and I will do it for thee' [John 15:7]. But oh, what can I ask! I have nothing to ask equal to holiness."

B. *Ars Moriendi*: Accounts of Triumphant Death

Nov. 11. She labored much to speak, and at last said, "I cannot tell you what sweet communion I had last night with my Jesus. He seemed very near and loving. I was praising him for all my mercies. Christ is mine and I am his to all eternity O, what comfort! No matter for this body."

On the 13th. She told me she was overcome with the goodness of God.

Nov. 14. With difficulty, but much energy, she repeated these lines,

> Come death, shake hands; I'll kiss thy bands
> 'Tis happiness for me to die.
> What do you think, that I will shrink?
> I'll go to immortality.[94]

The 19th. After a sore night with her cough and many complaints, she observed, "What a sweet night I have had in the love of God! Such nearness to Jesus, such willingness to suffer with him did I feel that I praised the Lord for every fit of coughing. Continually I am pointed to look at the dying Savior in these words,

> See from his head, his hands, his feet,
>   Sorrow and love, flow mingled down!
> Did e'er such love and sorrow meet,
>   Or thorns compose so rich a
>   crown."[95]

Indeed she was such a pattern of patience as I scarcely ever saw and often said with a smile, "Well, if it will glorify God, I am ready to suffer all this forty years. His will is all in all."

Mrs. Yates coming in, she said, "God bless Mrs. Yates and all her family." I said, "My dear love, after all your trials you now prove the faithfulness of God." She answered with the full exertion of all her strength, "There is no cloud can arise.[96] All is fair, all clear." I said, "Have you any sight opened of the invisible world?" She replied, "Yes. Paradise! Heaven is opened. O what has Jesus bought for me!" And then added, "I believe the blood of Jesus cleanseth me from all sin [see also 1 John 1:7], me, vile me, I come to him as the chief of sinners and he has washed me and made me all fair." After a pause, she said, "Give my love to the society, to all the societies." I answered, "My dear, I will, and tell them what God has done for your soul." She replied, with vehemence, "It is beyond compare." Her speech now greatly failed, but on my saying "a convoy of ministering spirits will attend you," she earnestly said, "They do minister; ready winged; ready winged;" meaning she had a perception of it. She remained some hours in the pangs of death, but seemed quite sensible. I asked her if she was not in great pain? She answered, "No." A little before her departure, I said, "Have you the same sweet views you had in the morning?" She immediately lifted up her head as high as she could, the sign we had agreed on for "yes," and at seven o'clock, Wednesday, Dec. 3, 1800, without a further struggle, her happy spirit took its flight to feast with Jesus' priests and kings.

SOURCE:

Mary Fletcher, *An Account of Sarah Lawrence* (London: Printed by Thomas Cardhouse, 1820).

B. ARS MORIENDI: ACCOUNTS OF TRIUMPHANT DEATH

7. ANN TRIPP

"ACCOUNT OF SARAH CROSBY"

Editor's Introduction

For an introduction to the life and work of Ann Tripp, see letter 16 above. At the time of Sarah Crosby's death, certainly no one had any more intimate knowledge of her life and witness than her friend of so many years, Ann Tripp. First linked in ministry with Mary Bosanquet in London, these two women had been active in Christian work over the course of nearly a half century, particularly in the north of England. Their life together among the "Female Brethren" of Leeds defined their life together in many ways. The loss of Sarah Crosby, the first woman preacher of Methodism, was a severe blow to this community in particular and to the Wesleyan movement as a whole. Sarah had given guidance and direction to countless women, providing a model to all of constant devotion to Christ, courageous response to God's call, and confident discipleship in the Wesleyan spirit.

* * * *

In compliance with your request I will now endeavor, in as brief a manner as I can, to give you an account of the Lord's dealings with my beloved friend a short time previous to her decease. But as I had not the least thought, even to the last hour of her life, of that event taking place so soon, many of her sayings which were strongly expressive of her confidence in the Lord and joy in the opening prospect, which she had of soon being with him, have quite slipped my memory. But "her record is on high" [Job 16:19]. Glory be to God, the stroke, though in some respect sudden and unlooked for by me, was not so to her. All the week preceding her death she was often indisposed, but did not abate anything of her usual exercises, and her spirit seemed often on the wing for glory. For she frequently sung more than she had done for months, so that she said, "I think, my dear, you have tuned your harp afresh." One verse she sung with great delight, as I well remember, was

> Heaven is my inheritance,
> I shall soon be taken hence;
> As the stars in glory shine,
> God and Christ and all are mine.[97]

Several times in the week she said, "If I die soon, remember such and such things." Thursday and Friday she met both her classes as usual.... In one of the classes she said her time here would not be long, and repeated, "Who first shall be summoned away, my merciful God, is it I?" and said that she found herself more allied to heaven than earth, for though she had many friends here, she had more in glory.

On Saturday she wrote two letters, went to the select band in the evening, and bore a blessed testimony for their Lord. Though very poorly, she rose on Sunday morning and went to the preaching at seven. She said that she found her spirit sweetly refreshed under the word. At breakfast she began again the subject of dying soon, mentioned some little things she could like to have done, and some concerning which it had given her pain that she had not been able to accomplish. I think it was then she said, "I have nothing that holds me here now, but you, my dear. But God will be with you." She went again to the preaching in the evening and stayed for the Society meeting, but returned very ill with a pain in her chest. We gave her something which relieved her, but in the night the pain returned again with violence, attended with shivering and cold sweats as if she were dying. We sent for the doctor who said she was very bad, although he hoped she would be brought through. But she said, "Without a change, I cannot continue long."

She began praying for her bands, classes, friends, and the church of God, that they might all meet above. Being requested to spare herself, she said, "My dear, if I go now, I have neither doubt, nor cloud. I know I am going to glory. I have been asking my Lord for a promise, and he says, 'I will never, never leave thee'" [Heb. 13:5]. Her weakness was such that she could scarce be kept from fainting

B. *Ars Moriendi:* Accounts of Triumphant Death

during the greater part of the day. Towards evening we conceived great hopes of her recovery as the doctor said her pulse was good, and she began to breathe with less difficulty. A little before she expired, she said to one that was present, "If I had strength, how I could praise him!" But at eight o'clock, without a groan or struggle, she closed her own eyes and mouth, and sweetly fell asleep in Jesus. This was October 29, 1804,[98] on the eve of her spiritual birthday, which was fifty-five years ago, and she was aged 75 (within a week). So composed was her countenance that when dead, not the least trace of death was discernible on it.

> Fill'd up with love and life divine,
> The house of clay, the earthly shrine
> Dissolves, and sinks to dust:
> Without a groan the body dies,
> Her spirit mounts above the skies,
> And mingles with the just.[99]

Mr. Taylor[100] preached her funeral sermon to a crowded audience from Rev. 21:4, a text she had chosen for the purpose soon after she was justified.

To draw a just character of her would require a more able pen than mine, but after so many years close intimacy and thorough knowledge of her, I think it a tribute due to her memory to say she was a sincere lover of truth, a pattern of Christian simplicity, and had such ardent love to Jesus and zeal for his glory as have been possessed by few. "Being dead," she "yet speaketh" [Heb. 11:4] and will live long in the affections of those who had the happiness of her particular instructions and intimacy. Most of the first Methodists are gone to their reward, but the residue of the Spirit is with the Lord. O! that he may pour it down upon the present and rising generation of Methodists, that we may imitate those that are gone in their self-denial, deadness to the world, love to God and zeal for his glory.

Thus you see, my dear friend, I have endeavored, though in a very feeble and imperfect manner, to give you a short sketch of the last moments of one whose loss I deeply feel and whose memory I revere. Much more might have been said with truth. But may he, who only can, accompany this with his blessing, and to him shall be the glory. Believing you will unite your prayers with mine,

I remain, with sincerity and respect,
Your obliged and affectionate Friend,
Ann Tripp

SOURCE:

WMM 29 (1806): 615-17.

B. *Ars Moriendi*: Accounts of Triumphant Death

8. Mary Tooth

"Account of Mary Fletcher"

Editor's Introduction

The following account of Mary Fletcher's death, which took place on December 9, 1815, at Madeley, is drawn from *Letter to the Loving and Beloved People of the Parish of Madeley, and its Vicinity, Who Have Lost a Friend to Piety in the Death of Mrs. Fletcher, Widow of the Rev. J. W. Fletcher*.[101] In the Methodist Archives and Research Centre of the Rylands Library, Manchester, one will find the extensive Fletcher-Tooth correspondence, in addition to the miscellaneous correspondence and commonplace books of Mary Tooth. Virtually nothing is known of Tooth outside these references; much remains to be explored in these materials. The depth of the two Marys' mutual affection is revealed in Miss Tooth's obituary letter of her friend, requested by Joseph Benson, then editor of the *Methodist Magazine*, and published in the 1816 issue, pages 157-59:

> To me she was more than a mother. I have felt for her all that a child can feel for a parent; and her death has occasioned me the most painful conflict I have ever endured. I miss her day by day, and cannot but deeply mourn the loss of such a counsellor and friend; though, through divine grace, I do not murmur at the dispensation. For twenty years, I had the unspeakable advantage of her friendship, her maternal love, and prayers; for more than the last fifteen of which, I was so highly privileged as to abide under her roof, and be scarcely separated from her for one day during the whole time. Her affection to me was so great, that she often said, to lose me would be the heaviest earthly affliction that could befall her; but she believed the Lord would never call her to drink that bitter cup. In this, and many other things of a similar nature, our gracious Lord was pleased to give her the desire of her heart.[102]

* * * *

Knowing that it is your desire to hear something respecting the close of the life of my invaluable friend Mrs. Fletcher, now in glory, and being assured that none but myself can undertake the work, as I alone was her constant companion, being separated scarcely a day for more than fifteen years, I have endeavored to set down a few circumstances relative to the close of a life surpassing in usefulness most of her fellow mortals. For the last month of her life her breath was more oppressed than usual. It had been much affected for years upon motion. Yet when she sat still or laid herself down at night, she could breathe quite easy. But the middle of November last, her breathing was affected both while she sat still and when she was laid down. She had also a troublesome cough that disturbed her rest at night. And when this was the case, her strength quickly declined. Yet with all that she went through, how did she labor for the good of souls! Many times she has gone to speak to the people, when she has said, "It is like as if every meeting would take away my life, but I'll speak to them as long as I can. While I've any breath and power to get out, I'll not spare myself." And truly she did not, as will be readily testified by many hundreds who have been in the habit of attending her meetings.

I am inclined to think the twenty-fourth of last July will not be forgotten by a large proportion of the great numbers who crowded to hear her. She explained the twenty-fifth chapter of Matthew's Gospel. It was the last Monday night she was able to speak to a listening crowd of attentive hearers, some of whom had come many miles, but did not think much of the pains they took because of the spiritual good they derived from the opportunity. I remember she spoke in a peculiarly striking manner on the necessity of being born again. When she came to the thirteenth verse, "Watch therefore, for ye know neither the day nor the hour wherein the Son of Man cometh," and from the following verses respecting the talents, she enlarged much, powerfully insisting upon the right use of the understanding, will, mind, or memory, with every affection, the right application of time, with every penny of money, and the watching over the tongue, which she observed might enjoy the honor of being God's advocate, but for want of watchfulness was, as the Apostle expresses it, "set on fire of hell."

Among the numerous company that will have to ascribe glory to our God for the good received through her instrumentality...I can-

B. *Ars Moriendi:* Accounts of Triumphant Death

not forbear saying, my hope is, that I shall stand among the ransomed of the Lord, and say, "I was born there." Yes, my friends, I must say the good Lord made her the means of the awakening, conversion, and deepening the work of grace in my soul. And while I give all the glory to my God for the grace received, I cannot but feel much love to the channel through which that grace was communicated. Nor are my feelings in this peculiar, they are the feelings of a number of lively souls who bless God that the sound of her voice ever reached their ears, and in whose affections she will long live, and though dead, yet speak [see also Heb. 11:4]. Thus did she, whether sick or well, labor for the increase of spirituality in the hearts of the people. Her eyes were always heavenward, and whether at home or abroad, she was ever endeavoring to draw souls to a closer walk with God.

[When unable to fulfil a preaching appointment due to illness, she sent a letter to the people to be read by Miss Tooth, an excerpt of which follows:]

"O that you would therefore do as Jacob did, be earnest with the Lord that his love may fill your heart; as the Scripture expresses it, the love of God shed abroad in your hearts by the Holy Ghost given unto you. If you get your hearts full of the love of God you will find that is the oil by which the lamp of faith will be ever kept burning. Love makes all our duty easy. A soul united as one spirit to the Lord, if temptation presents, has a ready answer. Such a one instantly cries out, How shall I do this great wickedness and sin against God? against Him in whom my soul delighteth? Pray, my friends, pray much for this love; and remember that word, 'He that dwelleth in love dwelleth in God, and God in him'" [1 John 4:16]!

One day, I think the sixth of December, when waking out of a doze, she said, "I am drawing near to glory," and soon after, "there is my house and portion fair," and again, "Jesus come, my hope of glory," and after a short pause, "He lifts his hands, and shows that I am graven there." On the seventh of December, taking my hand in hers, she said, "My precious, my invaluable friend, I have prayed that light and wisdom may guide you in all, in every difficulty and it will be so. I know it will. My prayer for thee is heard, my choice friend." The day following, the eighth, was as the day before, a day of praise for fulness of blessing. All this day her breathing was exceedingly difficult. But through all her mouth was full of the loving kindness of the Lord. We always prayed together before we went into the chamber, her breath being so greatly oppressed. She prayed very sweetly, but short, and then said, "Now you call upon the Lord. I can enjoy your prayer, though not able to speak." I did so, and found an uncommon degree of liberty while pleading the gracious promises made to the people of God. When I had ended, she said it had been to her soul a peculiar time of enjoyment while I was calling upon the Lord, and concluded saying, "O this has done me good." When we were ready to go into the chamber, and it was after ten, I got her into the chair, but she was now weaker than at noon. However, I wheeled her to the bedside and could not but look upon her as dying. And indeed so she considered herself, for when got into bed, she said, "My love, this is the last time I shall get into bed. It has been hard work to get in, but it is work I shall do no more. This oppression upon my breath cannot last long, but all is well. The Lord will shower down ten thousand blessings upon thee, my tender nurse, my kind friend."

After these and many more kind expressions to the same effect, and having embraced her, and put all her things as usual, she desired I would make haste to bed. I entreated her to let me sit up, repeatedly saying, "Do let me watch with you this one night." But with all the tenderness imaginable, yet with that degree of firmness which made me unwilling to urge the request further, she said, "Go to bed. You have done all for me you can do, and you know you can be with me in a moment if I want you. But if you sit up, it will make me uncomfortable. I cannot rest without you going to bed." I told her I had a few things to do before I could get into bed. She replied, "Then make haste and do them, for I want you in bed. I cannot rest till I know you are in bed." After I had made all the excuses I could for remaining up, and looking upon her dear countenance as long as her kind concern for me would admit, she still urged my going to bed, and I therefore laid me within the bed clothes, without taking my own off. And when she again put the question, "Are you my love in bed?" I answered, "Yes." She then said, "That's right, now if I can rest I will. But let our hearts be united in prayer, and the Lord bless both thee and me."

These were the last words her beloved lips uttered. For an hour after this, about one o'clock in the morning of December 9th, the noise her breath had so long made ceased. I thought, is she

B. *Ars Moriendi*: Accounts of Triumphant Death

dropped asleep? It immediately came to my mind, "Asleep in Jesus. See a soul escaped to bliss." I went directly to her bedside where I found the beloved body without the immortal spirit, which had entered the realms of endless day. My feelings are not to be described. I clung to the casket of the saint, knelt down by the side of it, and cried to him who had just now called home the spirit of my friend, that the mantle might rest on me. At length I thought I should injure her dear remains if I did not call the family up. I therefore went and called my sister and the servant at half past one, after which I sent for Mrs. Perks, who kindly came over immediately. I never left the chamber while anything could be done for her. I had promised to be with her to the last and the Lord enabled me so to do.

Her countenance was as sweet a one as was ever seen in death. There was at last neither sigh, groan, or struggle, but all the appearance of a person in the most composed slumber. When I first undrew the curtain and saw her dear head dropped off the pillow, and looking so sweetly composed, I could not persuade myself the spirit was fled, till I took her in my arms and found no motion left. I then perceived, the moment she had so much longed for had arrived. For I think I have heard her some hundreds of times exclaim, with the most vehement desire, "O, my Jesus, when shall I fly to thy arms!" She was always looking and waiting for the happy moment when she should gain the blissful shore.

SOURCE:

Mary's more widely known *Letter*, from which the following excerpt is drawn, may be consulted in the Methodist Archives, but is quoted with extensive editorial alteration in Moore, *Mary Fletcher*; and again, in part, in Taft, *Holy Women*, 1:31-36.

ABBREVIATIONS

AM	*The Arminian Magazine: Consisting of Extracts and Original Treatises on Universal Redemption.* Edited by John Wesley. London: Fry et al., 1778–97 (continued as *WMM*).
AM (BC)	*The Arminian Magazine: Consisting of Extracts and Original Treatises on Universal Redemption.* Edited by James Thorne. Devon: Arminian Bible Christians, 1822–27?.
BCP	*The Book of Common Prayer.* London, 1662.
Christian Library	John Wesley. *A Christian Library: Consisting of Extracts from, and Abridgements of, the Choicest Pieces of Practical Divinity which have been Published in the English Tongue.* 50 vols. Bristol: F. Farley, 1749–55.
Funeral Hymns*	[Charles Wesley]. *Funeral Hymns.* 2d Series. n.p., [1759].

Abbreviations

HLS*	John and Charles Wesley. *Hymns on the Lord's Supper*. Bristol: Farley, 1745.
HSP (1739)*	John and Charles Wesley. *Hymns and Sacred Poems*. London: Strahan, 1739.
HSP (1740)*	John and Charles Wesley. *Hymns and Sacred Poems*. London: Strahan, 1740.
HSP (1742)*	John and Charles Wesley. *Hymns and Sacred Poems*. Bristol: Farley, 1742.
HSP (1749)*	John and Charles Wesley. *Hymns and Sacred Poems*. Bristol: Farley, 1749.
John Wesley	*John Wesley*. Edited by Albert C. Outler. New York: Oxford University Press, 1964.
Journal CW	*The Journal of the Rev. Charles Wesley, M.A.*, ed. Thomas Jackson, 2 vols. London: Wesleyan-Methodist Book Room, 1849; reprinted Grand Rapids: Baker Book House, 1980.
Letters (Telford)	*The Letters of the Rev. John Wesley, A. M.* Edited by John Telford. 8 vols. London: Epworth Press, 1931.
Meth. Arch.	The Methodist Archives and Research Centre, John Rylands University Library of Manchester.
MethH	*Methodist History*.
Poet. Works	*The Poetical Works of John and Charles Wesley*. Edited by George Osborn. 13 vols. London: Wesleyan Methodist Conference Office, 1868–72.

PWHS	*Proceedings of the Wesley Historical Society.*
Redemption Hymns*	[John? and Charles Wesley]. *Hymns for Those that Seek, and Those that have Redemption in the Blood of Jesus Christ.* London: Strahan, 1747.
Scripture Hymns*	Charles Wesley. *Short Hymns on Select Passages of the Holy Scriptures.* 2 vols. Bristol: Farley, 1762.
WMM	Refers to quarterly theological journal of the (British) Wesleyan Methodist Church published as *The Methodist Magazine* (1798–1821) and *The Wesleyan Methodist Magazine* (1822–1913).
Works	*The Bicentennial Edition of the Works of John Wesley.* 35 volumes projected. Eds., Frank Baker and Richard P. Heitzenrater. Nashville: Abingdon Press, 1984–. (Volumes 7, 11, 25, and 26 originally appeared as the *Oxford Edition of the Works of John Wesley.* Oxford: Clarendon Press, 1975–83).
Works (Jackson)	*The Works of John Wesley.* Edited by Thomas Jackson. 14 vols. London, 1872; Grand Rapids: Zondervan, 1958.

* These works are included in *Poet. Works*, and quoted from there.

NOTES

Introduction

1. Quoted in Mary Tooth, *A Letter to the Loving and Beloved People of the Parish of Madeley* (Shiffnal: Printed by A. Edmonds, [1815]), 17-18.

2. See Philip Sheldrake, *Spirituality and History*, 2nd ed. (London: SPCK, 1995), for a description of the range of meaning accruing to the term "spirituality" in the Christian context.

3. Gordon Wakefield, ed., *The Westminster Dictionary of Christian Spirituality* (Philadelphia: Westminster, 1983), v. Wakefield has also written a helpful introduction to the spirituality of British Methodists entitled *Methodist Spirituality* (Peterborough: Epworth, 1999).

4. Geoffrey Wainwright, "Types of Spirituality," in *The Study of Spirituality*, ed. Cheslyn Jones, Geoffrey Wainwright, and Edward Yarnold (New York: Oxford University Press, 1986), 592.

5. Sheldrake, *Spirituality and History*, 50.

6. Ibid., 52.

7. This depiction of early Methodism draws on my discussion of "The Methodist Ethos" in *Her Own Story: Autobiographical Portraits of Early Methodist Women* (Nashville: Kingswood Books, 2001), 18-28; and on similar treatments in *The Wesleyan Tradition: A Paradigm for Renewal* (Nashville: Abingdon Press, 2002), 23-37; and *Recapturing the Wesleys' Vision: An Introduction to the Faith of John and Charles Wesley* (Downers Grove, Ill.: InterVarsity Press, 2004). See also the primary history of the movement (Richard P. Heitzenrater, *Wesley and the People Called Methodists* [Nashville: Abingdon Press, 1995]); and one of the more recent biographies of its founder, Henry D. Rack (*Reasonable Enthusiast: John Wesley and the Rise of Methodism* [Nashville: Abingdon Press, 1992]).

8. For a clear and judicious analysis of the English social scene, see Roy Porter, *English Society in the Eighteenth Century* (New York: Penguin Books, 1982).

9. One of the most helpful analyses of the Church of English in this period, providing a corrective to the stereotypical images left by nineteenth- and early twentieth-century scholars, is the incisive "Introduction: The Church and Anglicanism in the 'Long' Eighteenth Century," by John Walsh and Stephen Taylor, in *The Church of England c. 1689–c. 1833: From Toleration to Tractarianism*, ed. John Walsh, Colin Haydon, and Stephen Taylor (Cambridge: Cambridge University Press, 1993), 1-66.

10. Historian Barrie Tabraham has observed: "For the most part, Anglican clergy went about their duties quietly and conscientiously, but with perhaps little enthusiasm or conviction. There is a general sense of the Church of England having lost its 'nerve,' and being ill-equipped to respond to the developments that were soon to change the face of the country" (Tabraham, *The Making of Methodism* [London: Epworth Press, 1995], 5). On the state of the church throughout this period, see Alan D. Gilbert, *Religion and Society in Industrial England: Church, Chapel, and Social Change, 1740–1914* (London: Longman, 1976); E. Gordon Rupp, *Religion in England, 1688–1791* (Oxford: Clarendon Press, 1986); and the earlier classic study of Norman Sykes, *Church and State in England in the Eighteenth Century* (Cambridge: Cambridge University Press, 1934). See also J. Gregory and J. S. Chamberlain, eds., *The National Church in Local Perspective* (London: Boydell Woodbridge, 2003), 1-27, for a brief summary of sources and historiography.

11. Walsh, *Church of England*, 51.

12. Rack, *Reasonable Enthusiast*, 21.

13. See the broad discussion of the identity of Anglicanism in the eighteenth century in Walsh, *Church of England*, 51-60.

14. See Geoffrey Rowell, Kenneth Stevenson, and Rowan Wiliams, *Love's Redeeming Work: The Anglican Quest for Holiness* (Oxford: Oxford University Press, 2001), xx. The compilers of this massive anthology of Anglican sources identify Thomas Cranmer, Richard Hooker, and George Herbert as key exemplars of this Anglican trajectory of the spiritual quest.

15. For an illustration of the influences upon Charles Wesley, see John Lawson, "Charles Wesley: A Man of the Prayer-Book," *Proceedings of the Charles Wesley Society* 6 (1999–2000): 85-117.

16. On the development of English traditions of spirituality during this period, see Rowell, *Love's Redeeming Work*, 185-93; see also the earlier standard analyses of Martin Thornton, *English Spirituality* (London: SPCK, 1963); C. J. Stranks, *Anglican Devotion* (London: SPCK, 1961); and H. R. McAdoo, *The Spirit of Anglicanism* (London: Black, 1965).

17. Martin Thornton offers an excellent overview of their spirituality in "The Caroline Divines and the Cambridge Platonists," in Jones, *Study of Spirituality*, 431-37.

18. See Joseph Summer, *George Herbert: His Religion and Art* (Cambridge, Mass.: Harvard University Press, 1954); Margaret Bottrall, *George Herbert* (London: John Murry, 1954); and John N. Wall Jr., ed., *George Herbert* (New York: Paulist Press, 1981).

19. See Richard Baxter, "To the Reader," in *Poetical Fragments* (London: T. Snowden, 1681), ix.

20. See H. Trevor Hughes, *The Piety of Jeremy Taylor* (London: Macmillan, 1960); and Thomas K. Carroll, ed., *Jeremy Taylor* (New York: Paulist Press, 1990).

21. One of the best modern editions of the *Serious Call* and *The Spirit of Love* is by Paul G. Stanwood: *William Law* (New York: Paulist Press, 1978).

22. On the Puritan tradition of spirituality in England, see Gordon S. Wakefield, "The Puritans," in Jones, *Study of Spirituality*, 437-45.

23. See Arthur P. Davis, *Isaac Watts: His Life and Works* (London: Independent Press, 1948); and Selma L. Bishop, ed., *Hymns and Spiritual Songs, 1707–1748* (London and Glasgow: Faith, 1962).

24. Henry Scougal (1650–78), Scottish theologian and mystic. Albert Outler includes him among Wesley's four great mentors in piety (*John Wesley*, viii).

25. A Spanish Benedictine monk (c. 1536–99), whose highly esteemed devotional treatise, *De pugna spiritualis*, was falsely attributed to Juan de Castaniza, in Wesley's day.

26. Henry Scougal, *The Life of God in the Soul of Man*, ed. W. S. Hudson (Philadelphia: Westminster, 1958), 30.

27. There were also influences, in the end more negative than positive, from the Quietist mystic tradition of France and Spain, most notably the writings of Francis de Sales, Miguel de Molinos, Madame Guyon, and Fénelon. What Wesley appreciated most in these mystics was their doctrine of pure love and their aspirations of union with God; what he absolutely detested in the end was their strong bias in the direction of antinomianism.

28. The *Imitatio Christi*, of which Thomas à Kempis (c. 1380-1471) was the reputed author. Probably written between 1420 and 1427, the *Imitatio* is, next to the Bible, the most popular of Christian devotional classics. In his famous memorandum of May 24, 1738, Wesley wrote: "When I was about twenty-two my father pressed me to enter into holy orders. At the same time, the providence of God directing me to à Kempis's *Christian Pattern*, I began to see that true religion was seated in the heart and that God's law extended to all our thoughts as well as words and actions" (*Journal* [May 24, 1738], *Works* 18:243).

29. See his lengthy correspondence with his mother, Susanna, in relation to these questions, in *Works* 25:159-60, 162-90.

30. He published two different redactions of the treatise under the titles *The Christian's Pattern* (1735) and *An Extract of the Christian's Pattern* (1741), both based largely on the Worthington translation of 1677. The last edition of the former, larger work appeared in 1763; the *Extract* saw nineteen editions in England over the course of fifty years, the final form being published in 1791, the year of Wesley's death.

31. Letter to the Societies at Bristol (Oct. 1764), *Letters* (Telford) 4:272; see also Letter to Samuel Wesley Jr. (30 Oct. 1738), *Works* 25:576; Letter to George Merryweather (24 Jan. 1760), *Letters* (Telford) 4:83; Letter to Sarah Wesley (31 Mar. 1781), *Letters* (Telford) 7:54.

32. See Sermon 55, "On the Trinity," *Works* 2:373-86. On both figures, see David Butler, *Methodists and Papists* (London: Darton, Longman, and Todd, 1995), 137-54.

33. Gregory Lopez (1542–96) was an obscure Spanish mystic. Wesley, who abridged and published Lopez's life in the *Christian Library* (vol. 50), must have been impressed by his conversion account, his missionary exploits in the New World, and his attainment to such a high degree of virtue in life. There were also many striking parallels in their personal lives.

34. Gaston Jean Baptiste de Renty (1611–49), an affluent French Catholic turned ascetic, had been converted while reading the *Imitation of Christ* and devoted himself exclusively to piety and charity. In 1741, Wesley published an extract of his life, which he later included in *Christian Library*, vol. 29.

35. See Eamon Duffy, "Wesley and the Counter Reformation," in *Revival and Religion Since 1700*, ed. Jane Garnett and Colin Marshall (London: Hambledon, 1993), 1-19.

36. As reported by Butler, *Methodists and Papists*, 143.

37. Pseudo-Macarius was a fourth-century monk and spiritual writer. An excellent introduction to his thought is Marcus Plested, "The Macarian Homilies: A Wellspring of the Christian Mystical Tradition," *One in Christ* 40.3 (2005): 73-89.

38. See also Mark T. Kurowski, "The First Step Toward Grace: John Wesley's Use of the Spiritual Homilies of Macarius the Great," *MethH* 36 (1998): 113-24.

39. Ephraem Syrus (c. 306–73) was an obscure Syrian biblical exegete and controversial writer. Most of his voluminous exegetical, theological, controversial, and ascetic works are poetic in form. For a modern edition of his hymns, see Kathleen E. McVey, ed., *Ephrem the Syrian: Hymns* (New York: Paulist Press, 1989).

40. See in particular Gordon Wakefield, "John Wesley and Ephraem Syrus," *Hugoye: Journal of Syriac Studies* (syrcom.cua.edu/hugoye) 1.2 (July 1998); and Section IV, "Other Eastern Sources and Charles Wesley," in *Orthodox and Wesleyan Spirituality*, ed. S T Kimbrough Jr. (Crestwood, N.Y.: St. Vladimir's Seminary Press, 2002), 205-85.

41. See Paul W. Chilcote, *Praying in the Wesleyan Spirit: 52 Prayers for Today* (Nashville: Upper Room Books, 2001) and *Wesley Speaks on Christian Vocation* (Nashville: Discipleship Resources, 1986)

42. Gordon Wakefield, *Fire of Love: The Spirituality of John Wesley* (London: Epworth Press, 1976) and *Methodist Devotion: The Spiritual Life in the Methodist Tradition* (London: Epworth Press, 1966).

43. Frank Whaling, ed., *John and Charles Wesley: Selected Prayers, Hymns, Journal Notes, Sermons, Letters and Treatises* (New York: Paulist Press, 1981), 62.

44. Ibid., 63.

45. David Lyle Jeffrey, ed., *English Spirituality in the Age of Wesley* (Grand Rapids: Eerdmans, 1994), 28-35.

46. David Lowes Watson, "Methodist Spirituality," in *Protestant Spiritual Traditions*, ed. Frank Senn (New York: Paulist Press, 1986), 217-73.

47. Sondra Higgins Matthaei, *Making Disciples: Faith Formation in the Wesleyan Tradition* (Nashville: Abingdon Press, 2000).

48. Tom Albin, "An Empirical Study of Early Methodist Spirituality," in *Wesleyan Theology Today*, ed. Theodore Runyon (Nashville: Kingswood Books, 1985), 277.

49. Ibid, 278.

50. Ibid, 279.

51. See as well the chapter on the Wesleys in James Gordon's *Evangelical Spirituality: From the Wesleys to John Stott* ([London: SPCK, 1991], 11-40), which elevates the themes of salvation, poetry, Christian perfection, love, and the means of grace. More recent works highlight specific aspects of Wesleyan spirituality. Steve Harper's *Devotional Life in the Wesleyan Tradition* (Nashville: Upper Room Books, 1983) provides a popular discussion of Wesley's means of grace. For a more definitive discussion, see Henry H. Knight III, *The Presence of God in the Christian Life: John Wesley and the Means of Grace* (Lanham, Md.: Scarecrow Press, 1992). In *As If the Heart Mattered: A Wesleyan Spirituality* (Nashville: Upper Room Books, 1997), Gregory S. Clapper provides a popular analysis of this theme based upon the Wesleyan order of salvation. It is also my understanding that John Newton is preparing a new volume on Methodist spirituality, but I have not been able to consult it.

52. See Thomas A. Langford, *Practical Divinity: Theology in the Wesleyan Tradition* (Nashville: Abingdon Press, 1983), 24-48.

53. See Sermon 85, "On Working Out Our Own Salvation," *Works* 3:199-209.

54. One of Wesley's few catechetical publications, this small tract was a revised English extract from an early eighteenth-century French work by the prominent mystic, disciple, and biographer of Antoinette Bourignon, Pierre Poiret, entitled *Les Principes solides de la Religion et de la Vie Chretienne* (1705).

55. See Sermon 110, "On Free Grace" (*Works* 3:544-63), in which Wesley describes God's grace as a free gift, in all, and for all.

56. Most of the quotations from Methodist women in this introduction are from the sources included in this volume. Only those that are not will be given full citation.

57. See Chilcote, *Her Own Story*, 14-18, 39-41 in particular. This section is based in large measure upon that research. A helpful study of the developing genre of spiritual autobiography among women and the emergence of gendered subjectivity is Felicity Nussbaum, *The Autobiographical Subject: Gender and Ideology in Eighteenth-Century England* (Baltimore: John Hopkins University Press, 1990); see also her article, "Eighteenth-Century Women's Autobiographical Commonplaces," in *The Private Self: Theory and Practice of Women's Autobiographical Writings*, ed. Shari Bentock (Chapel Hill: University of North Carolina Press, 1988), 147-71. See also Cynthia S. Pomerleau, "The Emergence of Women's Autobiography in England," in *Women's Autobiography: Essays in Criticism*, ed. Estelle C. Jelinek (Bloomington: Indiana University Press, 1980), 21-38.

58. See the collection of transcribed manuscript materials in *Reformation and Revival in Eighteenth-century Bristol*, ed. Jonathan Barry and Kenneth Morgan (Stroud: Printed for the Bristol Record Society, 1994), 75-104; and similar collections in D. Bruce Hindmarsh, *The Evangelical Conversion Narrative: Spiritual Autobiography in Early Modern England* (New York: Oxford University Press, 2005). For an interesting but overly provocative analysis of some of this material, see John Kent, *Wesley and the Wesleyans: Religion in Eighteenth-Century Britain* (Cambridge: Cambridge University Press, 2002).

59. Reginald Ward observes that "the sheer bulk of the surviving evangelical self-representation and confession is a broad hint of the huge volume of class-meeting testimony and the like which never moved from oral to literary form" (*Works* 18:24). See also D. Bruce Hindmarsh, " 'My chains fell off, my heart was free': Early Methodist Conversion Narratives in England," *Church History* 68 (1999): 910-29.

60. Ted A. Campbell, *The Religion of the Heart: A Study of European Religious Life in the Seventeenth and Eighteenth Centuries* (Columbia: University of South Carolina Press, 1991), 2-3.

61. On the schematic design of these conversion narratives, see Reginald Ward's comments in *Works* 18:14.

62. *Principles of a Methodist Further Explained*, VI.4, *Works* 9:227.

63. From the homily of the Church of England entitled "Of True Christian Faith," quoted in *John Wesley*, 130.
64. See my introduction to the Christian perfection corpus in *Works*, vol. 12 (forthcoming).
65. Sermon 17, "The Circumcision of the Heart," II.10, *Works* 1:413-14.
66. *WMM* 31 (1808): 465; see also Chilcote, *Her Own Story*, 62.
67. For a discussion of the history, purpose, and function of these groups, see David Lowes Watson, *Covenant Discipleship: Christian Formation Through Mutual Accountability* (Nashville: Discipleship Resources, 1989); and *Class Leaders: Recovering a Tradition* (Nashville: Discipleship Resources, 1991).
68. *Collection of Hymns* (1780), #489, vv. 3-4, *Works* 7:677.
69. Sermon 16, "The Means of Grace" (*Works* 1:376-97) was Wesley's effort to clarify the difference between the proper use and possible abuse of prayer (and fasting), Bible study, Christian fellowship, and the Sacrament of Holy Communion in faithful discipleship. These "means" were, in fact, the very foundation of Wesleyan spirituality and their rediscovery a powerful appropriation of ancient Christian practice. The most important recent work on this topic is Knight, *Presence of God*.
70. "The Experience of Mrs. Ann Gilbert, of Gwinear, in Cornwall," *AM* 18 (1795): 45-46.
71. *Journal* (18 Sept. 1764), *Works* 21:489. Edward Perronet identified the woman as Mrs. Garbrand of Brentford.
72. Joseph Sutcliffe, *The Experience of the late Mrs. Frances Pawson, Widow of the late Rev. John Pawson* (London: Thomas Cordeux, 1813), 104-5.
73. Quoted in Earl Kent Brown, "Women of the Word: Selected Leadership Roles of Women in Mr. Wesley's Methodism," in *Women in New Worlds: Historical Perspectives on the Wesleyan Tradition*, ed. Hilah F. Thomas and Rosemary Skinner Keller (Nashville: Abingdon Press, 1981), 1:72.
74. William Bramwell, *A Short Account of the Life and Death of Ann Cutler*, new ed. with appendix by Z. Taft, containing *An Account of Elizabeth Dickinson* (York: Printed by John Will, 1827), 2.
75. William Bennet, *Memoirs of Mrs. Grace Bennet* (Macclesfield: E. Bayley, 1803), 78.
76. Sermon 122, "Causes of the Inefficacy of Christianity," §12, *Works* 4:93. For a discussion of Wesley's view of scripture, see Scott Jones, *John Wesley's Concept and Use of Scripture* (Nashville: Kingswood Books, 1995). For further discussion of the dynamic Wesleyan conception of biblical authority, consult W. Stephen Gunter et al., *Wesley and the Quadrilateral: Renewing the Conversation* (Nashville: Abingdon Press, 1997).
77. *HLS*, Hymn 54, v. 4. See also J. Ernest Rattenbury, *The Eucharistic Hymns of John and Charles Wesley* (London: Epworth Press, 1948), 176-249. For a discussion of the sacrament as an "effective means of grace," see in particular Ole E. Borgen, *John Wesley on the Sacraments: A Theological Study* (New York: Abingdon Press, 1962), 183-217.
78. "An Account of Mrs. Hannah Harrison," *WMM* 25 (1802): 321.
79. For a modern Methodist expression of this theme, see Rosemary Skinner Keller, ed., *Spirituality and Social Responsibility: The Vocational Vision of Women in the United Methodist Tradition* (Nashville: Abingdon Press, 1993).
80. *General Rules*, §5, *Works* 9:72.
81. Sarah Peters pioneered prison ministry with Silas Told in London's Newgate Prison, where she helped organize Methodist Societies for the inmates as early as 1748. See "Some Account of Sarah Peters," *AM* 5 (1782): 128-36; see also Paul W. Chilcote, *John Wesley and the Women Preachers of Early Methodism* (Metuchen, N.J.: Scarecrow Press, 1991), 95-96.
82. Letter to Miss March (9 June 1775), *Letters* (Telford) 6:153-54.
83. S T Kimbrough Jr., ed., *Songs for the Poor* (New York: GBGMusik, 1993), 12.
84. Quoted in S T Kimbrough Jr., *Lost in Wonder* (Nashville: The Upper Room, 1987), 11-12.
85. Paul W. Chilcote, "Songs of the Heart: Hymn Allusions in the Writings of Early Methodist Women," *Proceedings of the Charles Wesley Society* 5 (1998): 99-114.
86. "Account of Hannah Harrison," 321.

87. In addition to my writings on the subject, see the extensive bibliography in Chilcote, *Wesley and Women*, 329-57. Of particular note are Earl Kent Brown, *Women of Mr. Wesley's Methodism* (New York: Edwin Mellen, 1983); Thomas M. Morrow, *Early Methodist Women* (London: Epworth Press, 1967); Leslie Church's two-volume set, *The Early Methodist People* (London: Epworth Press, 1948) and *More About the Early Methodist People* (London: Epworth Press, 1949); and the terse discussion of Methodist women's roles in David J. Boulton, "Women and Early Methodism," *PWHS* 43 (1981): 13-17.

88. Gail Malmgreen, "Domestic Discords," in *Disciplines of Faith: Studies in Religion, Politics, and Patriarchy*, ed. Jim Obelkevich, Lyndal Roper, and Raphael Samuel (London: Routledge & Kegan Paul, 1987), 55-70. See also the volume of essays Malmgreen edited, *Religion in the Lives of English Women, 1760–1930* (Bloomington: University of Indiana Press, 1986). K. Morgan analyzes the religious narratives of early Methodist women in Bristol but makes no attempt to create a group portrait of the women in "Methodist Testimonials," in Barry and Morgan, *Reformation and Revival in Eighteenth-Century Bristol*, 75-104.

89. See Albin, "Methodist Spirituality" (pp. 275-76), from which the following portrait is drawn. See also the articles of Clive Field, "Adam and Eve: Gender in the English Free Church Constituency," *Journal of Ecclesiastical History* 44 (1993): 63-79; and "The Social Structure of English Methodism, 18th–20th Centuries," *British Journal of Sociology* 28 (1977): 199-225.

90. See Paul W. Chilcote, "John Wesley as Revealed by the Journal of Hester Ann Rogers," *MethH* 20 (1982): 111-23.

91. Letter to Hester Ann Roe (9 Dec. 1781), *Letters* (Telford) 7:96.

92. Manuscript letter dated May 20, 1780, *Meth. Arch.*

93. Of the thirty-seven women writers included in this volume, only thirty have relatively clear birth dates. Those women of whom virtually nothing is known, or for whom I was unable to obtain the necessary information, include Mary Lyth, Miss T., Phillis Wheatley, Portia Young, Mary Anderson, Mary James, and Elizabeth Henson.

94. Vicki Tolar Collins has marshaled data to demonstrate the popularity of Rogers's *Experience* in "Perfecting a Woman's Life: Methodist Rhetoric and Politics in *The Account of Hester Ann Rogers*" (Ph.D. dissertation, Auburn University, 1993).

95. It is important to note that consonance of Methodist women with three highly influential women religious writers of the age: Mary Astell (*The Christian Religion as Professed by a Daughter of the Church of England*, 1705), Susanna Hopton (*Collection of Meditations and Devotions*, 1717), and Hannah More (*Practical Piety*, 1811). On the nature of their influence within the life of the church, see Rowell, *Love's Redeeming Work*, 190.

96. Generally drawn up by communities for the purpose of describing their common life, disciplines, and purposes, in the history of Christian spirituality, four rules have been recognized as "canonical": the rules of Benedict, Basil, Augustine, and Francis. In the western church it was the Rule of St. Benedict that consolidated the various monastic traditions and has provided continuing insight with regard to spiritual formation. See also Steve Harper, "Rule," in *The Upper Room Dictionary of Christian Spiritual Formation*, ed. Keith Beasley-Topliffe (Nashville: Upper Room Books, 2003), 240.

97. Ann Taves, *Fits, Trances, and Visions: Experiencing Religion and Explaining Experience from Wesley to James* (Princeton: Princeton University Press, 1999), 71. See also her discussion of dreams and visions in the Wesleyan tradition in ibid., 53-57, 73-74, 108-9.

98. For a nearly encyclopedic discussion of "the letter" during this period, see Frank Baker's Introduction to *Works* 25:11-28. See also Patricia Meyer Spacks, "Female Rhetorics," in *The Private Self*, ed. Bentock, 172-78; and Nussbaum, *Autobiographical Subject*.

99. The classical studies on this theme include Mary Catharine O'Connor, *The Art of Dying Well: The Development of the "Ars Moriendi"* (New York: Columbia University Press, 1942); Nancy Lee Beaty, *The Craft of Dying: A Study in the Literary Tradition of the "Ars Moriendi" in England* (New Haven: Yale University Press, 1970); David W. Atkinson, *The English "ars moriendi"* (New York: Lang, 1992); and Carlos M. N. Eire, *From Madrid to Purgatory: The Art and Craft of Dying in Sixteenth-Century Spain*, new ed. (Cambridge: Cambridge University Press, 2002). See also Matthew Levering, ed., *On Christian Dying: Classic and Contemporary Texts* (New York: Sheed & Ward, 2004).

100. See the seminal works, Mary Field Belenky et al., *Women's Ways of Knowing: The Development of Self, Voice, and Mind* (New York: Basic Books, 1986); Carol Gilligan, *In A Different Voice: Psychological Theory and Women's Development* (Cambridge: Harvard University Press, 1982); Sherna Berger Gluck and Daphne Patai, eds., *Women's Words: The Feminist Practice of Oral History* (London: Routledge, 1991); Nancy Goldberger et al., *Knowledge, Difference, and Power: Essays Inspired by Women's Ways of Knowing* (New York: Basic Books, 1996); Carol Heibrun, *Writing a Woman's Life* (London: Women's Press, 1989); Serene Jones, *Feminist Theory and Christian Theology: Cartographies of Grace* (Minneapolis: Fortress Press, 2000); the three-volume study of women's narratives, edited by Ruthellen Josselson and Amia Lieblich, under the general title *The Narrative Study of Lives* (London: Sage, 1993–95); and Jeanne Stevenson-Moessner, ed., *In Her Own Time: Women and Developmental Issues in Pastoral Care* (Minneapolis: Fortress Press, 2000); to name just a few.

101. See Carol P. Christ, *Diving Deep and Surfacing: Women Writers on Spiritual Quest*, 2nd ed. (Boston: Beacon Press, 1986); Joann Wolski Conn, ed., *Women's Spirituality: Resources for Christian Development* (New York: Paulist Press, 1986); Maria Harris, *Dance of the Spirit: The Seven Steps of Women's Spirituality* (New York: Bantam, 1989); Carol Lakey Hess, *Caretakers of Our Common House: Women's Development in Communities of Faith* (Nashville: Abingdon Press, 1997); Mary Hunt, *Fierce Tenderness: A Feminist Theology of Friendship* (New York: Crossroads, 1991); Ursula King, *Women and Spirituality: Voices of Protest and Promise* (Basingstoke: Macmillan Education, 1989); Nicola Slee, *Women's Faith Development* (Burlington, Vt.: Ashgate Pub. Co., 2004); Charlene Spretnak, ed., *The Politics of Women's Spirituality: Essays on the Rise of Spiritual Power within the Feminist Movement* (New York: Anchor/Doubleday, 1982); and Katherine Zappone, *The Hope for Wholeness: A Spirituality for Feminists* (Mystic, Conn.: Twenty-Third Pub., 1991).

102. Slee, *Women's Faith Development*, 81.

103. Ibid., 107.

104. See ibid., 135-61.

105. Janet L. Surrey, "Self-in-Relation: A Theory of Women's Development," in Judith V. Jordan et al., *Women's Growth in Connection: Writings from the Stone Center* (New York: Guildford Press, 1991), 51-66.

106. Slee, *Women's Faith Development*, 160.

107. Ibid., 109-34.

108. Jones, *Feminist Theory*, 6-7.

109. See in particular her article "'Intimate Egoism': Reading and Evaluating Noncanonical Poetry by Women," *Victorian Poetry* 33 (1995): 13-30.

110. Ingrid Hotz-Davies, *The Creation of Religious Identities by English Women Poets from the Seventeenth to the Early Twentieth Century* (Lewiston: Edwin Mellon, 1996), 51.

111. See Kathleen Norris, *The Quotidian Mysteries: Laundry, Liturgy and "Women's Work"* (New York: Paulist Press, 1998).

112. J. Raymond, *A Passion for Friends: Towards a Philosophy of Female Affection* (London: Women's Press, 1986), 205.

113. Elsewhere I have discussed the connection between holiness and happiness in the writings of early Methodist women. Their conception of the Christian life could equally be described as a spirituality of happiness or blessedness. See Paul W. Chilcote, "Sanctification as Lived by Women in Early Methodism," *MethH* 34 (1996): 93-95.

114. Sermon 44, "Original Sin," III.5, *Works* 2:185. Commenting on this passage (fn. 70), Albert Outler describes the "recovery of the defaced image of God" as the "axial theme of Wesley's soteriology."

115. Quoted in Adam Clarke, *Memoirs of the Late Eminent Mrs. Mary Cooper, of London*, new ed. (Halifax: William Nicholson and Sons, [c. 1910]), 170-71.

116. "An Account of Mrs. Sarah Ryan," *AM* 2 (1779): 309-10.

117. Sarah Crosby, Manuscript Letterbook, 1760–74 (Perkins Library, Duke University), 37. The poem has not been identified.

Part One: Autobiography as Theology

1. See Richard P. Heitzenrater, *The Elusive Mr. Wesley*, 2nd ed. (Nashville: Abingdon Press, 2003), esp. the introduction in which the author discusses the quest for the real Wesley.
2. See Anne Ross Collinson, *Memoir of Mrs. Agnes Bulmer ... to which is subjoined Mrs. Bulmer's Last Poem, "Man the offspring of divine benevolence"* (London: Rivington, 1837). See also George John Stevenson, *City Road Chapel and Its Associations* (London: Stevenson, 1872).
3. Mrs. Rowley, "Memoir of the late Mrs. Agnes Bulmer," *WMM* 63 (1840): 801-10.
4. Quoted in ibid. 804.
5. Ibid.
6. See *AM* 11 (1788): 557.
7. Letter to Agnes Bulmer (28 Mar. 1788), *Letters* (Telford) 8:50.
8. See William W. Stamp, *The Orphan-House of Wesley; with Notices of Early Methodism in Newcastle-upon-Tyne* (London: J. Mason, 1863), 42-53.
9. J. Augustin Leger, *Wesley's Last Love* (London: J. M. Dent & Sons, 1910), 118.
10. On this complex relational crisis, see Frank Baker, "John Wesley's First Marriage," *London Quarterly Review* 192 (1967): 305-15; and Leger, *Wesley's Last Love*.
11. George Whitefield (1714–70) was the most widely venerated orator of the Methodist revival. In 1734, he became a member of the Oxford Holy Club, under the leadership of John and Charles Wesley. Following education at Oxford and missionary service in America, he established a chapel in Bristol in 1741 and later, through the patronage of Selina, Countess of Huntingdon, opened a Tabernacle in London, which became a center for the proclamation of his Calvinistic brand of evangelical Christianity for many years. He was the means of leading John Wesley to begin field-preaching at Bristol in 1739. See Wesley's *Journal* account, 10 March through 8 April 1739, *Works* 19:36-48.
12. An affluent London suburb where Whitefield and the Wesleys preached on a number of occasions; see also Wesley, *Journal* (14 June 1739), *Works* 19:69.
13. Most likely Charles Delamotte (ca. 1714–96), who resolved to accompany the Wesleys on their missionary journey to America. He later founded a school for free religious instruction in Georgia. Upon return to England in 1738, he became a Moravian and settled at Barton-upon-Humber.
14. On this central theme in Wesleyan preaching, see Sermon 18, "The Marks of the New Birth," *Works* 1:417–30; Sermon 19, "The Great Privilege of Those That Are Born of God," *Works* 1:431-43; and Sermon 45, "The New Birth," *Works* 2:187-201.
15. Whitefield embarked from England on February 2, 1738.
16. In April 1739, George Whitefield preached in Upper Moorfields with spectacular results. John Wesley followed suit on June 17, preaching to some six or seven thousand people, the first of many occasions. Wesley's Foundery, located in Upper Moorfields, soon became the center of London Methodism. It was the first solely Methodist society organized in London by John Wesley toward the end of 1739, to which he later withdrew with his supporters from the Moravian Fetter Lane Society when the Stillness Controversy divided the fledgling community. This remodeled royal foundry for cannon in Moorfields provided rooms for small group fellowship, a school, Wesley's living quarters, and a spacious room accommodating as many as fifteen hundred people. Regular services were held daily in the early mornings and early evenings. On the Foundery, see Frank Baker, *The Methodist Pilgrim in England*, 3rd ed. (Rutland: Academy Books, 1976), 35-36.
17. The final lines of stanza 2 of Isaac Watts's "When I survey the wondrous cross." Written for use in the Communion Service and inspired by Galatians 6:14, the hymn was originally published in 1707 with sacrifice "to his blood" rather than "to his cross." See also Isaac Watts, *The Works of the Reverend and Learned Isaac Watts, D.D.*, ed. David Jennings and Philip Doddridge (London: John Barfield, 1810–11), 4:349.

18. The bands were small, homogeneous groups of four to seven persons—divided by gender and marital status—organized for the purpose of mutual accountability and nurture in the Christian faith. In December 1738, Wesley drew up *Rules of the Band Societies*. For Wesley's description of the bands, see *A Plain Account of the People Called Methodists*, VI.3-8, Works 9:267-68. See also Rupert Davies's discussion of the development of the bands and the critical role of the band leader in early Methodism in *Works* 9:9-14. Concerning the preponderance of women in these roles, see Paul W. Chilcote, *John Wesley and the Women Preachers of Early Methodism* (Metuchen, N.J.: Scarecrow Press, 1991), 46-50, 68-72.

19. Another critical office within early Methodism in which women excelled. Wesley describes the business of a "visitor of the sick" in *A Plain Account of the People Called Methodists*, XI.3, *Works* 9:274. In 1786, he published Sermon 98, "On Visiting the Sick" (*Works* 3:385-98), in which he praised the work of women in this ministry. For a discussion of this office among early Methodist women, see Chilcote, *Wesley and Women*, 22-23, 72-75.

20. See Stamp, *Orphan-House*, 12-58.

21. In two letters in particular, dated November 8 and 22, 1757, Wesley provides instructions concerning Sarah's position at Kingswood and delineates her responsibilities as housekeeper; see also *Letters* (Telford) 3:239-41.

22. The school, conceived originally in 1748 by George Whitefield for the sons of colliers in Kingswood, became the largest and most permanent of John Wesley's many educational projects. The curriculum included courses in the classical languages, Hebrew, philosophy, and mathematics (see also *Journal* [27 Nov. 1739], *Works* 19:124-25). According to A. G. Ives, Sarah's work as housekeeper at the Kingswood School would have included "meeting a hundred persons every week in Methodist class or band, and also making excursions into the country around Bristol" (*Kingswood School in Wesley's Day and Since* [London: Epworth Press, 1970], 50-51).

23. Meaning a more informal Bible study or prayer group, as distinguished from parish worship.

24. On March 11, 1741, Whitefield returned to England from his second mission tour to the American colonies.

25. During this period, Whitefield published an exposition of the parable (Luke 15:11-32), entitled *The Prodigal Son. A Lecture* (Glasgow: Gallowgate Printing-House, 1741).

26. Unidentified.

27. The doctrine according to which human free will and cooperation are totally eliminated from the process of redemption, salvation being determined exclusively by the sovereign predestination and foreknowledge of God. Based upon the teachings of John Calvin, this view was republished by George Whitefield at this time. Wesley published the sum of his rejection of the predestinarian position in his *Predestination Calmly Considered* in 1752, but the so-called Calvinistic controversies continued, albeit sporadically, until his death. Sarah demonstrates through her own experiences how this theological tension between "Calvinistic" and "Arminian" parties touched the lives of many at the grassroots of the Methodist revival. On the theological controversy that arose between Whitefield and the Wesleys at this time, see Allan Coppedge, *John Wesley in Theological Debate* (Wilmore, Ky.: Wesley Heritage Press, 1987), 157-74; and Eric W. Baker, "Whitefield's Break with the Wesleys," *Church Quarterly* 3 (1970): 103-13.

28. See the account of her life and spirituality in the next selection.

29. Spitalfields, the childhood home of Susanna Wesley, was an immigration center for Huguenot refugees fleeing from France at the end of the seventeenth century. They built no fewer than eleven chapels in the district, the chief of which became Methodist property in 1750. It is undoubtedly this chapel to which Sarah refers. Note the similarity with John Wesley's account of his so-called Aldersgate experience: "In the evening I went very unwillingly to a society in Aldersgate Street, ... while he was describing the change which God works in the heart" (*Journal* [24 May 1738], *Works* 18:249-50). Note in particular the emphatic presentation of the personal pronouns, as in Wesley's account, which follows.

30. *Hymns on God's Everlasting Love* (1741), Hymn 15 [1 John 2:1, 2], v. 3 (*Poet. Works* 3:22).

31. Wesley notes in his *Journal* that he began officiating at this chapel near the Seven Dials in the west end of London on Trinity Sunday, May 29, 1743 (*Works* 19:326). Opened for French Protestants in 1700 and purchased for the purpose of renting it out in 1728, it was most likely offered to John Wesley by the rector, Thomas Blackwell. See also John Telford, *Two West-End Chapels: Or a Sketch of London Methodism, 1740–1886* (London: Methodist Book-Room, 1886), 8-10.

32. *HLS* (1745), Hymn 105, v. 1; see also *Collection of Hymns* (1780), #73, v. 1, *Works* 7:172.

33. See my more extensive introduction to her diary in Paul W. Chilcote, *Her Own Story: Autobiographical Portraits of Early Methodist Women* (Nashville: Kingswood Books, 2001), 77-78. See also the account of her life and work in Chilcote, *Wesley and Women*, 118-34, 149-71, 200-207, 243-59; Frank Baker, "John Wesley and Sarah Crosby," *PWHS* 27 (1949): 76-82; Earl Kent Brown, *Women of Mr. Wesley's Methodism* (New York: Edwin Mellen Press, 1983), 166-75; Paul W. Chilcote, *She Offered Them Christ* (Nashville: Abingdon Press, 1993), 62-93; and Thomas M. Morrow, *Early Methodist Women* (London: Epworth Press, 1967), 9-26. For an extensive bibliography, consult Chilcote, *Wesley and Women*, 256-59.

34. She carried on a lengthy correspondence with Wesley for some thirty-two years (1757–89), a couple of her letters included in part 3 of this volume.

35. See her letter to Frances Pawson in part 3 of this volume.

36. The *Appeals* represent John Wesley's first major attempt to explain and defend his movement. Published in 1743 at the outset of the revival, *An Earnest Appeal to Men of Reason and Religion* is an unusually clear, simple, and direct apology, distinguished from its sequel, *A Farther Appeal*, published in three parts in 1745, and urged upon him at the first Methodist Conference of the preceding year. For the definitive presentation of these texts, see *Works* 11:37-325.

37. Included among the doctrinal standards of Methodism, Sermon 39, "Catholic Spirit" (*Works* 2:79-96) was first published in volume 3 of Wesley's *Sermons on Several Occasions* in this same year, 1750. It was republished separately in 1755 and in 1770 with his brother's hymn "Catholic Love." It may have been Wesley's point that true religion lies deeper than our ability to articulate our experience of God that struck a resonant chord within Sarah Crosby.

38. George Whitefield's primary preaching house in London; see also note 11 above.

39. Most likely the third or fourth Sunday in February 1750. At this time, a series of earthquakes shook London, which occasioned considerable panic. On Sunday, February 18, Wesley observed in his *Journal*: "Today, likewise, wherever we assembled together, God caused his power to be known, but particularly at the love-feast. The honest simplicity with which several spoke, in declaring the manner of God's dealings with them, set the hearts of others on fire" (*Works* 20:321).

40. Wesley and Christopher Hopper set out for Ireland on March 19, 1750, but were unable to sail to Dublin from Holyhead until April 6. During the ensuing months, Wesley was only in London for a brief visit of several days in September, but returned on October 24, remaining thereafter in London through the end of the year.

41. First published in 1741 and subsequently reprinted in Wesley's *Sermons on Several Occasions* in 1750 and 1787, excerpts of which he included in his *Plain Account of Christian Perfection* (1766), a history of his thoughts and writings on this central doctrine of the Methodist theological heritage over the course of forty years. For the definitive edition of the sermon, see *Works* 2:97-124. For a larger collection of Wesley's perfection texts, see *John Wesley*, 251-305.

42. *HSP* (1749), "After a Recovery," Hymn 4, v. 9 (*Poet. Works* 4:446).

43. In Sermon 110, "Free Grace," (*Works* 3:544-63), based upon Romans 8:32, Wesley enunciates the essentially Arminian principle that the grace or love of God is free in all and free for all. This epoch-making sermon, issued as a separate publication in 1739, went through no fewer than ten editions during Wesley's lifetime.

44. The poetical writings of Charles Wesley were not published in a complete edition until 1870-72 in the thirteen-volume set *The Poetical Works of John and Charles Wesley*, compiled by George Osborn. While the editor documented Charles's publication of no fewer than 4,480 hymns during his lifetime, subsequent studies place the number of his hymns and religious verse closer to 9,000. Prior to 1749, all of the hymnbooks used by the Methodists were jointly published by both brothers. Of the nearly twenty collections of hymns published by the Wesleys between 1739 and 1749, the four editions of *Hymns and Sacred Poems* contained the great hymns of the Methodist revival. These hymns, as Sarah indicates, were not only sung, but also put to devotional use as well.

45. *Redemption Hymns*, Hymn 42, v. 8 (*Poet. Works* 4:265).

46. First John 1:7. In his magisterial study *The Path to Perfection*, William Sangster notes that "a full third of the texts on which Wesley chiefly relies for his doctrine of Christian Perfection are taken from the First Epistle of John" ([London: Epworth Press, 1943], 48). Note how Sarah "enpersonalizes" the biblical text by changing the original plural pronoun to the personal *me*.

47. *HSP* (1749), vol. 2, part 1, "For Watchnight. The Same Innocent Diversions," hymn 17, v. 8 (*Poet. Works* 5:284).

48. Zechariah Taft, *Biographical Sketches of the Lives and Public Ministry of Various Holy Woman* (London: Kershaw, 1825), 2:23-115.

49. Letter to Lady Maxwell (22 Sept. 1764), *Letters* (Telford) 4:264. D'Arcy, Lady Maxwell (1742?-1810), one of the most devout and influential Methodist leaders in Edinburgh, became friendly with John Wesley in 1764 (the same year he published Jane Cooper's *Letters*) and maintained a regular correspondence with him until his death in 1791. For similar references to Wesley's high esteem for Cooper, see Letter to Miss March (May 1769), *Letters* (Telford) 5:135; Letter to Mary Bishop (5 Nov. 1769), *Letters* (Telford) 5:154; Letter to Mary Stokes (17 Mar. 1771), *Letters* (Telford) 5:230; Letter to Ann Loxdale (10 June 1781), *Letters* (Telford) 7:67; and Letter to Ann Loxdale (12 Apr. 1782), *Letters* (Telford) 7:120.

50. In Letter to Miss March (11 Feb. 1775), *Letters* (Telford) 6:139-40. These are vivid memories and a living consciousness of someone who had died more than a decade before.

51. [John Wesley], *Letters Wrote by Jane Cooper: To Which Is Prefixt Some Account of Her Life and Death* (London: [Strahan], 1764), Preface, §3. See her letter included in part 3 of this volume. Wesley refers to her *Letters* in his Letter to Thomas Rankin (11 Sept. 1765), *Letters* (Telford) 4:312. Likewise, in a letter to Ann Bolton of December 29, 1770, he writes: "Now you may profit by Jenny Cooper's Letters and the Plain Account of Christian Perf." (*Letters* [Telford] 5:216).

52. Wesley, *Plain Account of Christian Perfection*, ¶24, *Works* (Jackson) 11:409. For an interesting discussion of Cooper's life and letters, see Susan J. Malin, "Jane Cooper: A Pattern of All Holiness," First Prize, United Methodist Women's History Writing Award 1995 (deposited at the General Commission on Archives and History, UMC, Drew University).

53. See *Journal* (19-25 Nov. 1762), *Works* 21:398-99. "I buried the remains of Jane Cooper," he notes, "a pattern of all holiness and of the wisdom which is from above, who was snatched hence before she lived five and twenty years."

54. Wesley developed a distinctive view of repentance as "true self-knowledge," which leads to contrition and eventual trust in Christ as the foundation of the Christian life. Variations on this basic theme are scattered throughout the Wesleyan sermon corpus, but see in particular Sermon 7, "The Way to the Kingdom," *Works* 1:217-32; and Albert Outler's incisive note on section II.1 (p. 225, n. 55).

55. A fascinating premonition that was fulfilled, in fact, by her death in 1762.

56. Most likely, either Rev. Thomas Jones, M.A., evangelical priest of St. Saviour's Church, Southwark, and closely linked to the Wesley, Whitefield, Romaine circle; or Dr. John Jones (c. 1719-85), who joined the Wesleys in 1746, and was for twenty years Wesley's best-educated lay helper and was in substantial charge of the London Societies from 1758 to 1767.

57. William Romaine (1714–95), the son of a French Protestant and one of the leading evangelical, Calvinistic clergy who abandoned his original Arminian views to become a staunch supporter of Whitefield, was, at this time, serving as Curate of St. Olave's, Southwark. For many years, the only evangelical clergyman in London, he concluded his distinguished career as Rector of St. Anne's, Blackfriars, a position he held from 1766 until his death in 1795.

58. A London parish church, frequented by the Wesleys in the late 1730s.

59. More than likely, Thomas Walsh (1730–59), the Irish preacher/scholar, during one of his three visits to London. Wesley held a very deep affection for him and frequently noted his amazing linguistic skills, especially his unparalleled abilities as a Hebraist. See John Telford, *Wesley's Veterans: Lives of Early Methodist Preachers*, 7 vols. (London: Robert Cully, Ch. H. Kelly, 1909–14), 5:34-35.

60. See note 31 above.

61. *HSP* (1739), part 1, "A Prayer Under Convictions," v. 6 (*Poet. Works* 1:77).

62. Note the emphatic personal pronouns so typical of early Methodist experience and reminiscent of John Wesley's own experience.

63. John Wesley spent much of the month of March 1759 working with the Society in Norwich where he had found the Methodist work "mouldered into nothing." His *Journal* notes that on the evening of Wednesday, March 7, he "desired that those who were willing to join in a society would speak with me the next evening. About twenty did so, but the greater part of these appeared like frightened sheep. And no marvel, when they had been so long accustomed to hear all manner of evil of me" (*Works* 21:179).

64. In his *Plain Account of the People Called Methodists* of 1749, Wesley describes his practice of reading "the accounts I received from time to time of the work which God is carrying on in the earth" on prescribed "letter days" each month in the context of the Societies, a development that, he observes, was "a time of strong consolation to those who love God" (§V, *Works* 9:266).

65. See this sentiment expressed in the same language of piety by Hester Ann Rogers in her journal in the next section (Part I, C.2) of this volume.

66. *HSP* (1742), part 2, "Pleading the Promise of Sanctification" [Ezekiel 36:23], v. 22 (*Poet. Works* 2:322). Originally, "While my full soul ...".

67. Note the similarity here with Wesley's statement concerning his first venture into field-preaching: "At four in the afternoon I submitted to 'be more vile', and proclaimed in the highways the glad tidings of salvation" (*Journal* [2 Apr. 1739], *Works* 19:46). Referring in 2 Samuel 6:22 to David's dance before the ark of the covenant, this phrase soon became a standard component of evangelical discourse.

68. See also Chilcote, *Wesley and Women*, 99-100, for original text and commentary.

69. Letter to Hannah Ball (7 June 1783), *Letters* (Telford) 7:180.

70. Surely a reference to Thomas Walsh, *A Collection of Sermons* (London: Foundry, 1764), which were published under Wesley's sponsorship. Like Hannah, Walsh had a particular interest in reaching children. John Wesley considered him to be the best Hebrew scholar he had ever met. Walsh was one of Wesley's most gifted preachers, often admired as well for his calm spirit.

71. Most certainly his visit in January 1765, during which time he preached on several occasions. See *Works* 21:498.

72. Thomas Hanson (1734–1804), of Horbury, Yorkshire, an apprentice clothier who became an itinerant preacher under Wesley in 1760, according to the Conference Minutes, a "plain, honest, faithful, zealous man."

73. *Scripture Hymns*, "But how much pleasanter to see" [Eccles. 11:7] (*Poet. Works* 9:358).

74. John Wesley's most extended discussion of this Reformed notion of the offices of Christ is to be found in Sermon 36, "The Law Established through Faith, II," I.6, *Works* 2:37-38. See also his allusion to the offices in the landmark Sermon 43, "The Scripture Way of Salvation," II.2, *Works* 2:161.

75. Most likely the curate, Rev. Williams, as John Wesley was in London at this time; see also *Journal* (6-30 Nov. 1769), *Works* 22:210-11.

76. *HSP* (1749), vol. 1, part 2, "Sinners, obey the gospel word," Hymn 155, v. 10 (*Poet. Works* 5:64).

77. Most likely Richard Henderson, an Irishman who emigrated to England in 1762 and served as one of Wesley's itinerant preachers from 1763 to 1771. He later settled in Hanham, near Bristol, where he established a famous asylum for the mentally disabled. See also *Journal* (29 Sept. 1781), *Works* 23:224.

78. *HSP* (1749), vol. 1, part 1, "Temptation," Hymn 105, v. 7 (*Poet. Works* 4:470).

79. For some months, Hannah felt compelled to offer herself for confirmation, which normally admitted members of the Church of England to the Sacrament. It was not totally unusual that a candidate of forty-three years of age would be confirmed in this way, the *BCP* even providing for mature confirmands such as Hannah.

80. See *BCP*; the prayer spoken over each mature candidate, kneeling before the bishop, reads: "Defend, O Lord, this thy Servant with thy heavenly grace, that she may continue thine for ever; and daily increase in thy holy Spirit more and more, until she comes unto thy everlasting kingdom. Amen."

81. Francis Wolfe, the Methodist itinerant preacher appointed to Oxfordshire in 1774. See John Wesley's letter to Hannah Ball concerning him; (12 Aug. 1774), *Letters* (Telford) 6:105-6.

82. That is, participated in the Sacrament of the Lord's Supper.

83. Wesley's original plan, from a letter to Hannah, dated October 23, 1779, was to arrive in High Wycombe on Tuesday, November 9, preach in the evening, and return to London thereafter (*Letters* [Telford] 6:359-60). There is no reference to this event in the published *Journal*.

84. Unidentified.

85. *HSP* (1740), part 1, Micah 6:6, v. 8 (*Poet. Works* 1:277).

86. See Paul W. Chilcote, "John Wesley as Revealed by the Journal of Hester Ann Rogers," *MethH* 20 (1982): 111-23.

87. With regard to literary and interpretive matters related to her *Experience*, see Vicki T. Collins, "Perfecting a Woman's Life: Methodist Rhetoric and Politics in *The Account of Hester Ann Rogers*" (Ph.D. dissertation, Auburn University, 1993). On her life and work, see Annie E. Keeling, *Eminent Methodist Women* (London: Charles H. Kelly, 1889), 103-17.

88. Macclesfield, originally "Maxfield," was a market town some thirty miles east of Chester, noted in the day for its evangelical clergy and associations with Methodist women; see B. Smith, *Methodism in Macclesfield* (London: Methodist Conference Office, 1875).

89. David Simpson (1745–99), evangelical Anglican clergyman, educated at Cambridge and appointed as curate of St. Michael's, Macclesfield, in 1772. When he failed to gain nomination to the vicarage of St. Michael's in 1779, he built Christ Church and remained its first incumbent until his death in 1799. The purpose of his four-volume work entitled *Sacred Literature* (1788–90) was to demonstrate the superiority of scripture over other ancient writings.

90. *BCP*, the words drawn from 1 John 2:1 immediately preceding the *sursum corda* at the beginning of the Prayer of Great Thanksgiving.

91. Samuel Bardsley (d. 1818) entered the Methodist ministry in 1768 and was one of the most well-traveled itinerants of his generation. He was noted for his sermons couched in simple language. A close friend of John Wesley, he was always addressed as "Dear Sammy" in their correspondence.

92. Not a publication of John or Charles Wesley.

93. Note the allusion here to John Wesley's rescue from the burning Epworth rectory.

94. *HSP* (1749), vol. 1, part 2, "Hymns for Believers," Hymn 18 (*Poet. Works* 5:25).

95. John William Fletcher, originally Jean Guillaume de la Fléchère (1729–1785), saintly vicar of Madeley, in Shropshire, one of a small circle of Methodist Ministers (i.e., ordained Anglican clergy affiliated with the Wesleyan revival) and designated successor of John Wesley. He married Mary Bosanquet in 1781. Rogers was reading Fletcher, *Christian Letters* (Manchester: C. Wheeler, 1775), a brief set of pastoral letters giving spiritual advice. The best current study of Fletcher is Patrick P. Streiff, *Reluctant Saint? A Theological Biography of Fletcher of Madeley* (Peterborough: Epworth, 2001).

96. *HSP* (1742), part 2, concluding hymn, v. 10 (*Poet. Works* 2:364).

97. In 1766, Wesley published a full-length treatise, *A Plain Account of Christian Perfection, as Believed and Taught by the Rev. Mr. John Wesley, from the Year 1725 to the Year 1765*, in which he collected extracts from almost all he had ever written or said on the subject, and wove them into a sort of cumulative exposition, stressing the continuity and cruciality of the doctrine. See also *Works* (Jackson) 11:366-446; a critical edition of this vital text will soon be published in *Works*, vol. 12.

98. *Scripture Hymns*, "Give me that enlarged desire," Psa. 131:10, v. 1 (*Poet. Works* 9:312).

99. The following paragraph is excerpted from her manuscript journal and has been modernized so as to conform to the style of her printed life; Rogers, Manuscript Journal, 1:72ff.

100. The occasion of Hester's first personal encounter with John Wesley. The two-day whirlwind that followed left an indelible impression upon this youthful Methodist. Between his arrival on Monday and his departure early Wednesday morning, Wesley preached three times, met with the bands and the select band, and celebrated a Love Feast. His parallel *Journal* account of the visit reads: "Monday, April 1 [1776]. I went on to Macclesfield. That evening, I preached in the house; but it being far too small, on Tuesday 2, I preached on the Green, near Mr. Ryle's door. There are no mockers here, and scarce an inattentive ear. So mightily has the word of God prevailed" (*Works* 23:7). See Chilcote, "Wesley as Revealed by Rogers," 113-14.

101. Mayor of Macclesfield.

102. The following three paragraphs are taken from original material written by Hester and included in James Rogers's Appendix to Thomas Coke's funeral sermon, Hester Ann Rogers, *An Account of the Experience of Hester Ann Rogers* (New York: Hunt & Eaton, 1893), 128-29.

103. *HSP* (1739), part 2, John 16:24, v. 1 (*Poet. Works*, 1:192).

104. Ann Loxdale (d. 1812), of Shrewsbury, closely associated with the Eden family of Broadmarston and a correspondent of John Wesley as well. She married Dr. Thomas Coke in 1811 but died the following year. See the series of letters to Loxdale from 27 March 1781 through 8 October 1785 in *Letters* (Telford) 7:52, 59, 66, 73, 80, 113, 120, 128, 130, 197, 200, 264, 295.

105. The following paragraphs are excerpted from Hester's manuscript journal and have been modernized so as to conform to the style of her printed life.

106. James Rogers (1749–1807), one of Wesley's faithful preachers who commenced his itinerant ministry around 1774. In 1783, his wife died and left him with two young sons while he was appointed to Macclesfield. He married Hester on August 19, 1784.

107. The common friend of Hester and Elizabeth Ritchie, and distant relation of an alienated member of the Holy Club at Oxford.

108. Wesley describes the events of these momentous days in his *Journal*:

> Good Friday, March 29 [1782]. I came to Macclesfield just time enough to assist Mr. Simpson in the laborious service of the day. I preached for him morning and afternoon, and we administered the Sacrament to about thirteen hundred persons. While we were administering, I heard a low, soft, solemn sound, just like that of an Aeolian harp. It continued five or six minutes, and so affected many that they could not refrain from tears.... In the evening, I preached at our room. Here was that *harmony* which art cannot imitate.
>
> Saturday 30. As our friends at Leek, thirteen miles from Macclesfield, would take no denial, I went over and preached about noon to a lovely congregation.... Easter Day, March 31. I preached in the church morning and evening, where we had about eight hundred communicants. In the evening we had a love-feast, and such an one as I had not seen for many years" (*Works* 23:233-34).

109. *HSP* (1740), part 1, "The Resignation," v. 4 (*Poet. Works* 1:267).

Notes to Pages 114-25

110. In his *Plain Account of Christian Perfection*, Wesley deals with this question at length. He summarizes his position in *Brief Thoughts on Christian Perfection*: "I believe this perfection is always wrought in the soul by a simple act of faith; consequently in an instant. But I believe in a gradual work both preceding and following that instant" (*Works* [Jackson] 11:466). His basic conception of perfection in the Christian life was dynamic, and not static, in nature. One of his most characteristic descriptions of those who have attained Christian perfection was that they were adult—or mature—Christians. Christian perfection is dynamic in the sense of being both instantaneous and processive. It is also dynamic in the sense that it can be lost. But Wesley assumed that growth in holiness would continue within Christian perfection and not just before it.

111. See the introduction to Jane Cooper earlier in this volume.

112. It is impossible to determine which Christian writers are being referred to here specifically. While Wesley held many of the great devotional masters in high regard, he also expressed concern about the tendency of some (particularly those of a mystical bent) to devalue the essential connection between faith and good works. In a memorandum concerning his spiritual state, he described the "mystic writers" as those "whose noble descriptions of union with God and internal religion made everything else appear mean, flat, and insipid. But in truth they made good works appear so too; yea, and faith itself" (*Works* 18:213, n. 95). In Wesleyan circles, therefore, this term usually meant those who leaned in an antinomian direction as a consequence of their dependence upon God's grace apart from works of mercy and piety.

113. This paragraph is transcribed from Hester's manuscript journal.

114. The Methodist Conference was held in Dublin, beginning on Friday, July 3. They embarked for their return to England on Sunday, July 12, aboard the packet *Princess Royal*. They landed in England in the early morning, Tuesday, July 14. See also *Journal* (3-12 July 1789), *Works* 24:145-47.

115. "We were then constrained to slacken sail," Wesley observed concerning the passage, "and to lie by for some hours, not having water to pass the bar" (*Works* 24:147).

116. The English Methodist Conference commenced on Tuesday, August 28. The issue of separation from the Church of England dominated the conference, but Wesley's indefatigable defense of loyalty to the Church prevailed.

117. James Rogers was appointed to this station at the preceding Conference session.

118. Excerpts from the published *Experience* resume at this point.

119. Edward Young, *The Complaint; or Night Thoughts*, 5th ed. (London: Dodsley, 1743), Night 2, p. 75; probably citing from Wesley's abridged reprint in his *Collection of Moral and Sacred Poems*, 3 vols. (Bristol: Farley, 1744), 2:259.

120. *Select Psalms*, Psalm 128, v. 7 (*Poet. Works* 8:245).

121. William Entwisle, ed., *Memoir of the Rev. Joseph Entwisle*, 9th ed. (London: Wesleyan Conference Office, 1867), 82.

122. See Wesley's Sermon 98, "On Visiting the Sick" (*Works* 3:385-97), first published in the *AM* in 1786.

123. Referring to the ensuing birth of her first child, a son, John, on March 8, 1793.

124. The allusion to Isaac Watts's (1674–1748) great hymn, "I'll Praise My Maker," on the lips of John Wesley at this death, is unmistakable:

> I'll praise my God who lends me breath;
> And when my voice is lost in death,
> Praise shall employ my nobler powers.

See also Bernard L. Manning, *The Hymns of Wesley and Watts* (London: Epworth Press, 1942), 78-105.

125. See the conclusion of the *Te Deum* (We Praise Thee, O God) of the Morning Prayer Office of the *BCP*: "O Lord, let Thy mercy be upon us as our trust is in Thee. O Lord, in Thee have I trusted; let me never be confounded." See also Psa. 22:5.

126. Joseph Entwisle records in his diary: "Frid. March 8th. About two o'clock this morning my dear wife presented me with a fine boy—my first-born—the beginning of my strength. My soul was filled with joy and gratitude. I felt overpowered with a sense of the goodness of God" (Entwisle, *Memoir*, 94).

127. Impossible to identify from this limited reference, but possibly the same Miss Rhodes whose journal extracts were published in James Sigston, *A Memoir of the Life and Ministry of Mr. W. Bramwell*, 2 vols. (London: Printed for James Nichols, 1821, 1822), 2:162-82. She became a revivalistic preacher associated with the evangelistic ministry of William Bramwell.

128. The "covenant meeting" refers to an annual worship experience using the Service of Covenant Renewal, urged upon all of Wesley's followers as early as 1747, but held formally for the first time at the French Church in Spitalfields on August 11, 1755. Culminating in a celebration of Holy Communion, these corporate reaffirmations of individual discipleship have usually been held on the first Sunday of the New Year since 1762. See also David Tripp, *The Renewal of the Covenant in the Methodist Tradition* (London: Epworth Press, 1969).

129. In 1762, Wesley had found it necessary, with the rise of increasing fanaticism around his doctrine of Christian perfection, to publish *Cautions and Directions Given to the Greatest Professors in The Methodist Societies*. Many decried Wesley's concept of perfection in this life as "enthusiastic," and the fact that there were some whose personal professions of "entire sanctification" disturbed Wesley compelled him to redress the imbalance. Mrs. Entwisle's concern reflects this tension. An abridgment of *Cautions and Directions* was incorporated into Wesley's *Farther Thoughts on Christian Perfection* (1762) and, in turn, was further abridged and woven into *A Plain Account of Christian Perfection* the following year; see also *John Wesley*, 298-305.

130. From 1743, one of the major centers of Methodism in the north of England. In 1751, the first chapel, the "Boggard House," was built; it was the scene of many momentous Conferences over the course of the century.

131. A market town in the parish of Whalley, thirty-five miles southeast of Lancaster, situated, in Wesley's day, on the top of a high round hill, at the edge of Pendle Forest and, as he had correctly presumed, formerly a Roman colony; see also *Journal* (20 July 1759), *Works* 21:209.

132. Marmaduke, probably born in September 1794.

133. For her prayer on this occasion, see part 3 below.

134. The years following the death of Wesley in 1791, as could well be expected, were tumultuous for the Methodist Connection. Dissension in many forms quickly arose in the succession of annual conferences, the strongest statements of dissent, democracy, and local power coming from Alexander Kilham. The conference of 1795, herein referred to, marked a critical turning point in this new era for Wesleyan Methodism. While the so-called Plan of Pacification, a triumph of the Wesleyan spirit in terms of its pragmatism and compromise, was accepted by the majority, the die was cast for schism. Subsequent to his trial at the ensuing conference of 1796, Kilham left his Wesleyan home to found "The Methodist New Connexion" in 1797, the first major schism in the Methodist family. On the various dimensions of this division and others to follow, see John T. Wilkinson, "The Rise of Other Methodist Traditions," in *History of the Methodist Church*, ed. Rupert Davies and E. Gordon Rupp, 4 vols. (London: Epworth Press, 1965-88), 2:276-329.

135. She refers here to the continuing controversy surrounding the administration of the sacrament of Holy Communion, which arose in Bristol in 1792. The "Bristol Controversy" arose when Henry Moore (who had been ordained by Wesley in 1787) celebrated Eucharist at Portland Chapel according to permission granted by the conference. "His actions," according to Heitzenrater, "were opposed by the trustees of the other two Methodist chapels in Bristol" who "suggested that such actions contradicted the 'Old Plan' of Methodism and implied separation from the Church" ([Richard P. Heitzenrater, *Wesley and the People Called Methodists* (Nashville: Abingdon Press, 1995], 315).

136. A third pregnancy.

137. Village in the West Riding of Yorkshire. Wesley notes opening the "new house" there on Thursday, April 28, 1774, the old chapel being succeeded by West Parade Chapel in 1801.

138. Her third, a daughter, Mary, most likely born in the late summer or early fall of 1796.

139. John Pipe, "Memoir of Miss Isabella Wilson," *WMM* 31 (1808): 462.

140. Watts, "The Psalms of David," Psa. 63, "Longing after God," v. 2 (Watts, *Works*, 4:171).
141. The opening line of Charles Wesley's famous hymn, first appearing in *HSP* (1742), Hymn 27, v. 1; see also *Works*, 7:114.
142. *HSP* (1742), part 2, concluding hymn, v. 15 (*Poet. Works* 2:365).
143. *HSP* (1740), part 1, "I Thirst, Thou wounded Lamb of God" (tr. German), v. 2 (*Poet. Works* 1:265). Originally, "Take my poor heart and let it be."
144. For the continuation of this prayer, see part 2, section C below.
145. John Pipe concludes: "Her eyes, her countenance, her whole manner spoke the inward rapture of her mind, with an eloquence greater than words: calmly waiting for her change, rejoicing in the convulsive throes of nature which were dislodging the soul, and looking forward with unshaken confidence and holy triumph to her everlasting home. No temptation to doubt or fear was suffered to approach her, but she was made to drink of the choicest cup of Divine consolations. Had I not been informed of her close walk with God, her benevolence, her activity in the service of her Master, and her affectionate concern for her fellow creatures, and longings for their salvation, I might easily have gathered that such had been her character, from the last dispensations of God to her soul, according to that word, 'Them that honour me, I will honour.' She fell asleep in Jesus that night, and her happy spirit was received by him her soul loved, to enjoy his presence more perfectly, and to celebrate in everlasting songs with all the redeemed, the unsearchable riches of his grace.... Her life has convinced me that we may live pure, and I believe her death has convinced many that they may die happy" (597).

Part Two: Writings in Practical Divinity

1. See the account of Leytonstone above in the Introduction, pp. 40-41.
2. See Chilcote, "An Early Methodist Community of Women," *MethH* 38 (2000): 219-30.
3. Volume 9 of Wesley's *Works* contains most of the regulatory documents of the early Methodist movement. Among the most important are *The Principles of a Methodist* (pp. 47-66), *The Nature, Design, and General Rules of the United Societies* (pp. 67-76), *Rules of the Band Societies* (pp. 77-79), *Advice to the People Called Methodists* (pp. 123-31), and *The Principles of a Methodist Farther Explained* (pp. 160-237).
4. *General Rules*, §§4-6, *Works* 9:70-73. Specific examples are provided under each rule, such as: (1) forbidding slaveholding, (2) enjoining provision of food to the hungry and clothing for the naked, and (3) stressing faithful participation in the life of the worshiping community.
5. *Journal CW* 2:334-35.
6. *Letters upon Sacred Subjects, by a person lately deceased* (London: n.p., 1757).
7. [John Wesley], *An Extract of Letters by Mrs. L*** (Bristol: William Pine, 1769).
8. See relevant references in *Journal CW* 2:217, 334; and the comments in *Letters* (Telford) 3:139-40.
9. Henry Moore, *The Life of Mrs. Mary Fletcher, Consort and Relict of the Rev. John Fletcher, Vicar of Madeley*, 2 vols. (Birmingham: J. Peart, 1817), 23.
10. In the original design of this volume, I did not intend to include any of the writings of Mary Bosanquet Fletcher simply because they deserve a volume(s) of their own. However, it proved inconceivable to compile a volume dedicated to the spirituality of the early Methodist women that did not include several pieces from her pen.
11. These vows, also known as the "evangelical counsels" in the monastic tradition, reflect the disciplined renunciation or asceticism that characterizes this form of spirituality. Profession of these three vows dates from around the thirteenth century, being made especially central by Francis of Assisi. The purpose of these vows is freely to center one's whole being and love in God and thereby pursue the fundamental baptismal vocation to love others as Christ has loved us.
12. Isaac Watts, *The Works of the Reverend and Learned Isaac Watts, D.D.*, ed. David Jennings and Philip Doddridge (London: John Barfield, 1810–11), 4:349. The closing lines of "When I survey the wondrous cross" (v. 2).
13. That is, into the close fellowship of a band or select band meeting of the Methodist Society, in which deeply confidential aspects of life were openly shared.

14. *Funeral Hymns*, Hymn 29, "On the Death of Mrs. L..., July 6, 1756," part 2, v. 5 (*Poet. Works* 6:266).
15. I.e., those who profess to have been perfected in love.
16. This value placed upon a "conscience void of offence to God and man" was rooted deeply in the English Puritan tradition and central to the spirituality of Susanna Wesley and her sons. John published several sermons on the subject, the most important of which are "The Witness of Our Own Spirit" (Sermon 12, *Works* 1:299-313) and "On Conscience" (Sermon 105, *Works* 3:480-90). Of more critical importance here is how the conscience functioned as a means to female liberation and even served to justify disobedience to oppressive structures and forces in both church and society. See the interesting study of Patricia Crawford, "Public Duty, Conscience, and Women in Early Modern England," in *Public Duty and Private Conscience in Seventeenth-Century England*, ed. John Morrill, Paul Slack, and Daniel Woolf (Oxford: Clarendon Press, 1993), 57-76.
17. In 1752, John Wesley published the pamphlet *Serious Thoughts Concerning Godfathers and Godmothers*, a general appeal admonishing the faithful seriously to consider the important role of baptismal sponsors, and for the church to take greater responsibility through them for the nurture of the baptized; see also *Works* (Jackson) 10:506-9.
18. *BCP*, drawn from the baptismal interrogation prior to the act of baptism. The original language differs slightly, but the general meaning is retained here.
19. *HSP* (1742), part 2, "Fight the good fight of faith" [1 Tim. 6:12], v. 15 (*Poet. Works* 2:314).
20. *HSP* (1740), part 2, "The Love-Feast," v. 3 (*Poet. Works* 1:350).
21. *HSP* (1739), part 2, "Isaiah 43:1, 2, 3," v. 4 (*Poet. Works* 1:136). Originally, "Still be Thy arm my sure defence/Nor earth nor hell shall pluck me thence."
22. Alexander Pope, "The Universal Prayer," lines 1, 39-40; Norman Ault, ed., *Alexander Pope: Minor Poems* (New Haven: Yale University Press, 1954), 148.
23. Stanza 6 of "A Penitential Hymn," which John Fletcher compiled and slightly revised from three hymns at the end of the *BCP*; see Fletcher, *The Penitent Thief* (London: R. Hawes, 1773), 32.
24. Mary expresses here the ancient concept of "faith seeking understanding," articulated most cogently by Anselm of Canterbury.
25. *Hymns to be Sung in a Tumult*, IV. The Fourteenth Chapter of Hosea, "Sinners obey the gracious call," v. 19 (*Poet. Works* 4:56).
26. Her commentaries include expositions of Luke 10:41 (published herein), Matt. 15:16, 1 John 2:15, Psa. 37:16, Mal. 2:7, Lev. 22:2, Matt. 3:11, 1 Pet. 1:5, Gen. 49:19, Rom. 12:14, Psa. 11:6, Isa. 33:14, and Luke 13:5.
27. See Joseph Beaumont, ed., *Memoirs of Mrs. Mary Tatham, Late of Nottingham* (London: Simpkin & Marshall, sold by John Mason, 1838), 375-402.
28. Wesley had insisted on a parallelism between justification and sanctification, both by faith. This insistent correlation between the goal and the foundation of the Christian life represents one of the most original contributions of Wesleyan theology to the Protestant tradition. See Wesley's most definitive statement of these principles, herein reiterated by Tatham, in Sermon 43, "The Scripture Way of Salvation," *Works* 2:153-69.
29. "Analogy of faith" is a technical theological term and certainly drawn here by Tatham directly from John Wesley. Generally referring to the "wholeness of scripture" or the "general tenor of scripture" and applied to biblical hermeneutics, the reference here is more generic, referring to the whole doctrine of salvation, namely, repentance, justification, and holiness of heart and life. Tatham and Wesley's concern is to maintain the integrity of the whole vision of the Christian life or the full doctrine of salvation through faith in Christ. For a full discussion of Wesley's use of this term, see Scott J. Jones, *John Wesley's Conception and Use of Scripture* (Nashville: Kingswood, 1995), 45-49.
30. John Lyth, *The Blessedness of Religion in Earnest: A Memorial of Mrs. Mary Lyth* (London: The Book Society, 1861), 19.
31. Lyth, *Memorial*, 13-14.
32. See Richard P. Heitzenrater, *The Elusive Mr. Wesley*, 2nd ed. (Nashville: Abingdon Press, 2003), 1:50-62; *General Rules of the United Societies* (*Works* 9:69-75); and *Rules of the Band Societies* (*Works* 9:77-79).

33. John Wesley's constant rule was, "sleep early, rise early." See Sermon 93, "On Redeeming the Time," II.13, in which he quotes at length from William Law's *Serious Call to a Devout and Holy Life*: "If you was to rise early every morning as an instance of self-denial, as a method of renouncing indulgence, as a means of redeeming your time and fitting your spirit for prayer, you would soon find the advantage" (*Works* 3:329).

34. On the central theme of eudaemonism in Methodism, see Paul W. Chilcote, "Sanctification as Lived by Women in Early Methodism," *MethH* 34 (1996): 93-95; and Albert Outler, *Theology in the Wesleyan Spirit* (Nashville: Tidings Press, 1975), 81.

35. Note here echoes of the medieval synthesis of Thomas Aquinas who argued that all people can know God exists, as well as know something about God's power, wisdom, and goodness, by reason alone, but that we only know who God is by means of revelation received through faith. See A. M. Fairweather, *Nature and Grace: Selections from the Summa Theologica of Thomas Aquinas* (Philadelphia: Westminster, 1954).

36. There can be no doubt of Charles Wesley's influence here. As Frank Baker has observed: "The most prolific of all was his favourite form of six eights—8.8.8.8.88, rhyming ABABCC. In this metre he composed over eleven hundred poems, a total of nearly twenty-three thousand lines, most of them with a vigour, a flexibility, yet a disciplined compactness, that proved this to be the instrument fittest for his hand" (Baker, *Charles Wesley's Verse* [London: Epworth Press, 1964], 70).

37. Wesley's source for this poem was Phillis Wheatley, *Poems on Various Subjects, Religious and Moral* (London: A. Bell, 1773), 25-26.

38. A transcription of this poem and Wesley's inscription are held in the Wesley Historical Society Library Collection. Wesley and Methodist Studies Centre, Westminster Institute, Oxford Brookes University, Oxford.

39. Quoted in S. W. Christophers, *The Poets of Methodism* (London: Hodder and Stoughton, 1877), 270.

40. Psa. 85:10.

41. John 17:3.

42. Luke 15:10.

43. Multiple images from Revelation 5-7.

44. Her son had died at six weeks of age in the year 1789.

45. Quoted in C. H. Crookshank, *History of Methodism in Ireland*, 3 vols. (Belfast: R. S. Allen, Son and Allen, 1885), 1:182-83; see also *Journal* (1 May 1765), *Works* 21:506.

46. Edward Smyth, ed., *The Extraordinary Life and Christian Experience of Margaret Davidson, as Dictated by Herself* (Dublin: Dugdale, 1782), 97.

47. In terms of poetic diction, there are clearly unmet challenges here. Agnes Bulmer experimented with this form with greater success, for example, in her hymn for Ancoat's Chapel above, while Margaret struggled with this favored Methodist meter (7.6.7.6.7.7.7.6). As in Charles Wesley's hymn "God of Unexampled Grace," the poem is cross-rhymed throughout, but with a group of three consecutive trochaic lines opening the second half and breaking the alternating trochaic-iambic sequence. The rhythms break down, however, as Margaret shifts occasionally from sevens to eights, particularly in the second half of each verse.

48. See my discussion of these developments in *John Wesley and the Women Preachers of Early Methodism* (Metuchen, N.J.: Scarecrow Press, 1991), 228-32.

49. See the excerpt in *Works* 26:634.

50. Note the comment from Thomas Jackson quoted in *Works* 23:108, n. 37. See also Elizabeth Ritchie's biographical sketch, *An Account of Mrs. Elizabeth Johnson* (1799).

51. See *WMM* 21 (1798): 46-47.

52. See *Journal* (12 Sept. 1780), *Works* 23:186.

53. See *PWHS* 4 (1903): 57-59. A later issue of the *AM* (13 [1790]: 223-24) did carry an elegy on her death.

54. On the family, see Frank Baker, "The Origins of Methodism in the West Indies: The Story of the Gilbert Family," *London Quarterly Review* 185 (1960): 9-17; and Edgar W. Thompson's biographical study, *Nathaniel Gilbert: Lawyer and Evangelist* (London: Epworth, 1960).

55. John Wesley, *An Extract of Miss Mary Gilbert's Journal*, 2nd ed. (London: Henry Cock, 1768), ix.
56. See *Journal* (6-11 March 1765), *Works* 21:502-3.
57. He corrected his extract during his visit to Chester in April 1768; see also *Journal* (2 April 1768), *Works* 22:124.
58. On the so-called offices of Christ, particularly as articulated in the sermons of John Wesley, see Sermon 14, "The Repentance of Believers," III.4, *Works* 1:352; Sermon 36, "The Law Established through Faith, II," I.6, *Works* 2:37-38; Sermon 43, "The Scripture Way of Salvation," II.2, *Works* 2:161; and the comment on variants to Sermon 1, "Salvation by Faith" in *Works* 4:433.
59. *Hymns on the Four Gospels* (1762), "What avails it God, to know" [John 13:17], final lines (*Poet. Works* 11:505).
60. See also Wesley, *Collection of Psalms and Hymns* (London: Strahan, 1741), "A Morning Hymn," st. 5 (p. 51):

> May we this Life improve,
> To mourn for Errors past,
> And live this short revolving Day
> As if it were our last.

61. *AM* 4 (1781): 35-40, 94-97, 148-52, 195-98, 256-59, 309-11, 372-75.
62. *Works*, 23:187.
63. This meditation, probably from the year 1780, originally written in the third person, has been reformulated into second person and adapted slightly for devotional use. See my treatment of this prayer in "Sanctification," pp. 90-103.
64. William Bramwell, *A Short Account of the Life and Death of Ann Cutler; A Pious Character, and Useful Instrument in the Work of God* (York: Printed by John Hill, 1827), 2.
65. Ibid., 6.
66. Ibid., 19-20.
67. See also Tripp, *Renewal of the Covenant*.
68. That is, paradise, where God is.
69. Edward Young, *The Complaint; or Night Thoughts*, 5th ed. (London: Dodsley, 1743), Night 4, p. 126; probably citing from Wesley's abridged reprint in his *Collection of Moral and Sacred Poems*, 3 vols. (Bristol: Farley, 1744), 2:266.
70. This language, with regard to the "disposition of the heart," meaning a holistic governing force in a person's life, is typical Wesleyan terminology. For a discussion of the importance of and distinctions between affections and tempers or dispositions, see Randy L. Maddox, *Responsible Grace: John Wesley's Practical Theology* (Nashville: Kingswood, 1994), 69-70.
71. See the account in Paul W. Chilcote, *Her Own Story: Autobiographical Portraits of Early Methodist Women* (Nashville: Kingswood Books, 2001), 173-87.
72. Quoted in Leslie F. Church, *More about Methodist People* (London: Epworth Press, 1949), 162.
73. Leslie F. Church, *The Early Methodist People* (London: Epworth Press, 1948), 19.
74. Sarah seems to be conflating and adapting lines from two Wesley hymns; at least the text as cited has not been located. But compare the following: "Empty me of self and pride" (*HSP* [1740], "Father I Have Sinned," st. 4 [*Poet. Works* 1:321]); and "With All Thy Fulness Fill!" (*HSP* [1739], "Grace after Meat," st. 4 [*Poet. Works* 1:34]).
75. *Select Psalms*, Psa. 128, "Bless'd is the man," v. 9 (*Poet. Works* 8:245).
76. Unidentified.
77. See part 1, n. 29 above.
78. See the introduction to Mrs. Lefevre in the section on spiritual instruction above.
79. Her niece, about whom, see part 3, B.6 in this volume.
80. *Hymns of Intercession for All Mankind*, Hymn 37, v. 4 (*Poet. Works* 6:141).
81. Possibly the daughter of Benjamin Colley (d. 1767) of Tollerton, Yorkshire, one of Wesley's ministers, receiving episcopal ordination and assisting him as a priest in the London chapels.

82. See my account of this in *Wesley and Women*, 192-98.//
83. *Works* 23:426-27.//
84. In the early nineteenth century, Zechariah Taft possessed the original document and reproduced it in his *Biographical Sketches of the Lives and Public Ministry of Various Holy Women*, 2 vols. (London: published for the author, 1825), 1:84; see also *PWHS* 3 (1902): 74.//
85. Most likely, James M. Byron, one of Wesley's itinerant preachers.//
86. John Wesley opened the new preaching house there on November 19, 1776; see also *Works* 23:37 and *WMM* 48 (1825): 365.

Part Three: The Art of Living and Dying

1. See Paul W. Chilcote, *Her Own Story: Autobiographical Portraits of Early Methodist Women* (Nashville: Kingswood Books, 2001), 191-218. See particularly pp. 191-92, on which I discuss female rhetoric and literary portraiture, as background for this present section.//
2. One of the most important collections of early Methodist correspondence is Zechariah Taft, *Original Letters* (Whitby: George Clark, 1821), which includes many selections by significant women leaders within the movement.//
3. See the judicious discussion of these complexities in Hilary Hinds's account of "silences in radical sectarian women's writings," in *God's Englishwomen: Seventeenth-Century Radical Sectarian Writing and Feminist Criticism* (New York: St. Martin's Press, 1996), 51-79.//
4. See Mary Catherine O'Connor, *The Art of Dying Well: The Development of the "Ars Moriendi"* (New York: Columbia University Press, 1942); Nancy Lee Beaty, *The Craft of Dying: A Study in the Literary Tradition of the "Ars Moriendi" in England* (New Haven: Yale University Press, 1970); and David W. Atkinson, *The English "ars moriendi"* (New York: Lang, 1992).//
5. According to O'Connor, most texts consisted in variations of six basic themes: "(1) a collection of questions on death from Christian authorities; (2) advice to the dying person on ways of resisting the five sins of faithlessness, despair, impatience, pride, and worldliness; (3) catechetical questions that had to be answered correctly in order to gain salvation; (4) prayers and rules to assist in the imitation of the dying Christ; (5) advice to those who were present around the deathbed; (6) prayers to be said by those who were present at the moment of death" (*Art of Dying*, 157).//
6. See David W. Atkinson, "The English *ars moriendi*: Its Protestant Transformation," *Renaissance and Reformation* 6, 1 (1982): 1-10.//
7. See the groundbreaking work of Philippe Ariès, *The Hour of Our Death*, trans. Helen Weaver (New York: Oxford University Press, 1991).//
8. Atkinson, "The English *ars moriendi*," 7-8.//
9. See Sermon 133, "Death and Deliverance," *Works* 4:204-14.//
10. Sermon 149, "On Love," III.5, *Works* 4:387. See also Sermon 109, "The Trouble and Rest of Good Men," in which he stresses the notion that while death is the effect of sin, it is also appointed by God as the cure of sin (*Works* 3:531-41).//
11. See also the influential work of Puritan divine, William Perkins, *A Salve for a Sicke Man* (1595).//
12. The *Journal* of John Wesley is filled with such accounts; see also *Works* 19:206-8, 246; 20:82-84, 114, 430-31, 436-37, 442; 21:57, 58-60, 96-98, 153, 295, 371, 463; 22:7, 20-21, 23, 65, 94-95, 100, 114, 169-70, 174-75, 194, 214, 218, 222, 257, 297, 308, 384, 397, 435, 442, 462-63; 23:79, 111, 258, 262, 276-77. Of the various accounts of death that he published, Wesley included those of at least five women: Hannah Richardson (1741), Mary Langson (1770), Alice Gilbert (1773), Elizabeth Hindmarsh (1777), and Jane Newland (1790).//
13. *Redemption Hymns*, Hymn 25, "The Musician's Hymn," v. 4 (*Poet. Works* 4:244).//
14. Answer to Question 29. In 1753, John Wesley published an extract of the *Assembly's Shorter Catechism* in *Christian Library* (31:109-48). He removed a number of questions completely, both deleting what he considered harmful doctrinal teaching and abridging other parts of this important text, *The Confession of Faith ... approved by the General Assembly of the Kirk of Scotland*, originally published in 1651. With regard to the matter of justification by grace through faith, Wesley and his Calvinistic predecessors were absolutely kindred spirits.

15. The central issue at stake here is the doctrine of assurance, or the witness of the Spirit. Under the influence of Moravian Pietism, both Wesley brothers initially affirmed that full assurance was essential to justification, a radical view that was soon called into question. In later years, they allowed for a more robust doctrine of degrees of assurance. This more mature view can be seen in John's Sermon 89, "The More Excellent Way," *Works* 3:263-77; and Sermon 106, "On Faith," *Works* 3:492-501; see also the important sermon trilogy, Sermons 10-12, "The Witness of Our Own Spirit," "The Witness of the Spirit, I," and "The Witness of the Spirit, II," *Works* 1:267-313. On the development of Wesley's thought in this regard, see A. S. Yates, *The Doctrine of Assurance* (London: Epworth Press, 1952); and Colin W. Williams, *John Wesley's Theology Today* (Nashville: Abingdon Press, 1960), 102-14.

16. On Ann Bolton, see John Banks, *Nancy Nancy* (Manchester: Penwork [Leeds] Ltd., 1984); and Maldwyn Edwards, *My Dear Sister* (Manchester: Penwork [Leeds] Ltd., [1975]), 101-14.

17. Letter to Francis Wolfe (11 January 1775), *Letters* (Telford) 6:136.

18. See n. 15 above.

19. Until her marriage in 1792, she lived with her brother, Edward Bolton (1747–1818) at Blandford Park.

20. Crosby, Manuscript Letterbook, 46.

21. That is, Wesley's *Plain Account of Christian Perfection*.

22. Drawn from the question in Paragraph 19, from a meeting held in Bristol in August 1758. Wesley's full response is: "A. It was expressed in these words: (1) Every one may mistake as long as he lives. (2) A mistake in opinion may occasion a mistake in practice. (3) Every such mistake is a transgression of the perfect law. Therefore, (4) Every such mistake, were it not for the blood of atonement, would expose to eternal damnation. (5) It follows, that the most perfect have continual need of the merits of Christ, even for their actual transgressions, and may say for themselves, as well as for their brethren, 'Forgive us our trespasses'" (*Works* [Jackson] 11:395).

23. See selections from Sarah Ryan elsewhere in this volume.

24. That is, those of a Calvinistic persuasion who strongly denied the possibility of "Christian perfection" in this life.

25. See Sermon 76, "On Perfection," *Works* 3:71-87. This sermon, published originally in 1784, provides a final summary of his doctrine of Christian perfection. The whole issue, he had come to believe, hinged upon two particular matters: (1) the definition of "perfection" in terms of love of God and neighbor, and (2) the definition of sin as deliberate.

26. Sarah first heard Wesley preach at the Foundery in London in February 1750. There is no record of his sermon, text, or the specific event. It is possible, however, that the occasion was the watch-night service recorded in his *Journal* on Wednesday, February 14 (see *Works* 20:321).

27. *HSP* (1742), part 1, "After a Recovery," v. 2 (*Poet. Works* 2:123).

28. See also Rupert Davies and E. Gordon Rupp, eds., *A History of the Methodist Church in Great Britain*, 4 vols. (London: Epworth Press, 1965–88), 4:178-81.

29. Hester articulates a clear objective or Latin theory of atonement, based upon the teachings of Anselm of Canterbury in his classic work of 1098, *Cur Deus Homo*, without question the most considerable contribution to the theology of the atonement in the medieval church. It interpreted the doctrine in terms of the satisfaction due God for the dishonor that sin brought upon the Creator. Anselm strongly repudiated the notion that Satan had rights over humankind, for which the cross exacted payment. See Eugene R. Fairweather, ed., *A Scholastic Miscellany: Anselm to Ockham* (New York: Macmillan, 1970), 100-183.

30. In addition to the multiple references in the works of John Wesley to this issue, Hannah may have been aware of his correspondence with Eliza Bennis, an important Irish Methodist. Upon two separate occasions, Wesley dealt with this theological point in detail. "But we all maintain we are not saved without works," he wrote on March 1, 1774, "that works are a condition (though not the meritorious cause) of final salvation. It is by faith in the righteousness and blood of Christ that we are enabled to do all good works; and it is for the sake of these that all who fear God and work righteousness are accepted of Him" (*Letters* [Telford] 6:76-77). On May 2, 1774, he reiterated: "The Methodists always held, and have declared a thousand times, the death of Christ is the meritorious cause of our salvation—that is, of pardon, holiness, and glory; loving, obedient faith is the condition of glory" (*Letters* [Telford] 6:79-80).

31. These Articles deal respectively with "Of the Justification of Man," "Of Good Works," and "Of Works before Justification." John Wesley published his edited version of "Homilies of the Church of England" on these subjects as well; see also *John Wesley*, 123-33.

32. See the discussion of this point in Randy L. Maddox, *Responsible Grace: John Wesley's Practical Theology* (Nashville: Kingswood Books, 1994), 188-89.

33. This is consistent with John Wesley's definition of sin for the purposes of his doctrine of Christian perfection, namely, "a willful transgression of a known law of God."

34. See excerpts from her journal in my volume, *Her Own Story*, 106-14.

35. Elizabeth, in fact, recorded in minute detail the events leading up to the very moment of his death. See also Richard P. Heitzenrater, *The Elusive Mr. Wesley*, 2nd ed. (Nashville: Abingdon Press, 2003), 2:143-50.

36. There are no explicit references to this in John Wesley's letters or journal.

37. Matthew Mayer (1740–1814) of Portwood Hall, Stockport, was one of the most notable local preachers, spiritual advisers, and evangelists in early Methodism and was the founding father of the greatest of all nondenominational Sunday schools at Stockport. At this point, he and his wife had been John Wesley's faithful friends for nearly twenty years. The Mayer's house became one of the most significant bases for the expansion of the Methodist movement. See *WMM* 39 (1816): 3-11, 161-70, 241-51; W. Reginald Ward, *Religion and Society in England, 1790–1850* (London: Batsford, 1972), 32-33; and *Works*, 21:419.

38. See George Holder, *A Short Account of the Life of Mrs. Mary Holder. Mostly taken from Her Journal* (Whitby, 1836); and Zechariah Taft, *Biographical Sketches of the Lives and Public Ministry of Various Holy Women* (London: published for the author, 1825), 1:100-128, 2:89-107.

39. To cite just one example among many, on May 2, 1767, Wesley wrote: "I doubt only whether you are so useful as you might be. But herein look to the anointing which you have of God, being willing to follow wherever He leads, and it shall teach you of all things" (*Letters* [Telford] 5:46).

40. An intimate member of the Leytonstone circle of women, Anne became the governess of the community when the numbers increased beyond the capacity of her two friends, Mary Bosanquet and Sarah Ryan. See her account of Sarah Crosby's death later in this collection.

41. *Select Psalms*, Psa. 133, "Behold how good thing," v. 1 (*Poet. Works* 8:250).

42. This is a quote from Miguel de Molinos's *Spiritual Guide*, most likely drawn from the extract of the same name that Wesley published in *Christian Library*, vol. 38 (see quote on p. 262).

43. See also *BCP*, prayer of consecration in the eucharistic liturgy.

44. Taft, *Holy Women*, 1:181. Subsequent to her preaching in the Methodist Chapel at Sunderland on October 22, 1775, she became embroiled in a controversy over the propriety of her actions and exchanged letters with Joseph Benson (emerging antagonist to the women preachers), John Wesley, and Robert Empringham concerning her work. For an account of this incident, see Paul W. Chilcote, *John Wesley and the Women Preachers of Early Methodism* (Metuchen, N.J.: Scarecrow Press, 1991), 156-59.

45. Taft, *Holy Women*, 1:178.

46. See Chilcote, *Her Own Story*, 85-101.

47. Alexander Kilham (1762–98) had been censured by the Methodist Conference in 1792 for his defense of Joseph Cownley's celebration of the sacrament. He produced a stream of broadsheets and circulars, drawing upon the explosive rhetoric of Tom Paine and the French Revolution, arguing for democratic reform within the life of the movement. Looking back to England's own dissenting traditions, he also espoused separation from the Church of England and assumed an openly nonconformist position. Matters came to a head late in 1795 when he published *The Progress of Liberty Amongst the People Called Methodists*. He was formally expelled from Wesleyan Methodism in 1796 and subsequently founded the Methodist New Connexion in 1797.

48. From a German hymn translated by John Wesley and published in *HSP* (1739), part 2, "Trust in Providence," v. 7 (*Poet. Works* 1:126).

49. Frances married John Pawson on August 14, 1785. Since the time of their marriage, Frances and Elizabeth had not had any communication, owing in large measure to their itinerant life. This letter, therefore, breaks a decade of silence in terms of their correspondence.

50. *HSP* (1749), part 2, Hymn 13, "Thou God of Truth and Love," v. 5 (*Poet. Works* 5:423).

51. *HSP* (1739), "Grace before Meat," v. 6 (*Poet. Works* 1:33).

52. It is noteworthy here that Elizabeth refers to the Methodist Societies as a "church." The reference is actually quite early, but reflects the growing autonomy of the Methodists after Wesley's death and the establishment of a new institutional identity as Wesleyan Methodism moved into the nineteenth century.

53. That is, the itinerant preachers.

54. That is, the Methodist New Connexion.

55. See the treatment of Mary Tatham in part 2 above.

56. William Bramwell (1759–1818), noted revivalist and advocate for women preachers, became a traveling preacher in 1785, serving primarily in the North of England. In association with Ann Cutler (1759–95), whose *Account* he later published, he enjoyed particular success during the great Yorkshire Revival of 1792–96. His failure to rise through the ranks of the preachers after Wesley's death was due primarily to acts of disloyalty to the established leadership of Wesleyan Methodism, his 1803 resignation from the ministry in order to unite with dissident revivalist elements in Leeds, and certain divisive elements in his theology. Described by some as a precursor of the great revivalist Charles Finney, he died at Leeds on August 13, 1818.

57. See Chilcote, *Wesley and Women*, 221-37 for a full discussion of these developments.

58. That is, Sally Lawrence, the niece of Sarah Ryan and "adopted" daughter of the Fletchers.

59. Mary Taft's full account of Mary Fletcher's death was later published and is included later in this collection. Joseph Benson, editor of the *Methodist Magazine* at this time, was a noted antagonist to women's preaching. He was notorious in the editorial elimination of references to the work of women in this sphere.

60. Women's preaching was not prohibited per se but was permitted only under the following regulations: "1. They shall not preach in the Circuit where they reside, until they have obtained the approbation of the Superintendant [sic] and a Quarterly Meeting. 2. Before they go into any other Circuit to preach, they shall have a *written* invitation from the Superintendant of such Circuit, and a recommendatory note from the Superintendant of their own Circuit" (*Minutes of the Methodist Conferences* [London: Printed at the Conference Office, 1812–], 2:188-89).

61. See a discussion of this issue in Chilcote, *Wesley and Women*, 141-81; see also Mary's important letter of June 1771 to John Wesley, in ibid., 299-304.

62. See Chilcote, *Wesley and Women*, 198-201.

63. Near to the heart of Methodism in Leeds, Sarah Crosby was buried nearby in St. Peter's churchyard.

64. See letter 9 above.

65. Shortly after the death of her husband, Mary Fletcher published a tract entitled *Thoughts on Communion with Happy Spirits* (Birmingham: Printed by William Rickman King, n.d.), in which she reflected upon the communion of saints and their continued presence in the community of faith.

66. The connection of Leeds to the annual meeting of Conference through the years was especially critical. Discussions related to the separation of the Methodist Societies from the Church of England were held there in 1755 and 1762. The 1769 Conference sent the first pair of missionaries to America. In 1784, it was the Leeds Conference that approved Wesley's Deed of Declaration and laid plans for the establishment of the new Methodist Church in America.

67. See Taft, *Holy Women*, 2:115-39; Leslie F. Church, *More About the Early Methodist People* (London: Epworth Press, 1949), 156-59; and Chilcote, *Wesley and Women*, 186-89, 205, 211, 284-85.

68. John Norris, "The Resignation," as found in John Wesley, *A Collection of Psalms and Hymns* (London: Strahan, 1741), 30; *Poet. Works* 2:11.

69. In the last year of his life, Wesley published Sermon 127, "On the Wedding Garment" (*Works* 4:139-48), which was to be the last of his expositions of the doctrine of holiness of heart and life. This sermon marks a return full circle to the vision of salvation first articulated in Sermon 17, "The Circumcision of the Heart" (*Works* 1:401-14).

70. This is a nuanced, Arminian interpretation of divine decrees, standing in opposition to a Calvinistic soteriology. On this understanding of election, see Carl Bangs, *Arminius: A Study in the Dutch Reformation* (Nashville: Abingdon Press, 1971), 193-205 in particular.

71. This event is not included in the published *Memoirs* of Mary Taft.

72. Their London home, in Islington.

73. D'Arcy, Lady Maxwell (c. 1742–1810), a highly educated Scottish aristocrat, remained faithful to the Church of Scotland even though she joined the Methodist Society in Edinburgh in 1764. She was a valued correspondent and friend of John Wesley. Left a wealthy widow at only nineteen years of age, her life was methodical, full of worship and praise in both Methodist Society and Scottish Kirk. She led her own household worship daily, established a boys' school, supported the Sunday school movement, and provided spiritual direction to leaders and laity. See Robert Bourne, *A Christian Sketch of Lady Maxwell* (London: Hatchard, 1819); and John Lancaster, *The Life of Darcy, Lady Maxwell*, 2nd ed. (London: Kershaw, 1826).

74. Located about twenty-five miles east of Lincoln, Raithby became a major Methodist center due to the influence of Robert Carr Brackenbury, one of Wesley's great friends and a pioneer of Methodism in the Channel Islands.

75. Unidentified.

76. See Paul W. Chilcote, "John Wesley as Revealed by the Journal of Hester Ann Rogers," *MethH* 20 (1982): 111-12.

77. John Newton, *Olney Hymns* (London: Oliver, 1779), Book 2, Hymn 74, "The Tolling Bell," st. 3 (p. 270).

78. Watts, *Hymns and Spiritual Songs*, Book 2, Hymn 75, "Spiritual and Eternal Joys," v. 6 (Isaac Watts, *The Works of the Reverend and Learned Isaac Watts, D.D.*, ed. David Jennings and Philip Doddridge, 6 vols. of the Reverend and Learned Isaac Watts, D.D., [London: John Barfield, (1810–11], 4:319).

79. Philip Doddridge, *Hymns Founded on Various Texts in the Holy Scriptures* (Salop: Eddowes & Cotton, 1755), Hymn 363, "An Evening Hymn," st. 3 (p. 317).

80. *HSP* (1749), vol. 2, part 2, "Hymn for Christian Friends," v. 3 (*Poet. Works* 5:447).

81. *HSP* (1749), vol. 2, part 1, Hymn 22 (*Poet. Works* 5:169).

82. *HSP* (1749), vol. 2, part 1, Hymn 12, v. 1 (*Poet. Works* 5:147).

83. *Redemption Hymns*, "Musician's Hymn," Hymn 25, v. 10 (*Poet. Works* 4:245).

84. See Chilcote, *Her Own Story*, 42-45.

85. *Journal* (12 Aug. 1745), *Works* 20:82-83.

86. *HSP* (1742), part 2, "Zechariah 4:7," v. 5 (*Poet. Works* 2:291).

87. There is no direct allusion to the event in either Wesley's diary or published *Journal*.

88. This is the title of a short hymn that became popular in Methodist circles and that traces back to Joseph Hart (1712–68), an ardent Calvinist and the most popular eighteenth-century hymn writer among independents other than Isaac Watts. The hymn is actually stanza 7 of Hart's Hymn 123, "No Prophet, nor Dreamer of Dreams," in *Hymns Composed on Various Subjects* (London: Everingham, 1759), see p. 98.

89. The closing line of Charles Wesley's "Love Divine, All Loves Excelling"; see also *Works* 7:545, 547.

90. Ann's epitaph, engraved on copper and fixed on the tombstone in Macclesfield, reads: Underneath lie the remains of ANN CUTLER, Whose simple manners, solid piety, and extraordinary power in prayer, distinguished and rendered her eminently useful in promoting a religious revival wherever she came. She was born near Preston, in Lancashire, and died here December 29th, 1794, AE. 35.

91. In addition to the account of Mary Fletcher, see also Taft, *Holy Women*, 1:41-48.

92. *HSP* (1742), part 2, "I will hearken," v. 5 (*Poet. Works* 2:265).

93. Watts, *Hymns and Sacred Songs*, Book 2, Hymn 110, "Triumph over Death," v. 2 (Watts, *Works* [1810], 4:330).

94. The original source of this hymn stanza is unclear; but it may have been known to Sarah from its quotation in a popular account of David Brainerd, a missionary to the native tribes in North America; see also *Account of the Life of the late Reverend Mr. David Brainerd* (Edinburgh: Gray & Alston, 1765), 78 (his journal entry for 23 August 1743).

95. Watts, *Hymns and Spiritual Songs*, Book 3, Hymn 7, "When I Survey," v. 3 (Watts, *Works* [1810], 4:349).

96. See *HSP* (1749), vol. 1, part 2, Hymn 130, "For Believers," v. 5 (*Poet. Works* 5:25).

97. *Hymns for Children* (1763), Hymn 75, Part II, v. 8 (*Poet. Works* 6:445).

98. Correcting the improper date of October 24 as published in the *WMM*. Wesley Swift was the first to point out the discrepancy between the printed version of Ann Tripp's account and the inscription on her tombstone. Other evidence confirms the date of October 29. See Frank Baker, "John Wesley and Sarah Crosby," *PWHS* 27 (1949): 82.

99. *Funeral Hymns*, (1759), Hymn 14, Part 2, v. 7 (*Poet. Works* 6:243).

100. Possibly, Thomas Taylor (1738–1816), a native of Yorkshire and one of the first Methodist preachers appointed to Wales. Later appointed to Ireland, Scotland, and in twenty-two circuits in England, his itinerant career carried him further than Wesley in his own day. He was ordained by John Wesley in 1791 and elected President of the Methodist Conference in 1809.

101. Printed by A. Edmonds at Shiffnal, undated, but presumably 1815, or early 1816.

102. *WMM* 39 (1816): 158.

SELECTED BIBLIOGRAPHY

1. Primary Sources

Beaumont, Joseph, ed. *Memoirs of Mrs. Mary Tatham, Late of Nottingham.* London: Simpkin & Marshall, sold by John Mason, 1838.

Bennet, William, ed. *Memoirs of Mrs. Grace Bennet.* Macclesfield: Printed and sold by E. Bayley, 1803.

Bosanquet, Mary. *Jesus, Altogether Lovely; or a Letter to Some of the Single Women in the Methodist Society.* 2nd edition. Bristol: s.n., 1766.

———. *A Letter, Written to Elizabeth A—ws, On Her Removal from England.* Leeds: James Bowling, 1771.

Bramwell, William. *A Short Account of the Life and Death of Ann Cutler; A Pious Character, and Useful Instrument in the Work of God.* York: Printed by John Hill, 1827.

Bulmer, Agnes. "Poem for the Rev. John Wesley." Dated February 6, 1790. Transcribed by B. F. Fielding. Wesley Historical Society Library Collection. Wesley and Methodist Studies Centre, Westminster Institute, Oxford Brookes University, Oxford.

———. *Thoughts on a Future State, Occasioned by the Death of Mrs. Hester Ann Rogers.* Birmingham: J. Belcher, 1795.

Bulmer, Agnes, ed. *Memoirs of Mrs. Elizabeth Mortimer.* Second Edition. London: J. Mason, 1836.

Clarke, Adam. *Memoirs of the Late Eminent Mrs. Mary Cooper, of London.* New Edition. Halifax: William Nicholson and Sons, [c. 1910].

Selected Bibliography

Cole, Joseph, ed. *Memorials of Hannah Ball*. Third Edition, revised. London: Wesleyan Conference Office, 1880.

Cooper, Jane. "Christian Experience." *AM* 5 (1782): 408-9, 489-90.

Crosby, Sarah. "An Account of Mrs. Crosby, of Leeds." *WMM* 29 (1806): 418-23, 465-73, 517-21, 563-68, 610-17.

———. "An Account of Mrs. Sarah Ryan." *AM* 2 (1779): 296-310.

———. Manuscript Letterbook, 1760–74. Perkins Library, Duke University.

[Design, Susannah]. Manuscript Journal of Susannah Design. *Meth. Arch.*

Entwisle, Mary. Manuscript Diary. *Meth. Arch.*

Fletcher, Mary. *An Account of Sarah Lawrence*. London: Printed by Thomas Cardhouse, 1820.

———. *Thoughts on Communion with Happy Spirits*. Birmingham: Printed by William Rickman King, n.d.

Hall, Bathsheba. "An Extract from the Diary of Mrs. Bathsheba Hall." *AM* 4 (1781): 35-40, 94-97, 148-52, 195-98, 256-59, 309-11, 372-75.

[Hall, Martha]. "A Discourse on Meditation." Martha Hall Manuscripts. *Meth. Arch.*

Holder, George. *A Short Account of the Life of Mrs. Mary Holder. Mostly taken from Her Journal*. Whitby, 1836.

[Lefevre, Mrs.]. *Letters upon Sacred Subjects, by a person lately deceased*. London: n.p., 1757.

Leger, J. Augustin. *Wesley's Last Love*. London: J. M. Dent & Sons, 1910.

Lyth, John. *The Blessedness of Religion in Earnest: A Memorial of Mrs. Mary Lyth*. London: The Book Society, 1861.

[Mallitt, William]. "An Account of S[arah]. Mallitt." *AM* 11 (1788): 91-93, 238-39.

Moore, Henry. *The Life of Mrs. Mary Fletcher, Consort and Relict of the Rev. John Fletcher, Vicar of Madeley, Salop: Compiled from her Journal and Other Authentic Documents*. 2 vols. Birmingham: J. Peart, 1817.

Pipe, John. "Memoir of Miss Isabella Wilson." *WMM* 31 (1808): 372-75, 410-15, 461-69, 516-18, 562-67, 595-97.

Rogers, Hester Ann. *An Account of the Experience of Hester Ann Rogers.* New York: Hunt & Eaton, 1893.

———. Manuscript Journals, 1775–84. 3 volumes. *Meth. Arch.*

Smyth, Edward, ed. *The Extraordinary Life and Christian Experience of Margaret Davidson, as Dictated by Herself.* Dublin: Dugdale, 1782.

Stokes, Mary. "The Experience of Miss Mary Stokes, in a Letter to Mr. Tho[mas] Rankin." *AM* 18 (1795): 99-101.

Sutcliffe, Joseph. *The Experience of the late Mrs. Frances Pawson, Widow of the late Rev. John Pawson.* London: Printed at the Conference Office, by Thomas Cordeux, 1813.

Taft, Mary. *Memoirs of the Life of Mrs. Mary Taft; Formerly Miss Barritt.* 2 vols. London: Printed for and sold by the author, 1828–31.

Taft, Zechariah. *Biographical Sketches of the Lives and Public Ministry of Various Holy Women.* 2 vols. London: Published for the author, and sold by Kershaw, 1825.

———. *Original Letters.* Whitby: George Clark, 1821.

Tooth, Mary. *A Letter to the Loving and Beloved People of the Parish of Madeley.* Shiffnal: Printed by A. Edmonds, [1815].

Wallace, Charles, Jr., ed. *Susanna Wesley: The Complete Writings.* New York: Oxford University Press, 1997.

Watts, Isaac. *The Works of the Reverend and Learned Isaac Watts, D.D.* Edited by David Jennings and Philip Doddridge. 6 vols. London: John Barfield, 1810–1811.

[Wells, Mary]. *The Triumph of Faith ... Exemplified in the Life, Death, and Spiritual Experience of ... Mrs. Joanna Turner.* Bristol: Religious Tract Society, 1787.

[Wesley, John]. *An Extract of Letters by Mrs. L***.* Bristol: William Pine, 1769.

[Wesley, John, ed.]. *An Extract of Miss Mary Gilbert's Journal.* Second Edition. London: Henry Cock, 1768.

Wesley, John. *Letters Wrote by Jane Cooper: To which is Prefixt, some Account of Her Life and Death.* London: [Strahan], 1764.

SELECTED BIBLIOGRAPHY

2. Books

Atkinson, David W. *The English "ars moriendi."* New York: Lang, 1992.

Barker-Benfield, G. J. *The Culture of Sensibility: Sex and Society in Eighteenth-Century Britain.* Chicago: University of Chicago Press, 1992.

Beasley-Topliffe, Keith, ed. *The Upper Room Dictionary of Christian Spiritual Formation.* Nashville: Upper Room Books, 2003.

Beaty, Nancy Lee. *The Craft of Dying: A Study in the Literary Tradition of the "Ars Moriendi" in England.* New Haven: Yale University Press, 1970.

Beddoe, Deirdre. *Discovering Women's History: A Practical Manual.* London: Pandora, 1983.

Belenky, M. F. et al. *Women's Ways of Knowing: The Development of Self, Voice, and Mind.* New York: Basic Books, 1986.

Bentock, Shari, ed. *The Private Self: Theory and Practice of Women's Autobiographical Writings.* Chapel Hill: University of North Carolina Press, 1988.

Brown, Earl Kent. *Women of Mr. Wesley's Methodism.* New York: Edwin Mellen Press, 1983.

Butler, David. *Methodists and Papists.* London: Darton, Longman, and Todd, 1995.

Carroll, Berenice A., ed. *Liberating Women's History: Theoretical and Critical Essays.* Urbana: University of Illinois Press, 1976.

Chilcote, Paul W. *Her Own Story: Autobiographical Portraits of Early Methodist Women.* Nashville: Kingswood Books, 2001.

———. *John Wesley and the Women Preachers of Early Methodism.* Metuchen, N.J.: Scarecrow Press, Inc., 1991.

———. *Praying in the Wesleyan Spirit: 52 Prayers for Today.* Nashville: Upper Room Books, 2001.

———. *Recapturing the Wesleys' Vision: An Introduction to the Faith of John and Charles Wesley.* Downers Grove, Ill.: InterVarsity Press, 2004.

———. *She Offered Them Christ.* Nashville: Abingdon Press, 1993.

Christophers, S. W. *The Poets of Methodism.* London: Hodder and Stoughton, 1877.

Selected Bibliography

Church, Leslie F. *The Early Methodist People*. London: Epworth Press, 1948.

———. *More About the Early Methodist People*. London: Epworth Press, 1949.

Clapper, Gregory S. *As If the Heart Mattered: A Wesleyan Spirituality*. Nashville: Upper Room Books, 1997.

Collins, Vicki Tolar. "Perfecting a Woman's Life: Methodist Rhetoric and Politics in *The Account of Hester Ann Rogers*." Ph.D. dissertation, Auburn University, 1993.

Conn, J. W., ed. *Women's Spirituality: Resources for Christian Development*. New York: Paulist Press, 1986.

Crookshank, C. H. *Memorable Women of Irish Methodism in the Last Century*. London: Wesleyan-Methodist Book-Room, 1882.

Cunningham, Valentine. *Everywhere Spoken Against: Dissent in the Victorian Novel*. Oxford: Clarendon Press, 1975.

Davies, Rupert, and Rupp, E. Gordon, eds. *A History of the Methodist Church in Great Britain*. 4 vols. London: Epworth Press, 1965–88.

Eliot, George. *Adam Bede*. London: Tallant, 1859.

Eltscher, Susan M., ed. *Women in the Wesleyan and United Methodist Traditions: A Bibliography*. Madison, N.J.: General Commission on Archives and History, 1992.

Gilligan, C. *In A Different Voice: Psychological Theory and Women's Development*. Cambridge: Harvard University Press, 1982.

Goldberger, N. et al. *Knowledge, Difference, and Power: Essays Inspired by "Women's Ways of Knowing."* New York: Basic Books, 1996.

Gordon, James. *Evangelical Spirituality: From the Wesleys to John Stott*. London: SPCK, 1991.

Harper, Steve. *Devotional Life in the Wesleyan Tradition*. Nashville: Upper Room Books, 1983.

Heilbrun, Carolyn. *Writing a Woman's Life*. New York: W. W. Norton, 1988.

Heitzenrater, Richard P. *Wesley and the People Called Methodists*. Nashville: Abingdon Press, 1995.

Hess, C. L. *Caretakers of Our Common House: Women's Development in Communities of Faith*. Nashville: Abingdon Press, 1997.

Selected Bibliography

Hindmarsh, D. Bruce. *The Evangelical Conversion Narrative: Spiritual Autobiography in Early Modern England.* New York: Oxford University Press, 2005.

Hotz-Davies, Ingrid. *The Creation of Religious Identities by English Women Poets from the Seventeenth to the Early Twentieth Century.* Lewiston: The Edwin Mellon Press, 1996.

Hunt, M. *Fierce Tenderness: A Feminist Theology of Friendship.* New York: Crossroads, 1991.

Jeffrey, David Lyle, ed. *English Spirituality in the Age of Wesley.* Reprint Edition. Grand Rapids: William B. Eerdmans Pub. Co., 1994.

Jelinek, Estelle C., ed. *Women's Autobiography: Essays in Criticism.* Bloomington, Ind.: Indiana University Press, 1980.

Johnson, Dale A., ed. *Women in English Religion, 1700–1925.* New York: Edwin Mellen, 1983.

Johnson, Dale A. *Women and Religion in Britain and Ireland: An Annotated Bibliography from the Reformation to 1993.* Lanham, MD: Scarecrow Press, Inc., 1995.

Jones, Cheslyn, et al., eds. *The Study of Spirituality.* New York: Oxford University Press, 1986.

Jones, Serene. *Feminist Theory and Christian Theology: Cartographies of Grace.* Minneapolis: Fortress Press, 2000.

Jones, Vivien, ed. *Women in the Eighteenth Century.* London: Routledge, 1990.

Keeling, Annie E. *Eminent Methodist Women.* London: Charles H. Kelly, 1889.

Keller, Rosemary Skinner, ed. *Spirituality and Social Responsibility: The Vocational Vision of Women in the United Methodist Tradition.* Nashville: Abingdon Press, 1993.

Kimbrough, S T, Jr., ed., *Orthodox and Wesleyan Spirituality.* Crestwood, N.Y.: St. Vladimir's Seminary Press, 2002.

King, U. *Women and Spirituality: Voices of Protest and Promise.* Basingstoke: Macmillan Education, 1989.

Knight, Henry H. III. *The Presence of God in the Christian Life: John Wesley and the Means of Grace.* Lanham, MD: Scarecrow Press, 1992.

Selected Bibliography

Lloyd, Gareth. *Sources for Women's Studies in the Methodist Archives.* Manchester: John Rylands Library, 1996.

Maddox, Randy L. *Responsible Grace: John Wesley's Practical Theology.* Nashville: Kingswood Books, 1994.

Malmgreen, Gail. *Religion in the Lives of English Women, 1760–1930.* Bloomington: University of Indiana Press, 1986.

Matthaei, Sondra Higgins. *Making Disciples: Faith Formation in the Wesleyan Tradition.* Nashville: Abingdon Press, 2000.

Matthews, William, comp. *British Autobiographies: An Annotated Bibliography of British Autobiographies Published or Written Before 1951.* Berkeley: University of California Press, 1955.

McAdoo, H. R. *The Spirit of Anglicanism.* London: Black, 1965.

McClendon, Jr., James W. *Biography as Theology.* Nashville, Abingdon Press, 1974.

Morrow, Thomas M. *Early Methodist Women.* London: Epworth Press, 1967.

Newton, John. *Susanna Wesley and the Puritan Tradition in Methodism.* London: Epworth Press, 1968.

Nussbaum, Felicity. *The Autobiographical Subject: Gender and Ideology in Eighteenth-Century England.* Baltimore: John Hopkins University Press, 1990.

O'Connor, Mary Catharine. *The Art of Dying Well: The Development of the "Ars Moriendi."* New York: Columbia University Press, 1942.

O'Malley, Ida B. *Women in Subjection: A Study of the Lives of English Women before 1832.* London: Duckworth, 1933.

Rattenbury, J. Ernest. *The Eucharistic Hymns of John and Charles Wesley.* London: Epworth Press, 1948.

Rowbotham, Sheila. *Hidden From History: Rediscovering Women in History from the Seventeenth Century to the Present.* New York: Pantheon Books, 1974.

Rowe, Kenneth E. *Methodist Women: A Guide to the Literature.* Lake Junaluska, N.C.: General Commission on Archives and History, 1980.

Senn, Frank, ed. *Protestant Spiritual Traditions.* New York: Paulist Press, 1986.

Sheldrake, Philip. *Spirituality and History.* Second Edition. London: SPCK, 1995.

Selected Bibliography

Slee, Nicola. *Women's Faith Development*. Burlington, Vt.: Ashgate Pub. Co., 2004.

Spretnak, C., ed. *The Politics of Women's Spirituality: Essays on the Rise of Spiritual Power within the Feminist Movement*. New York: Anchor/Doubleday, 1982.

Stevens, Abel. *The Women of Methodism: Its Three Foundresses—Susanna Wesley, the Countess of Huntingdon, and Barbara Heck*. New York: Published by Carlton and Porter, 1886.

Stevenson-Moessner, J., ed. *In Her Own Time: Women and Developmental Issues in Pastoral Care*. Minneapolis: Fortress Press, 2000.

Stranks, C. J. *Anglican Devotion*. London: SPCK, 1961.

Tabraham, Barrie. *The Making of Methodism*. London: Epworth Press, 1995.

Taves, Ann. *Fits, Trances, and Visions: Experiencing Religion and Explaining Experience from Wesley to James*. Princeton: Princeton University Press, 1999.

Thomas, Hilah F. and Keller, Rosemary Skinner, eds. *Women in New Worlds: Historical Perspectives on the Wesleyan Tradition*. 2 vols. Nashville: Abingdon Press, 1981–82.

Thornton, Martin. *English Spirituality*. London: SPCK, 1963.

Wakefield, Gordon. *Fire of Love: The Spirituality of John Wesley*. London: Epworth Press, 1976.

———. *Methodist Devotion: The Spiritual Life in the Methodist Tradition*. London: Epworth Press, 1966.

———. *Methodist Spirituality*. Peterborough: Epworth, 1999.

Wakefield, Gordon, ed. *The Westminster Dictionary of Christian Spirituality*. Philadelphia: Westminster, 1983.

Walsh, John, et al., eds. *The Church of England c. 1689–c. 1833*. Cambridge: Cambridge University Press, 1993.

Ward, W. R. *Religion and Society*. London: Batsford, 1972.

Watson, David Lowes. *Covenant Discipleship: Christian Formation Through Mutual Accountability*. Nashville: Discipleship Resources, 1989.

Whaling, Frank, ed., *John and Charles Wesley: Selected Prayers, Hymns, Journal Notes, Sermons, Letters and Treatises*. New York: Paulist Press, 1981.

3. Chapters and Articles

Albin, Tom. "An Empirical Study of Early Methodist Spirituality." In *Wesleyan Theology Today: A Bicentennial Theological Consultation*, 275-90. Edited by Theodore Runyon. Nashville: Kingswood Books, 1985.

Atkinson, David W. "The English *ars moriendi*: Its Protestant Transformation." *Renaissance and Reformation* 6.1 (1982): 1-10.

Baker, Frank. "John Wesley and Sarah Crosby." *PWHS* 27 (1949): 76-82.

———. "John Wesley's First Marriage." *London Quarterly Review* 192 (1967): 305-15.

Bates, E. Ralph. "Sarah Ryan and Kingswood School." *PWHS* 38 (1972): 110-14.

Boulton, David J. "Women and Early Methodism." *PWHS* 43 (1981): 13-17.

Brown, Earl Kent. "Standing in the Shadow: Women in Early Methodism." *Nexus* 17.2 (1974): 22-31.

Chilcote, Paul W. "The Blessed Way of Holiness." *Journal of Theology (UTS)* 100 (1996): 29-51.

———. "An Early Methodist Community of Women." *Church History* 38 (2000): 219-230.

———. "John Wesley as Revealed by the Journal of Hester Ann Rogers." *MethH* 20 (1982): 111-23.

———. "Sanctification as Lived by Women in Early Methodism." *MethH* 34 (1996): 90-103.

———. "Songs of the Heart: Hymn Allusions in the Writings of Early Methodist Women," *Proceedings of the Charles Wesley Society* 5 (1998): 99-114.

Harrison, A. W. "An Early Woman Preacher: Sarah Crosby." *PWHS* 14 (1924): 104-9.

Hindmarsh, D. Bruce. "'My chains fell off, my heart was free': Early Methodist Conversion Narratives in England," *Church History* 68 (1999): 910-29.

Jones, Margaret. "Whose Characterisation? Which Perfection? Women's History and Christian Reflection." *Epworth Review* 20.2 (1993): 96-103.

Morgan, K. "Methodist Testimonials." In *Reformation and Revival in Eighteenth-Century Bristol*, 75-104. Edited by J. Barry and K. Morgan. Bristol: Bristol Record Society, 1994.

Selected Bibliography

Rosen, Beth. "Sexism in History or, Writing Women's History Is a Tricky Business." *Journal of Marriage and the Family* 33 (1971): 541-44.

Surrey, J. L. "Self-in-Relation: A Theory of Women's Development." In *Women's Growth in Connection: Writings from the Stone Center*, 51-66. Edited by J. V. Jordan, et al. New York: Guildford Press, 1991.

Watson, David Lowes. "Methodist Spirituality." In *Protestant Spiritual Traditions*, 217-73. Edited by Frank Senn. New York: Paulist Press, 1986.

Index

Adam Bede, 141, 234
Adlington, 105
Albin, Tom, 12, 36
Allen, Mr., 207
Anderson, Mary, 305-6
Andrews, Lancelot, 5
Anglican, 2, 4, 6, 12, 19, 23, 28, 34, 36, 37, 95, 159, 202, 323
Antigua, 40, 218
Appeals to Men of Reason and Religion, 82
Ariès, Phillipe, 252
Arminian Magazine, 42, 45, 62, 66, 140, 188, 250, 314
ars moriendi, 45-46, 249, 251-53, 309-39
ars vivendi, 255-308
Ashbourne, 234
Aspen, Dr., 318
Atkinson, David, 252
Aunt's Advice to a Niece, 148
autobiography, 13, 16, 37, 43, 61, 207

Backburn, 318

Ball, Hannah, 14-15, 25-26, 27, 29, 33, 39, 41, 43, 49, 56, 64, 95-103, 250-51, 260-61, 262-63
Ballinderry, 41, 202
band meeting, 23-25, 40, 71, 74, 110, 202, 209, 280, 332
Bardsley, Samuel, 37, 106
Barritt, Mary, 41, 207-8, 289, 291. *See also* Taft, Mary
Batting, Mr., 101
Baxter, Richard, 6-7
Bedford, Miss, 260-61
Bennet, Grace, 71
Bennet, John, 71
Benson, Joseph, 123, 335
Berridge, Rev. J., 286
Biographical Sketches of Various Holy Women, 62, 178
Blackheath, 72
Bolton, 278
Bolton, Ann ("Nancy"), 95, 262-63
Book of Common Prayer, 5, 161
Bosanquet, Mary, 32, 41, 44, 63, 75, 81, 111, 137-38, 144, 148-

57, 240, 250, 258-59, 279, 282, 295, 298, 331. *See also* Fletcher, Mary
Bradshaw, Samuel, 116
Brammah, William, 279
Bramwell, William, 27, 228, 289, 318
Bremerton, 5
Bristol, 39, 40, 42, 75, 178, 209, 215, 226, 314, 316
Bulmer, Agnes (née Collinson), 42, 44, 47, 53, 63, 65-70, 140, 188-201
Bulmer, Joseph, 65, 188
Bunting, William M., 65
Bunyon, John, 6
Burdsall, Mary, 171. *See also* Lyth, Mary
Butterfield, Herbert, 3
Byron, James, 244-45

Cambridge, 5
Campbell, Ted, 16
Carport, 323, 327
Castle-Donnington, 282
Chapman, Patty, 95
Cheshire, 36-38
Chester, 112, 218
Church of England, 3, 4, 37, 67, 68, 100, 104, 117, 144, 202, 268, 271-72, 288
Church, Leslie, 234
Church, Thomas, 17
Church Fenton, 207
Clarke, Adam, 65, 173, 215, 301
class meeting, 12, 23-25, 38, 40, 71, 74, 77, 84, 119, 131, 138, 161, 207, 215, 280, 314
Classics of Western Spirituality, 11

Clewlow, Mrs., 112
Clonmel, 178
Coalport-House, 328
Coke, Thomas, 104, 173, 273, 301
Collet, Elizabeth (née Tonkin), 298-300
Colley, Sister, 45, 240, 242
Collinson, Agnes, 188. *See also* Bulmer, Agnes (née Collinson)
Collinson, Edward, 65
Collinson, Elizabeth, 65
Colne, 123, 128, 207
Colston, Sarah, 40, 314-15
Comber, 202
communion, 7, 11, 25, 29, 31, 105
conversion, 16-17, 19, 20, 37, 55, 58, 63, 111, 118, 123, 168, 229, 234, 271, 309
Cook, Joanna, 44, 141, 215-17. *See also* Turner, Joanna
Cook, Mary, 215
Cooper, Jane, 22, 29, 40, 43, 55, 57, 63, 87-94, 117, 251, 257
Cooper, John, 173
Cork, 39, 119-21
Cornwall, 144
covenant, 7, 11, 44, 53, 112, 126, 132, 141, 152, 194-96, 215, 231, 276
Crosby, Sarah, 14, 24, 27, 30-31, 37, 40-41, 43, 55, 63, 78-79, 81-86, 87, 141, 224-25, 238, 250, 254, 264-67, 279-81, 295, 297, 331-34
Cross Hall, 40, 54, 75, 264, 295, 324

Cutler, Ann ("Praying Nanny"), 27, 41, 123, 141, 228-30, 254, 318-22

Davidson, Margaret, 39, 41, 49, 54, 57-58, 140-41, 202-6, 222-23
Delamotte, Charles, 72
Derby, 41, 229, 234
Derbyshire, 41, 286
Design, Susannah, 40, 141, 209-11
Dewsbury, 228
Dickinson, Elizabeth, 318
discipleship, 11-13, 23-25, 43, 226, 250, 331
Doyle, Mrs., 316
dreams, 44-45, 137, 141-42, 237-46, 324-26
Dublin, 39, 118-19, 121
Dudley, Robert, 178
Dunsford, 202
Dyer, Mr., 89

Early Methodist People, 234
Edinburgh, 277
Eliot, George, 41, 234. *See also* Evans, Mary Ann
English Spirituality, 12
Entwisle, Joseph, 123, 148
Entwisle, Mary, 14, 25-26, 42-43, 49-52, 55, 57, 65, 123-30, 141, 233. *See also* Pawson, Mary
Ephraem Syrus, 9
Epworth, 158, 292
Eucharist (sacrament), 13, 29-31, 63, 78-79, 88, 118, 132, 151
Evans, Elizabeth, 41, 141, 234-35. *See also* Tomlinson, Elizabeth

Evans, Mary Ann, 41, 234. *See also* Eliot, George
Evans, Samuel, 234
Experience of Frances Pawson, 286
Experience of Hester Ann Rogers, The, 41, 43, 64, 104, 254, 268, 309

fasting, 26-28
Fifty Spiritual Homilies, 9
Fire of Love, 11
Fletcher, John, 39, 41, 108, 111, 161, 292, 295, 320, 323, 325, 326, 335
Fletcher, Mary, 1, 39-41, 44-45, 55, 64, 111, 137, 141-42, 148, 240-42, 250-51, 254, 282-85, 291-92, 293-94, 295, 298-300, 323-30, 335-39. *See also* Bosanquet, Mary
friendship, 54-55, 131, 335
Furley, Samuel, 144

"General Rules," 32, 137
Georgia, 72
Gilbert, Ann, 26, 298
Gilbert, Francis, 218
Gilbert, Mary, 40, 42, 141, 218-21
Gilbert, Nathaniel, 218
Gloucester, 41, 95
Grace Abounding to the Chief of Sinners, 6
Great Duty of Believing, The, 106
Gwinear, 298

Halifax, 161
Hall, Bathsheba, 42, 117, 141, 226
Hall, John, 226

Hall, Martha ("Patty"), 27, 39, 43, 138, 158-60
Hall, Westley, 158
Hanson, John, 173
Hanson, Mary, 15, 20, 42-43, 51-52, 55-56, 138, 141, 173-77, 236, 301-4
Hanson, Thomas, 96
Hardon, Mrs., 296
Harper, Joseph, 244
Harrison, Hannah, 30, 35
Harrison, Mr., 128
Harrison, Mrs., 296
Heitzenrater, Richard, 34
Henderson, Richard, 98
Henson, Elizabeth, 317
Herbert, George, 5
Hervey, James, 253
Hickok, Kathleen, 48
High Wycombe, 33, 39, 41, 95-96, 102, 262
Highfield, Ann, 40, 41, 254, 318-22
Hill, John, 318
Hobbs, Thomas, 4
Hodgson, Mrs., 296
Holder, George, 279
Holder, Mary (née Woodhouse), 279-81
Holiness, 5-6, 10, 12, 17, 20-23, 35, 45, 55-56, 58, 81, 89, 104, 114, 116, 131, 133, 137, 148, 152-53, 167, 168, 240-41, 251, 275, 282
Holland, Mary, 306-8
Holy Life of Gregory Lopez, The, 8
Horncastle, 305
Hotz-Davies, Ingrid, 48
Hudson, Rev., 202

Hull, 123
Humphries, Thomas, 103
Hurrell, Elizabeth, 41, 81, 286-88
hymns, 7, 10-12, 14, 34-35, 43-44, 72, 83, 112, 137-38, 140, 171, 178-80, 183-84, 191-92, 194-97, 202, 203-8, 222, 314, 324
Hymns on the Lord's Supper, 31

Imitation of Christ, 8, 161
Instructions for Children, 14
Introduction to a Devout Life, 159
Isle of Wight, 65

Jackson, Thomas, 62
James, Mary, 316
Jeffrey, David, 12
Jesus, Altogether Lovely, 137, 148
Johnson, Elizabeth, 40, 215
Johnson, Robert, 112
Johnson, Samuel, 158
Jones, Serene, 47-48
Jones, Thomas, 88
justification, 17, 20-22, 82, 84, 97, 113-17, 161, 163-66, 167, 251, 253, 260, 268, 270, 301-2, 325

Ken, Thomas, 5
Kendal, 218
Kilham, Alexander, 286
Kimbrough, S T, Jr., 9
Kingswood, 33, 75
Kirkstall-Forge, 279, 318

Lancashire, 41, 207, 228, 286
Laud, William, 5
Law, William, 6-8
Lawrence, Sarah ("Sally"), 33, 241, 254, 294, 323-30

INDEX

Leadbetter, Mary, 218
Leeds, 39, 41, 81, 112, 123, 128, 161, 295, 323-24, 331
Leek, 113, 115, 229
Lefevre, Mrs., 15, 18, 40, 43, 138, 141, 143-47, 212-14, 240, 251, 255-56
Leicestershire, 234, 282
Letters upon Sacred Subjects, 144
Letters Wrote by Jane Cooper, 87
Leytonstone, 32, 40-41, 44, 54, 75, 81, 138, 148, 240, 241, 293, 295, 323
Life of Gaston de Renty, 9
Life of God in the Soul of Man, 8
Life of Mary Fletcher, 148
Lincolnshire, 292
Lisburn, 41, 202
Liverpool, 278
Lives of the Early Methodist Preachers, 62
London, 16, 32, 33, 39-40, 45, 63, 65, 71-72, 75, 88, 117, 120-21, 137, 142, 158, 173, 215, 218, 226, 240, 286, 295-96, 331
Long Stratton, 243
Lopez, Gregory, 8
love feast, 116
Lowestoft, 245
Loxdale, Ann, 111, 273-76
Lutheran, 16
Lyth, John, 171
Lyth, Mary, 44, 138, 171-72. *See also* Burdsall, Mary

Macarius (Pseudo-Macarius), 9
Macclesfield, 37, 38-39, 104, 110, 115, 117-19, 123, 228-29, 268, 278, 318, 321
Madeley, 39, 41, 293, 298, 323, 326, 335
Mahoney, Mary, 119
Making Disciples, 12
Mallet, Sarah, 39, 44-45, 141-42, 243-46
Mallitt, William, 244
Malmgreen, Gail, 36
Manchester, 110, 119, 123, 189, 229, 243-44, 291, 335
Matthaei, Sondra, 12
Maxfield, Thomas, 295
Maxwell, Lady D'Arcy, 87, 307
Mayer, Matthew, 278
Mayer, Mrs. Matthew, 278
McVey, Kathleen, 9
means of grace, 12, 25-26, 30-32, 62, 79, 95, 131-32, 140, 314
meditation, 6-7, 12, 20, 27-28, 42, 44, 95-96, 98, 101, 137-38, 143-48, 150, 158-60, 173-77, 212
Meditations Among the Tombs, 253
Memoirs of Elizabeth Mortimer, 63, 65-70
Memoirs of Grace Bennet, 71-74
Memoirs of Mary Cooper, 301
Memoirs of Mary Taft, 131
Memoirs of Mary Tatham, 44, 161
Messiah's Kingdom, 42, 65, 188
Methodist Devotion, 11
Methodist Magazine, 43, 65, 131, 282
Methodist Spirituality, 11
Mitchell, Mr., 89
Montgomery, James, 188
Moorfields, 72
Moravian, 16
Morris, Dinah, 141, 234

Mortimer, Elizabeth, 26-27, 42, 48, 65-70, 250, 277, 296, 306-8. *See also* Ritchie, Elizabeth
Mortimer, Frances, 286. *See also* Pawson, Frances
Murray, Grace, 17, 24, 27, 34, 40, 43, 49, 63, 71-74. *See also* Bennet, Grace

Nantwich, 273
narrative, 13, 15-23, 29, 31, 34, 43, 45-47, 51, 62, 209, 226, 250, 277
Naylor, Mary, 33
new birth, 16
Newbold, 234
Newcastle upon Tyne, 24, 71, 74
Newfoundland, 234
Newtownards, 202
Night Thoughts, 65, 188, 253
Norfolk, 39, 243
Norwich, 89, 91
Nottingham, 161, 289

Oddie, James, 202
Oldham, 229
Orthodox and Wesleyan Spirituality, 9
Otley, 277
Oxford, 7, 39, 95, 117, 158

Pawson, Frances, 27, 286-88, 295-97. *See also* Mortimer, Frances
Pawson, John, 123, 295
Pawson, Marmaduke, 123
Pawson, Mary, 123. *See also* Entwisle, Mary

perfection, Christian, 12, 17, 21-22, 33, 35, 43, 63, 81, 83, 90, 98, 118, 126, 151-52, 167, 181, 214, 224, 251, 253, 264-66, 273-75
Peters, Sarah, 33
Pietist, 16, 23
Pilgrim's Progress, The, 6
Pipe, John, 131
Plain Account of Christian Perfection, 7, 8, 87, 108, 161, 264
Plea for the Bible, 105
Portwood, 278
prayer, 2, 6, 7, 10, 13, 26-28, 30, 35, 37, 39, 41, 43-44, 49, 55, 63, 74-75, 90, 92, 95-99, 101, 106, 108, 117-19, 122, 126, 131-32, 137-38, 140-41, 149, 153-55, 156, 158-59, 162-63, 171, 175, 188, 202, 207, 209-36, 251, 255, 282-83, 285, 338
Preston, 228
Priest to the Temple, 5
Proctor, Mrs., 296
Protestant Spiritual Traditions, 12
Puritan, 5-7, 9, 12, 16, 215

Rack, Henry, 5
Raikes, Robert, 41, 95
Raithby, 26, 307
Ratcliffe, 289
Raymond, J., 54
regeneration, 16-17
Renty, Gaston de, 8-9
repentance, 16-19, 140, 311, 328
Rhodes, Miss, 126
Ritchie, Elizabeth, 39, 250, 277-79. *See also* Mortimer, Elizabeth

Roche, 144
Roe, Charles, 106
Roe, Hester Ann, 15, 19-21, 37-38, 55, 141, 227, 250, 268-72, 273-76, 309. *See also* Rogers, Hester Ann
Roe, James, 104
Roe, Joseph, 112
Roe, Robert, 112, 115-18
Rogers, Hester Ann, 18, 28-29, 31, 37-39, 41-43, 64-65, 104-22, 123, 189, 227, 250-51, 253, 268, 273, 277, 309-13. *See also* Roe, Hester Ann
Rogers, James, 38-39, 104, 112, 118-20
Rogers, Martha, 38-39
Romaine, William, 88-89
Roseland, 298
Rowley, Mrs., 65
Ryan, Sarah, 30, 33, 35, 43-45, 56, 63, 75-80, 141-42, 237-39, 265, 295, 323-24
Ryles, Mayor, 110, 112, 117
Rules and Exercises of Holy Living and Dying, 6, 7, 253

St. Dunstan's, 89
St. Erme, 298
Saints' Everlasting Rest, 7
Sales, Francis de, 44, 138, 159
Salisbury, 5, 158
Salmon, Miss, 112
sanctification, 17, 20, 21, 30, 56, 58, 92, 95, 110, 113-14, 116-17, 155, 161, 165-68, 182, 214, 225, 232, 271, 274, 323
Scougal, Henry, 7-8

Scripture, 11, 13, 26, 28-29, 95, 107, 161-62, 189, 209
Scupoli, Lorenzo, 8
Select Letters of Agnes Bulmer, 66
Sellars, John, 112, 118
Senn, Frank, 12
Serious Call to a Devout and Holy Life, A, 6, 7
Sermons of George Whitefield, 89
Sheffield, 112, 207
Sheldrake, Philip, 2
Short Account of the Life and Death of Ann Cutler, 318
Shropshire, 39
Simpson, David, 31, 37, 104-5, 118
Sinnethwaite, 131
Slaithwaite, 144
Slee, Nicola, 46-47
Smith, George, 234
Smith, Mr., 111
Smyth, Edward, 41, 202
Smyth, Mrs. Edward, 41, 202
Southwark, 88
Spiritual Combat, 8
Spiritual Letters of Hester Ann Rogers, 254, 268, 309
Spitalfields, 56, 78, 231, 239
Stockport, 278
Stokes, Mary, 18, 40, 140, 178-80
Stonehewer, Mrs., 116
Strickland, Mary, 161. *See also* Tatham, Mary
Sturton Grange, 207
Surrey, J. L., 46
Sutcliffe, Joseph, 286
Syrus, Ephrem, 9
Sutton, Mrs., 305

Taft, Mary, 39, 131, 140, 289, 291-92, 293-94, 305-306. *See also* Barritt, Mary
Taft, Zechariah, 27, 41, 62, 178, 207, 228, 243, 250, 286, 305, 318
Tatham, John, 161
Tatham, Mary, 20, 22, 29, 42-43, 58, 138, 161-70, 289. *See also* Strickland, Mary
Taves, Ann, 44
Taylor, Jeremy, 5-8, 253
Taylor, Joseph, 298
Taylor, Thomas, 333
Tedford, 305
Temple, The, 5
Thomas à Kempis, 6, 8, 161
Thomas, Mary, 314-15
Thorner, 123
Thornley, 228
Thoughts on Communion, 148
Thoughts on a Future State, 189
Tomlinson, Elizabeth, 234. *See also* Evans, Elizabeth
Tooth, Mary, 39-41, 55, 335-39
Tripp, Ann, 24, 33, 40, 254, 280, 295-97, 331-34
Trowbridge, 215
Turner, Joanna, 40, 215. *See also* Cook, Joanna

Veryan, 298
virtue, 6, 95, 138, 187
visions, 44-45, 137, 141-42, 237-46

Wade, Mr., 207
Wainwright, Geoffrey, 2
Wakefield, 51, 123, 129
Wakefield, Gordon, 1, 11

Walsh, John, 4
Walsh, Thomas, 89, 96, 103
Wandsworth, 218
Watlington, 95
Watson, David Lowes, 12
Watts, Isaac, 7
Wesley, Charles, 2, 6, 7, 9-12, 15-16, 19, 23, 27, 29-31, 33-35, 39-40, 43, 45, 56, 66, 71, 73, 82-83, 138, 143, 158, 181, 188, 189-90, 209, 253, 314
Wesley, John, 2, 6-10, 12-13, 16-17, 19, 21-22, 24, 26-30, 32-33, 37-40, 42-43, 45, 56, 62-63, 65-67, 71-72, 75-78, 81-83, 95-97, 102, 104, 108, 110, 112-13, 115-20, 138, 140, 144, 161, 171, 188, 190-91, 202, 209, 215, 219, 226, 237, 243-44, 250-51, 253, 260, 262, 264-67, 277-78, 279, 286, 288, 291, 293, 295, 302, 314, 317, 320
Wesley, Kezziah, 158
Wesley, Matthew, 158
Wesley, Susanna, 7, 158
West Indies, 218
Whaling, Frank, 11-12
Wheatley, Phillis, 40, 185
Whitby, 279
Whitefield, George, 40, 72, 75-76, 82, 89, 215
Whitehead, John, 277
Whittlebury, 317
Williams, Rev., 97-98
Wilson, Isabella, 15, 23, 25, 30, 35, 37, 43, 55, 57, 64, 131-34, 141, 231-32, 289-90
Wilson, Mr. and Mrs., 289
Wirksworth, 234

Witney, 95, 262
Wolfe, Francis, 100, 262
Women's Faith Development, 46
Wood, Mrs., 296
works of mercy, 13, 32-34, 250-51, 318
works of piety, 13, 25-32, 250-51, 318
worship, 7, 34, 40, 61, 71, 131, 154, 212, 218

Yates, Mrs., 329
York, 35, 123, 171, 277
Yorkshire, 39, 40-41, 63, 75, 81, 277, 286, 293, 295
Young, Edward, 65, 121, 188, 253
Young, Portia, 186-87
Youth's Instructor, 65

Index of Scripture References

Genesis
1:3 176
3:19 309
5:3 269
22:2 153
49:18 101

Exodus
6:6 74
16 263
17:12 152
20:3 240
33:19 90

Numbers
6:24 262
11:29 279

Deuteronomy
5:32 211
6:5 109
11:12 283
30:6 114
32:30 280
33:27 .... 150, 242

Judges
11:35 153

2 Samuel
12:23 153

2 Kings
2:12 312
2:15 325

1 Chronicles
4:10 282-85

2 Chronicles
10:16 288

Job
3:17 292
16:19 331
23:10 84

Psalms
1:2 232
4:6 256
8:4 273

Index of Scripture References

12:4 287
17:8 .... 227, 324
22:5 126
23:1 .... 154, 175
23:6 126
32:8 294
32:9 155
34:8 210
40:17 165
42:1 108
42:5 317
46:1 125
51:10 108
62 256
62:11 91
63:1 145-47
73:25 .... 165, 325
85:10 195
103:2 124
103:12 150
107:30 311
116:12 129
116:13 224
118:28 165
119:13 98

Proverbs
3:6 296
3:17 275
14:10 90

Ecclesiastes
1:14 173
2:14 153
4:12 151

Song of Solomon
1:2 156
2:4 224

2:10 315
2:13 312
2:15 258
2:16 156
5:16 .... 133, 149

Isaiah
1:22 287
1:25 .... 155, 222
12:1-6 261
12:3 134
14:23 238
30:20 90
40:1 106
40:11 84
40:15 176
40:31 280
41:10 125
46:4 280
48:18 .... 100, 167
50:6 256
51:1 288
52:2 157
53:4-6 269
55:1 245
55:3 82
55:6 310
57:1 245
60:4 284
60:18-20 85
62:7 210
64:6 164
64:8 224
66:8-9 117

Jeremiah
17:7 175
18:6 .... 108, 279, 298
31:12 219

Ezekiel
20:19-20 114
33:11 310
36:25 . . . . 275, 285

Daniel
3:26 99
12:3 210

Hosea
11:1 288
11:9 115
13:1 288
14:5 298

Joel
2:6 110

Habakkuk
3:17-18 84

Zephaniah
3:14-20 92

Malachi
3:1 92
3:17 151
4:2 220

Matthew
1:21 157
4:8 274
5:6 113
5:8 209
5:11-12 94
5:29 259
5:39 162
6:9-13 154
6:11 263
6:22 283
6:34 296
7:2 154
7:7 . . . . 257, 285, 303
7:24 110
8:3 325
8:8 210
9:29 284
9:38 210
10:8 266
11:12 154
11:28 . . . . 107, 145
11:29 . . . . 220, 285
13:1-9 78
13:58 157
15:28 96
18:3 271
19:13 241
19:26 213
22:12 302
22:13 110
22:40 166
24:13 150
24:35 145
25 . . . . 302, 336
25:21 94
25:23 94
26:39 119
26:41 303
26:42 . . . 80, 133, 222, 233, 299

Mark
1:15 113
1:41 115
3:1-3 157
4:39 212
10:15 177
10:45 269
12:30 275
16:16 245

Index of Scripture References

Luke
1:38 209
1:73-75. 275
1:77 96
2:10 126
2:52 . . . . 118, 274
5:39 288
8:50 . . . . 241, 280
9:23 . . . . 263, 303
10:27 152
10:39 . . . . 210, 284
10:39-42. 236
10:41. 168-70
12:11-12. 94
15:10 198
15:18-21. 216
19:9 238
19:40 280
22:42 214
22:54 305
23:34 235
24:32 235
24:34 115

John
1:29 97
1:47 287
3:3 . . . . 72, 271
3:8 188
3:17 150
3:21 99
4:6-15. 235
4:10 . . . . 102, 152
4:14 177
4:24 97
5:40 235
6:28 164
6:35 155
6:44 90
6:55 118
7:37 245
10:11 317
10:28-29. 302
11:25 79
14:6 115
14:13 224
14:15 302
15 166
15:3 325
15:4 109
15:5 . . . . 153, 267
15:7. . . . . 109, 328-29
15:16 156
16:13 167
16:33 132
17:3 . . . . 198, 283
17:21 210
20:27 77
20:28 . . . . 115, 275
21:17 . . . . 84, 255
21:20 239

Acts
2 111
2:41 117
4:4 117
7:60 162
16:31 . . . . 106, 113, 115
24:16 152

Romans
3:10 163
3:10-12. 270
3:20 164
3:20-26. 270
3:24 302
3:25 163
3:26 269

INDEX OF SCRIPTURE REFERENCES

3:27-29 270
3:28 164
4:3 270
4:4-8 270
4:5 163
4:23-25 270
5 73
5:2 102
5:5 . . . . 107, 116, 156
6:6 167
6:22 165
6:23 . . . . 116, 269
7:24 . . . . 165, 310
8:1 . . . . 79, 107
8:7 91
8:15 . . . . 165, 275
8:17 . . . . 260, 298
8:28 . . . . 132, 279
8:39 . . . . 239, 302
12:21 163
13:10 275
15:13 177

1 Corinthians
1:23 102
1:27-29 318
1:30 . . . . 92, 166
1:30-31 271
2:9 189
6:13 299
6:15 299
6:19 149
6:20 110
12:31 284
13 316
13:1 284
13:12 313
15:53-54 213
15:55 256
15:58 312

2 Corinthians
1:12 222
1:20 . . . . 29, 111, 125, 155
3:17 294
4:6 85
5:17 271
5:21 269
7:1 152
8:9 112
12:2 231

Galatians
3:17 127
4:6 115
5:1 165
5:6 . . . . 168, 302
5:22-24 271
6:14 271

Ephesians
2:1 166
2:9 98
3:15 154
3:17 . . . . 127, 283
3:18 283
3:19 168
3:20 . . . . 157, 209, 256
6:11 221
6:16 167
6:18-19 98

Philippians
1:21 254
1:26 285
2:5 232
3:8 166
3:13 110
3:14 . . . . 100, 207
4:7 . . . . 100, 167, 175
4:13 303

Index of Scripture References

Colossians
1:9 283
1:12 220
1:27 .... 226, 261
3:1 100
3:4 116

1 Thessalonians
5:16 93
5:17 .... 93, 274, 283, 285
5:18 .... 93, 274
5:22 303
5:23 275
5:24 275

Titus
3:7 256

Hebrews
1:3 269
4:15 274
7:25 .... 263, 280
10:37 262
11:1 253
11:4 .... 333, 337
12:1 127
12:14 .... 89, 114
12:24 92
12:26 111
13:5 332
13:8 132

James
1:17 307
1:23 219
1:25 275
14 91

1 Peter
1:8 .... 90, 256
1:16 259

2:1 112
2:2 156
2:9 305
2:10 241
2:11 112
2:24 269
3:15 152
3:18 164
4:18 245
5:5-6 115

2 Peter
2:10 287
3:8 115
3:18 211

1 John
1:3 275
1:7 .... 84, 152, 154, 325
1:9 167
3:8 126
4:16 .... 317, 337
4:18 .... 86, 102, 116, 165, 275,
                              283, 317
4:19 102
4:21 275
5:3 275
5:4 .... 157, 284
5:18 167

Jude
1:8 287
1:24 91
1:25 80

Revelation
3:1 98
3:20 245
20 88
22:11 271
22:20 .... 222, 312

www.ingramcontent.com/pod-product-compliance
Lightning Source LLC
Chambersburg PA
CBHW011139290426
44108CB00020B/2682